THE GREAT NORTH
OF SCOTLAND RAILWAY
A NEW HISTORY

David Ross

Aberdeen Harbour: a busy scene at Waterloo Quay. *(Aberdeen University Library)*

Stenlake Publishing Ltd

ISBN 978-1-84033-701-3

Printed in China

Ah me! what perils do environ
The man that meddles with cold iron.
Samuel Butler, *Hudibras*, Part 1, canto 3,
quoted in *Caledonian Mercury*, 22 January 1846,
of certain persons who had speculated in GNS shares

A Railway Carol
For the Cutting of the First Turf
of the Great North Railway

What ho! ye sturdy burghers,
Or by the wand'ring Dee,
Or where the Ness down the broad firth
Rolls onwards to the sea;
Or ye who dwell upon the Don,
Or Ury's classic shore,
Or ply your crafts with stalwart arms
In the borough of Kintore; –
Ho! ye who dwell in Huntly town
By Bogie's silver side,
And fling the flashing shuttle,
Or tan the tough ox-hide;
Or watch from out the tortur'd worm
The sparkling aquae flow;
Or on the ringing anvil make
The red brands dance and glow; –
Ho! dwellers in fair Elgin,
Ho! denizens of Keith,
And ye who wone in Forres town
Beside the "blasted heath" –
Rouse up! ye burghers one and all,
Put on your best array,
This day the first turf's to be cut
Of the GREAT NORTHERN WAY!

First stanza of five, written in 1854 by William Cadenhead (1819-1904), "the Bard of Bon-Accord"

Also by David Ross:

The Highland Railway
The Caledonian: Scotland's Imperial Railway
The North British Railway: A History
The Glasgow & South Western Railway: A History

CONTENTS

FOREWORD

Of Scotland's five main railway companies, the Great North was the smallest in terms of route mileage, though it vied with the Highland Railway for fourth place in some respects. Unlike the others, which extended in relatively long trunk lines, its original main line was only 53 miles, but extensions and branches raised its final route length to 336 miles. A combination of circumstances confined it in the north-east corner of the country, Aberdeenshire, Banffshire and Moray, with a few miles in Inverness-shire and Kincardineshire, though the original intention, as its name indicated, had been to make it the principal, and preferably the only, railway company in the entire north of Scotland. This ambition was rooted in a perception of the role and status of Aberdeen as a regional capital with a hinterland extending far beyond its own county, but it met resistance in Inverness, which though a much smaller town did not consider itself to be a sub-location to Aberdeen. Rivalry between the Great North and the Highland companies exerted a powerful influence on the economic development of the wider region.

The nature of the Great North of Scotland Railway was summed up by William Acworth in his *Railways of Scotland*, published in 1890. He wrote of it as a very bad company up to the late 1870s, which had become a very good company after 1880; and this ugly duckling-to-swan transformation has been broadly accepted ever since. Acworth's view was reiterated in W.J. Scott's short account of the line, *Little and Good*, published in 1898, and echoed by E.L. Ahrons's derisive comments in the *Railway Magazine* on earlier GNS services, "glacial expresses" travelling at minimal speed through post-glacial countryside: "Why it was ever allowed to be called a railway passed comprehension." Like all long-established generalisations, their view needs to be challenged, and its validity is explored in the following pages.

Whatever its previous record, there is no doubt that from the early 1880s, the GNS became an efficient and innovative railway operation. It was an early protagonist of integrated transport, and though its attempt to take over Aberdeen's tramway system was frustrated, it was one of the first railway companies to use buses and lorries to complement its country train services. A significant element in the story is the company's relationship with the growing city of Aberdeen, its council, its mercantile community, and its harbour commissioners – to say that there was sometimes less than a perfect understanding among these bodies is to make a considerable understatement.

This book also records the histories of the companies absorbed by the Great North, and since its early history is intimately linked with that of the Aberdeen Railway and the Scottish North Eastern Railway, there is also much about them, although the SNER ultimately became part of the Caledonian system. Some topics treated in detail, notably that of goods carriage in the 1880s and 1890s, are relevant to all five Scottish railway companies. Selective as it must be, the amount of detail required in order to give a reasonably substantial account of the Great North's activities and involvements may make demands on the reader, but it is hoped that the extent and intrinsic interest of the information will make close perusal worthwhile. A detailed index helps in tracing specific topics. Readers will find numerous supplementary details included among the notes and references.

Currency and measurements

Sterling currency during the GNS's existence was in pounds, shillings and pence (12 pence to a shilling, 20 shillings to a pound. The old penny (abbreviated to *d*) was divided into two halfpence, and four farthings: at a time when skilled men earned a pound a week, farthings were significant. Measurements were in miles, furlongs, chains, yards, feet and inches (8 furlongs to the mile, 10 chains to the furlong, 22 yards to the chain). Ground measurements were in acres (1 acre=4,840 square yards). Heavy weights were measured in hundredweights (112 lbs to one cwt) and tons (20 cwt). Herring catches were measured in crans (a cran was equivalent to around 750 fish).

ACKNOWLEDGEMENTS

Many hours were pleasantly spent in the reading rooms of the National Archives of Scotland, the National Library of Scotland, the Wolfson Room of Aberdeen University Library, the Aberdeen City Archives, the Aberdeen Central Library, and the Postal Museum, London, in order to gather information for this book, and I am very grateful to the helpful and expert staff in all these places.

Chapters 1-21 were read in draft by Peter Fletcher and Keith Fenwick (who also read chapters 22 and 23), and I am extremely grateful to them for many corrections, helpful comments and suggestions. Dr Fletcher has also kindly allowed me to draw on his 2007 thesis, 'Strategy, Solvency and the State: the development of the railway system of northern Scotland, 1844-74'. Any errors in the text, along with all judgements, are exclusively the responsibility of the author.

Dr Mike Cooper and Keith Fenwick provided the images from the Great North of Scotland Railway Association's collection, and thanks are extended to them and to the Association, as also to Ferryhill Railway Heritage Trust, Aberdeen City Art Gallery, Aberdeen University Library, Moray Libraries, the *Northern Scot* and Richard Stenlake.

The Great North of Scotland Railway Association, founded in 1964 to encourage interest in and study of the Great North and the continuing story of the line, welcomes new members. It publishes a regular journal and occasional books and papers (see its website).

Aberdeen Railway

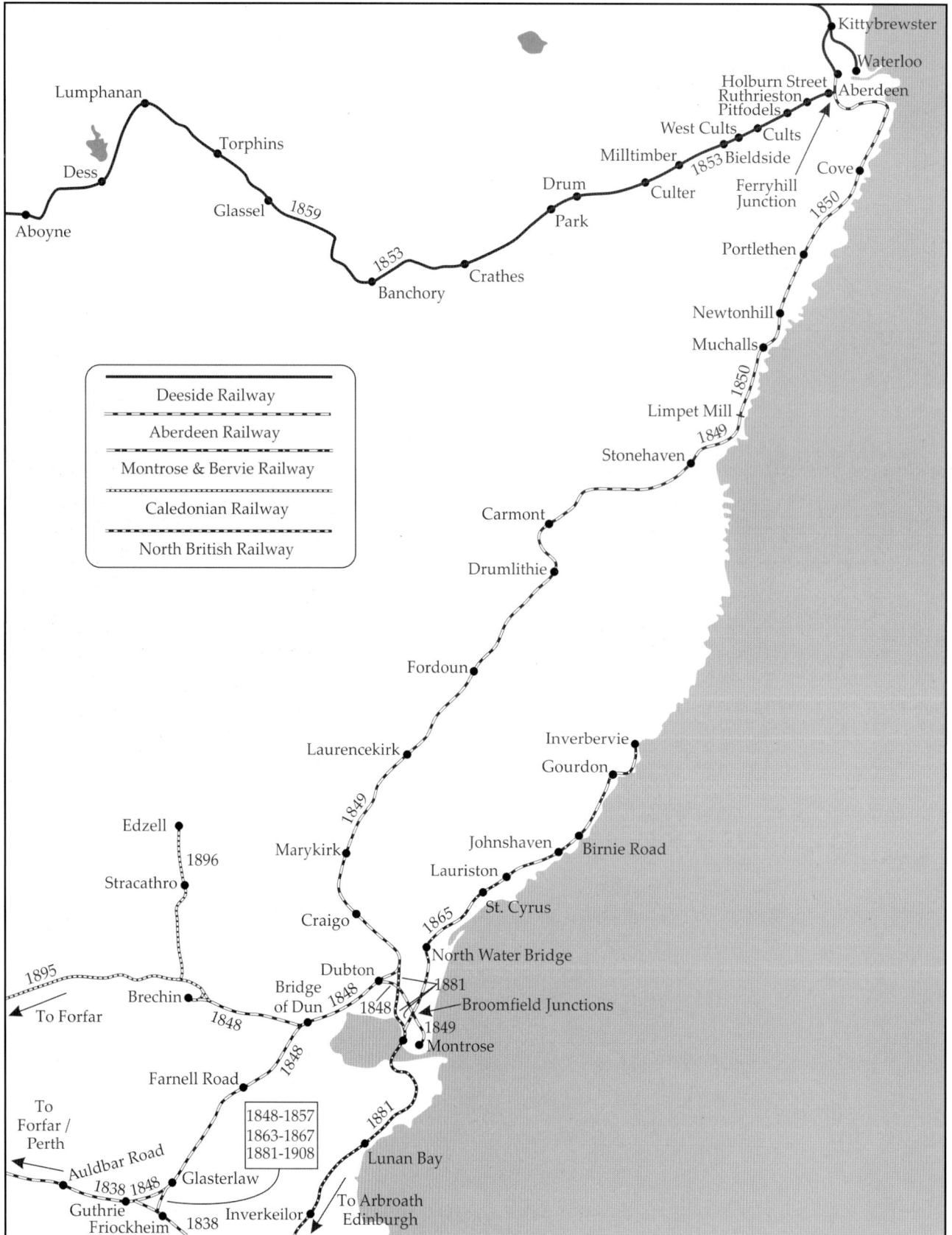

Kittybrewster
Waterloo
Holburn Street
Ruthrieston
Pitfodels
Aberdeen
West Cults
Cults
Milltimber
1853 Bieldside
Cove
Drum
Culter
Ferryhill
Junction
1850
Park
Portlethen
Lumphanan
Torphins
Newtonhill
Dess
Glassel *1859*
Muchalls
Aboyne
1853
Crathes
1850
Banchory
Limpet Mill
Stonehaven *1849*

Legend:
Deeside Railway
Aberdeen Railway
Montrose & Bervie Railway
Caledonian Railway
North British Railway

Carmont

Drumlithie

Fordoun

Inverbervie
Laurencekirk
Gourdon
1849
Edzell
Johnshaven
Birnie Road
Stracathro *1896*
Marykirk
Lauriston
St. Cyrus
Craigo
1865
1895
North Water Bridge
Brechin
Dubton
1881
To Forfar
Bridge *1848*
of Dun
Broomfield Junctions
1848
1848
1849
Montrose
Farnell Road
1848
To
Forfar /
Perth
1881
| 1848-1857 |
| 1863-1867 |
| 1881-1908 |
Auldbar Road
Lunan Bay
1838 *1848* Glasterlaw
Guthrie
Friockheim *1838* Inverkeilor
To Arbroath
Edinburgh

Great North of Scotland Lines East.

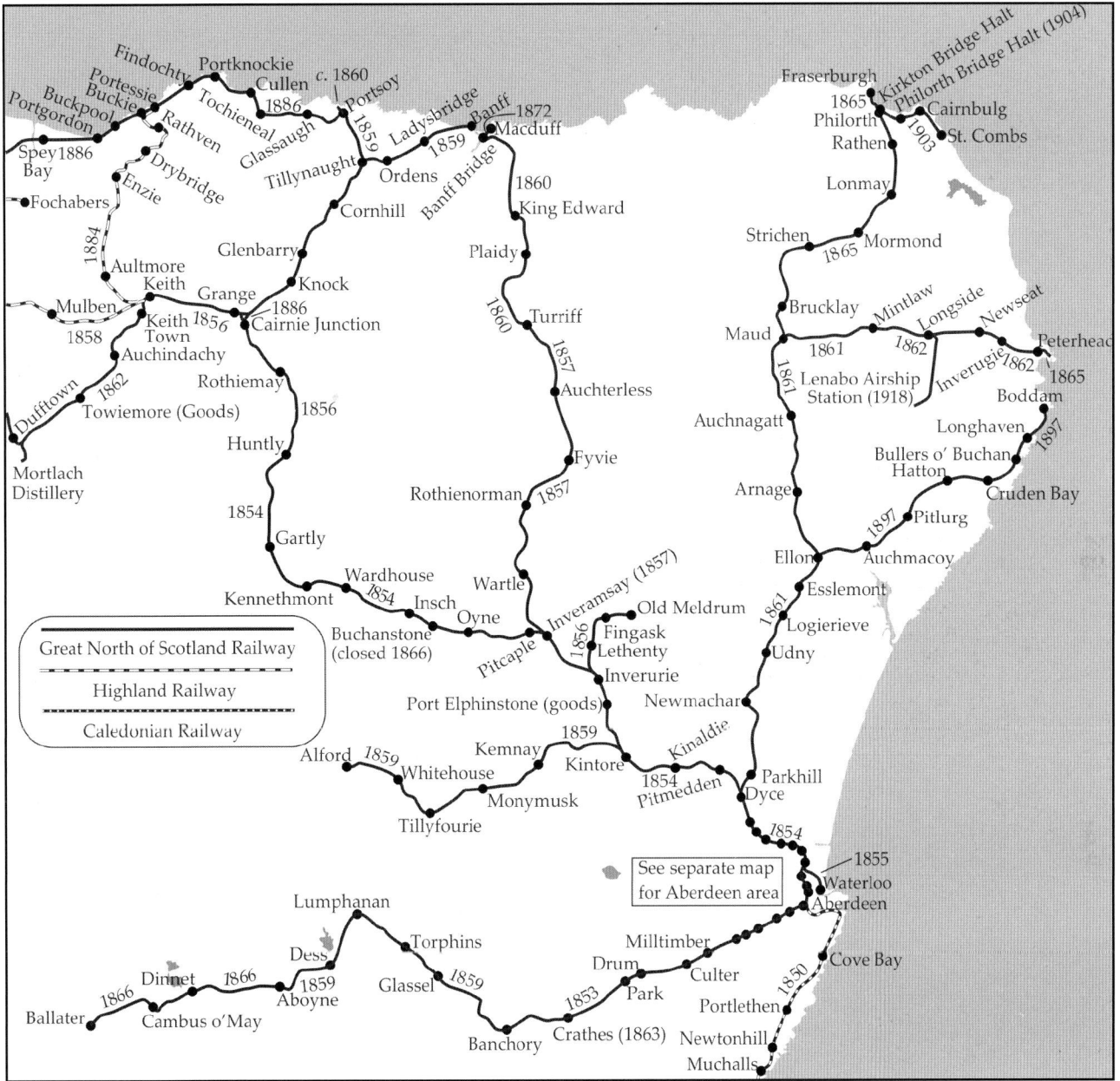

Portgordon
Buckpool
Buckie
Portessie
Findochty
Portknockie
Cullen *c.* 1860
Rathven
Tochieneal
1886
Portsoy
Spey 1886
Bay
Drybridge
Enzie
Glassaugh
1859
Ladysbridge
Banff — 1872
1859
Macduff
Fochabers
1884
Tillynaught
Ordens
Banff Bridge
Aultmore
Keith
Cornhill
1860
Glenbarry
Knock
King Edward
Mulben
Grange
1886
Plaidy
Keith 1856
Town
Cairnie Junction
1858
Auchindachy
Turriff
1860
Dufftown
1862
Rothiemay
1857
Towiemore (Goods)
1856
Auchterless
Huntly
Mortlach
Distillery
1854
Fyvie
Rothienorman
1857
Gartly
Wardhouse
Wartle
Kennethmont
1854
Insch
Oyne
Inveramsay (1857)
Old Meldrum
Buchanstone
(closed 1866)
Pitcaple
1856
Fingask
Lethenty
Great North of Scotland Railway
Highland Railway
Caledonian Railway
Port Elphinstone (goods)
Inverurie
Newmachar
Alford 1859
Kemnay
1859
Kinaldie
Whitehouse
Kintore
Monymusk
1854
Pitmedden
Tillyfourie
Parkhill
Dyce
1854
Lumphanan
See separate map
for Aberdeen area
1855
Waterloo
Aberdeen
Dess
Torphins
Milltimber
Dinnet
1866
1866
Glassel
1859
Drum
Culter
Cove Bay
Ballater
Aboyne
1859
1853
Park
Cambus o'May
Portlethen
1850
Crathes (1863)
Newtonhill
Banchory
Muchalls

Fraserburgh
1865
Kirkton Bridge Halt
Philorth Bridge Halt (1904)
Philorth
Cairnbulg
Rathen
1903
St. Combs
Lonmay
Strichen
Mormond
1865
Brucklay
Mintlaw
Longside
Newseat
Maud
1861
1862
Peterhead
1861
Inverugie
1862
Lenabo Airship
Station (1918)
1865
Auchnagatt
Boddam
Longhaven
Bullers o' Buchan
1897
Arnage
Hatton
Cruden Bay
1897
Pitlurg
Ellon
Auchmacoy
1861
Esslemont
Logierieve
Udny

Great North of Scotland Lines West

Hopeman
Burghead
1892
Coltfield
1862
Mosstowie
Alves
1858
Kinloss
Forres
1858
Brodie
Auldearn
Nairn
To Inverness

Lossiemouth
Greens of Drainie (1853)
1852
Linksfield (1853)
1896 To Buckie
Garmouth
Calcots
1884
Spey Bay
Urquhart
Elgin
Elgin (HR)
Lhanbryde
Balnacoul
Glenlossie Distillery
Longmorn
1893 Fochabers
Orbliston
Coleburn
1862
1858
Birchfield (1871)
Orton
Sourden
Mulben
1858
Rothes
To Keith
1858

1863
Dunphail

Dandaleith
1863
Craigellachie
Towiemore
Knockando House (Private, 1869)
Aberlour
1863
1862 To Keith
Knockando (1899)
Dufftown
Carron
Dailuaine Distillery
Mortlach Distillery
Blacksboat
1863
Dava
Ballindalloch
1863
Advie
Dalvey (1863-68)

Cromdale
Balmenach Distillery
Grantown on Spey (HR)
Grantown on Spey
1863
To Inverness
Broomhill
Carrbridge
1898
1866
Nethybridge
Boat of Garten
To Perth
Aviemore

| Great North of Scotland Railway |
| Highland Railway |

Aberdeen

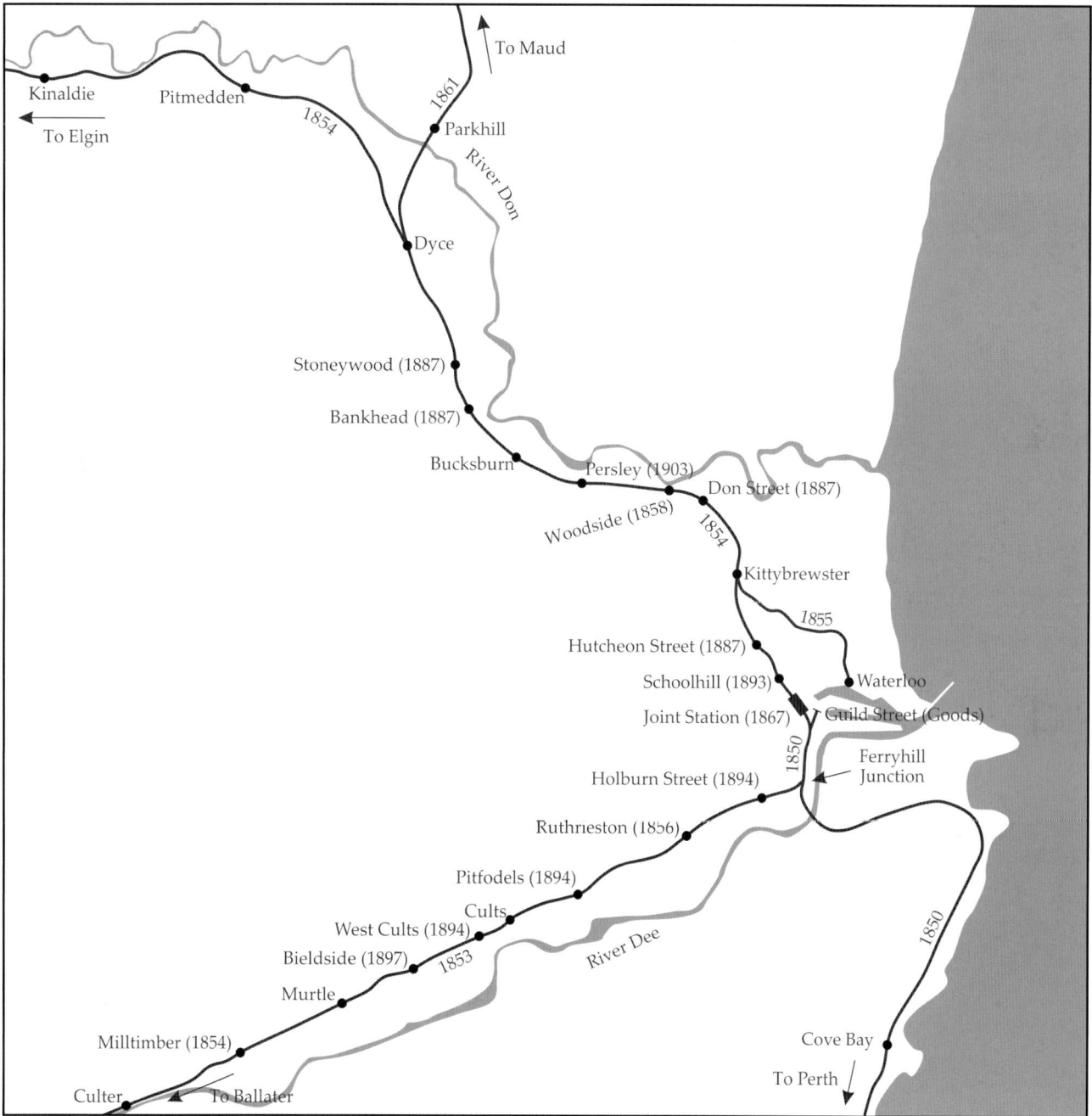

To Maud

Kinaldie

Pitmedden

1861

Parkhill

To Elgin

1854

River Don

Dyce

Stoneywood (1887)

Bankhead (1887)

Bucksburn

Persley (1903)

Don Street (1887)

Woodside (1858)

1854

Kittybrewster

1855

Hutcheon Street (1887)

Waterloo

Schoolhill (1893)

Joint Station (1867)

Guild Street (Goods)

Holburn Street (1894)

1850

Ferryhill
Junction

Ruthrieston (1856)

Pitfodels (1894)

Cults

West Cults (1894)

Bieldside (1897)

1853

River Dee

Murtle

Milltimber (1854)

1850

Cove Bay

Culter

To Ballater

To Perth

Locations of Proposed Railways
Central Buchan and Banffshire

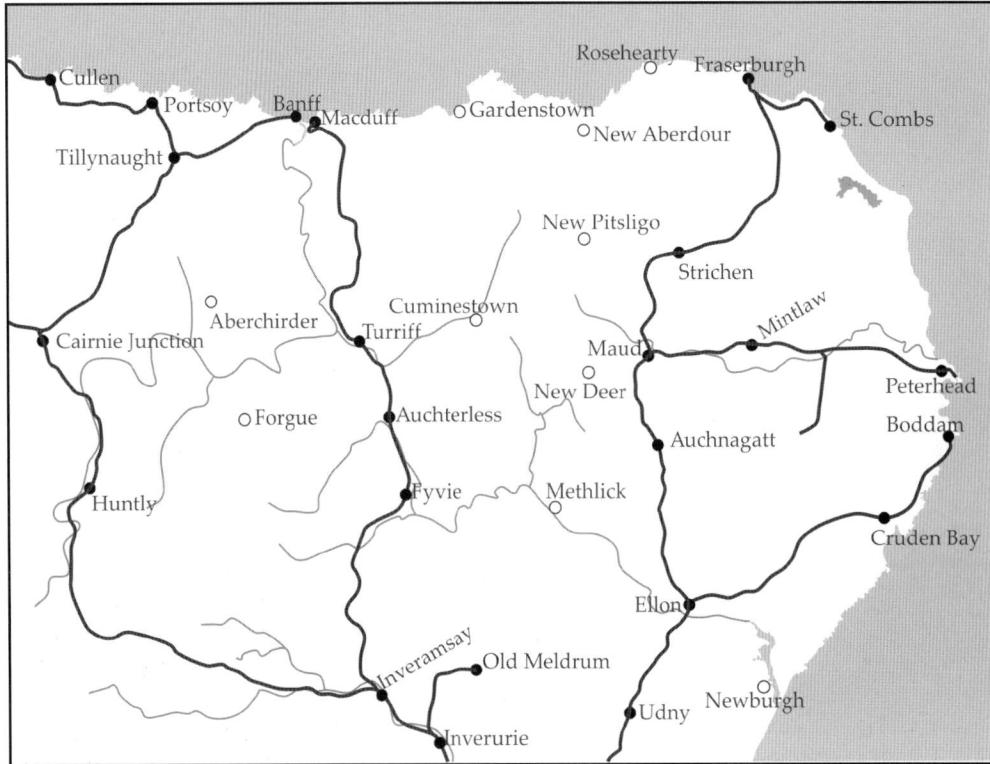

Cullen
Portsoy
Banff
Macduff
Tillynaught
Rosehearty
Fraserburgh
St. Combs
Gardenstown
New Aberdour
New Pitsligo
Strichen
Mintlaw
Aberchirder
Cuminestown
Turriff
Cairnie Junction
Maud
Peterhead
Boddam
Forgue
Auchterless
New Deer
Auchnagatt
Huntly
Fyvie
Methlick
Cruden Bay
Ellon
Inveramsay
Old Meldrum
Udny
Newburgh
Inverurie

Tomintoul Area

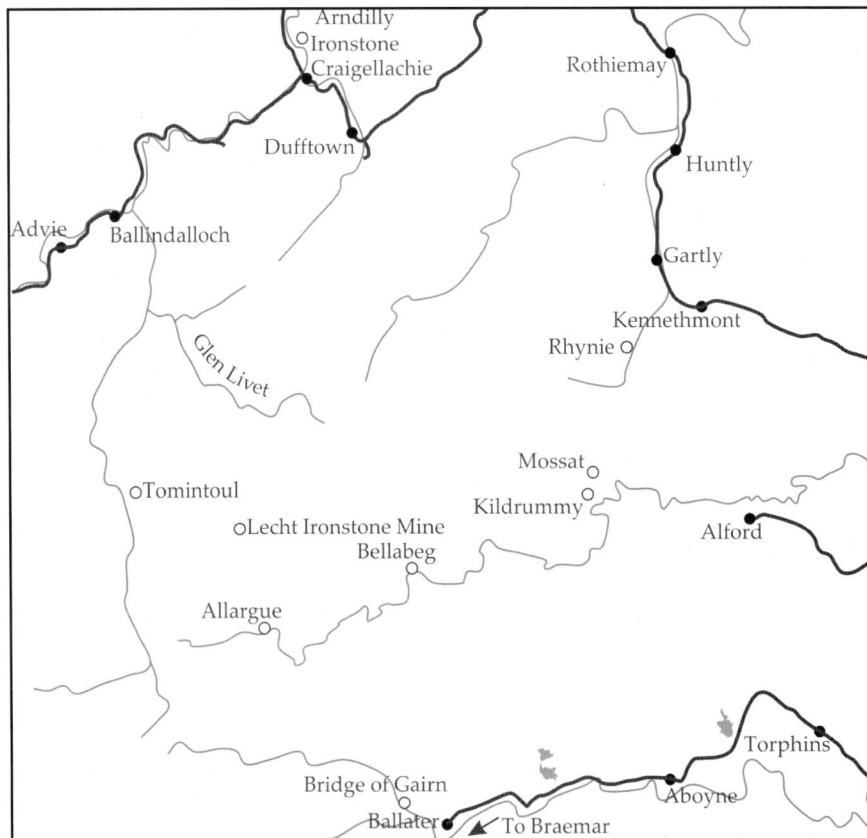

Arndilly
Ironstone
Craigellachie
Rothiemay
Dufftown
Huntly
Advie
Ballindalloch
Gartly
Kennethmont
Rhynie
Glen Livet
Mossat
Kildrummy
Tomintoul
Alford
Lecht Ironstone Mine
Bellabeg
Allargue
Torphins
Bridge of Gairn
Aboyne
Ballater
To Braemar

CHAPTER 1
First Moves 1830s – 1846

Early initiatives

'Bon Accord' has been the motto of Aberdeen since medieval times, though conduct of the city's affairs has not always lived up to it. If the civic harmony it implies had been present in railway matters, this would be a much shorter book. The beginning was auspicious, however. Scotland's third-largest city was a comparative late-comer in promoting railways; from Dundee a railway reached Newtyle and the flax fields of Strathmore in 1831, the Dundee & Arbroath Railway opened in 1838, and in the late 1830s other railways were made in Angus. By then several lines were at work on the eastern side of Glasgow, first laid to carry coal from pit-heads to canal wharves, and the Glasgow-Ayr railway was being built. Aberdeenshire had no coal mines, and the county town had easy communication with its hinterland, along the Don, Dee and Ythan valleys. Mobility around 1840 was supplied by some twenty road coaches: eight on the south road, four each on the north (Elgin) and north coast (Buchan) roads, two on Deeside, and two to the Midmar area[1]. There was also the Aberdeenshire Canal, opened in 1805, extending from Aberdeen Harbour to Port Elphinstone, near Inverurie, and used for both goods and passengers. Sailing vessels and a few steamships linked Aberdeen to other east coast ports and to places across the North Sea: in 1838 185 vessels were registered at Aberdeen, with a total tonnage of 31,063[2]. Railways to both north and south had been discussed during the 1830s; an Aberdeen-Perth line had been surveyed in 1837 and in 1839 an Aberdeen Railway Bill had got to a second reading in the Commons before failing[3]. A hint of the future came when Robert Davidson, pioneer of electric propulsion, exhibited a two-person "electromagnetic carriage" on rails in Aberdeen in 1840[4], but it was only when the concept of an Anglo-Scottish main line became a reality that the prospect of railway links was really embraced, with the city seen as as the natural northern terminus. By 1844 two trunk lines were being actively planned: the Edinburgh & Northern Railway cutting across Fife from Burntisland to the Firth of Tay; and the Scottish Central Railway, from Greenhill, south of Larbert, to Perth. The Edinburgh & Northern would form an extension of the East Coast route – when finished – from London via York and Berwick, with ferries at the Forth and Tay water gaps; the Scottish Central would meet the Caledonian and Edinburgh & Glasgow Railways at Greenhill, as elements in the West Coast route to London by way of Preston and Carlisle. With both envisaging Aberdeen as the terminus, these schemes were of course potential rivals.

In early 1844 the city's mercantile community was buzzing with interest as new plans were aired. On 23 March an advertisement in the *Caledonian Mercury* from the Adam & Anderson legal practice in Aberdeen noted that as a matter of certainty a London-Edinburgh-Glasgow railway would be established, and so, "The time has therefore arrived when steps should be taken for securing the same advantages to Aberdeen and the intervening districts." They called for a fresh route survey to be made[5]. Now that the time seemed right, competing schemes arose, with potential names bandied about and altered freely. The first mention of a Great North of Scotland

Railway came from a provisional committee formed in Perth, to continue the Scottish Central line all the way to Aberdeen, "so as to give the Public the benefit of an unbroken chain of Railway Communication from Aberdeen to London"[6]. A prospectus was published on 24 April, and its interim secretary, David Clark, a Perth lawyer, rubbished the Edinburgh & Northern project, with its ferry crossings. In Aberdeen, two southward lines were advertised: the Aberdeen & East Coast Railway was to extend past Stonehaven, Bervie and Montrose to Arbroath or, keeping its options open, to meet the Arbroath & Forfar Railway (opened in January 1839) at Friockheim. The Dundee & Arbroath Railway directors gave this plan their cordial support[7]. The rival Aberdeen, Perth & Dundee Railway was to follow the River Dee west to Crathes and then swing southwards through Laurencekirk and Brechin, to meet both the Arbroath & Forfar and Dundee & Arbroath lines. Clearly only one of these lines would be authorised by Parliament, and rather than compete expensively, their promoters agreed to combine in a single project, the Aberdeen Railway Company, with the route to be re-surveyed. Announced in the Aberdeen newspapers on 3 April 1844, the united enterprise had the comfortable prospect of its track being required by both the East and West Coast systems. Assuming mistakenly that the Aberdeen Railway would share the Angus lines' 5ft 6in gauge rather than the West Coast's 4ft 8½in, Clark claimed "it is manifest that the great Midland chain of communication is to be stopped at Perth", and called the line "a perfect disconnection"[8].

At the same time, Aberdeen's railway entrepreneurs were looking north and north-west, at a line which would run as far as Inverness. Advertised as a continuation of the southern line, though under the aegis of a separate company, its plan was developed simultaneously with the Aberdeen Railway's, and the core group of promoters and planners was the same for both. Each had its own provisional committee, an important body in these preliminary stages because the approval and backing of landowners whose land would be traversed, and of towns which would be passed through, was a vital element in convincing a parliamentary committee, and potential investors, that the proposed railway was both viable and desirable. The Aberdeen-Inverness line used the name 'Great North Railway' at first, but by March 1845 was calling itself the Great North of Scotland Railway[9] (Clark's Perth project had failed to establish itself). It was to have £1,100,000 of capital, in £50 shares, and its committee was headed by the Earl of Errol, Lord Lieutenant of Aberdeenshire and his relative Lord James Hay, second son of the 7th Marquis of Tweeddale. It included the Earl of Moray, Lord Lieutenant of Banffshire, Sir Robert Elphinstone, an Aberdeenshire landowner, Thomas Blaikie, Lord Provost of Aberdeen and ironworks proprietor, James Grant, the Elgin lawyer who would also be founder of the Morayshire Railway, Henry Paterson, manager of the North of Scotland Bank, and many others[10]. The Aberdeen Railway's committee was headed by Lord Provost Blaikie and also included numerous notables as well as a strong contingent of Aberdeen businessmen. Both companies retained the legal services of Adam & Anderson, and Alexander Anderson would remain a central figure in the Great North's affairs.

Both also used the engineering services of John Gibb & Co. of Aberdeen, provided by Alexander Gibb[11]. The Aberdeen Railway also appointed the experienced Scottish railway engineers Grainger & Miller, but the connection appears to have quickly lapsed in favour of William Cubitt, of London. Seeking unity on the southward line, the committee hired Cubitt as a consultant in July 1844, to survey and recommend a route. His report, delivered on 2 October, recommended that the line should start from a two-level station at Market Street, Aberdeen (passengers above, goods below), run to Ferryhill on a granite viaduct of 171 arches, with a parallel line joining from the harbour level, and follow the coast to Stonehaven before swinging inland via Laurencekirk, to pass between Brechin and Montrose, with a branch to each, joining the Arbroath and Forfar Railway at Friockheim, from where a line would also fork off to Forfar. Estimating the capital required at £900,000, he reckoned an annual 8% return on that would be forthcoming[12]. His proposal was in accordance with the philosophy of the West Coast route, which aimed at as direct a line as possible, but it was not at all to the liking of a committee formed to make the Scottish Midland Junction Railway between Perth and Forfar. At an earlier stage the Aberdeen, Perth & Dundee promoters had agreed with this committee that their main line would come via Brechin to Forfar. Now Brechin was to be on a branch and it seemed clear that north-south traffic was to be diverted either via the Edinburgh &

Sir Thomas Blaikie, first chairman of the GNSR, 1846-1849. *(Aberdeen City Libraries)*

Northern line, or via the proposed Dundee & Perth Railway – in either case bypassing the Scottish Midland Junction. An SMJ meeting in Coupar Angus in late October resolved that if the Aberdeen Railway did not revert to the Brechin route, it would promote its own "direct line" northwards, and noted darkly that "there can be no doubt under what influence" the switch to favour the East Coast had been achieved. A deputation travelled to Aberdeen to urge retention of the agreed route[13]. The Aberdeen directors disputed the existence of any agreement, claiming it had merely been a provisional arrangement.

At this time, across the country, hundreds of provisional committees were being set up to propose new railways to the investing public. Every proposal had to lodge a Bill with Parliament, to be scrutinised before it was accepted or refused; and a deposit of 5% (raised to 10% in 1845) of the total capital had to be lodged. Late in November 1844, a well-attended public meeting in the Court House, Aberdeen, discussed railway issues. Thomas Blaikie offered to stand down as chairman because of his connection with the Aberdeen Railway, but was retained by acclamation. Announcing that the AR subscription list was nearly full, he said that another railway to the north (presumably what was later proposed as the Great North of Scotland Eastern Extension Railway) was under consideration. The mood was bullish and though some suggested that the meeting should not back one particular route south, support for the Aberdeen Railway and Cubitt's route was overwhelming[14]. By now the business of buying and selling shares in joint stock companies, mostly railways, was big enough for Aberdeen to have stockbrokers: in 1844 James Black & Co. advertised their readiness to buy and sell shares in 26 enterprises, including the Aberdeen Railway, the North of Scotland Bank, and the Aberdeen Steam Navigation Company[15]. In 1845 the Aberdeen Stock Exchange was established.

Financing the lines, and the rise of competition

Two million pounds, over a period of five years, would have to be raised in order to build the Aberdeen and Great North railways, and it was natural to look first at local resources, especially when the lines were being promoted by local people. Aberdeen was not short of banks – the Aberdeen Banking Company had been established in 1767 and an original £150 share was said to be worth £3,000 in 1845; there were also the National Bank, the Aberdeen Town & Country Bank, and the North of Scotland Bank, founded in 1836, with a capital of £200,000[16]. Agricultural improvement had been going on for a century and both estate owners and larger tenant farmers were able to accumulate capital and to invest in further modernisation, not only in crop growing but in cattle and sheep stocks: at this time the Aberdeen Angus was becoming the pre-eminent beef breed. Aberdeen's railway promoters had close links with the banks, and confidence remained strong throughout the winter of 1844-45, while the Aberdeen-Inverness line's prospectus was in preparation. Introduced to the public on 4 February 1845 and hailed by the *Aberdeen Journal*, it had a strong selling point in the approval of the Railway Board[17], lately appointed to review new proposals: "… appears well laid-out … and the importance of it is increased by the consideration that a cheap and easy line is stated to have been surveyed between Aberdeen and Inverness"[18]. Almost simultaneously a prospectus for the Morayshire Railway was issued, for a line from the Bridge of Craigellachie via Rothes to meet the 'North of Scotland Railway' at Orton and use that line for ten miles to Elgin, then continue on its own rails to Lossiemouth Harbour, from where it would have a steamer to ply across to Sutherland. Its capital was set at £75,000[19]. The Scottish Midland Junction could draw some encouragement from the Railway Board's view that the Strathmore line was to be regarded as the north-south trunk route, rather than the lines via Dundee, 5½ miles longer to Perth, and with no proper connection in central Dundee.

In July 1845 the Aberdeen, Scottish Midland Junction, Scottish Central, and Caledonian Railway Bills all received the royal assent. Construction could begin. The Aberdeen Railway was to join the Arbroath & Forfar at Guthrie for Forfar, and Friockheim for Arbroath. Its capital was reduced to £830,000, of which £645,000 was already subscribed, with 71 locally-based individuals in to the tune of £276,000, or an average of £3,880 each; and 236 from elsewhere, representing £376,000[20], an average of £1,593 each, though of course only a £2 10s deposit per share had as yet been paid. An early start to operations was announced at its first ordinary general meeting, held on 11 September 1845, with Thomas Blaikie in the chair, along with the intention of amalgamation with the not yet authorised Great North of Scotland Railway. This had also been noted at the GNS provisional committee's meeting on 31 March: "… a suggestion … that an Amalgamation with the Aberdeen line may ultimately be considered desirable"[21].

Alexander Gibb's preliminary survey of the Great North's route was considered by the provisional committee on 3 March 1845. Diverging from the Aberdeen Railway at Marywell Street (the AR was to end at the gasworks site on Gas Street), it went up the west side of the Denburn stream and on to Kittybrewster. Gibb offered four possible lines between Kittybrewster and Huntly[22] and a single option from there to a point "a little west of Nairn" where double track would end and two single lines continue, one to Inverness and one to Fort George. The latter was not because of its military importance but to reach a pier where traffic to and from the far north could be exchanged. Gibb foresaw traffic in passengers, lime, coals, farm produce, livestock, stone and slate (there were slate quarries at Gartly, Foudland and Tillymorgan), minerals (the iron and manganese deposits in Glenavon and Glen Livet were being talked up), salmon and other fish, timber, manufactured goods, distillery traffic, manures, drainage tiles, etc., and estimated a total construction cost of £749,000[23]. A revised prospectus was issued on 8 March, listing potential branches to Banff and Portsoy, Speymouth, and Lossiemouth or Burghead. The Fort George line "may be so constructed as afterwards to form part of a leading line of railway to the four northern counties", which suggests that the committee was considering bridges or embankments across two navigable firths. The demand for shares was such that Adam & Anderson announced that no applications would be entertained after 29 March 1845, and by that date applications for 75,000 shares had been received[24]. The *Aberdeen Courier* on 9 April 1845 reported that 200,000 shares had been applied for. By then, however, the promoters no longer had the field to themselves. An alternative scheme, the 'Aberdeen Banff & Elgin Railway, with Branches to Peterhead and Fraserburgh' was being pushed by the Aberdeen solicitors Stronach & Grainger, with its own provisional committee. Its line would follow the Don to Inveramsay, then turn north to Banff, and westwards along the coast.

Unlike the southern schemes, there was neither combination nor compromise between these two: a propaganda war opened up, and both were presented to Parliament. The GNS committee set out to exclude all possibility of competing lines, presenting two Bills, one for the Great North of Scotland Railway to Inverness, with branches to Burghead, Portsoy, and Banff; the other for the Great North of Scotland Eastern Extension Railway, from Dyce to Fraserburgh, with a branch to Peterhead. Other Bills were lodged by promoters of the Alford Valley Railway, the Banffshire Railway, the Banffshire Extension Railway[25], the Deeside Railway (all supported by the GNS committee) and – of some concern to the Aberdeen Railway board – the East of Scotland Junction Railway, promoting a line from Arbroath through Bervie and Montrose to Stonehaven.

This sudden plethora of north-east regional lines reflected the national picture: 115 Bills for Scottish railways had been lodged and the number for England was naturally far greater. As with the GNS and Aberdeen Banff & Elgin, many of these proposed lines were competing for the same territory, but almost all the railways subsequently made in Scotland were first proposed in the 'railway mania' of 1845-46, though it took more than fifty years to complete them. If private greed to make a fast buck out of rising railway shares, and the anxiety of towns not to be left off the railway network were prime factors, so also was the policy of railway companies or committees. Whenever a line was proposed by someone else in 'their' territory, they opposed it by putting forward their own scheme. At a gathering of gentlemen to celebrate the opening by the Earl of Fife's Trustees of the Banff Hotel, 'Success to the Railways' was proposed by James Adam of the *Aberdeen Herald*, who noted James Grant hard at work on the Morayshire Railway, and Mr Stronach pushing forward the Aberdeen Banff & Elgin, but ended by coupling the name of Alexander Anderson, of the Aberdeen Railway, with the toast. Replying, Anderson expressed confidence that the line would be completed within three years[26]. Two other proposed railways were also of concern to the Aberdonians: news of the Great North project had prompted parties in Inverness to propose a T-shape of lines, from Inverness to Elgin, and from Nairn to Perth. There was to be no welcome in the Highland capital for a railway from Aberdeen. Relatively few of the 136 named persons on the GNS provisional committee came from west of Forres. In October 1845, however, a meeting between Great North and Perth & Inverness projectors was arranged in London, with the aim of making an amicable agreement on a shared Inverness-Nairn line, but it never took place because Edward Ellice MP, who had arranged it, was away. In March 1846 the GNS committee resolved to oppose the Perth & Inverness Bill[27].

Sir Alexander Anderson, a founder, director and law agent of the GNSR. *(Aberdeen City Libraries)*

**Lines north of Aberdeen Joint Station in the 1930s. Schoolhill Station platforms
can be seen in the distance.** *(LGRP)*

The Canal, the Turnpikes, and Gaining of the Acts

In the summer of 1845 the directors, as they were already calling themselves, of the GNS were considering the purchase of the Aberdeenshire Canal. At a stroke it would provide an easy line from Kittybrewster almost as far as Inverurie and remove a competitor (and a possible opponent to their Bill[28]). On 2 September they resolved to buy it. The canal company's Act in 1796 had authorised capital of £20,000, of which £17,800 was paid up; in 1800 it had run out of money and a second Act authorised a further £20,000, which it failed to raise and instead took out a mortgage of £10,000[29]. Its annual revenue was noted as £2,553 16s 4d, its expenditure, before interest payments, at £1,337 0s 7½d, and it had never earned enough to pay a dividend. The agreed price was £36,000, a large sum in the circumstances, but the deal was commended by Blaikie as "desirable and advantageous for both parties." Certainly, for anyone owning shares in the canal company, it was a highly favourable transaction. Alexander Jopp, an Aberdeen lawyer, member of the GNS committee and also agent for the canal proprietors, handled the sale, which was contingent on the railway receiving its Act[30].

Railways might be a new thing for Aberdeen but its businessmen were alive to the money-making opportunities involved. Some of the promoters of the Aberdeen Banff & Elgin had been early recipients of GNS shares, which they had sold on at a profit. In the bitter war of words between the two schemes they were accused of setting up the AB&E project purely as a way to repeat the operation on a larger scale. But the involvement of the engineer Thomas Grainger, perhaps a kinsman of the Aberdeen lawyer Charles Grainger[31], suggests that it was more than a phantom company. Sizeable sums were at stake here. Investors had signed up for large holdings, whose profitability was predicated on engineers' assessments of a likely return on capital. A competing line could erode that return and make the investment a risky one. Gibb's estimate of 7% on the Aberdeen Railway would allow an investor to borrow at 4% in order to pay the successive instalments of his shares and still have a clear profit margin. But if the return fell to 4% or less it would be another story – thoughts of this kind were beginning to preoccupy the minds of many people who had signed up blithely for large amounts of railway stock. With the railway mania beginning to implode, the euphoria of 1845 was fading fast when in December, with construction going on at each end of the line, the Aberdeen Railway called up a further instalment of £5 per share from its investors, many of whom failed to respond.

In May 1846 all the north-eastern railway projects were listed in a single group for consideration by a House of Commons committee. By 20 May, the two Inverness Bills had been thrown out, and the Aberdeeen Banff & Elgin and Banffshire Railway Bills had been withdrawn[32]. The Deeside Railway was unopposed, and both Great North Bills had survived the first stages of scrutiny[33]. Lord Provost Blaikie and a posse of directors were stationed in London to join negotiations outside Parliament, to pacify or buy off opponents, among them the Aberdeenshire and Banffshire turnpike road trusts, which were anxious about their ability to pay off their debts from a diminished toll income. The trusts held out for a ten-year guarantee of annual payments to make each year's revenue up to their average annual net income in the ten-year period before the passing of the railway's Act. Some landowners were accommodating, including the Duke of Richmond & Lennox, who was willing to allow a low price for the line across his extensive grounds, but the Earl of Fife required £20,000 compensation for injury to his amenities. Brodie of Brodie was induced to withdraw his opposition by the payment of £500 plus £1,000 for temporary loss of his amenities during construction[34]. The hopes of allies had sometimes to be damped down, as when the Caithness Commissioners of Supply asked the company to improve the harbours at Lossiemouth and Burghead and set up steam packet services – then and later, the GNS would refrain from sinking its money in harbours[35].

On 26 June 1846 the Great North of Scotland Railway Act was given the royal assent, and the Eastern Extension followed on 14 July, with the Alford and Deeside Railways. All competitors were out of the running – what could be more promising? The directors met on 7 July, when Lord Provost Blaikie was elected as chairman and William Leslie was appointed interim secretary[36]. Payment of £18,000 on account for the services of Adam & Anderson was approved. A first ordinary general meeting of the shareholders was held on 21 August, but an immediate start was not in prospect. The directors recommended holding back for a time, because of pressure on the capital and labour markets, and it was agreed to defer work until the Aberdeen Railway had reached a more advanced stage; at that time its opening was anticipated in spring 1848. If this decision came as a blow to communities expecting an early railway link, it suited the shareholding group who were spared an immediate call on their £50 shares. For the same reason, delays were agreed for the Eastern Extension, Alford Valley and Deeside Railways. In the meantime the directors were to receive limited fees of £100 (to be shared), the secretary / treasurer £100, and the two auditors £10 10s each, per annum, though on 21 July they had also voted themselves attendance fees of £1 1s for meetings (£1 11s 6d for the chairman) and daily allowance of £3 3s when in London for the company[37]. Some information as to the holdings in GNS shares emerges from a scripholders' meeting held on 18 May noted "as now required by Parliament" before the Bill was passed. Although the original proposal was for 22,000 £50 shares, a further 5,776 were issued, on the supposition that not all subscribers would pay up, and considering the "great inconvenience and loss from a second allotment"[38], but deposits were paid on all 27,776 and the authorised capital was raised to £1,500,000. Fifty-four shareholders held 22,172 shares. They included William Gordon, sharebroker of Aberdeen, with 3,505; George Cruickshank, advocate, Aberdeen, 1,195, Thomas Blaikie 1,380, David Blaikie 540, John Blaikie 1,000, George Thompson Jnr, 780, N. T. Christie, secretary of the Aberdeen Railway, 500, James Hadden 570, Alexander Anderson 1,575, Robert Allan, sharebroker, Edinburgh, 1,715, Alex Pirie 500, Patrick Pirie 500. Hadden and the Piries were textile and paper manufacturers in Aberdeen. It was very much an Aberdeen company, and as Joseph Mitchell, projector of the Inverness railways, observed, the promoters had kept almost all the stock for themselves or their friends, "calculating …that when they obtained their Bill the stock would run up to a premium". He believed, correctly, that their deposit money had been advanced by the banks, chiefly the North of Scotland Bank. Unfortunately, the railway mania had run its course and the value of shares was sliding. At the time, Great North £50 shares, with £2 10s deposit paid up, could be had for £2 7s 6d[39].

CHAPTER 2.
Acts and Inaction, 1846 – 1850

Amalgamation Agreed

A statement of accounts to date in August 1846 told the Great North shareholders that their Act had not come cheaply. The engineers had been paid £5,545, advertising and printing amounted to £23,406 10s 6½d, payments to witnesses at the enquiry were £4,861 6s 2d, and to agents £4,790 13s 3d, while brokers received £3,664 10s. Attendance fees for directors were £418 19s. An unusual item was £936 4s 11d for 435 shares in the rival Aberdeen Elgin & Banff Railway, whose affairs were now being wound up. These had been passed to a Mr Yeats, "agent for certain opponents of the AE&B Company, acting in concert with the Great North", who was to retain the proceeds on account of "certain claims against this company" – from such details emerge hints of the semi-covert dealings inseparable from competitive Bills. Lord Moray had been paid £860 to withdraw his opposition to the Bill. In all, £161,852 17s 1d had been spent, while deposits on shares amounted to £142,565. Unsurprisingly, the board was seeking to defer payment for the canal until their railway had "broken ground". Despite being financially in the red, the GNS agreed to acquire 6,395 £50 shares in its Eastern Extension Railway, currently held by the Aberdeen Railway, at £1 a share. The company had no legal authority to make this purchase. In December it had to arrange a bank overdraft of £11,000 to buy the Woodside estate north of Aberdeen, through which its line had to pass; the purchase made necessary by the obduracy of its owner, Mr Kilgour, who would otherwise have opposed the company's Bill[1].

To the south, the Aberdeen Railway had taken a lease of the Arbroath & Forfar line, intending to convert it to double track and reduce its gauge to 4ft 8½in. An annual dividend of 5½% on the A&F capital of £223,500 was guaranteed to its proprietors[2]. Just outside Aberdeen, the Dee Viaduct was under construction. On 28 September, three arches collapsed, after the centering was prematurely removed, killing seven workmen and seriously injuring four. Thomas Blaikie was among the first to arrive on the scene, and it was noted that the railway directors "in the most liberal manner" had undertaken to defray funeral expenses and grant temporary aid to widows and dependants[3]. On 17 October 1846 the Aberdeen Railway company held an ordinary general meeting, with James Hadden in the chair. Completion by 1848 was still anticipated. So far, it had raised actual capital of £217,209 17s 5d and spent £170,025 16s 3½d. Much more than £47,000 was needed for completion, and the two boards discussed the possibility of the AR being leased by the London & North Western, which they understood (incorrectly) to have already leased the Scottish Central Railway and Scottish Midland Junction railways and to be "in treaty" for the Caledonian line. It was agreed that no deal should be made which did not also embrace the Great North, and that meanwhile a Bill for merging the AR and GNS should be introduced[4].

In January 1847 the companies held special meetings of shareholders on consecutive days to consider and vote on the amalgamation plan, unanimously approved in each case. The Aberdeen board had other business, including rearrangement of lines for through running at Forfar, where the Arbroath & Forfar station was a terminus, and purchase of ground from Aberdeen Harbour Commissioners at Upper Inches, for workshops. This item ran into trouble when at a routine inquiry held by the Admiralty, Alex Torrie, a town councillor and harbour commissioner, claimed that the railway board was using influence to buy the land cheaply. James Hadden (Dean of Guild), Thomas Blaikie (Lord Provost), and Alexander Hadden, brother of James, were all both railway directors and members of the harbour commission. Another director, Alex Pirie, had a brother on the commission. The inquiry officer undertook to report back to the Admiralty, which in turn left the decision to Parliament, which was due to consider the harbour commission's Bill to allow the sale. Despite Torrie's opposition, the Bill was passed, but the commissioners agreed to submit the land price to arbitration to ensure a fair deal[5].

On 9 July 1847 the Amalgamation Bill of the Great North and Aberdeen Railways received the royal assent, with the proviso that it should not take effect before half the capital of each company had been called up and expended. By now, the AR had raised £422,797 of its authorised £830,000, but the GNS had raised only £142,565 of its authorised £1,500,000. The combined company would take the name of the Great North of Scotland Railway[6].

The Scottish Midland Junction was still trying to get powers to build its "direct" line from Forfar to Brechin but its Bill was suspended until the 1848 session of Parliament, while the Aberdeen Railway was making good progress at its southern end. In July 1847 Mr Ingram of the Star Inn, Montrose, sold his 26 horses – his mail contract was taken over by the AR on a five-year agreement, using horses until the line should open. Brown & Murray, contractors on the southern section, were enlightened employers, refusing to operate truck or tommy shops (many contractors paid their men partly in vouchers only exchangeable at the tommy shop, and over-charging for goods sold) and not reducing the wages in winter. On 25 September, in an unusual gesture, their workmen presented them each with a silver snuffbox. By mid-October, the Montrose Branch was almost finished to a temporary terminus at Rotten Row outside the town, and a locomotive – the first one built in Aberdeen, by Simpson & Co., ironfounders – was delivered by road to Dubton on the 23rd[7].

Neo-classical pavilions with linking wings formed the façade of the original joint station at Aberdeen. A view from the corner of Guild Street and Gas Street. (Great North of Scotland Railway Association)

Openings, and money problems

Problems were building up, however. By now, share prices had tumbled, interest rates had soared, and a general disillusionment with railways as an investment had arisen. Thousands of people who had paid deposits on railway shares were unable, or unwilling, to pay the further instalments that the companies needed for construction (and to pay interest on their own borrowings). The AR, with a small number of shareholders holding large amounts of stock, was badly affected. At the annual general meeting on 30 November 1847, James Hadden revealed that the company was heavily indebted to its bankers. So far, £664,000 of the £830,000 capital had been called up, and another £5 call was announced. In 1847, £450,000 had been spent, and to avoid bankruptcy, the contractors' operations had had to be cut back. A further £300,000-worth of capital was needed to complete the line. On the same day the a.g.m.s of the Great North, Eastern Extension, and Alford Valley companies were held, and it was resolved to postpone commencement of work for another year, as also with the Deeside Railway. Deeside £50 shares, with £5 already paid up, were being quoted at £3, while Aberdeen Railway £50 shares, with £45 paid up, were at £27, and Great North, with £2 10s paid up, were at £0 17s 6d[8]. The GNS managed to stave off payment for the Aberdeenshire Canal, first to 1 April 1848, then for an open-ended period, though having to pay 5½% interest on the £36,000[9].

Industrial relations were less good in the north, exacerbated by the AR's financial troubles: pay had been reduced, men had been laid off, and the price of provisions raised. On 5 January 1848 the navvies, mostly Highlanders, rioted in Stonehaven, breaking windows and beating up people who could not reply to them in Gaelic. One man was killed and some twenty injured. Next day the militia arrived, eleven ringleaders were arrested, and an uneasy peace restored. Against this alarming background, the southern section of the Aberdeen Railway was opened on 1 February. The directors' party left Aberdeen by road coach at 6 am, reaching Montrose five hours later. At Rotten Row two engines were waiting with a train of seventeen "splendid" first class carriages, which ran to Brechin in 20 minutes. A group from Forfar joined the party, and the train set off for Arbroath before returning to Montrose, for a luncheon laid on for 400 people, a convivial occasion when "the viands disappeared with great rapidity". James Hadden noted that the Aberdeen Railway's lease of the Arbroath & Forfar Railway had begun on the previous day. The mode of working was four mixed trains daily between Montrose and Arbroath, with connections for Brechin at Bridge of Dun, and Forfar at Friockheim, plus two Brechin-Forfar trains[10]. Expressing a hope that the Great North line would soon be started, he said its directors were merely waiting until they could obtain materials and money at moderate expense[11]. Before long, it was apparent that the Aberdeen Railway's progress had stalled, for the same reason. By May, Hadden was asking for a loan from the Government to complete the line, and in June the AR was one of seven Scottish railway companies petitioning the Treasury to provide £1,000,000 at "a moderate rate of interest" to enable them to carry on, since in "the present embarrassed state of mercantile affairs" they were unwilling to make further calls on their shareholders. County meetings in Aberdeenshire, Banffshire and Kincardineshire supported the plea, but the Government declined to assist. The AR was also advertising for loans, at 6% interest[12].

On 2 August, the Scottish Midland Junction opened for passengers between Perth and Forfar, with goods services four weeks later. Little work was now being done on the Aberdeen line. The *Scottish Railway Gazette* commented that the Aberdeen Railway had now expended more than £1,000,000 and "we understand that the Company have paid not less than £300,000 more than contemplated for land. But in this respect they have suffered from the same kind of extortion and injustice which has added so largely to the embarrassment of other companies"[13]. The company, though running trains between Arbroath, Forfar, Montrose and Brechin, had run out of money to complete its line to Aberdeen. At 31 August 1848 its expenditure was £1,000,547 12s 2d, with capital and loans amounting to £997,466 4s 3½d[14]. Insolvency led to board changes, with Hadden departing and the election of five new directors including Lord James Hay as chairman, James Westland, new manager of the North of Scotland Bank[15], and Alex Pirie. Rescue by richer companies seemed the only option, and directors went to London to negotiate with the London & North Western Railway, which offered to pay the AR £80,000 on account, against valuation of its assets, and to work the line for five years, at a mileage rate to be fixed by the engineer Joseph Locke[16]. This would have drawn the Aberdeen line into the West Coast system, but while the offer was still under discussion, another proposal emerged from the East Coast companies, via the Edinburgh & Northern. Seeing the final section of their route in jeopardy, they offered two options: either the E&N, North British, and York Newcastle & Berwick Railways would take up £276,000 of Aberdeen Railway guaranteed preference stock at an annual dividend of 6% for five years, thereafter at 5% plus a share of surplus profits; or they would lease, complete and work the line for 21 years, taking 40% of the gross revenue. All options were laid before an extraordinary general meeting of AR shareholders on 31 October. Chairman Lord James Hay's motion favoured the East Coast. It was noted that the extent of present claims on the company was £80,000, to meet which there was £40,000 in unpaid share calls, and £58,000 in unused borrowing powers. The board's motion was carried without opposition, and on the same day an Edinburgh & Northern special meeting agreed by a majority decision to accept the rescue plan.

Crisis in the Aberdeen Railway

Financial straits invariably prompted shareholders to seek close inspection of company affairs, and the board agreed to appoint Quilter, Ball, Jay & Crosbie, accountants in London, to look through the company's accounts from the beginning, and make a report. Before this was received, at the AR's annual meeting on 30 November 1848 a major row erupted. Lord James had one or two positive points to note: the Scottish Midland Junction's northern extension Bill had been thrown out by a parliamentary committee, and preliminary information from the investigators suggested nothing amiss with the company's past accounts, but interest focused on the rescue plan and the state of the company's affairs, with £40-45,000 of share calls remaining unpaid, conversion work on the Arbroath & Forfar line unfinished, likewise the line to the terminus in Montrose, and only limited work going ahead between Dubton and Stonehaven. The board had decided to take the first of the East Coast options in preference to the West Coast proposal, as its £276,000 would enable full activity to resume. The number of directors was to rise from eleven to thirteen to include representatives from these companies. Sir James Elphinstone, deputy chairman, a former naval officer who had inherited his baronetcy in 1848, congratulated the board, saying that the AR's position "was now better than that of any railway in Scotland", but the mood changed dramatically when Mr Spicer, a London shareholder, brought up "certain rumours" about the company's affairs. He did not object to the East Coast arrangement, as the best thing in the circumstances, but opposed the re-election of three directors "whom I consider to be involved in a transaction not at all creditable to them, and which renders it not in the interest of the Company that they should remain in the direction".

It emerged that back in July 1846, the Aberdeen Railway board desperately needed to borrow money, but its Act did not allow borrowing until half the capital, £415,000, had been raised. A further £150,000 was needed to reach this, and Adam & Anderson undertook to see that it was done by 20 December. It was proposed that the directors should guarantee the necessary funds, "looking to the proprietary for indemnification", but a minority refused to participate and the proposal was dropped. The others, including John Blaikie, privately bought up £130,000-worth of forfeited Aberdeen Railway £50 shares at the highly advantageous price of £39,000, or £15 a share. During a brief easing of the share market, some of these 2,600 'club shares' were sold on at a profit. The price subsequently fell sharply, and the 'club' were now trying to get the company to relieve them of the shortfall on the value of the shares they still held, amounting to £92,000 at present prices[17]. A rift opened between the directors who had known about (or were part of) the 'club' and the new arrivals on the board, who were shocked by this cosy win-win arrangement. The London accountants' report disappeared from sight in a welter of accusations and counter-accusations. John Blaikie described the share purchases as the action of public-spirited men sustaining the company through its difficulties. Alex Pirie pointed out that the purchase had never been mentioned until the price fell and the 'club' tried to get relief from the company[18]. Meanwhile, in December, two Edinburgh & Northern directors appeared at the Aberdeen Railway board meeting on the 19th. They were prepared to pay over a first instalment of £20,000 on the subscription of £276,000, on the understanding that their entire shareholding would be immediately registered and that they would have six directors on the Aberdeen Railway board. To Sir James Elphinstone and three of his colleagues this was acceptable, but six directors, headed by Lord James Hay, demanded a delay, pointing out that only heads of agreement had been signed and the E&N had not yet produced a full draft. They were not hostile to the proposal, but felt formal consent should await the full details; and that these details should be considered by a board that did not have a phalanx of East Coast directors already installed on it.

Tumult in the company's affairs continued into the new year, with stormy meetings in Aberdeen and London. Spicer maintained his attack, and further issues emerged. One was the habit of the company's law agents, Adam & Anderson, of charging a 'slump sum' for services rather than providing a clearly itemised account. The other involved the AR's need to show that half its capital was raised by 20 December 1846. Arrears of calls still amounted to £40,000 and Adam & Anderson filled this gap by a loan to themselves of £40,000, half from each of the Aberdeen and North of Scotland Banks. They used this money to pay off outstanding arrears on a whole range of Aberdeen Railway shares which had not yet been paid up to the required £25 level, without informing the owners. As the owners paid up, the money was repaid by the AR to Adam & Anderson, with interest – £40,548 11s 4d was returned to them by 31 August 1847. Adam & Anderson, and their associates, could have paid the £40,000 against future calls on their own shares, but as Pirie pointed out, this would have made their shares unmarketable. With this dubious arrangement in place, the Aberdeen Railway was put in a position to borrow

Staff at Craigellachie in the early years of the twentieth century.
(Great North of Scotland Railway Association)

on the money market[19]. In another twist, Thomas Blaikie, who had withdrawn temporarily from the board while his company was tendering for ironwork (his nephew John remained a director) had written to the company expressing the hope that "they would have a preference for the work, at fair prices." No other tenders were sought and they got the contract, but Spicer demonstrated from figures given him by the engineer Joseph Locke, that it was given at £2 a ton over the market price, yielding excess profits of £18,000[20].

The Aberdeen Railway board, it seemed, had contained a nest of directors whose dedication to the company came second to their exploitation of opportunities it offered for their enrichment. Under heavy pressure, the entire board offered to resign and stand for re-election. At the adjourned extraordinary general meeting on 26 December, when it became obvious that only Spicer's nominees, including Lord James Hay and Alex Pirie, were going to be elected, Elphinstone and his discredited colleagues walked out[21]. With their removal, the Aberdeen and Great North companies ceased to be run by the same people, and the ousted directors from the AR board, still with their GNS seats, were bitterly resentful against their former company. Thomas Blaikie and Alexander Anderson both later received knighthoods and were considered highly respectable persons, and their dealings with the Aberdeen Railway were not untypical of what other railway directors did in the 1840s. Business ethics of the time allowed them to profit from their positions (and exertions on behalf of the company) in a way which would be considered unacceptable in the 1860s and which even in the 1840s was deplored by shareholders.

By January 1849 the East Coast companies had withdrawn their offer, blaming the Aberdeen Railway board for its refusal to act promptly. On its side, the Aberdeen board blamed the southern companies and hinted broadly that their urgency showed a concealed motive to get control before unveiling the terms of the agreement[22]. With astute and acquisitive figures in the background like the North British chairman John Learmonth, and the York, Newcastle & Berwick's George Hudson, such a motive is likely enough. Meanwhile, AR shares were trailing at £16 10s, and the new board, facing an uphill struggle to find extra capital, resolved on getting parliamentary authority to raise £549,377 6s 8d in 6% preference stocks. To a chorus of ex-directors proclaiming the futility of this measure and the imminent bankruptcy of the company, it embarked on what Spicer called "a vigorous and manly effort", while the GNS board protested that the share issue, requiring the conversion of unissued ordinary shares into preference stock, was illegal and would seriously damage its own interests.

Aberdeen Railway completed, Great North and Deeside not yet started

Commerce in Aberdeen had slumped in 1848. The Hadden mills closed for two years and others went out of business. In that year the Great North of Scotland took advantage of an 1848 Act to extend its building time by two years (also that of the branches) but did nothing towards making a start. Its current obligations were already exceeding its resources when at the end of January 1849 Mr Adam presented it with a demand for £73,800, on account of 1,630 shares held by him, on which £45 out of £50 had been paid up. This was not a personal investment but an agreed ploy to get the company's parliamentary deposit up to the required 10% of capital without troubling the scripholders, which "for obvious reasons" was not recorded in board minutes at the time. Now Adam wanted to be relieved. After some dickering, the North of Scotland Bank raised a credit to pay him and the shares were transferred to the company. Meanwhile Alex Gibb was pressing for a long-delayed £1,923 9s 3d, which the board continued to defer[23]. Prospects for the Great North were not looking bright, and doubtless those who had backed the Aberdeen Banff & Elgin were happy to jeer at its apparently endless inertia. In March three directors, including Alex Pirie resigned, and shareholders were increasingly restive, with Adam's and Anderson's role as both directors and law agents a focus of criticism. With the company in no position to make its line, Anderson had seen the big contractor Thomas Brassey in London and spoken also with Joseph Locke and the Duke of Richmond & Lennox. It was agreed that Brassey, together with the contractor J.R. Davidson, should tender for construction and operation of the line. Suddenly, things seemed to be moving. Thomas Blaikie resigned as chairman, pleading pressure of other commitments, and Sir James Elphinstone was elected in his place, with Blaikie remaining as "senior director"[24]. Late in August, the GNS board considered three tenders for a single line to Inverness starting from Kittybrewster, on the northern edge of the city, and with no link to the Aberdeeen Railway; the lowest, £527,296 3s 3d, was offered by the consortium of Mitchell & Dean, who also tendered separately for the link line to the Aberdeen Railway, at £29,058, with a maximum gradient of 1 in 100, or £21,328 with a maximum gradient of 1 in 70. By the end of August, their main tender was accepted subject to Cubitt's approval, with the provisos that the company had the option to stop the line at Keith, if thought expedient, and that Mitchell & Dean would acquire and hold 7,500 £50 shares, to be held on their behalf by Gibb, and deposit £50,000 to be applied as calls on their shares. A finance and general purposes committee was set up, under Elphinstone, who also chaired a land acquisition committee. Landowners' fleecing of the Aberdeen Railway had not been forgotten, and a circular went out to shareholders, referring to the improved state of the money market and the reduction in labour costs, but "…we cannot expect returns… sufficient to justify the board offering a price beyond the actual value of the land, converted into a moderate Feu Duty"[25].

During the spring of 1849, with the economic climate easing somewhat, things were also looking up for the Aberdeen Railway. The preference share issue was fully subscribed, mostly by English investors, and work had resumed, with Locke & Errington as engineers. At a special meeting on 31 May, Alexander Anderson complained that his firm's role as company solicitors debarred him from assisting the return to the board of the ousted directors, who despite their prophecies of doom had retained their shareholdings. But Adam & Anderson were dropped by the Aberdeen Railway, whose new board was still disputing their charges, and had no wish to share its confidences with the Great North's law agents. In March the AR had been coaxed into completing the Montrose Branch by the combination of a low ground price from the council, with payment deferred for five years, and an offer by Mitchell, the contractor, to defer two-thirds of his charge until a year after completion[26], and by September the line was completed to the terminus on Erskine Street, with a tramroad to the quay. On the 18th a trainload of guests was taken from Montrose as far as Stonehaven[27]. From 1 November trains ran as far as Limpet Mill, three miles past Stonehaven[28], and at the half-yearly ordinary general meeting meeting on 29 November, Lord James announced that a single track had been laid as far as Portlethen. To save costs, it had been intended to make the Aberdeen terminus outside the city on the south bank of the Dee, but now it had been decided to complete the Dee Viaduct and make a terminus at Ferryhill, still a mile south of the centre and the harbour. This would enable the Deeside Railway to share the station. Rolling

Sir James Dalrymple Horn Elphinstone, chairman of the GNSR, 1849-1867: a 'Spy' cartoon of 1878.

stock was ordered, to the value of £90,000. A curious item at this meeting was a statement in the directors' report that £16,843 13s 7d shown in the accounts as payment for Deeside Railway shares was in fact the repayment to the Deeside Railway of a £16,000 loan made in 1847, plus interest. The repaid sum was to be divided among the Deeside shareholders, who would then make over their Deeside shares to the Aberdeen Railway: "In other words, the Deeside Shareholders agreed to hand over their undertaking to this Company," an arrangement which would prevent it from "falling into the hands of other and perhaps hostile parties," and the AR shareholders were informed that "you now hold the [Deeside Railway] Act, either to let its powers expire, or turn them to advantage should an opportunity offer"[29]. Why they should have handed over their shares merely in return for the repayment of what they were owed is not clear; but the Deeside company's £16,000 can only have come from its parliamentary deposit of £17,675, paid in January 1846, and refunded after passage of its Act. This sum, like the GNS deposit, was probably raised as a lawyers' and bankers' ploy, without the shareholders having to pay anything. Like the Great North, the Deeside board had yet to lay a foot of rail. Deeside £50 shares were being quoted at only £2 2s. Lord James also announced that the Aberdeen Railway would seek repeal of the Amalgamation Act with the GNS, since the two companies no longer had the same directors, the GNS had not made a start on construction, and once it was running, the AR would benefit anyway from through traffic from the north. The most cogent reason – the two boards were locked in enmity – was obvious but unstated.

Relations had bumped along at a low level throughout 1849. The intention of a joint central station remained, though the prospect was a remote one. Locke & Errington had criticised the Market Street site as requiring very expensive works and anyway being too small[30], and the Aberdeen Railway lodged a Bill to alter the station and to move the junction with the GNS further to the west. Meanwhile the AR was being sued by Blaikie Bros., who had been dropped as a supplier but claimed that they had a valid contract for providing all the company's ironwork. At the fourth ordinary general meeting of the Great North, on 28 November, the directors proposed immediate execution of a line from Kittybrewster to Keith, single tracked but with provision for doubling, made by Mitchell & Dean, to cost £380,000 plus £40,000 for the canal and £50,000 for other costs. The resolution was passed by acclamation, though if anyone expected instant action they were to be disappointed. Another two years would go by before work started.

On 16 March 1850 the Aberdeen Railway directors travelled on the first train to reach Aberdeen (Ferryhill), where a large crowd had gathered to witness the arrival. The Scottish Central and Scottish Midland Junction Railways had been working since 1848, as had the Edinburgh & Northern (renamed Edinburgh Perth & Dundee Railway in 1849), and rail connections to the south now existed both via the Forth and Tay ferries and the inland route via Forfar, Perth and Stirling. Public opening of the Aberdeen Railway took place on 1 April for passengers, with goods services beginning from 1 May.

CHAPTER 3
Companies at War, 1850 – 1853

Amalgamation repealed

By contrast, the Great North of Scotland had not put a spade into the ground. Its board's explanation for the protracted delay had been that they were waiting for more propitious economic circumstances, and also for the southern access line to be complete. But building of many other railways had continued, despite the tight money market and high costs of labour and materials. The true reason for inaction lay with the expensive £50 shares issued with such confidence five years before. Even more than with the Aberdeen Railway's, a high proportion had been allotted to the directors and their business associates, and the board's reluctance to make calls on the shareholders had a hefty element of self-interest: they themselves might have to borrow substantial sums in order to pay, and their belief in a handsome dividend had waned. When in 1849 the GNS directors at last decided that a start must be made, they appealed not to the shareholders but to one of the region's great magnates, the Duke of Richmond & Lennox. The key issue was the price of land. A widespread belief, with much evidence to back it up, was that the demands of greedy landowners had forced the costs of railway building up to levels of capital cost which hugely reduced their profitability. For the GNS, contemplating a line of 108 miles, a new approach was essential, even though in the first instance it was proposing to build only as far as Keith, 53 miles from Aberdeen. Encouraged by the duke, a committee of Aberdeenshire landlords agreed they were "not unfavourably disposed" to a yearly rent at agricultural rates, rather than a sale. The duke himself agreed provisionally to provide land for the railway by permanent annual rental (a feu, in Scottish legal terminology) at a price that reflected agricultural, not 'development' value. Other landowners followed his example, including Sir James Elphinstone. In November Adam and Anderson and also David Blaikie resigned from the board, making room for new landowner-directors[1].

Completion of the Aberdeen Railway prompted the *Aberdeen Journal* to urge the Deeside company into action. A local accountant, Robert Russell Notman, had just published a lengthy *Letter to the Landed Proprietors of Deeside*, setting out the advantages of a railway and suggesting that a single-track line as far as Banchory could be made for a relatively modest £75,292. At this time, three horse coaches and 33 carriers were operating on the Deeside roads. Notman acted as secretary to a committee formed on 22 August, with Alexander Kinloch of Park as chairman, to resuscitate the Deeside project. It hoped to have a Bill lodged for the 1851 parliamentary session[2], and though this did not materialise, preparations went on, with the engineer John Errington giving his services free in a fresh survey as far as Banchory.

Unfortunately for the Aberdeen Railway, completion of its line did not bring the expected surge in income. Goods and passengers had always come and gone by sea, and the steamer companies, faced with new competition, immediately reduced their rates, so that the railway drew only a limited amount of traffic away from the traditional route. With low traffic, high working costs, high interest charges, and, not least, the obligation to pay the guaranteed lease of the Arbroath & Forfar Railway all fuelling shareholders' dissatisfaction, a committee of inquiry was appointed. The committee recommended that £200,000 of additional capital be raised, £150,000 in 5% preference shares, the rest in debentures; also that a general manager should be appointed, and the board cut to nine or even seven members. Against opposition from the New Market company, which had asked £50,000 for its site, from the harbour commissioners, and from the Great North, the Aberdeen Railway obtained an Act on 29 July for relocating the central joint station from the original Market Street location to Guild Street, south of a proposed new road running west from the harbour[3]. The GNS had to borrow another £5,000 from its bankers to meet the cost of opposing this proposal and getting clauses inserted to protect its position, including one compelling the Aberdeen Railway, when the Great North should come to within 200 yards of its line, to extend the line to meet the GNS at the junction originally intended rather than at the new level it proposed. Piers for Cubitt's long viaduct had been erected and some arches finished, but these were now taken down. Another important item in the Act, not opposed by the Great North, was for repeal of the Amalgamation Act of 1847[4]. Personal hostilities aside, neither company could see any commercial value in a merger.

The Great North and Morayshire refinanced, the Aberdeen Railway struggles

At this time, the GNS finances were hanging on a shoestring. Repayment of the £5,000 loan was to be made out of a first call on shares, which might be made either for the purposes of winding up the company or proceeding[5]. Further aid was got from the Duke of Richmond on 2 May 1850, when he chaired a meeting in London to consider a Guarantee Fund initiated by two new directors, Mr Morison of Bognie, and the lawyer G.D. Sandford. The duke guaranteed £15,000-worth of shares, with repayment not demandable until two years after opening of the line to Keith. The guarantee was set at £20 per share, which was considered sufficient despite the nominal £50 value. In the hope of contributions from other wealthy parties, local committees were set up along the line to help the guarantee and rental schemes, and Elphinstone wrote numerous letters seeking support[6]. These initiatives did

GNS mechanics and busmen with a Caledon 45 hp 18-seater bus at Kittybrewster. This vehicle was in service with the GNS from 9 July 1915. Its chassis was transferred to the LNER southern Scottish area on 12 April 1926. *(Stenlake collection)*

The interior of Peterhead Station in 1963, little changed from GNSR days. New posters, of course, and maybe one new coat of paint, but it was still gas-lit. *(G N Turnbull/Great North of Scotland Railway Association)*

not have the desired effect, and finally in October the company's rickety finances were firmly grasped. On the advice of a London-Scottish solicitor, J.N. Farquhar, a scheme already tried out successfully by the Shrewsbury & Hereford Railway was adopted: the company's capital limit was to be cut from £1.5 million to £1 million and the crippling £50 shares replaced by 100,000 new shares at £10. Every registered holder of a £50 share on which £2 10s had already been paid up would receive five £10 shares plus an additional share with £2 10s already credited to it. The new shares were to be marketed at a discount of 10%. This recapitalisation, which also allowed losses to be written off, leaving only survey costs and parliamentary expenses relating to the Great North line, required parliamentary approval which was obtained in an Act on 3 July 1851, and so did not immediately transform the situation, but with the growing Guarantee Fund, and the feeling that land prices were "largely safe", it encouraged the board to go ahead with the patiently waiting Mitchell & Dean. The contract was finally signed in March 1851, though for a line only as far as Huntly. The 40 3/4 miles to Huntly, if feued at £16 a mile per year, would cost £652 a year, a very manageable figure[7]. Benjamin Hall Blyth, of Edinburgh, was appointed engineer to the line, at £55 per mile exclusive of travel and other expenses. William Leslie resigned as interim secretary in December and his salary, hitherto unpaid, was handed over. Alexander Anderson, ex-director, temporarily replaced him[8].

Its own lack of capital – only £29,700 worth of shares had been sold – and the improbability of the GNS ever building between Keith and Elgin also cut the Morayshire Railway's ambitions down to size. Although its prospectus had assured investors that it would be completed within a year of its Act being granted, it had been unable to make a start. At an extraordinary general meeting on 21 September 1850 its shareholders approved of a plan to abandon the proposed line between Orton and Rothes and concentrate on making the railway between

Elgin and Lossiemouth, a less ambitious exercise estimated at around £3,000 a mile for its 5 ½ mile length. A further notice in June 1851 confirmed the abandonment as between Orton and Craigellachie[9]. Even the short line was too much for a group of Edinburgh shareholders, who tried in the following summer to get the company wound up, but the doughty James Grant, Provost of Elgin from 1848 to 1863, saw them off, by 1,586 voting shares to 712. The company's intended capital of £75,000 was cut back to £29,700, with the 2,970 £20 shares reduced to £10; and borrowing of £9,900 allowed once half the capital was paid-up[10].

The Aberdeen Railway was fighting its contractors, who were claiming damages of £40-50,000 for the stoppages inflicted by the company's lack of funds – the arbitrator ruled in favour of the railway company – and also its erstwhile law agents Adam & Anderson, who, having claimed £67,165 5s 2d, were awarded £1,047 19s 1d by arbitration. £61,026 8s 3d of their claim, described as "Advances to Company", was exposed as consisting of Adam & Anderson's losses in the share market. A longer-running case was that of Blaikie Bros against the Aberdeen Railway, claiming that they had a legal contract for the supply of all the company's ironwork. Having sacked Blaikies, the new board was mounting a counter-case for repayment of excess profits, claiming that the contract had been illegal and that Alexander Gibb, who had been appointed arbitrator for the contract, was ineligible because of his links with Blaikies. The Court of Session ruled that the contract was valid but the AR immediately appealed[11]. A general manager had been appointed, James Tasker, from the SCR, but he died in January 1851. Despite sabbatarian pressure from both outside and inside the board, the company was running Sunday trains at the Post Office's behest, for both mail and passengers.

The struggles of the Aberdeen Railway to achieve profitability, and of the GNS to raise capital, forced the two companies into a state of communication if not amity. The AR's new share issue was a flop. A year after opening it was still running at a loss, and an agreement was made with the Scottish Central to work both the AR and the Scottish Midland Junction lines, using these companies' plant, at cost, for a year from 1 February 1851, cutting out any through service to the Edinburgh Perth & Dundee Railway (Edinburgh & Northern until 1849) via Broughty Ferry and Tayport. Some of the AR's creditors had a trust conveyance made out in their names, as trustees for all creditors, of "the whole rolling stock and service and other materials", plus 7% of fully paid-up stock, against their claims. At the half-yearly meeting on 30 April 1851, Lord James Hay expressed his keenness to see the Great North in operation, in the hope that its traffic would offset the heavy competition of the steamship companies[12].

In August Robert Milne was appointed as full-time secretary to the GNS. Trained as a civil engineer, he would represent the company through thick and thin for 29 years. Even without a mile of track the Great North had problems to cope with. One of the immediate issues was the canal purchase: as the canal had been set up by an Act of Parliament, parliamentary sanction should have been sought for its purchase and demolition. An Edinburgh lawyer gave his opinion that the purchase appeared to have gone beyond the directors' statutory powers. The error resulted in the GNS being obliged to pay compensation of some £10,000 to bargemen and tenants on canal ground, and a boardroom row broke out over who was to blame. An inquiry, at the instigation of a landowners' meeting, looked at the proceedings of the provisional committee, which had been criticised as irregular in certain respects and which might have left the board without legal authority to make calls on the shareholders. Originally 29,316 shares been allotted, of which 12,141 had been returned for registration, and 17,715 had not been returned. The company had not attempted to chase up these shareholders and so its share register was incomplete. Another questionable matter was the company's expenditure of £8,371 1s 1d on shares in the GNS Eastern Extension Railway. It was explained that it was thought necessary at the time for the Great North to own enough shares to ensure complete control of the Eastern Extension, but that in present circumstances the board did not consider it advisable to proceed with the line[13].

A new broom on Deeside; the Great North flirts with the Great Northern

Queen Victoria and Prince Albert had leased Balmoral Castle in the Upper Dee valley since 1848; in October 1851, returning to Windsor, they took the Royal Train (LNWR carriages) from Stonehaven, where the hard-pressed Aberdeen Railway had built two dining rooms, a drawing room and other apartments for the Queen's party[14]. The Deeside Railway at that time existed only on paper, but in November the company gave notice of a Bill to supersede its original Act of 1846, with a revised line as far as Banchory. It had acquired a new, vigorous chairman in John Duncan, an Aberdeen advocate who had recently become chairman (1850-52) of the Caledonian Railway, introducing a policy of strict economy to pull the Glasgow company out of dire trouble[15]. Duncan announced a reform programme including reduction of the capital to £106,250 and cutting the share price from £50 to £10, though he did not expect calls on the shareholders to exceed £5 a share, and boldly stated his expectation that the cost per mile of the line, 16 miles 1 furlong, would be around £5,000[16]. Not far away, the Alford Valley Railway quietly wound up its affairs in December. Only £4,344 of its £100,000 capital had been paid up, and subscribers got back only £2 16s of their £5 deposit on each £50 share[17].

With the Amendment Act of 3 July 1851, the Great North's authorised capital was reduced to £1,107,440, and its loan limit cut to £300,000[18]. The turn-round had begun, though initially progress was slow. Aberdeen's stock market continued to list the old £50 shares, with £2 10s paid up, at the giveaway price of 1s 6d until the end of 1852[19]. The problem of raising actual capital still remained, and the directors had to make a more tempting offer. An ambitious issue, of 83,058 preference shares priced at £10, to yield a dividend of 5% a year, was promoted. When the GNS published a prospectus for this issue in November 1851, the Aberdeen Railway board objected to the Kittybrewster-Keith line being put as a priority over a link to the southern line, but the GNS board emphasised its wish to build the cheapest line, and one that would "secure the traffic"[20]. The Aberdeen Railway board responded by refusing to recommend the GNS share issue to its large constituency of English shareholders (its own £50 shares at the time could be had for £10[21]. Much discussion and little real action went on into 1852. In late spring Adam raised the GNS's hopes after a meeting with Edmund Denison, chairman of the Great Northern Railway, to discuss

An early portrait of John Duncan, chairman of the GNSR, 1867-1871.

"pecuniary assistance" to the GNS if all its through traffic to places south of York were booked through the English company, unless specifically consigned by some other route. This would be impossible without the co-operation of the Aberdeen Railway, and a proposition was made to the AR that if the Great North were to build the connection with the Aberdeen Railway, the AR "… will enter into a formal mileage agreement with the Great North of Scotland and companies comprising the Eastern route." The Aberdeen Railway replied positively, ready "even at some sacrifice" to co-operate if the Aberdeen link line were to become a reality, and on being assured that the GNS was in a position to build a northern line at least as far as Elgin. During the summer of 1852 the Great North even allowed itself to be "inspected" by Alex Pirie and George Leslie on behalf of the AR, as a preliminary to the Aberdeen board recommending Great North shares to its larger shareholders. They felt that a line going no further than Keith would be unlikely to bring much traffic to the AR, and wanted an extension to Burghead. In their view the GNS would need at least £350,000 more capital subscribed than the £395,000 it had so far reached; and they noted that no final agreements on land prices had been signed. As a price for its backing, the Aberdeen Railway wanted to have representation on the Great North Board. The Great North was quite amenable to building as far as Elgin or Burghead, if finance could be arranged, considered its land costs fairly estimated at £53,000, and agreed it was fair and reasonable for parties taking stock in large amounts to be represented on its board[22].

A Great North deputation to London followed in July, but discussions with the Great Northern, York Newcastle & Berwick and North British companies yielded only a willingness to give a percentage on through traffic rates when the line was working. What the GNS wanted was cash up-front. But the East Coast companies did want to secure their route to Aberdeen, and a visit followed by Seymour Clarke, the GNR's general manager, John Balfour and Henry Chaytor of the North British Railway, and Leeman and Hunter of the York Newcastle & Berwick, and things became a little more positive: the visitors recommended that the GNS create £150,000 in £10 shares to receive the ordinary dividend, plus a percentage to be derived from the traffic sent over the East Coast route. Refinements and confirmations of this proposition went on into September. Chaytor, now vice-chairman of the North British, was invited to join the Great North board, but he was a Londoner, and the affairs of the North British at this time were quite problematic enough to remove any allure from a directorship of another cash-strapped Scottish railway[23].

John Duncan, awaiting the passing of his Deeside Railway Bill, felt that the Deeside company, closely allied to the Aberdeen Railway, should "look to a much wider sphere than the Aberdeen Railway – namely, to the North,"

OPENING OF THE MORAYSHIRE RAILWAY.—THE TERMINUS AT LOSSIEMOUTH.

The opening of the first railway in the north of Scotland, in August 1852, attracted the attention of the *Illustrated London News* which published this engraving of the scene at Lossiemouth.
(Keith Fenwick collection)

and proposed a new line to the west of Aberdeen, joining the Great North at Kintore with the Deeside Railway at Murtle, "so as to open a new line of communication between Kintore and Aberdeen" and also to bring "the traffic, not only of Deeside, but the whole North of Scotland" along five miles of the Deeside line between Murtle and Ferryhill. Such a line would bring all three Aberdeen railways into a central joint station, from the south. Claiming it could be made for £60-80,000, Duncan said his proposal was not hostile to the Great North but would "relieve their minds of a heavy incumbrance"[24]. Though it knew the out-of-town location of its terminus at Kittybrewster was unpopular, the GNS board dismissed the idea, following a report from Benjamin Hall Blyth, describing it as traversing "bleak, barren territory", and took a feu of ground at the south-west side of Union Bridge (later the site of the Palace Hotel) as its preferred site for a joint central station. The Aberdeen Railway was less negative, and suggested to the GNS that independent arbitration should be sought to recommend the most economical and advantageous route[25]. The Deeside company got its new Act on 28 May and the first turf of the line was cut at Park by Mrs Kinloch, on 5 July, in the presence of a large crowd come to witness the "commencement of a new era on Deeside." Duncan announced that he expected the contractors, Leslie & Davidson, to complete the job in a year. Reporting the event, including the usual "sumptuous but elegant *déjeuner*", the *Aberdeen Journal* referred to Duncan as "a gentleman whose clear-headed ability and dauntless energy has raised to at least a well-founded prospect of success an extensive concern which had become a byword for prostration and ruin in the railway world"[26]. On 10 August it was the Morayshire Railway's turn to put up the bunting, with the opening of its line from Elgin to Lossiemouth, the first railway north of Aberdeen[27].

A stab in the back – the Waterloo Quay extension

As time went on and the Aberdeen Railway revenues continued to fall short of costs and the GNS's capital remained short of what was required, attitudes hardened once again, and both the Great North's flirtation with the East Coast companies, and the rapprochement with the Aberdeen Railway, petered out. In October 1852 the GNS began chasing up unregistered holders of scrip (allocated shares). The original allottees were listed in the Share Register and a call of £1 10s per share was made. On behalf of a large group of allottees, John Clark, an Aberdeen advocate, wrote to deny any ownership and to reject the call[28]. On 25 November the long-awaited day came when the first sod of the Great North of Scotland line was cut, by Lady Elphinstone, at Westhall, near the Elphinstone mansion. The line was only to Huntly, but William Cadenhead, Aberdeen's bard, celebrated the event in verse (see page 2) as if the whole Inverness railway were under way. Under the umbrella of the Mitchell-Dean contract, seven contractors were at work with the 40-mile line divided into fourteen sections.

Relations with the Aberdeen Railway had relapsed: George Reith, the AR secretary, wrote to say that the GNS directors' report to the 7th ordinary meeting of chareholders did not fairly represent the discussions between the companies, and that the Aberdeen directors declined to recommend the purchase of Great North shares to their shareholders. The GNS board resolved "that no notice whatsoever be taken of the said letter"[29]. At the end of the year the AR introduced a Bill to raise further funds, and to make alterations to its line into Aberdeen city, and the GNS resolved to oppose it unless its rights and privileges were safeguarded[30]. Through 1852 the Aberdeen Railway had continued to run at a loss, despite efforts to increase its traffic. Advertisements in June announced Aberdeen-London within one day, by a train leaving Ferryhill at 6.06 am and reaching Euston at 11.15 pm. A first class return to London (not on the express) cost 30s. Return tickets to stations on the AR's own line were reduced to single fare plus a half. Goods traffic was improving but this necessitated expenditure on additional wagons, especially coal wagons. The board also wanted to get authorisation for a relocated joint station, despite unsatisfactory discussions on the subject with the Great North. In October the House of Lords ruled against Gibb having power to award damages to Blaikies against the AR, whereupon Blaikies instituted a case "for random amount of damages". That month John Stirling of Kippendavie, chairman of the Scottish Midland, was elected to the Aberdeen Railway board, in what turned out to be a significant move[31].

It was March 1853 before the Aberdeen Stock Exchange began listing the Great North's £10 ordinary and preference shares, at £0 5s and £1 respectively[32], but this was already an improvement on the previous share prices. Investors had begun to buy, and the prices climbed slowly but steadily. In February the Great North had raised Robert Milne's salary to £350 a year, backdated to 1 January 1852. By now the company was paying some of its bills, selectively. When Sir James Elphinstone sent in an account for £1,000 for his expenses between January 1849 and December 1851, his board suggested £650 in full settlement. It also resolved to tighten up on directors' expenses. Sir James's claims would be a recurrent minor theme in the Great North story[33]. In spring 1853 the Aberdeen Railway had to defer payment on its 6% and 7% preference shares, issuing warrants to the holders. Its

The coast line between Buckie and Portessie, with Gordonsburgh sawmill siding. *(Stenlake collection)*

passenger numbers remained disappointing and Alex Pirie, chairing the half-yearly meeting on 20 April, bemoaned "the general disinclination of northerners to move from home". The Scottish Central was still working the Aberdeen Railway and Scottish Midland Junction lines. With opening of the Deeside Railway imminent, the Aberdeen Railway again raised the question of the junction line with the Great North: it was willing to put forward a joint Bill, and to allow the Great North to charge a local rate equivalent to four miles for all goods carried on the mile-long line between Kittybrewster and the joint station. Robert Milne replied that his board needed more time to consider, and that the four-mile rate was not enough[34]. It was not unusual to make such additional charges in special cases: Milne had checked that the high-level Tyne Bridge at Newcastle was charged as if it were three miles, but the Aberdeen Railway doubted that the Denburn line would be eligible for a special toll on through rates, and instead offered the Great North 6% of its own revenue from through traffic over the junction line. While the Aberdeen company continued to press for a joint Bill to be lodged for the 1854 parliamentary session, the Great North temporised, making a claim that the Denburn line was anyway objectionable because "intervention of the main line of the Aberdeen Railway deprives the Great North of free access to the Station ground at the top of the Harbour …" It required free use of Aberdeen Railway tracks to reach the harbour: "a concession which would really cost you nothing"[35]. The AR accepted this, but the Great North's delaying tactics were successful in preventing any Bill being prepared for 1854.

A new director, John Stewart, had joined the GNS board on 29 November 1852, and would be a dynamic if also difficult and finally impossible member. He had established the Aberdeen Comb Works in 1830, by now the largest comb factory in the world, powered by steam, and a pioneering example of mass production. Stewart's views influenced and probably moulded the Great North's attitude to the proposed junction line with the Aberdeen Railway. While this remained a nominal commitment, the GNS board seems to have become increasingly convinced that for a large outlay, it would have relatively little to gain from the link while passing on substantial traffic to the Aberdeen Railway. Traders in the city were still sending and receiving the bulk of their goods by sea. For the next ten years or so, the central link through the Denburn Valley would be seen primarily as a bargaining counter to use against the Aberdeen Railway rather than a firm part of the Great North's own future strategy. And late in 1853 the GNS disclosed a new scheme – a short railway of 1 mile 6 furlongs from Kittybrewster to Waterloo Quay at the northern end of the harbour, using the canal bed, at an estimated cost of £10,000. At a stroke this would bring the company into the city (if not the centre) with its own terminus, and give it access to the quays. To the Aberdeen Railway, which had been negotiating in good faith and with some generosity for a shared station and shared access to the harbour, this was a stab in the back. The GNS could claim it was only making effective use of its ownership of the canal, and insisted that a junction line with the Aberdeen Railway was still proposed (though no-one now expected any early action on that) but it was obvious that it had been playing the other company along.

The Deeside Line opens; Inverness springs a surprise

Progress on the Deeside line was rapid and relatively smooth, with an 1853 amendment to the Act to bring it ¾ of a mile closer to Banchory than had at first been planned. Duncan noted that most landowners had been co-operative, with only a few smaller proprietors holding out for feus that would have been more appropriate to a city centre[36]. One of these proprietors was Alexander Anderson, who demanded £1,507 10s 3d for part of a field cut across by the railway. The company offered £112 10s. Arbitration failed to resolve matters and eventually a Sheriff court jury awarded Anderson £455 plus his costs[37]. Enough ground had been acquired to allow for double track between Murtle and Aberdeen, in case the Kintore link became a reality, though Robert Milne came along to a Deeside Railway special general meeting on 25 February 1853 in order to reiterate the Great North's negative opinion. The first train to Banchory carried a party of directors and guests on 20 August, and 200 invited guests attended the inaugural ceremony on 7 September, with the Aberdeen City Band in attendance. Toasts were drunk both to the Aberdeen Railway and to the Great North, represented by George Milne of Kinaldie. Public services began on 8 September, with three trains each way daily, worked by the Scottish Central in an extension of its agreement with the Aberdeen and Scottish Midland companies. The timing between termini was one hour. Only first and third class carriages were provided – although the GNS usually receives credit for being first to dispense with second class, it seems that the Deeside line takes precedence[38].

Following the problem over transfer of the Aberdeen Canal, the railway company had had to make separate contracts with each shareholder, offering shares rather than cash whenever possible. In November 1853, before this process was complete, Erskine & Carstairs, contractors for the southern section of the line, took unauthorised possession of the canal and drained it into the River Don at Dalweary, near Kintore, stranding numerous barges. The canal company went to the Court of Session, which compelled the contractors to restore and refill the waterway[39]. With the Huntly line progressing, the Great North board was considering the provision of locomotives and rolling stock. Adamson & Gordon, coal merchants, proposed to put 40 wagons on the line if they were guaranteed a preferential rate which would undercut carting from harbours. A Scottish engineer, Daniel Kinnear Clark, was retained first as a consultant to provide specifications for locomotives, then as locomotive superintendent, at £250 a year, and on his recommendation an offer from Blaikie Brothers to sell an engine they had on hand was refused. Tenders for seven passenger and five goods engines were considered, with the secretary instructed to contact the lowest tenderers, Fairbairn's of Manchester, at £2,250 for the passenger, and £2,220 for the goods types, and ask what proportion of shares they would accept as part-payment. A deal was done on 500 preference shares, not to be sold at a discount until a year after delivery of the engines. The Aberdeen Bank was agitating for payment of balances due plus interest, and the company paid up, also resolving to "strike off the Aberdeen Bank from the list of the Company's bankers". Efforts were being made to sort out the share register: 14,376 shares on which calls had not been paid up were declared forfeited and sold to unspecified purchasers at a giveaway price of £5, including a provision of £4 against future calls and at a discount not to exceed £1 10s a share[40].

What turned out to be a temporary easing of the money market brought other railway schemes back into the market-place. A new line from Inverurie to Turriff and Banff was proposed, impelling the GNS board into resuscitating its own line, only to cancel Blyth's survey as soon as it heard that the other project had been dropped. A Peterhead Railway, via Auchnagatt in central Buchan, also proposed by independent backers[41], did not last, but more ominous was the resumption of railway promotion in Inverness, for a 15-mile line to Nairn. The Great North's powers to build between Elgin and Inverness, and the Fraserburgh-Peterhead lines, were not further extended after 1850[42]. Failure to renew is unlikely to have been an oversight; more probably any re-application would have been refused, as the company had done nothing towards making a start, but the company's reaction to the Inverness project shows that the original aim had not been abandoned. Indeed, Benjamin Hall Blyth had re-surveyed the ground between Keith, Elgin and Burghead in the summer of 1853[43]. But having struggled to assemble enough funds for the line to Huntly, the GNS was in no condition to re-promote railways west of Elgin: at the ordinary general meeting on 25 November 1853 total receipts were reported as £188,210 9s 11d, and expenditure as £200,340 17s 10½ d. There was a credit balance with the banks of £33,000[44], but many claims had to be met, including the cost of the proposed harbour line. Diplomacy was needed, and late in 1853 Alexander Anderson met Inverness & Nairn promoters in Edinburgh and was reported to have wished them success, receiving assurances that the Great North would be granted "every facility consistent with the interests of their own [I&N] shareholders". In February 1854 these expressions of goodwill were overtaken by a GNS decision to oppose the Nairn Bill on the ground that it did not conform with parliamentary standing orders. This tactic brought further negotiations in London, resulting in an agreement made on 25 February, granting the GNS running powers between Nairn and Inverness from such time as the companies' lines met, with a booking office at Inverness, and on this basis the Great North withdrew its opposition. The status of this document was to cause dispute in the future. Correspondence in July between Adam & Anderson and G&P Anderson of Inverness, the I&N solicitors, shows that the latter were to produce a deed which both companies would seal, but the I&N seal would not be ready for nine or ten days. The Inverness & Nairn company got its Act on 24 July 1854, and with that accomplished, it does not appear that its solicitors ever produced the deed[45].

CHAPTER 4
The Opening, At Last 1854 – 57

The Great North prepares

In Aberdeen two railway companies were now active and the third's line was under construction. Traffic on the Deeside line was exceeding forecasts, earning around £10 per mile per week, and the passenger accommodation at Banchory had to be expanded, as had the goods depots there and at Culter. Introduction of goods services, and building of goods sheds, had been delayed until well after the opening to passengers. The Deeside directors, unhappy with the service provided by the Scottish Central, and preferring to have things under their own control, had resolved to operate the trains themselves. Two engines were on order in October, and 30 goods wagons were already on the line. On passenger carriages, John Duncan told the company's second ordinary general meeting, on 26 October, that the directors thought "open carriages, well fitted-up, was a desideratum for this line"[1] One hopes he had summer tourist traffic in mind. The Morayshire Railway also returned an optimistic report, with a gross revenue of £3,484 17s 9d since its opening on 10 August 1852, and expenses of £1,760 9s 7d; and a 5% dividend was declared[2].

The GNSR crest featured the three castles from Aberdeen's city arms quartered with the lion rampant of Scotland.

Gradually, the Aberdeen Railway's position was improving. At its half-yearly meeting in October 1853 its first operating surplus was announced, of only £274 19s 4 ½ d, but six months later the surplus had risen to £3,232, after interest and debenture payments – still not enough to pay the 6% and 7% preference shares, whose arrears now amounted to £181,412. Additional rolling stock was still needed, and the board was authorised to issue £40,000 of 4% debenture stock among the proprietors, with a committee of shareholders to help the directors raise the funds. The Great North had assets of £434,453 in May 1854, but liabilities totalling £573,856. A loan of £64,000 from the North of Scotland Bank was made conditional upon no extension beyond Huntly being made without the bank's consent until it was fully repaid[3].

In November 1853 a first order for Great North rolling stock was placed, with Brown & Marshall of Birmingham, who agreed to take a third of the cost in shares: eight first, 16 second and 20 third class carriages, four luggage vans, two horse boxes, two carriage trucks, four goods brake vans, 20 covered vans, 50 cattle trucks, 200 open wagons and four sheep vans. On 6 January 1854 it was decided to have first and third class carriages only – the GNS was the first, and for almost 20 years the only, main line railway company in Britain to do without second class[4]. Its line was to be worked by the most up-to-date means and a contract was offered by the Electric Telegraph Co. for 40 miles at £4 per mile per year, with two wires, and five double needle instruments[5]. Five wooden and one stone-built (Huntly) goods sheds were ordered, along with a terminal train shed over the platform at Huntly. The decision to build the Waterloo Quay line was confirmed in January 1854, and a contract was placed with David Mitchell of Aberdeen, for £7,493[6], also with William Leslie for a locomotive shed at Kittybrewster (£1,440). Kinnear Clark's staff list was approved: a head foreman at £130 a year, an under-foreman at Huntly, £72 15s, six drivers at £109 6s, six stokers at £52, five cleaners, two who were also firelighters at £36 8s and three at £26; two cokemen at £70 14s, two fitters at £65, two boys at £10 8s, one smith at £62 8s, one striker at £31 4s, one coppersmith at the same, five wrights at £54 12s, one storekeeper at £70 6s, a boy at £13, and a gatekeeper-timekeeper at £36 8s.

Through the first half of 1854, everything was coming together for the Great North, with the passenger engines due by the end of July, and the goods engines following in August and September. The canal closed finally on 15 February; the telegraph contract was confirmed in May[7]. A Bill had been lodged with Parliament for the Waterloo extension, and three directors, Stewart, Alexander Jopp and Newell Burnett were delegated to negotiate with the Aberdeen Railway and the harbour commissioners. For once, all parties appear to have collaborated and it was agreed that the commissioners should arrange for dock rails to be laid and maintained between Waterloo and Guild Street stations, with the railway companies paying the board an annual 7½% of its outlay, estimated at £7,500. The town council and harbour commissioners had been concerned to ensure that there should be not just a rail link between the two goods stations but rails all round the Victoria Dock. Horse haulage only was to be employed[8]. The Bill received the royal assent on 24 July.

Opening of the Great North

While the board had been aiming for an opening date of 1 July for the Huntly line, Mitchell and Dean declared that 1 August was the earliest possible date, and that would require an extra £2,000, which was reluctantly given. Although the contract specified completion within 24 months, they had only had occupancy for 16 months. The line was divided into four portions, Kittybrewster-Dyce, Dyce-Inveramsay, Inveramsay-Insch, Insch-Huntly, with the working arrangement that only one engine at a time should be on any portion[9]. A preliminary Board of Trade inspection found shortcomings: there was no turntable yet at Huntly and engines had to run backwards to Aberdeen; and the signalling was incomplete, but Captain Yolland gave his approval on 15 September, and on Tuesday 19 September the line formally opened, though goods trains had run on it for a week before. Public services began on the 20th[10]. On the 19th a special train of 25 four-wheel carriages carried some 400 people from Kittybrewster to Huntly, most of whom had paid the ordinary fare plus a half. At Huntly a banquet was laid on for the directors and special guests, with the Duke of Richmond & Lennox presiding. For anyone who cared to remember the first prospectus ten years before, with its line to Inverness, double track almost all the way, the construction of a single line as far as Huntly can only have seemed a modest achievement, with other companies claiming the ground between Inverness and Elgin. At last, though, the Great North of Scotland Railway was a reality, with plans for further extension. There was even a *Guide* to the line, published that year in Banff, almost wholly concerned with local history, but noting of Huntly Station that its front presented an elegant curve, with a "smart and commodious" booking office, and masonry walls supporting an overall roof 170ft long and 40ft wide, above two tracks, one for arrivals, one for departures[11].

The events of the day were duly recorded: "Tuesday, 19th September, 1854, was selected as the day for the formal opening of the railway. Arrangements were made for a special train starting from Kittybrewster at eleven o'clock a.m. It was drawn by two engines, and consisted of twenty-five carriages. By it there travelled the directors and leading officials, as well as a number of prominent Aberdeen citizens, amounting in all to about four hundred. The various stations en route were tastefully decorated, and each contributed its quota of neighbouring proprietors and burgh functionaries to the party, whilst at every station the whole population turned out. In several instances the pupils belonging to the schools in the vicinity of the line were ranged in military-like order, to witness the new and fascinating sight. The train was advertised to arrive at Inverurie Station at 11.50, and, true to a minute, it steamed in, in grand style, amid the shouts of applause and demonstrations of wonder and delight of the large and motley group assembled. The inhabitants, young and old, were stationed at every point of the long town from which they could catch a glimpse — if not a full view — of the passing train; and while it was standing at the station to take up the Earl of Kintore, Provost Davidson, and others, as well as to admit of the engines being watered, the members of the Aberdeen City Band, who were accommodated in one of the carriages, struck up in splendid form 'Scots

OPENING OF THE GREAT NORTH OF SCOTLAND RAILWAY.—THE HUNTLY STATION.

The opening of the line at Huntly in September 1854 as depicted in the *Illustrated London News*.
(*Keith Fenwick collection*)

wha hae' — the inspiriting strains of which were heard above the snorting thunder of the engines on the resumption of the journey, until distance drowned the intervening sound.

On arriving safely at Huntly, amidst the plaudits of an immense concourse, an adjournment was made to a field near the railway station, where a public banquet was held in a large marquee specially erected for the auspicious occasion. The Duke of Richmond presided, and amongst the leading speakers were the Earl of Kintore, Sir James Elphinstone, Sir Andrew Leith Hay, and Mr. Lumsden of Auchindoir. The toast of 'Success to the Great North of Scotland Railway and to its early further extension to the North' was pledged with the utmost enthusiasm, to the unique accompaniment of the whistle of the engines which had been drawn up alongside"[12].

Less than a week later, Kittybrewster Station was the scene of a fatal accident. On 23 September a mixed train of eight goods wagons, three first and three third class carriages and a goods brake, which had left Huntly two hours and 20 minutes late, ran past a danger signal and failed to stop before colliding with carriages standing at the single platform, which already held passengers waiting to leave. An elderly woman was killed and several people were injured. Captain Yolland returned to investigate the cause and criticised the working arrangements at Kittybrewster. The incoming train was supposed to stop outside the station, where its engine with the goods wagons would transfer to the rear and push the passenger carriages alongside the platform. The driver of the engine had come from the Eastern Counties Railway of England – there was no pool of experienced railwaymen for the company to draw on in its own area[13].

From 20 September 1854 the timetable was as follows. Departure and arrival times included the proviso "not before".

	Goods	Passenger	Passenger/ Parliamentary	Passenger/ Mail	
Aberdeen dep.	5.15 am	8.35 am	1.30 pm	6.30 pm	
Huntly arr.	9.25 am	10.35 am	3.30 pm	8.30 pm	

	Mixed/mail	Passenger	Passenger/ Parliamentary	Passenger	Passenger/ Mail
Huntly dep.	4.25 am	6.15 am	11.00 am	4.00 pm	4.25 pm
Aberdeen arr.	7.25 am	8.15 am	1.00 pm	6.00 pm	7.25 pm

**Kinaldie was rather more elaborate than other wayside stations, perhaps because of
George Milne's residence nearby.** *(Stenlake collection)*

There was also a Sunday service, for mails and passengers, from Aberdeen at 6.30 pm to Huntly, arriving at 8.30; and from Huntly at 4.25 pm, arriving in Aberdeen at 7.25. Fares were $1\frac{3}{4}d$ a mile first class, $1\frac{1}{4}d$ a mile third class, and $1d$ a mile on the parliamentary service, with return fares available at one and a half times the single fare. An omnibus service from Union Square in Aberdeen connected with the trains at Kittybrewster, costing $4d$ for an inside seat and $3d$ for outside. Pickford & Co. had been appointed the carting agents; apart from Aberdeen they also delivered in Huntly, Banff, Portsoy, Fochabers, Keith and Elgin, with through rates available from Aberdeen to places beyond Huntly. In November the timetable was revised to provide four passenger trains each way daily, though still with a single parliamentary (one penny a mile maximum) service. There were fourteen stations, though Kinaldie, Buchanstone and Wardhouse did not open until 1 December[14]. Initially, mail was carried only for places as far as Huntly, and other mail still went north on the 'Defiance' coach, but haggling was going on with the Post Office on a full mail contract. The PO earned £960 a year on the Aberdeen-Inverness mails, carried by the 'Defiance' for £200. Now the coach operator wanted £200 for Huntly-Inverness, and the GNS wanted £410 10s 3d for Aberdeen-Huntly. By 24 February 1855 Milne reluctantly agreed to £205 8s 1d[15].

The first few months saw a rather irregular service, due to inexperienced staff and the gradual formation of an organised team. Also, by the end of November only half the rolling stock had been delivered and there were no cattle trucks until 6 December. Daniel Kinnear Clark's contract had specified residence in Aberdeen but he remained in London, sending instructions to the works foreman at Kittybrewster. On 2 August the Aberdeen Railway's terminus at Guild Street opened, giving a central passenger station. The goods depot alongside was almost finished. These facilities were also to be used by the Deeside Railway, at a charge of £700 a year for the first three years, and £1,000 a year thereafter, plus £25 for every £500 of revenue over £12,000 a year. The Deeside company, now working its own line, ran four passenger trains each way, on weekdays only:

	first/third	first/third	Mixed	first/third
Aberdeen dep.	7.40 am	11.00 am	2.10 pm	4.45 pm
Banchory arr.	8.33 am	12.00 am	3.30 pm	5.45 pm
	Mixed	first/third	first/third	first/third
Banchory dep.	6.00 am	8.50 am	1.00 pm	7.00 pm
Aberdeen arr.	7.05 am	9.45 am	1.55 pm	8.00 pm

No parliamentary service is shown, suggesting that all third class fares were $1d$ a mile. Specially cheap fares were offered on Wednesday and Saturdays[16].

Whose railway over the Spey to Keith?

Generally, 1854 was not a good year for industry and commerce, and the AR's half-yearly meeting in April drew attention to "the depressed state of manufacturers, especially in Aberdeen". The textile industry was in steep decline, and four factories had closed down. In the seemingly interminable lawsuit with Blaikies, the House of Lords rejected Blaikies' claim for £7,000 against the Aberdeen Railway, though this was not quite the end of the saga: in April 1855 a final extra-judicial settlement was made, in which both sides withdrew all claims and paid their costs. The moral victory was with the railway company[17]. As yet there was no electric telegraph to Aberdeen but the AR had been negotiating for two years with the Electric Telegraph Co. which was seeking to instal a line alongside the railway track. A deal was done in March 1855, helped by a donation of £200 from the Prince Consort (wires were also to follow the Deeside Railway) and of £50 from Aberdeen town council[18].

New proposals for branch lines to Oldmeldrum and Turriff were announced in late 1854, as separate enterprises to the Great North but to be worked by it at prime cost plus, in the case of the Banff, Macduff & Turriff Junction Railway, one quarter of the gross receipts of all traffic passing from it on to the GNS line.

The railway from Inverness to Nairn had been under construction since 21 September, and a committee had been formed to promote a continuation to Elgin. The Great North's initial decision to oppose this Nairn-Elgin line was swiftly followed by negotiation between the companies, and the Great North's lodging of a Bill for the 1855 session of Parliament for its own line from Huntly to Nairn[19] was no doubt to strengthen its hand in the negotiations, as the likelihood of its raising the necessary capital was extremely low. In December an agreement was reached with the provisional committee of the Elgin & Nairn Junction Railway, that its line would be continued as far east as the River Spey and join up with the Great North in the centre of a Spey Viaduct to be built at joint cost, with I.K. Brunel to supervise and apportion costs. The Elgin company would also contribute £1,000 to the Great North. John Stewart said he would have been happy to let the Inverness company come as far as Huntly[20].

Plans for extension from Huntly to Keith were well in hand by May 1855 and a special meeting of GNS shareholders approved a Bill for this purpose, along with the Bills for the Inverury & Old Meldrum Junction and Banff Macduff & Turriff Junction Railways, which included power for the company to invest £2,000 in the former

Kennethmont Station, with Ardmore Distillery. *(Stenlake collection)*

and up to £40,000 in the latter line. George Milne of Kinaldie, chairing the meeting in the absence of Elphinstone (who would be an increasingly absentee chairman) affirmed that the Great North still wished to reach Inverness. Though the "gentlemen of the North" would meet them at the Spey, he evidently anticipated running powers to Elgin and beyond. In October the directors published a "gratifying" half-year report:

Passenger revenue:	£16,334 14s 1½d
Carriages, horses, dogs:	£326 16s 10d
Mail:	£731 19s 4½d
Goods (after cartage deducted):	£16,330 16s 9d
Working expenses:	£12,846 16s 9d
Feus, rates, taxes:	£208 5s 8d
Passenger duty:	£617 17s ½d
Interest charges:	£3,196 19s 11d
Credit balance:	£17,253 8s 0½d

With £2,151 11s 6½d held over against compensation payments for the Kittybrewster crash, the 5% preference shares received their full dividend and 1¼% was paid on the ordinary shares. Share prices responded positively, with £10 ordinary now at £6 15s 9d and preference at £9 18s 9d[21]. The Great North's annual meeting in the Royal Hotel, Aberdeen, on 29 October was a confident occasion. The Keith extension and the Oldmeldrum and Turriff lines had all been approved by Parliament, on 25 May and 15 June. Elphinstone, presiding, reported that the harbour branch was already handling goods traffic and the passenger terminus would soon be ready. The quayside link to the Aberdeen Railway had also been completed. Four thousand £10 shares in the Banff, Macduff & Turriff Junction Railway had been subscribed for by the GNS, and building would begin early in 1856. Revised arrangements for the main line, proposed from the Inverness end, were now agreed: the former Inverness & Elgin (or Elgin & Nairn) Junction Railway had been renamed as the Inverness & Aberdeen Junction Railway and it was to build all the way to Keith, taking full responsibility for the Spey crossing. The GNS would invest £40,000 in the I&AJR and have two directors on its board. Sir James described this arrangement as "relief of no ordinary kind" and considered that the I&AJR would be able to deal more advantageously with the Morayshire proprietors than the GNS could. As proposed in the directors' report, their emolument of £400 for the past year was approved, and Sir James was awarded a payment of £400 "for services in promoting the interests of the Company before the opening of the line[22].

New competition, and formation of the Scottish North Eastern Railway

Two other projected lines faced competition. The powers acquired to build the GNS Eastern Extension had expired in 1853 and the railway was listed as an abandoned undertaking. Now it was to be re-promoted as the Formartine & Buchan Railway, to branch off at Dyce and run initially only to Strichen, though Peterhead and Fraserburgh were the ultimate termini. An investment of £15,000 from the Great North was proposed, and the new company would get free access to the GNS passenger terminal (unlike the Deeside Railway which was paying the Aberdeen Railway £1,000 a year for the use of Guild Street). A special meeting of GNS shareholders approved the proposal though David Mitchell (currently the contractor on the Keith section) queried the value of investment in the Formartine & Buchan line: "he did not know any railway that had meddled in branches, but regretted it"[23]. The Alford Valley Railway had also been revived, to branch off at Kintore and run to Bridge of Alford; this line too would receive a £15,000 investment from the Great North, which was to work the traffic on both lines. Sir James defined the aims of the company in making these investments as the smallest sums that could be advanced "to enable the proprietors and tenants to develop the traffic of a district". John Duncan, the Deeside Railway's chairman, mounted simultaneous rival schemes in each case. His Aberdeen, Peterhead & Fraserburgh Railway was to connect the city to the two fishing ports by a route nearer the coast than the Formartine & Buchan line, and his Deeside & Alford Extension Railway was to strike northwards from Lumphanan, on the Deeside line, to Alford. Each side put forward claims which minimised the likely capital cost and maximised the potential return, claiming 5% or even 6%, and each mustered impressive lists of local supporters (who incurred no obligation for the lending of their names)[24]. Negotiation and compromise might have been expected, since neither party could afford the costs of competition before a parliamentary committee, but both sides dug in for a battle. Other than insisting his were better routes, Duncan did not spell out his motive for competing with the Great North's plans, but he certainly felt, with the success of the Deeside line, that he understood what was needed to get a country railway built and to make it profitable. Indeed it is possible that the GNS schemes were in response to Duncan's, rather than the other way round.

On 31 August 1855 the Scottish Central "retired" from its working agreement with the Aberdeen Railway and handed back some well-worn locomotives and rolling stock. By then, AR merger talks with the Scottish Midland Junction were well advanced, with John Stirling very much the prime figure on both sides. Of all Scotland's railway chairmen, he would be the most committed to the principle of amalgamation. It was to be a full merger except that each company would pay for its own liabilities out of its share of the divisible funds, the latter to be split 70% to the AR, 30% to the Scottish Midland Junction. Until an Act was obtained, a joint committee would run both companies. A joint agreement to lease the Dundee & Arbroath railway was proposed, which would have given a single-company line from Aberdeen to Dundee, but though the D&A directors were willing, after three months of negotiation and a shareholder revolt, a new board repudiated the scheme and the Lease Bill had to be dropped[25]. The Aberdeen and Scottish Midland companies were united as the Scottish North Eastern Railway by an Act of 29 July 1856, with Stirling as chairman.

Openings – Waterloo, Oldmeldrum, and Keith

London had had its Waterloo Station since 1848 – now Aberdeen had one too. The steep harbour line (maximum gradient 1 in 59) had carried good trains since 24 September 1855, and on 1 April 1856 the Waterloo Quay passenger terminus was opened, on the former canal basin, an unassuming wooden building with three platform faces. Kittybrewster now became a through station. Offices for the company had been built alongside the new terminus, a single-storey granite building which would become increasingly cramped as time went on.

At the beginning of 1856, of the Great North's authorised capital of £1,407,440, £671,356 had been paid up, plus £108,300 in loans. Capital expenditure still exceeded funds, but by June 1856 revenue was approaching £1,000 a week. Takings for the week ending 14 June were: Passenger & mail: £400 17s 9d; goods £508 2s 11d, a total of £908 19s 10d compared with £770 18s 2½d for the same week in 1855. The Deeside line's figures were £126 15s 4d for passenger trains and £100 2s 11d for goods – the total of £226 18s 3d was slightly down on the same week in 1855: £236 16s 5d[26].

Although Waterloo's passenger service was withdrawn in 1867, the buildings survived in increasing dilapidation until the 1960s. In 1960, the station was visited by a railtour which can be seen at the platform, while the Gas Works engine stands at the head of a train of tank wagons.
(Harold Bowtell/Great North of Scotland Railway Association)

Aerial view of Aberdeen docks, showing Waterloo Quay and the original GNS terminus. Joint station to left, beyond the fish market. Fifteen years after the end of the GNS, the company's imprint on the city remains clear. *(RCAHMS)*

The Inverury & Old Meldrum Junction Railway's opening ceremony on Thursday 26 June 1856 saw "a large and gay assembly" at Oldmeldrum. Cakes and wine were followed by a dinner for 300 people, with fireworks and a bonfire: "such a day had never been seen in Oldmeldrum"[27] Its terminus was just to the west of the village. The 4 ½-mile line, engineered by John Willett, presented no constructional problems, with a 50ft span cast-iron girder bridge over the Ury being its main feature. A wayside station was provided at Lethenty, where there was a corn-mill, from 1 November, and a platform halt was set up at Fingask in 1866. Oldmeldrum was a farming village (parish population 2,343 in 1861), with a gasworks and a distillery, both of which brought their coal in by rail following opening of the goods depot three weeks later: goods traffic came in by the 5.15 am and 3.55 pm trains from Aberdeen and the 4.15 am and 11.50 am trains from Huntly, and left by the 11.40 am and 3.20 pm trains from Oldmeldrum. Three trains ran daily each way, one passenger-only, one mixed and parliamentary, one mixed, with no Sunday service. Passenger fares from Oldmeldrum to Inverurie were 10*d* (first class), 7*d* (third) and 5 ½ *d* (parliamentary) – the latter exceeding the statutory penny a mile. Public opening was on 1 July. At its second ordinary general meeting on 27 October, the Inverury & Old Meldrum Junction directors reported that £16,704 13*s* 9½*d* of capital had been expended, and only £12,722 10*s* of the authorised capital of £22,000 had actually been raised in shares. Borrowing powers of £7,000 had not yet been exercised, and they hoped for further share purchases[28].

On Friday 10 October the Keith extension was opened. Its main feature was a five-arched skew viaduct over the Deveron at Avochie (replaced by a double-track girder bridge in 1900). The Great North's arrival in Banffshire was celebrated by a dinner given by Keith's "principal inhabitants" to the directors of the company. Thomas Bruce of the Inverness & Aberdeen Junction Railway presided and praised the GNS's enterprise. Sir James Elphinstone replied, noting that "In 1850 the Great North had been in a manner abandoned, and it was with great difficulty that the vital energies of the country could be got to bring it into operation". Paying tribute to the Duke of Richmond's role, he again remarked that the Great North had been relieved of building beyond Keith by "the parties to whom the influence in that portion of the country legitimately belongs"[29]. For the time being, Keith was

The terminus at Old Meldrum, with a mixed train. The branch engine was said to be known as 'Meldrum Meg'. *(Stenlake collection)*

a terminus, though within two weeks of its opening, a preliminary meeting was held at Dufftown for the promotion of a Keith & Dufftown Railway. Alexander Gibb had been commissioned by a local committee to survey a line and prepare plans, and his cost estimate was £50,000. The committee was in touch with the GNS, which by December had agreed to contribute £1,000 and to work the line, nominating two of nine directors[30]: Elphinstone himself, with John Blaikie, represented the Great North's interest.

The branch policy and the almost-fatal error

Sir James's acceptance of Keith as the end of the line for the Great North was a realistic acknowledgement that the major landowners in Banffshire had preferred to support the Inverness railways. More relevant, though unmentioned, was the fact that the Great North, living from week to week on bank loans to complete its Keith extension, had been in no position to make a case for ownership, or even equal joint ownership, of the Junction project. It was a diplomatic defeat that might have happened anyway, but the company's financial difficulties made it inevitable.

Shut off to the north-west by the Inverness & Aberdeen Junction Railway, to the south by the Scottish North Eastern Railway, and with the Deeside Railway out to the west, the GNS could now only consider its future as serving the north-east – and that meant developing a system which would prevent competing companies from encroaching on that region. Investment in branch lines was already under way, as we have seen, and the policy was outlined by Sir James in October 1855: ". … where the proprietors and other parties in the various districts are unable of themselves to develop, by railway, their resources fully, we come forward to aid them, thinking that if we could direct their traffic into our own line, we would at once be serving them and the shareholders of our line"[31].

Company policy governed traffic operations, under the supervision of Robert Milne as *de facto* manager. With no competing line, determined to hold down its costs, and equally to maintain an attractive dividend, the GNS ran its services as economically as possible. The majority of trains were mixed passenger and goods, with twelve 2-4-0 locomotives available for main line service by October 1855. Average speeds were slow – faster trains meant increased coal consumption – coal was costing the GNS 14s a ton, and coke was 25s, while the Caledonian paid 4s and 12-14s respectively – and greater wear and tear on the tracks. Trains were infrequent. Fares and carriage

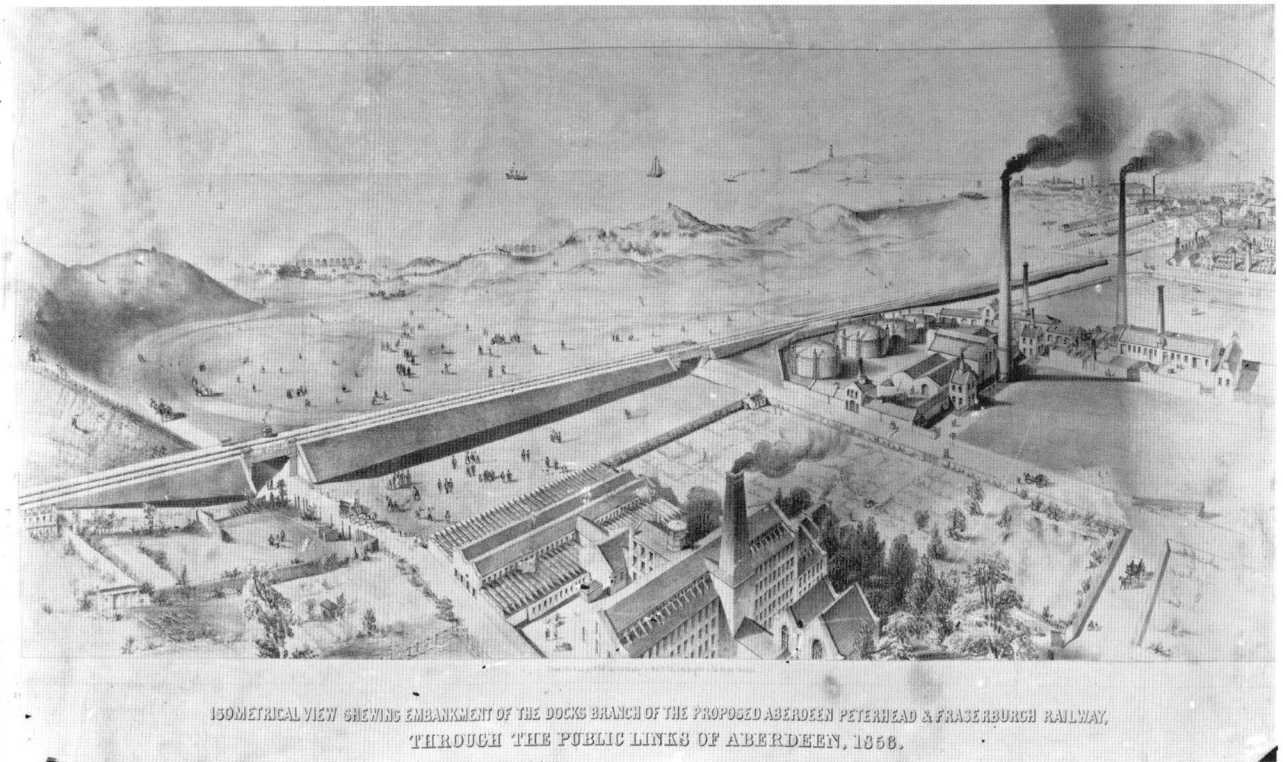

ISOMETRICAL VIEW SHEWING EMBANKMENT OF THE DOCKS BRANCH OF THE PROPOSED ABERDEEN PETERHEAD & FRASERBURGH RAILWAY, THROUGH THE PUBLIC LINKS OF ABERDEEN, 1856.

John Duncan's proposed railway through the links: this lithograph of 1857 also gives a part view of Aberdeen at the time. *(Aberdeen University Library)*

rates were comparatively high. Although the timetable allowed time for mixed trains to detach or add wagons along the way, the demands of shunting often made for delays. In February 1857 an anonymous 'Traveller' complained of irregular services and sudden alterations. Three trains ran from Keith to Aberdeen, two of them leaving before 10 am, the third at 4.45 pm, with nothing in between[32]. In part this was due to the infrequency of crossing loops, with the line divided into four sections.

In November 1856 the directors presented a positive report. The company now had a general manager, with Robert Milne acquiring the title, while also continuing as secretary. A parliamentary committee had rejected both the Formartine & Buchan and the Aberdeen Peterhead & Fraserburgh projects, for failing to comply with standing orders, but the board intended to re-apply in 1857, now proposing to put £50,000 into the project, to extend all the way to Peterhead and Fraserburgh (John Duncan was also re-proposing his line). The GNS-backed Alford Valley Railway from Kintore was preferred to the branch from Lumphanan, and received the royal assent on 23 June. The Inverness & Aberdeen Junction Railway also obtained its Act on 21 July. At Kittybrewster the workshops were almost finished, and four new engines were on order from Fairbairns. Between Inveramsay and Turriff, the contractor John Brebner was busy, and would soon start on the Alford Valley line. And the Denburn line was to be revived, as the Aberdeen Junction Railway, with a new Bill in 1857 – with an eye on through traffic coming from the north via Keith by 1858, and including a hotel and a joint station at the south-west corner of Union Bridge, but in fact no Bill was lodged[33].

Great North subscriptions to branch lines were by now up to £152,000, but Sir James was confident, informing the annual shareholders' meeting that some £400-500,000 of authorised capital had yet to be called up. In this lay his almost-fatal error: there was certainly a large amount of potential capital – £540,000 at the end of 1858 – and with the GNS beginning to pay good dividends, never less than 4% from 1857 to 1864, it could be raised. But he was pouring loans and subscriptions into companies which were incapable of repaying or yielding the necessary return, and in whose accounts, prepared by the GNS, the debts were kept concealed.

The Deeside Extension Railway and other plans

At an extraordinary general meeting of the Deeside company in November, John Duncan announced that local interests had come forward to propose an extension of the line from Banchory as far as Aboyne (population in 1861

1,200), a further 14 miles and 7 furlongs, and had asked the Deeside to promote a Bill on their behalf. In the event of the Bill failing, all expenses would be repaid, and the Deeside Railway was asked to contribute only £5,000 towards the venture; and to work the line on completion. The meeting agreed unanimously to support the plan[34]. Plans for the Deeside Extension were lodged in the Sheriff Clerk's office in December along with a range of other Bills, some competitive with each other:

The Aberdeen Junction Railway, 1 1/4 miles; capital £120,000 plus borrowing powers of £40,000. The GNS to subscribe £50,000 and the Scottish North Eastern Railway £40,000.

The Formartine & Buchan Railway, inland route from Dyce with lines to the harbours at Fraserburgh and Peterhead; capital £370,000 plus borrowing powers of £123,000.

The Aberdeen Peterhead & Fraserburgh Railway, from Aberdeen docks via Newburgh and Ellon to a junction at Mintlaw

The Banff Macduff & Turriff Extension Railway, to continue the line from Turriff to the coast, about 12 miles; capital £81,000 plus borrowing powers of £27,000.

The Banff Portsoy & Strathisla Railway, from a junction at Grange to Banff with a branch to Portsoy; capital £90,000 plus borrowing powers of £30,000.

The Keith & Dufftown Railway, a 9-mile line with a possible extension to mineral workings in Glenrinnes; capital £50,000 plus borrowing powers of £16,666. The Bill allowed for the line to be worked by either the GNSR or the Inverness & Aberdeen Junction Railway[35].

The capital requirement of this set of proposals was over £800,000. Even the most sanguine promoter can hardly have expected that such an amount could be raised from private individuals in north-east Scotland. By now, with industrial expansion going on apace, there were many companies other than railways competing for investment funds. In June 1857 a Great North shareholders' meeting approved the company's Bills, and agreed to subscribe £5,000 to the Banff Macduff & Turriff Extension and £1,000 to the Keith & Dufftown Railways.

The Buchan lines battle goes on

Lord Provost Blaikie, now Sir Thomas, presided more or less impartially over a noisy public meeting in Aberdeen on 25 June, called to express views on whether John Duncan's Aberdeen Fraserburgh & Peterhead Railway should be allowed to cut across the links to reach a terminus by the harbour, close to the GNS at Waterloo Quay. Eight thousand citizens had signed a petition against the plan. Hisses and claps greeted the speakers both for and against. Defending the route against arguments that his line should use the existing GNS Waterloo line, Duncan claimed that "Everybody knows that the dock branch of the Great North is an inconvenient one". Each side accused the other of forcing a parliamentary hearing and squandering city funds as well as their own. A show of hands came out against the links line[36]. Verses by a Peterhead bard, 'Peter Caput', give a whiff of the public's interest:

> *A rail, a rail. Brade Buchan for a rail.*
> *A land o' corn and nowt, seal oil and whale.*
> *A land o' rowth, o' gowd, o' stock and folk;*
> *We'll hae a rail. 'Tis now no more a joke …*
>
> *Preserve the links, the Northerns raise the cry;*
> *Here's work for all, the Duncanites reply[37].*

The dispute became a bitter one and Blaikie brought four cases in the Court of Session against John Duncan for libel. Duncan had said of the Formartine & Buchan promoters that "the North of Scotland Bank coffers are open to them for all purposes at all times" (the Bank's management committee had intimate links with GNS directors and ex-directors) and "they simply had to put their hands into the bank till and transfer any sum they chose to Mr Robert Milne [secretary of the Formartine & Buchan committee as well as of the GNS] without security". The juries gave judgement against Duncan, who was ordered to pay £250 to the pursuers on each count. An application for appeal to the House of Lords was refused, as was Duncan's request to be allowed to see the records of the GNS's transactions with the North of Scotland Bank, even though it was admitted in court that "it appeared there was some mismanagement – a very improper proceeding on the part of the then manager of the said Bank, with which the pursuer [the GNS] was connected – but not to do with the present directors." James Westland, who had replaced Paterson as manager of the Bank, denied that money had been lent to the railway company without security[38].

CHAPTER 5
Deeside and Beyond, 1857 – 1860

New Acts and a new opening, but stalemate in Buchan

A new phase of railway building was heralded by the royal assents given on 27 July 1857 to the Deeside Extension (Banchory-Aboyne), the Banff Portsoy & Strathisla, Banff Macduff & Turriff Extension, and Keith & Dufftown Railways. Parliamentary approval was one thing, albeit essential: now they had to set about raising capital. The Keith & Dufftown had contractors lined up in Mitchell, Ireland of Montrose, for a price of £43,125 partly payable in 750 £10 shares, but by the time of the first ordinary general meeting in September, subscriptions and guarantees amounted to only £4,970 plus the Great North's £1,000[1].

From 1 September the Great North began a perpetual lease of the Inverury & Old Meldrum Railway, replacing the former working agreement with an annual rental of £650. The Old Meldrum company did not disappear, though now vested in the GNS; it was authorised by the Leasing Act to raise £5,500-worth of new shares and to borrow up to £4,400 against the security of the rental payments. The GNS did not ask for parliamentary sanction and was obliged to obtain a retrospective Act, which got the royal assent on 11 June 1858. Commending the necessary Bill to shareholders, Elphinstone was rather dismissive about the Old Meldrum line: "We work [it] at prime cost, and I don't think the shareholders get much by it. We did not make the line, as we did not think it important to the district, but they were anxious to have it, and they work it on their own basis"[2]. Turriff became a railway terminus on 4 September 1857, when a train "of about 30 handsome new carriages" arrived from Waterloo with guests. A marquee had been attached to the engine shed and dinner was laid on for 400 people. John Brebner the contractor had died during construction and after a three-month delay Graham Monro had taken over. Sir James told the guests that "Our scheme is still incomplete …we contemplate running branches into all the chief districts of the country", and Robert Milne expressed confidence that the new line would yield 4 or 5% a year to its investors[3]. As part of the working agreement, the Banff Macduff & Turriff received a "drawback" or commission from the GNS on traffic passed on to the main line. Public services began on the 5th.

The constitution of the Deeside Extension was unusual. Effectively part of the Deeside Railway, its directors were those of the Deeside plus two specifically appointed to look after Extension shareholders' interests. But the share registers and accounts of Aberdeen-Banchory and Banchory-Aboyne were kept separately. This enabled dividends to be calculated separately, preserving the Deeside Railway's high level (never under 6% after 1859) from dilution by the less lucrative Extension. Provision was made for amalgamation of the stocks if the dividends of each section became equal – an event hardly to be anticipated. Construction began on 2 October.

The station at Turriff, terminus of the Banff Turriff & Macduff Junction Railway from 1857 until the Macduff extension opened in 1860. *(Stenlake collection)*

Yet again there was stalemate as far as the Buchan lines were concerned. On 11 November at a public meeting in Fraserburgh Lord Saltoun, formerly a proponent of the Aberdeen Peterhead & Fraserburgh, announced his backing for the Formartine & Buchan Railway. In the latest Bill, its capital requirement had been cut back to £300,000 with borrowings of £100,000, and it was proposed to bypass Ellon, putting the town on a branch line two miles 46 chains long. It was also to pass to the east, rather than the west, of Mormond Hill[4]. Alexander Anderson spoke up for the plan, admitting that the scheme had been unpopular in Fraserburgh for not including the town from the first, but all that was over. The Great North would guarantee rates on the Formartine & Buchan line to be no higher than on its own line. Anderson addressed meetings at Crimond, Peterhead, and New Deer in the attempt to win local backing in the next set of parliamentary hearings[5]. The Great North helped matters along with an encouraging half-year dividend of 4½% on the ordinary shares. Its passenger traffic had risen by 50% in the past two years, which the chairman ascribed to the low fares which, he contended, were 25% less than on any other railway. Goods traffic was also up, by a more modest 15%[6]. According to John Duncan, the Great North's Act required it to have second class carriages and it got round this by charging second class fares for first class seats[7]. Duncan had by no means given up on the rival plan, though he noted the uncertainty and proneness to panic of the money market. Meetings and counter-meetings went on into the spring of 1858, but in the end the Formartine & Buchan line was approved and the Aberdeeen Peterhead & Fraserburgh was thrown out. The battle had lasted three years and been hugely expensive, costing the Great North £25,000. Replying to those who wanted to know why, having got the Act for the Formartine & Buchan Railway, the board had not made a start, John Stewart declared that if the district provided £2,000 per mile, they would construct the whole 50-mile line. The community must come up with £100,000, or a quarter of the estimated capital requirement; and furthermore, "We shall not put a spade into the ground until we have obtained liberal and satisfactory land settlements"[8]. Earlier in 1858 the Great North had passed a significant marker, when its £10 ordinary shares were being sold at par[9], indicating investors' confidence in the company.

An incident at Waterloo, opening of the Inverness & Aberdeen Junction Railway and extension of the Morayshire

Letters in the *Aberdeen Journal* in August 1858 revealed an incident on the 5th, when the Scottish North Eastern Railway mail train arrived late at Guild Street, only a few minutes before the GNS Keith train was due to leave Waterloo. Only the mail bags and a few fast-moving through passengers were admitted before the gates were

Aboyne: the original terminus of the Deeside Extension Railway (1859). *(Aberdeen University Library)*

closed. A lady and her luggage were allowed through while her husband, held up in paying for their cab, was shut out. He was James Merry, a future director of the Highland, and one of his fellow-travellers was James Grant, chairman of the Morayshire Railway. Both were among the signatories of an angry letter deploring the officious behaviour of the GNS staff, the "factious motives and party squabbles" which inconvenienced the travelling public, and declaring that it was high time a more direct and *continuous* railway to the North was made. Robert Milne published an unapologetic reply, claiming that had the train waited for all the south train's passengers, "the whole of the Company's Train arrangements for the day would have been seriously interfered with" and suggesting it was unfair to complain about the Great North's respect for punctuality (incidentally the clock at Waterloo was set five minutes behind those of Guild Street, the Post Office and Town House). Merry's letter became an important weapon in the campaign for the Inverness-Perth line, and has often been quoted, but the actual number of occasions on which passengers were shut out in this way is not recorded[10].

On 18 August 1858 the entire Inverness & Aberdeen Junction Railway line was opened, and the GNS station at Keith ceased to be a terminus, with the Inverness company paying £500 a year for its use of the facilities[11]. The station agent was to take his instructions from the respective traffic managers and if their orders conflicted, to refer to the joint committee of directors, or if at a loss, to refer to the manager of the line to which the case applied, or to both managers. He was to show no partiality. Inter-company disputes were to be settled by an arbiter under the Railway Clauses Consolidation (Scotland) Act, 1845, with a £500 penalty for any departure from the agreement. Keith Station's staff at the time comprised the agent, two goods clerks, three goods porters, three passenger porters, three pointsmen, one night watchman, one woman "for cleaning", and one horse and man for shunting[12]. Despite the GNS investment and presence on the board, Aberdeen-Inverness was not operated as an 'inter-city' line but as two separate railways, with through passengers having to change trains at Keith. Before the opening, Elphinstone had written to the I&AJR chairman Alexander Matheson to suggest that GNS trains might go as far as Elgin "until the traffic shall be developed"[13] but to no avail. Goods trains also terminated here though wagons were necessarily passed on in both directions. If the GNS and Scottish North Eastern Railway had been joined by a proper passenger railway in Aberdeen, the case for operating through carriages between Inverness and the south would have been a great deal stronger. Railway expansion into Ross-shire and beyond was under way and the Great North was excluded from participation in this[14].

With the construction of the Inverness & Aberdeen Junction Railway, the Morayshire Railway had set aside its plan for a line between Elgin and Rothes (population in 1861 around 1,000), instead acquiring running powers on the Junction line between Elgin and Orton and obtaining an Act in 1857 for a line from Orton to Rothes with an extension southwards alongside the Spey to Dandaleith, on the north side of the river (the station was named Craigellachie until 1 June 1864). Completion of this line by 23 December 1858 was celebrated by a dinner at Rothes[15], with public services from the 24th. The Morayshire now connected Elgin with its southern hinterland, though there were problems with the I&AJR, which complained of the Morayshire's under-powered engines causing delays on the Elgin-Orton line, and after six weeks Morayshire carriages were attached to I&AJR trains, for an extra 10% of receipts. The Junction company also refused to give through bookings to Rothes from Elgin, so that passengers had to re-book at Orton[16].

Mixed news from the branches

Keith's other railway, to Dufftown, remained in abeyance through lack of capital, and the construction contract had been annulled. By its third ordinary general meeting in October 1858 the directors faced the choice of holding on for another year in the hope that the Great North would "take up" the line ("in consequence of the numerous engagements of that Company" it had declined to say what it might do), or of winding it up. With considerable personal liabilities in the enterprise, they decided to soldier on. The two GNS directors played a minimal role at this time[17]. Through 1859 the Keith & Dufftown company still struggled to assemble enough capital, but by October things looked more promising. The Duke of Richmond and the Earl of Fife guaranteed £7,500 and £5,000 respectively, through their agents Thomas Balmer and W.G. Tayler, and Major Gordon Duff of Drummuir a further £1,000 – if the Great North would take on the undertaking. This the Great North agreed to do, provided that half the cost was raised by *bona fide* local subscriptions (only £2,380 10s of the necessary £25,000 was subscribed as of 31 July), with the land required given at agricultural feu rates, that the Keith & Dufftown's present liabilities be ascertained and adjusted, and that if half the capital had not been raised locally by 1 December 1859, the GNS would have its costs reimbursed. Construction powers would expire on 1 July 1860, and a new Bill had be prepared to obtain an extension of time. The GNS undertook this, and the Bill also provided for a revised and cheaper line from the junction at Keith[18]. Keith's wooden goods shed and contents were totally destroyed by fire at the end of January 1859[19]. The GNS had no fire insurance policy, and charged the damage of £481 to revenue.

A busy moment at the Alford terminus in the 1900s. *(Stenlake collection)*

John Stewart had been quoted in the *Railway Times* in November 1857 on the subject of the Great North's branch policy: "The great secret why we have been so successful with the branches lies, I think, in this, that we help them to help themselves"[20]. Now, deputising for Sir James Elphinstone (elected that year as Conservative MP for Portsmouth) at the Great North's annual shareholders' meeting on 12 November, he gave a different view on what he called "this sore subject, the branches." He singled out the Turriff line, which having cost around £145,000 to build, and still needing a further £5,000 to complete its works, had since its opening yielded the "miserable amount of only £6,769," and could report a free balance, after costs and interest, of only £200 5s 8d. The local area had raised only £14- or £15,000 of the capital, less than the purchase cost of land for the line, £18,000. So few of its ordinary shares had been taken up that the Banff Macduff & Turriff Junction company had to apply to Parliament for authority to issue 5% preference stock. Having begun with a service of four passenger and one goods train daily, the Great North had cut it back to three mixed trains. The Alford Valley Railway, traversing a difficult stretch of country, had been expected to open in August 1858 but would not do so until 21 March 1859, and then to a terminus three quarters of a mile short of the original one. Stewart could still announce a dividend of 5% on the GNS ordinary shares, and boast that the company's ratio of working expenses to revenue was the lowest of any railway, at 31 1/2 %[21].

1859 was not an encouraging year for the railway investors of the north-east. Most results were poor. The Banff Macduff & Turriff Junction Railway changed its name to the Aberdeen & Turriff from 19 April, but its fortunes remained dismal. Building of its extension to Macduff was delayed by floods which destroyed newly-built bridges. The Banff Portsoy & Strathisla Railway opened on 2 August[22], and its report showed expenditure of £63,084 while only £46,175 of its £90,000 share capital had been subscribed. Its directors hoped for "the support of the public to make up the deficiency" in its capital account, but calls on the shareholders remained largely unanswered. These two lines, authorised by simultaneous Acts on 27 July 1857, terminated within a mile of each other. This adjacence does not seem to have been raised as a potential problem during the parliamentary hearings of the Bills. Although promoted by separate local groups, both sought support from the Great North, which was authorised to invest in both and to work their traffic. The Banff company however bought two small engines and its own rolling stock, and maintained an independent existence in its first few years. At the time, the function of a rural railway was seen as to 'open up' a section of country, and the two lines, traversing different districts, separated by the River Deveron, were more than twenty miles apart for most of their extent. Nevertheless, the

The approach to Banff Harbour gave passengers a fine view across the Moray Firth. *(Stenlake collection)*

opening of the Banff Portsoy & Strathisla line had an immediate adverse effect on the line to Turriff. At the Aberdeen & Turriff Railway's a.g.m. on 30 November 1860, John Stewart told the shareholders that though the opening of the Banff Harbour line from Grange had diverted much of the traffic, opening of the Banff, Macduff & Turriff Extension will "not only bring back the greater portion of the traffic thus diverted, but will probably add to its amount. And the working of that line and yours continuously under one system will prove mutually advantageous to both companies"[23]. This was wishful thinking of a high order.

Reduced revenue was also reported by the Deeside Railway in 1859. It had opened workshops at Banchory early in the year, to service its four locomotives and rolling stock; a fifth engine was delivered by Hawthorn's of Leith in July, in anticipation of the extension to Aboyne, approved by Captain Tyler of the Board of Trade on 29 November and opened on 2 December. Between Guild Street and Banchory four trains ran daily each way, with three between Banchory and Aboyne, giving a two-hour journey time for the 30 miles between Aboyne and Aberdeen. On the Buchan line, a rethink about Ellon, taking the line via the town, required an Amendment Act, obtained on 19 April[24].

Inverness & Aberdeen Junction Railway – the Great North opts out

On the Great North itself, 1859's revenue was down on 1858, but a 5% dividend was maintained, and the share price was now above par, with £10 ordinary at £11 5s and preference at £12 2s 6d in October[25]. A Consolidation Act, obtained on 21 July, brought the company into line with the practice of other railways, with half-yearly reports, accounts, dividends and meetings, and also authorised a new issue of preference shares at a dividend not to exceed 4%[26]. On the northern front, relations with the Inverness & Aberdeen Junction company were becoming difficult. The Inverness & Aberdeen Junction Railway was seeking to expand its capital by £200,000 in preference stock, in part to subscribe to the Ross-shire Railway, but also because £95,000 of its original capital was unsubscribed – something the Junction company had concealed by putting the shares against the name of its secretary. Alexander Anderson, now Lord Provost of Aberdeen, still the GNS's law agent, and no stranger to the trickeries possible in railway finance, expressed concern that the Great North's £40,000 of ordinary shares would be devalued by the new issue. At a Junction company shareholders' meeting, the engineer Graham Monro and John Stewart made an alternative proposal, that the Great North should get involved in the Ross-shire extension, buying the I&AJR plant, lending the money, and working the line. This brought an immediate flat negative from Alexander Matheson, the Junction company chairman: "It is quite useless, Mr Stewart. Nothing on earth would induce me to amalgamate", followed up by, "How do you happen to be so very flush with cash in Aberdeen? Did you not make application to Parliament some time ago for similar [capital enlargement] powers?" Stewart replied that "We have gone to Parliament not to increase our powers, but to diminish them; but we have a large margin"[27].

Territorial possessiveness and suspicion of the Great North's motives were evident in the *Inverness Courier*'s comment: "In any emergency or difficulty experienced by the Junction Company the Great North are pretty sure to pay us a visit, and they are always ready with an offer of help … We confess our own experience of the Great North is not such as to prepossess us greatly in their favour. Their trains are really the slowest in the Kingdom … They decline, also, to give through rates for goods traffic unless the goods go by their steamers from Aberdeen." It suggested that the GNS only managed to keep its 5% dividend because of traffic off the Junction line, and hoped "we shall have no more of these unseemly … exhibitions"[28].

At this time the Great North's weekly takings were around £1,100, almost exactly twice those of the Inverness & Aberdeen Junction Railway, and in 1859 it carried more than half a million passengers, a total of 509,955[29]. It was evident that the majority of the I&AJR board was resolved to make no concessions to the Great North, either in terms of through trains to and from Aberdeen, or in allowing it to operate north of Inverness; and that the same people were involved in a revived scheme for a direct line between Inverness and Perth. For the GNS there appeared little point in having two directors as a permanent minority on the Junction company board, and it appears to have taken the initiative in proposing to give up its interest in that concern[30]. The I&AJR followed up swiftly and by the end of January 1860 the Great North's £40,000-worth of shares was bought back at full value, to be paid in two equal instalments. At its half-yearly meeting on 2 April Sir James noted that a profit of 5% had been made on the transaction[31]. Now, however, the Aberdonians had no influence or leverage on the Inverness companies, and January 1860 marks the start of a forty-year period of rivalry and hostility which effectively determined the future pattern of railway development across north-east Scotland. If the GNS board saw the events of January 1860 as a tactical withdrawal, they were deceiving themselves. It was a second strategic defeat, following that of 1856. A sense of complacency reigned at Waterloo Quay, however. The shareholders approved

Paradise Quarry near Kemnay is one of the main sources of granite in Aberdeenshire. It was conveniently served by a siding on the Alford Branch. The tracks visible here are part of its internal railway system. *(Great North of Scotland Railway Association)*

a jump in investment in the Keith & Dufftown Railway, to £8,000 in shares and £16,000 in debentures, making it possible for construction to proceed. The Denburn link line was no longer a priority, with Elphinstone expressing the view that "the plan was not so much for the benefit of the Great North as for that of southern and more wealthy companies"[32].

In this matter the Great North was studying its own benefit, to the detriment of the southern companies, especially the Scottish North Eastern Railway. At this time it was not combining with other companies in offering a through rate for goods passing into or out of its system. Most railways were now doing this, using the Railway Clearing House (established in 1842) to monitor the traffic and collect and distribute the receipts. The GNS however did not join the Clearing House and insisted on charging its own rates. John Stewart, by now a very active vice-chairman, appears to have been the main architect of the policy of exchanging goods with steamships, rather than by transfer to the SNER[33]. At the April meeting he recalled that on the opening of the line there had been a "severe contest" with the Leith & Clyde and North of Scotland Steam Packet companies, and "It was never the wish of the Directors of this Company to be steam proprietors", but they put on a small steamer between Invergordon and Inverness to collect Ross-shire traffic, on a three-month trial. It lost money and was given up, replaced by a minimum-rate agreement with the shipping companies. In fact the operation lasted for the whole year of 1859 and involved five ships in all, chartered by the Great North at £200 a month per ship and operating from Granton and Aberdeen to Burghead, Banff, Cullen, Lossiemouth, Findhorn, Nairn, Inverness, Cromarty, Invergordon and Fort George. Clearly this was an alternative seaborne service to the Inverness & Aberdeen Junction Railway. From January 1859 until May the ships were *Xantho* and *Duke of Rothesay*; from May to the end of the year they were *Express*, *Hamburg* and *Kangaroo*, chartered from William Thompson & Co., Leith[34]. Involvement with steamship companies would take a controversial turn before long.

'Banff and Macduff': the network spreads

A dividend of 7% was declared for the January-July half-year. Working expenses were 37½% of gross revenue. The Great North's results were gaining it favourable comments in the financial press, and its shares stood above par, with £10 ordinary at £10 16s in Edinburgh on 21 July[35]. The Banff Macduff & Turriff Extension Railway, worked by the GNS as a continuation of the Aberdeen & Turriff line, opened to Gellymill, outside Macduff, on 4 June. The station was advertised as 'Banff & Macduff', and as the timetable of arrivals and departures from the various termini shows[36], the local inhabitants needed to choose between it and Banff Harbour, depending on their direction of travel.

Down Trains (to Elgin & Inverness)

	Passenger	Passenger/ Parliamentary	Spec Mail (first class only)	Passenger	Passenger
Aberdeen dep.	8.00 am	11.00 am	1.17 pm	4.35 pm	6.50 pm
Alford dep.	7.40 am	–	–	–	6.45 pm
Old Meldrum dep.	8.24 am	11.30 am	–	–	7.35 pm
Banff-Macduff dep. (via Turriff)	6.50 am	10.00 am	–	–	6.05 pm
Keith arr.	10.51 am	2.05 pm	3.57 pm	7.20	9.35 pm
Banff-Macduff arr. (via Turriff)	11.10 am	2.10 pm	–	7.15	9.50 pm
Banff arr. (via T'naught)	11.50 am	3.15 pm	–	8.17	–
Inverness arr.	1.45 pm	–	7.02 pm	10.15	–

Up Trains (to Aberdeen)

	Passenger	Spec Mail (first class only)	Passenger/ Parliamentary	Mixed	Passenger
Inverness dep.	–	6.40 am	–	10.15 am	3.15 pm
Banff dep. (via T'naught)	6.10 am	–	9.15 am	12.35 pm	5.00 pm
Banff-Macduff dep. (via Turriff)	6.50 am	–	10.00 am	1.00 pm	6.05 pm
Keith dep.	7.00 am	9.10 am	10.25 am	1.20 pm	6.15 pm
Old Meldrum dep.	8.24 am	11.30 am	11.30 am	–	7.35 pm
Alford dep.	7.40 am	–	11.30 am	2.25 pm	6.45 pm
Aberdeen arr.	9.45 am	11.55 am	1.35 pm	4.10 pm	9.00 pm

For the first time it was possible to go between Aberdeen and Inverness and return in one day, though rather more time was available in Aberdeen than in Inverness. But the best time between Aberdeen and Keith was still two hours and 40 minutes.

The townspeople of Banff, a year after acquiring their railway service, found that vigilance and agitation were needed to make the most of it. In July 1860 the first of numerous petitions or representations was raised, in this case for better mail services. Although the early southern mail arrived in Aberdeen at 3.30 am, it was not sent on to Banff until 8 pm; and the afternoon mail for Turriff and Banff went by train to Huntly, and onwards by gig. Yet there was now a railway all the way past Turriff to Banff. They wanted an early postal departure to Aberdeen, so that a reply could be received on the same day via the 1.17 pm train[37]. From 5 March 1859 two GNS carriages had compartments fitted with sorting boxes, and on the Special Mail a Post Office clerk sorted letters for points beyond Keith or Aberdeen. Between 1859-61 the price of the mail contract was in dispute – the PO officials did not find Robert Milne easy to deal with. In March 1859 he demanded 6s 6d per mile for the 'Special Mail' (by comparison the Great Western was receiving 3s 9d a mile for the much heavier London-Bristol mail train) and arbitration was resorted to[38].

Speyside and Morayshire

Various works were now in hand, with Charles Brand getting the Keith & Dufftown contract at £24,607, excluding cost of rails, for the 9$\frac{1}{2}$-mile line. Double track between Kittybrewster and Dyce was almost complete (opened in early October 1860). The directors' report made light of the proposal for an Inverness-Perth railway: "the value of through traffic between stations on the Inverness line and the south is apt to be over-rated", but they had a Bill in preparation for a 33$\frac{3}{4}$-mile continuation of the Dufftown line down the Spey as far as Grantown, which was on the proposed line to Perth. Presiding at the half-yearly meeting on 1 October, Stewart held out great hopes for this Strathspey line and its timber traffic in particular[39].

Seeking to put an end to its difficult relationship with the Inverness & Aberdeen Junction Railway, the Morayshire Railway obtained an Act on 3 July 1860 for a new direct line from Elgin to Rothes. This was of keen interest to the Great North, already backing the Dufftown line and planning the Strathspey continuation, which would pass very close to the Morayshire's southern terminus at Craigellachie. Though an expensive bridge over the Spey would be needed, a link between these lines would give the GNS its own access to Elgin. Even grander ambitions were held by the Morayshire Railway chairman James Grant – a letter to the Scottish North Eastern Railway set out a proposal for a line from Blairgowrie, terminus of a SNER branch, to meet the Morayshire at Craigellachie. The Morayshire could not afford to pay the survey costs, and the SNER declined to contribute, though its engineers made a survey between Blairgowrie and Dalnacardoch on the proposed Inverness & Perth Railway, to establish whether that line could be diverted via Blairgowrie. At the same time the Scottish North Eastern Railway was also in touch with the I&AJR about making a joint line from Keith to meet the SNER at Aberdeen, as an alternative to the Inverness & Perth railway[40]. The implication is of extreme frustration with the Great North.

That company was busy doing its own thing – taking the Keith & Dufftown Railway in hand, after the years of uncertainty. It now had four of the nine directors, and these with James Petrie the local chairman, formed a committee of management "with all the Powers of the Board". Robert Milne was secretary. A contract with Charles Brand had been made, for £24,609 8s 9d, and it was agreed to extend the line across the River Fiddich to Balvenie, as the original terminus was "quite unsuitable for Dufftown and district"[41], for an additional £12,723. The extension was also intended to link with the Strathspey Railway, and though made by the Keith & Dufftown, its cost was to be refunded by the Strathspey, with progressive interest at 5%, as soon as that company was in a

Wayside station: Monymusk, on the Alford Branch. *(Stenlake collection)*

position to do so, and no later than the opening of its line. In a scheme typical of the tortuously worked-out finances of these lines, if the Keith & Dufftown should open before the Strathspey, interest on the outlay connected with the Balvenie extension, at the rate of the current dividend on the ordinary stock of the Dufftown line, was to be credited to the Strathspey Railway. On the Strathspey line being opened, the cost of the extension and of the Dufftown Station – if not already repaid to the Keith & Dufftown – should be repaid to it, and the Keith & Dufftown would then use these facilities, paying interest to the Strathspey company on the capital cost of the extension exclusive of the station at the rate of its current dividend; and at 5% on half the cost of the station. Whichever company maintained the station was to be paid $2\frac{1}{2}\%$ on half the maintenance cost by the other, with wages borne equally. It was also optional to the Keith & Dufftown, at any time before repayment was made by the Strathspey, to apply for an Act constituting the extension as part of its own line[42]. This convoluted arrangement – both lines had a natural end at Dufftown Station – would be a source of future dispute. The Keith & Dufftown board also recommended to shareholders that "at the proper time" a subscription of £25,000 should be made to the Strathspey Railway, "in consideration of the great benefit it will confer on the Keith & Dufftown". Though the initiative for this surely came from the Great North, the directors who made the recommendation were all local and not the GNSR nominees, and on 21 December three of them signed for purchase of £25,000 of Strathspey shares "for behoof of and in trust for the [Keith & Dufftown] Company"[43].

Branch disappointments, and the navviesses of Buchan

In December 1860 the Alford Valley Railway held its fifth annual meeting, with John Stewart presiding. A poor harvest was blamed for a disappointing set of accounts. The net revenue was only £1,173 12s 11$\frac{3}{4}$d, but 5% interest on the company's borrowings, of £66,245, would amount to £3,312, leaving the company in the red. The GNS was working the line not on an agreed percentage of the gross revenue but at prime cost, i.e. its own reckoning of the actual cost, including £75 a year for the use of Kintore Station, described as "a pen". Speaking for the disappointed promoters, Dr Garden of Alford suggested that the AVR was being run by the Great North for its own benefit, to which Stewart rejoined that the GNS had "given" the Alford company £15,000 in shares and a £30,000 loan, for which it had to borrow money at $4\frac{1}{2}\%$. Of the authorised £76,500 capital, only £37,291 15s 0d had been paid up, and he asked why local proprietors had not bought more shares in the line. Stewart's forceful articulacy silenced the protesters. On the same day he chaired the Aberdeen & Turriff meeting, facing down similar complaints with the same answers. After the GNS had taken its costs, the Turriff's net revenue was only £59 4s 11$\frac{1}{2}$d, but he reminded the shareholders that the GNS had "half the undertaking on its shoulders"[44].

Work was proceeding on the Formartine & Buchan line between Dyce and Mintlaw, with an unusual element in the labour force: one subcontractor was apparently employing women, "… buxom navviesses wheeling their barrows, and still retaining that natural regard for their invincible charms, betokened by broad parapluie hats …"[45]. Landowners had not been particularly co-operative, and by March 1859 only half had accepted a feu arrangement. Authorised capital for the line was £300,000, but only £57,303 was paid up by August 1859. To invoke the Formartine & Buchan's borrowing powers, only possible once half the capital was subscribed, the Great North did exactly what it had criticised the Inverness & Aberdeen Junction Railway for doing: it got the contractor to put his name down for 15,648 ordinary shares, paying the 10% deposit with money already borrowed by the railway company from the North of Scotland Bank. One of the main structures, a four-arched stone viaduct over the Ythan, partially collapsed in the summer of 1860, but the keystone of its final arch was placed in October.

CHAPTER 6
Manoeuvres and Machinations, 1860 – 1862

Steamship links – Stewart's involvement

While the branches were recording meagre or negative results, the Great North declared a $6\frac{1}{2}\%$ dividend even for the "winter" half-year, August 1860-January 1861. At the half-yearly meeting on 1 April, Sir James Elphinstone stressed the continuing low level of working expenses, only 31% of total revenue in the half-year. While the Inverness & Perth Junction Railway's Bill was in Parliament, he had changed his views on the link with the Scottish North Eastern Railway, and appeared to regret the previous inaction, saying that if the link had been made before, the Inverness & Perth Junction Railway "would never have been called into existence". This indicated a breach, soon to widen, with John Stewart who, replying to a challenge about the company's links with steamboat operators, made "a few energetic remarks" which did not wholly clarify the position.

The situation was this: the established Aberdeen Steam Navigation Co., with John Stewart among its directors, had been operating ships from Aberdeen to Granton (for Edinburgh) and to Inverness, taking in the Moray Firth ports and also those at Chanonry Point (Fortrose), Cromarty and Invergordon. The Steam Navigation Co. was happy to exchange traffic with the Great North line at Portsoy, Banff and Aberdeen but refused to collaborate in offering a large rebate on goods carried by sea and rail. Sugar sent from London to Keith was used as an example: by sea to Lossiemouth and then by train, the railway company charged for 24 miles, while from Aberdeen Harbour it charged for 54 miles. The steamship company refused a request from the Great North to give the customer a 25% 'drawback' on its share of the traffic, which would be matched by the railway, and in a boardroom altercation Stewart and some others lost their ASN directorships on 9 March 1859. Stewart promptly set up the Northern Steam Navigation Co. in competition, and it of course acquired the Great North's traffic. A meeting in London of GNS, Scottish North Eastern, Edinburgh & Glasgow, and Scottish Central representatives on 31 March agreed on the experimental charter of a steamer on the Granton-Aberdeen-Inverness route for one month[1] The Scottish North Eastern Railway subsequently withdrew, considering the action to be *ultra vires* [beyond its legal powers]. By July 1861 the Northern Steam Co. was advertising weekly sailings to London, and through rates for goods and livestock off the GNS, Inverness & Aberdeen Junction Railway, and Banff Portsoy & Strathisla Railways, on its own steamer to Invergordon and the *Heather Bell* steamer from Burghead to Littleferry in Sutherland. The 'Northern' operated as a rogue company, seeking traffic by undercutting the ASN rates, which were fixed by the east coast steamboat 'pool', of which the ASN was a member. The ASN had to refuse a request from Henry Ormond, Liverpool cattle traffic manager of the LNWR, to raise its cattle rate from 15s to £1 a head, because the Northern Steam Navigation company was charging less than 15s. It was widely suspected that the Northern was being propped up by the

The railway in the landscape: The Keith & Dufftown line south of Keith, with Strathmill distillery, which had its own short goods spur. *(Stenlake collection)*

GNSR, and Stewart came clean in September 1861 with the admission that a subsidy of £1,500 a year was paid. He was unrepentant: "This has given a great impulse to your trade," he told the GNS shareholders, "you would not have got your 7% today had it not been for this traffic". By October the rival steamer companies were in process of amalgamation under the Aberdeen Steam Navigation name, with capital recorded as £37,000 (ASN) and £27,000 (NSN), the Inverness & Aberdeen Junction Railway was dropped from the advertisements, and the SNER was listed as a participant railway. Chairman of the combined company was John Stewart, and it maintained the old ASN's place in the east coast steamboat pool[2]. Stewart's action ensured that the GNS maintained an alternative route to and from the south, independent of what he called "the railway league"[3], at the cost of encouraging a sense of isolationism at a time when active participation in developing rail-borne traffic would have been a better strategic aim.

Operations in Moray and Banffshire

On 18 July 1861 the Formartine & Buchan Railway was opened to a temporary terminus at Mintlaw, its 29 miles of track laid with "improved fish-jointed rails"[4]. The main structural features were the Don Bridge of three 50ft span arches, and the rebuilt Ythan Bridge, of four 60ft spans. A year would go by before it was extended to Peterhead, and four years before it reached Fraserburgh. The Great North board was looking with more urgency at Strathspey. With its Act passed on 22 July 1861, the Inverness & Perth line ceased to be a potential threat and became a future menace. Opposition from the Great North had resulted only in some rather vague protective clauses being included in the Act. Aberdeen's lack of connection between its northern and southern railways had been held out as one reason for the new north-south railway, and talks resumed between the GNS and the Scottish North Eastern Railway on this topic, with the Denburn Valley still seen as the shortest and most obvious route, despite the expense of making a cross-city line. The Strathspey Railway, conceived, though not acknowledged, as a defensive measure against the Perth line's threat to GNS traffic, also was to go ahead, and the GNS, Strathspey, and Keith & Dufftown Railways held a joint meeting in Aberdeen on 1 August 1861, with John Stewart presiding. They approved a proposal from Alexander Gibb that H. Mills, engineer of the Morayshire Railway, should be appointed resident engineer to the Strathspey, with Gibb himself as supervising engineer receiving £100 a mile.

The Fiddich Viaduct near Dufftown, scene of two fatal accidents. *(Aberdeen University Library)*

On 9 July the Fiddich Viaduct on the Keith & Dufftown Balvenie extension had fallen, killing a workman and his daughter. A report from Thomas Elliot Harrison ascribed the collapse to premature removal of the arch centrings while the work was in "a green state". The contractor was required to rebuild it at his own expense[5]. Construction tenders were accepted by the Strathspey board in October from Ireland & Co., Laurencekirk, and Charles Brand, Montrose, for £23,960 (with 300 £10 5% preference shares as part-payment) and £11,841 10s (with 400 shares) for the Fiddich and Craigellachie sections respectively. Ireland also got the Aberlour section at £10,420, and A. Edward Preston of Elgin got Craigellachie-Abernethy at £82,000. Instead of an up-front subscription of £100,000 as authorised in the Strathspey's Act, the Great North guaranteed a cash account of £80,000 for the company with the National and North of Scotland Banks, at 4½% interest for three years; the remaining £20,000 being available as cash credits. Security against these was provided in the form of the 10,000 Strathspey shares plus collateral of £10,000 in GNS preference shares, the banks taking half each[6]. Great North share prices were still riding high, with ordinary shares worth a nominal £100 bought for £131, and preference shares at the same price[7].

On 30 December 1861, the Morayshire Railway opened its direct Elgin-Rothes line for goods trains, with passenger services from 1 January 1862. The Keith & Dufftown directors traversed their own line on 18 January in two carriages behind a "splendid new engine" and 12 wagons loaded with rails. Captain Rich approved the line for the Board of Trade on 19 February and it opened on the 21st, with the day made a public holiday in Dufftown[8]. Considerable engineering activity was still going on in southern Banffshire, with work proceeding both on the Strathspey Railway and the line across the Spey joining it end-on to the Morayshire Railway. The layout of Strathspey Junction (renamed Craigellachie Junction on 1 June 1864 , with the 'Junction' dropped in 1872), to cost £1,683 5s 1d, paid for jointly by the Morayshire and Strathspey Railways, was approved in February 1862. Sleepers for the Speyside line were bought from upstream suppliers and floated down-river, and in another cost-cutting exercise, five miles of track into Abernethy (renamed Nethy Bridge on 1 November 1867 to avoid confusion with the North British station of the same name) were laid with old rails supplied by the GNSR. Target date for completion of the lines was 1 June 1863 but the engineers reported that the contractors would need to employ substantially more men and equipment to meet this. Preston in particular was accused of being dilatory, replying that he had had a six-month delay getting on to Lord Seafield's land and citing other problems, but basically he had undercharged to get the contract. In October 1862 he was paid off with £12,000 and relieved of the contract, which was then completed by subcontractors watched over by Mills. Navvies were at a premium, with the Inverness-Perth line also being built: masons were receiving 30s a week and labourers 18s, 20% more than any previous workmen's rates north of Aberdeen[9].

Dividend at a peak

A few weeks later, John Stewart revealed various aspects of growth at the Great North's half-yearly meeting on 20 September 1861, with carefully-chosen but impressive statistics. In its first year the company had carried 61,555 tons of goods; in the 12 months to 31 July 1861 it carried 196,547 tons; passenger revenue in the first year had been £17,393; in the most recent year it was £42,244. GNS trains had run 136,147 miles in the first years, compared to 279,183 in 1860-61. Less welcome to the board was a rise in the rate of payments to parish poor rates, now £1,423 a year compared to £440 in the first year; "We bring prosperity and have to bear the burden of the poor," was Stewart's comment. He also remarked that "the principle on which we proceeded with our branch lines has been very much misunderstood. We helped them to help themselves."

An account had been kept over six months on through traffic between stations north of Keith and south of Aberdeen and it had been found to amount only to around £2,800, in a total goods revenue of £46,000. Intended to minimise the threat of the Inverness & Perth Junction Railway in the shareholders' eyes, this figure ignored the value of goods brought from, or to, places north of Keith via the harbour of Aberdeen. His hearers might have been a little confused by the company's new readiness to see the Denburn line built. Stewart asserted that "for years" the GNS had been ready to subscribe £50,000 towards it, but "our friends the Directors of the Scottish North Eastern Railway did not see their way to it. They do so now." However, the board would not go ahead until the town council and proprietors agreed to sensible prices for the ground: "If 95% of the proprietary, including the town council, deal fairly and liberally with us," then a Bill would be drafted for the next session of Parliament[10].

Stewart's defensive comments about branch policy were at variance with the Bill lodged by the Great North that winter, seeking authority for the company to subscribe further sums to the Alford Valley and Formartine & Buchan companies, and to guarantee payment of interest and principal on the mortgage debt of the Alford Valley, Aberdeen & Turriff and Keith & Dufftown companies. This was not helping them to help themselves but providing a lifeline to companies which would otherwise have gone under. The Formartine & Buchan had

Waiting for the train at Fyvie, on the Turriff line, *c*.1900. (*Stenlake collection*)

declared 14,000 shares forfeit through non-payment, the Aberdeen & Turriff paid no dividend, blaming the third bad harvest in a row; the Alford Valley had less traffic than in its second year, which itself had less than in the first. Two thirds of its gross revenue was being taken in working costs by the Great North. The relief sums involved were not small – the Great North was to provide £48,000 to the AVR and £100,000 to the Formartine & Buchan Railway, in addition to the £15,000 and £50,000 already committed. A further £300,000 was to be raised "for the general purposes of the Company", in 5% preference shares, along with borrowing powers of £100,000[11].

Shareholders in the GNS enjoyed their biggest dividend yet in March 1862, 7½%, and the ordinary share price touched a high of £140[12]. The Aberdeenshire Canal had vanished but was not forgotten: a long-running arbitration case finally apportioned payments to be made to the traders who had suffered because of the closure. Having sought £16,898 14s 6d, they were awarded £8,229 14s 3d. With a last payment of £1,300 to the contractors, this ended the company's liabilities on the original construction account.

The 'Scottish Northern Junction Railway' and acquisition of the Deeside line

Dramatic events were to come in early 1862. The issue of the junction line and central station in Aberdeen became a white-hot controversy. While always admitting that the project was an essential one, both the GNS and the Scottish North Eastern Railway had on different occasions put delays in the way of joint action. During 1861 discussions resulted in the engineers of both companies presenting the boards with five possible routes for the link. None were acceptable to the Great North directors, and it was also claimed that in one case, the cost had been underestimated by £16,000. Describing the plans as "immature", Robert Milne wrote to the SNER that there was not time to make satisfactory arrangements for a Bill in 1862[13], and asked for a 12-month delay in putting forward a Bill, adding that the Great North was willing to commit to a 50% contribution to the "cheapest and best" scheme that could be devised in the meantime. Benjamin Blyth had a hand in this: having made his own survey he claimed that a line could be built for £170,000, £30,000 less than the company engineers' lowest price.

Seeing the request for postponement as only a further delaying tactic, the Scottish North Eastern Railway reacted with a completely new scheme. On 4 December 1861 its board discussed a letter from John Webster, an Aberdeen advocate, which set out the potential advantages to the SNER of a railway from its line at Limpet Mill, 2½ miles north of Stonehaven, to the GNSR at Kintore, bypassing Aberdeen completely, and crossing the Deeside Railway

Aboyne Station from the east, after 1900. *(Stenlake collection)*

at Culter with junctions towards the city from both south and north. This 22-mile line – an expanded version of what John Duncan had proposed in 1852 – would offer a more direct and efficient through route for north-south traffic, as a rival to the Great North's practice of trans-shipping goods at Aberdeen Harbour. Greater speed and competitive rates would draw the customers. The SNER agreed to become joint promoters, to take £90,000-worth of stock, work the line for 45% of gross revenue (to be abated if this did not equate with a 4½% return on the capital), and to pay the preliminary and parliamentary costs[14]. Hailing the scheme as a good feeder to their line, Duncan and three other Deeside Railway directors joined the provisional committee. John Stirling and his SNER colleagues must have felt they had achieved a master-stroke.

To the Great North this 'Scottish Northern Junction Railway' was a serious threat. The new line could siphon off local traffic from the Kintore area to Aberdeen by way of the junction at Culter into the Scottish North Eastern Railway terminus at Guild Street, while passengers to and from south of Aberdeen would find it much more convenient to change trains at Kintore than make their way between Waterloo and Guild Street.

Soon, though, complications arose. The scheme required running powers over the Deeside Railway from Culter to Ferryhill, and application was made to the Deeside board in November, which agreed promptly, asking for a toll of 47% of the gross receipts per mile over its line. The Scottish North Eastern Railway, however, was unwilling to go beyond 35%. Focus of the discussion changed from running powers to a full lease of the Deeside Railway. Lack of surviving evidence, and contradictory statements from those involved, make it difficult to chart the exact progress of events in late January and February 1862, but the general course is clear, with John Duncan as the central figure. The Deeside board demanded an annual rental of 8% on its capital, and 4% on the Deeside Extension capital, for a permanent lease. These were considered high terms by the Scottish North Eastern, which was slow to make a formal response, but on 7 February its board decided to offer 7% on paid-up capital for two years, 7½% for a year from 1 September 1863, and 8% thereafter, plus 2% on the Deeside Extension for two years, then to rise by ½% a year to 4%[15]. In the interim, without informing the Scottish North Eastern Railway, Duncan had approached the Great North – claiming later that he had done so only because he believed the SNER had dropped out. The GNS was indeed interested, and a prompt bid was made for a permanent lease at 6% a year on the Deeside's capital, to be increased to match the GNS dividend if that should in any year exceed 6%. The Deeside Extension was not included and would be worked as at present, but Duncan had a substantial holding in the Extension and arranged with the GNS that it would buy 1,800 Extension shares owned by "certain parties", mostly himself, at par – £10 a share, the current market price being £3. When revealed, this deal, which left other Deeside Extension Railway shareholders out in the cold, was vehemently opposed by the two directors appointed to look after the interests of the Deeside Extension Railway[16].

The Scottish Northern Junction proposal had already prompted the Great North to seek a meeting with representatives of the Scottish North Eastern Railway on neutral territory, under the auspices of the Caledonian chairman Thomas Salkeld, to reconsider a Denburn Valley line. This took place in Glasgow on 11 February 1862, but by then the GNS had made its Deeside offer and the SNER knew of it. Its deputation refused to discuss the Denburn line unless the Great North gave up its bid for the Deeside. The GNS repeated its willingness to contribute half the cost of the "best and cheapest line" (meaning Blyth's), but the meeting "broke up without almost any further discussion"[17]. Events were moving fast, with both sides locked into competing plans. Bargaining centred now on the Deeside Extension Railway, open since December 1859 but which had never paid a dividend. Its capital had never been fully subscribed and 3,100 £10 shares were still unsold. Neither of the competing companies actually wanted the Extension: John Stewart had said "not a shilling" would be spent on it[18].

On 10 February the Scottish North Eastern Railway dramatically improved its offer by proposing to buy the 3,100 unsold Extension shares at par (£10). Duncan deferred any answer for a week between 12 and 18 February, during which time he and the GNS agreed that the £18,000 purchase would be dropped, and instead the SNER's offer of £31,000 for the unallocated shares would be matched. At a Deeside directors' meeting on 18 February, both offers were considered, and with his board evenly split on the issue, Duncan gave his casting vote for the Great North[19]. Next day, another meeting between GNS and SNER directors had been arranged, but with the Great North on the point of signing its lease on the Deeside Railway and refusing to back down, the SNER representatives walked out. On 22 February W.B. Ferguson, manager of the Deeside, wrote to Irvine Kempt, secretary of the SNER, to say that his directors had declined the SNER proposal but would put it to a general meeting of shareholders which would be called to approve the decision to go with the Great North[20]. In fact this was not done.

For the Great North, acquisition of the Deeside Railway was a triumph. The terms, 6% per annum on the capital of £106,250, plus "such additional rent as will enable the Deeside Railway dividend to be equal to the Great North's" (currently 7% plus), were high, but the Deeside had been paying a 6% dividend. Up till now, the Deeside company had been seen as very much an associate of the Scottish North Eastern, and Duncan's turnabout caused great surprise. W.B. Ferguson described the Deeside's atttitude in terms of *realpolitik*: "Menaced … as a small line 'twixt two great ones, at war with each other," and said it preferred to treat with the "Company which had the greatest power to injure them by new lines … if the shareholders only suspend their judgement until the proper time for full explanation comes, they will at once confirm [approve] what has been done"[21]. Duncan's motive in accepting the lower offer can only be guessed at, but he certainly believed in himself as a man who could run a big railway and perhaps saw involvement with the Great North as more likely to provide a platform for his abilities than the Scottish North Eastern Railway, where John Stirling sat securely.

Meanwhile, the Limpet Mill-Kintore project line was still possible, though with the Deeside Railway in the hands of the Great North, the likelihood of the Scottish North Eastern Railway being able to run trains from Kintore via Culter to Aberdeen was very small, and the scheme lost much of its appeal. Nevertheless, the SNER proceeded with its Bill, while also seeking a legal interdict against the Great North-Deeside Railway agreement. Despite W.B. Ferguson's assurance, when the Deeside Railway's extraordinary general meeting took place on 13 May, only the Great North's proposal was presented for approval. Of the Deeside Extension Railway's 319 shareholders, 240 opposed the deal, but they mustered only 1,3421 shares against 3,255 held by, or in favour of, Duncan, and the meeting simply approved the GNS offer[22]. Three dissident Deeside directors, and a Great North shareholder, Stephen Youden, officer of the Inland Revenue at Stonehaven, sided with the SNER and sought a legal interdict against the deal. Overwhelming approval of the agreement was given by the GNS shareholders at a meeting on 27 May, but in July the Court of Session imposed the interdict until Parliament should approve the agreement[23].

The Kittiwake line

At the GNS half-yearly meeting on 28 March 1862, George Milne of Kinaldie moved a resolution in favour of making conciliatory approaches to the Scottish North Eastern, but it was voted down[24]. Milne was evidently unaware that the GNS was taking other measures hostile to the Scottish North Eastern Railway. A railway locally promoted to link Montrose and Bervie had obtained its Act on 3 July 1860. At first it was regarded with suspicion by the SNER, until its promoters gave an assurance that it was purely a local branch. As with other north-east branch lines, great difficulty was found in raising capital, with only £25,000 of the necessary £70,000 in the bank by March 1862. Things looked up for the Montrose & Bervie when two benevolent gentlemen from Aberdeen came on the scene. At a meeting in London in March 1862 with Montrose & Bervie directors, John Stewart and Alexander Anderson offered to provide £35,000 if a further £10,000 were raised locally. There was a condition attached: that the Bervie company should apply for extensions at each end, to make a railway linking Arbroath, Montrose and Stonehaven. Blyth & Blyth would be the engineers. Anderson and Stewart promised to provide the deposit and expenses of the necessary Bill, the latter to be repaid if the Bill was successful. Of course the project, soon nicknamed the "Kittiwake Line" in Aberdeen, was hotly opposed by the SNER, which produced the letter pledging the Montrose & Bervie to be a local branch. In February 1863 the *Aberdeen Journal* published a letter from the joint secretaries of the Montrose & Bervie company, blankly denying that their company had broken faith with the Scottish North Eastern Railway, or that the Great North had anything to do with the Montrose & Bervie Bill[25]. While distortions of the truth were quite common in such controversies, blatant falsehood like this was rare. The Commons committee threw out the Montrose & Bervie Bill on 27 April 1863, leaving the Great North with 3,000 shares, nominally worth £30,000, in a small and unfinished railway twenty-five miles away from its own system, a purchase for which it had no parliamentary sanction[26]. The nature of the operation is revealing: Stewart and Anderson were purporting to act as private individuals, though the aim was to secure for the GNS a line which would compete with the SNER between Aberdeen and Dundee, and it was GNS money that they offered. Nothing of this was said to the shareholders or officially recorded.

A new mail contract was agreed with the Post Office in March 1862, worth £3,375 a year. To any observer, the Great North of Scotland company was doing extremely well. In March it again paid $7\frac{1}{2}$% on its ordinary shares. Its share price, on the Aberdeen stock market, was the highest of any railway at £136[27].

These manoeuvrings and machinations on Deeside and on the coast left the question of an Aberdeen link line wide open, and despite the bad relations, the mutually opposed Bills, and the lawsuits, a combination of past promises, commercial pressures, and demand both from the city's inhabitants and its council forced the companies to keep talking. This had the unexpected result of producing a second alternative to the Denburn line.

At the same time as the Montrose & Bervie's, the Scottish Northern Junction Bill was under parliamentary scrutiny. Inevitably the long-mooted Denburn line was drawn into the committee's deliberations, along with the GNS's attitude to it. In his evidence, William Walker, its traffic manager, maintained the line of playing down the value of through traffic, which he said was worth £3,275 a year to the company, of which he expected to lose half to the Perth line. Omnibus passengers between Aberdeen's two stations numbered 10,000 a year, or 32 per working day. Walker also insisted that the GNS sent on more goods by rail than by sea despite sea rates being a third cheaper. John Stewart, asked why the GNS did not join the Railway Clearing House, said that the company was quite willing to join, "if they will give us our local rates" – at this time the company was charging above the Clearing House scale on goods traffic. Stewart called the Denburn Valley route "not such as I approve of" and said he believed a better line could be found; it seems he already had an alternative in mind when he made a surprising proposal: that if rejection of the Scottish Northern Junction Bill were to depend on the Great North undertaking to construct a junction line at Aberdeen at its own expense, then the Great North was willing to do just that. The committee took him at his word. The Scottish Northern Junction Bill was passed, but its application was to be suspended for a year, and if within the year the GNS obtained an Act for a line from Kittybrewster to the Scottish North Eastern Railway, to be built at its own expense, then the Scottish Northern Junction was to be abandoned, though the SNER could apply for "protection and facilities" in the subsequent Act. In Aberdeen the Great North's next move was awaited with keen interest[28].

Kittybrewster Station, seen from Powis Terrace. A post-1923 but wholly GNSR view.

CHAPTER 7
The Branch Policy, 1862 – 1864

Unveiling of the 'Circumbendibus'

Even with the Montrose & Bervie intrigue going on, there was something of a rapprochement with the Scottish North Eastern in the summer of 1862 and in August the two companies got as far as drafting provisions for a joint committee and a joint purse, as preliminaries to complete amalgamation. These arrangements were not mentioned to the shareholders and by October they had come to an end, when the GNS refused to accept certain points raised by the Scottish North Eastern Railway[1]. The GNS declared a 5% ordinary dividend in September. At the half-yearly meeting it was noted that Aberdeen's two rival steamship companies had amalgamated, and John Stewart refunded the subsidy money that had been paid to his Northern Steam Navigation company[2].

Publication of Benjamin Blyth's plan for the alternative link-line reignited controversy. Avoiding the Denburn Valley completely, it ran south from Kittybrewster as far as Rosemount, then swung west to skirt the outer suburbs, with a proposed station at Albert Street, before curving eastwards, running in cuttings through new building developments around Albyn Place and entering the station at Guild Street from the south. Named the Aberdeen Junction Railway, it was an ingenious plan, though it speedily acquired the byname of 'Circumbendibus', reviving a jokey old word for something excessively circuitous or long-winded. Public opinion was largely against it, and 3,488 people signed a memorial opposing it. The town council was divided, with Alexander Anderson, still Lord Provost, and Alexander Gibb favouring the proposal, and a committee was appointed to consider it. The Scottish North Eastern, which had not been consulted, and which was also now fully aware of the Montrose & Bervie scheme (whose Bill, published in the same issue of the *Edinburgh Gazette* as that for the Circumbendibus, did not mention the Great North at all, but the Scottish North Eastern Railway knew very well who was behind it) expressed regret that the GNS had abandoned the Denburn line, and offered to contribute £30,000 if it were reinstated, which the GNS refused in a haughty letter from Robert Milne claiming there was no time for further consideration and stating that the GNS would seek compulsory powers of access to the station at Guild Street[3]. The Bill provided for joint or separate stations but the clear intention was that the SNER would have to concede the use of, and almost certainly enlarge, its Guild Street terminus. Heated exchanges at a packed public meeting on 15 December included descriptions of the Circumbendibus as "a monstrous evil" and the Lord Provost as "a paid agent of the Great North" and the gathering ended with three cheers for the Denburn route. Undeterred, the Great North lodged the Great North of Scotland Railway (Aberdeen Junction) Bill[4].

By May 1863, 10,398 people had signed a petition against the Circumbendibus route. The Bill was in committee and both sides had marshalled their witnesses. Although in theory the contest was between what John Stewart

Dyce: the four-platform station, looking north, with a train off the Buchan line. *(Stenlake collection)*

preferred to call the 'suburban' route and the Scottish Northern Junction line, the Denburn line was constantly referred to; John Stirling renewed the offer of £30,000 and offered to suspend the Scottish Northern Junction plan if a Bill for a Denburn line were introduced. The great and increasing problem of the Denburn line was the cost of land, not just for the track but for the new joint station which would be needed: neither side believed that the line would actually pay its way[5]. Nevertheless, the committee, ably led by Michael Hassard, Conservative member for Waterford Borough, effectively decided on 6 May that the Denburn line should be constructed. While the Circumbendibus Bill was passed, gaining the royal assent on 21 July, its effectiveness was suspended to give the Scottish North Eastern Railway time to bring in a new Bill for the Denburn route, and both the GNS and SNER were to apply the resources earmarked for their other schemes to this one. In the case of the Great North this meant the £125,000 estimated for the Circumbendibus. The baton was thus passed back to the SNER, which would manage construction of the line and of a new station, whose plan would be determined by a joint committee. The GNS would have no running powers south of the joint station (it was not yet operating the Deeside line) nor would the SNER have running powers north of it. The station itself would be managed by a joint committee which would set the tolls and rates for usage; after deducting 40% for expenses, the revenues would then be divided 75% to the Great North and 25% to the Scottish North Eastern. It would be situated in "the space extending from the ice-house near Messrs. Pirie's works at Poynernook to a new street formed by the extension of Guild Street in a direct westerly line to College Street". Considerable redevelopment of the area would be undertaken, with new and widened streets, including "a street leading to Union Street, crossing Windmillbrae by a high arch, and emerging on Union Street at the side of Messrs. A.&W. Ogilvie's shop. Windmillbrae will be slightly raised, and carried over the railway by a bridge"[6].

Branches – difficulties and developments

Branches continued to require, and receive, funds from the Great North's apparently large resources. A special meeting of shareholders chaired by John Stewart on 31 March 1862 approved payment of further amounts already authorised by Parliament, including the £100,000 for the Strathspey company, still referred to as a "subscription." This meeting also approved the £1,000 for the Keith & Dufftown under its original Act of 1857, and £25,000 under the Keith & Dufftown Deviation Act, 1860; and £20,000 to the Morayshire Railway (Morayshire Railway Act 1861)[7]. These sums were necessary to complete the works in hand, because of the almost total absence of local investment, and the inability of these fragile companies to raise loans on their own account.

An early view of Peterhead Station from the north, with harbour branch track in foreground, and level crossing gates made by Harper & Co. of Aberdeen. The low station building was enlarged in the early 1870s. Also notable are the guard's uniform and the transporter crane. (*Great North of Scotland Railway Association*)

The Great North's ability to provide was based on the amount of authorised capital and loans which had not yet been raised. At the end of 1862, the company's authorised capital amounted to £1,510,000, and loans to £420,000. Of this total of £1,930,000, the sum actually raised to date was £1,527,596 (of which £423,109 had already been invested in, or lent to, other companies[8]. Two calls on shareholders had been made by the Strathspey Railway, with minimal results. The Alford Valley Railway was trying to raise capital through a Bill for preference shares. Dr Garden, an assiduous inquirer, asked what had become of the original capital of the line, ostensibly £64,920 – there had been 163 shareholders, of whom four had signed up for £61,000 worth of shares but had never paid anything towards them. Adam explained that the unnamed four had transferred their shares before any call for payment was made, something the directors could not prevent. The persons in whose names the shares now stood were unable to pay, and the shares were now forfeited. So the Alford Valley Railway, with an authorised capital of £100,000, and built at a cost of well over £70,000, had an actual paid-up capital of £3,920. Made with borrowed money, the line could not hope to raise a penny unless the Great North guaranteed a return on the new preference shares. Only the Deeside was free of financial trouble, but it had other problems. John Duncan faced a difficult extraordinary general meeting on 13 May with typical bluffness, describing himself as "the best abused man in the North of Scotland". Controversy centred on the lease to the Great North and especially on the status of the Deeside Extension. The working agreement with the Great North still hung in abeyance, and the Deeside was still running its own services.

Peterhead finally became a railway terminus on 3 July 1862 with the completion of the line from Mintlaw, whose only large engineering work was the three-span cast-iron skew bridge over the Ugie. Vacillation by the town council and property owners over the siting of the terminus had been largely responsible for the year-long delay, and its final location at the west end of the town was criticised as being "practically in the country"[9]. A local author, William Anderson, wrote in the year of opening, " … the station buildings, which stand on the property of the Feuars of Peterhead, at the west end of Queen Street, are by no means pretending-looking erections, although durable enough and substantial in their build. The passenger station, for its size, is a very well-laid-off and commodious little place, having a platform upwards of five hundred feet in length. On a smaller scale (of

**Maud Junction looking north, *c*.1910. Manson No. 6, *Thomas Adam* (1887)
heads a train from Fraserburgh. (*Stenlake collection*)**

course) we have … all the advantages and facilities possessed in the large terminal stations in the south. The space is divided thus: luggage room, guard's room and closet, store-room, stationmaster's room, ticket office, gentlemen's waiting-room, ladies' waiting-room, boiler room, lamp room, and water-closets. A few yards to the south of the passenger-station is erected the carriage shed, a long and somewhat unshapely wooden building, but well enough fitted for its purpose — that of holding spare carriages. Then we have the goods station, the arrangement and build of which is all that could be wished for. Beside the goods station stands the engine house and water-tank, the water for the supply of which is brought all the way from Howe o' Buchan. The water is forced up by two powerful 'rams' (the design and work of Mr White, coppersmith, Peterhead) to the top of the brae on the old road overlooking Blackhouse, in order to give it sufficient fall. The 'rams' are well worthy of the inspection of the mechanically curious." At the time, Peterhead had a population of around 8,000, and still had some 20 or 30 sealing and whaling ships among the 50 vessels registered at the port, as well as 250 herring boats. There were three shipyards, a woollen manufactory, tanneries and the nearby quarries[10].

Shareholders become uneasy

If many shareholders were happy to take a 5% dividend and assume that everything must be fine, there were also critics. In December 1862 'A Shareholder' published an open letter which made a wide-ranging attack on 'The Past and Present Policy of the Directors and the Future Prospects of the GNSR'. Elphinstone was dismissed as supine, and John Stewart was the prime focus of criticism, for his role in putting off action on the Denburn Valley line in 1859, and for his backing of the Speyside Railway, which "begins and ends nowhere". For failure to maintain good relations with neighbouring lines, for spending £30,000 on the Deeside Extension, which yielded a 1% dividend in 1861, and for pouring £50,000 into the Alford Valley and £100,000 into Formartine & Buchan Railways as "advances", the board is roundly castigated, with the directors also accused of manipulating the accounts and paying dividends out of capital, of switching sums from Revenue to Capital and vice versa; and concealing large amounts of debt in suspense accounts. But if the author hoped to start a shareholders' revolt, he was disappointed.

Massive subsidisation of the Formartine & Buchan was indeed lined up. A Bill for the Fraserburgh Branch, now to diverge at Brucklay (later Maud Junction), lodged for the 1863 session, included authorisation to raise £100,000 preference stock at a maximum interest of 5% and to issue further 5% preference shares in replacement of 14,959 forfeited shares (nominal value £149,590). A letter to the *Aberdeen Journal* on 7 January 1863 from 'Investigator' asked who had subscribed these forfeited shares. Of the Formartine & Buchan's 30,000 ordinary shares only 11,736 had been fully paid up, and no more than £13,665 had been paid in calls on the other 18,264 shares. The writer pointed out that in addition to taking £50,000 of stock, the Great North had advanced £96,000 to the Buchan company "at high interest", and if this were to be converted into preference shares, as the Bill would allow, then the ordinary shareholders were unlikely to see any dividend. The Formartine & Buchan had paid a 1¼% dividend in 1862[11] while the other northern branches paid nothing.

At the GNS ordinary general meeting on 26 March, John Stewart, presiding, admitted for the first time that the Strathspey Railway had a "defensive" aspect, having previously talked up its potential economic strength. The dismal record of branch revenue might have been the main topic had it not been for a wordy dispute between Stewart and Dr Matthew, a shareholder but also a Scottish North Eastern Railway director, known to be author of the recent anonymous pamphlet attacking the Great North management. Asserting his right as a GNS shareholder, Matthew wanted to see the Great North's account books but Stewart insisted that the time was not appropriate and that Matthew was making "abuse of liberty"[12].

Opening of the Strathspey Railway, and the line to Elgin

The summer of 1863 brought several openings which significantly extended the activity of the Great North. From 1 February it had been working the Banff Portsoy & Strathisla Railway in anticipation of a merger agreement, at a charge of 60% of gross revenue, or 50% if the gross receipts exceeded £7 per mile per week. Colonel Yolland, for the Board of Trade, inspected the Strathspey lines on 22-23 June and expressed satisfaction, except for the use of old rails between Grantown and Abernethy, which he considered "a bad precedent". Milne wrote to say that the traffic would be extremely small and very slow, only three trains daily each way in summer, and two in winter, and not expected to earn more than £3 or £4 per mile per week. A 10 mph limit was imposed until new rails were laid (to be done within two months). On 25 June the directors had travelled the 34 miles from Dufftown to Abernethy to inspect their new line. Apart from the 70-yard Taminurie Tunnel between Aberlour and Strathspey Junction, its main works were bridges over the Spey at Carron and Ballindalloch, of iron in both cases. The Carron Bridge, a cast-iron three-ribbed arch, carried both the railway and a carriage road for Mr Grant of Carron. Built by Mackinnon & Co., it cost £3,277[13]. Overall building cost was £204,000, around £6,000 a mile. In the engine shed at

Carron, looking east, with the Imperial Distillery sidings in foreground. The GNS tended to lay crossing loops short enough to be worked from a single cabin, as here. *(Stenlake collection)*

The railway in the landscape: The Spey Bridge at Craigellachie, linking the Strathspey and Morayshire Railways, built 1866. *(Stenlake collection)*

Abernethy a luncheon for guests was provided, with John Stewart presiding, and the lines opened for public service on 1 July. At a joint meeting of Dufftown and Strathspey directors in Dufftown Station it was resolved that the Balvenie extension should be reckoned as part of the Keith & Dufftown line, with Dufftown station as joint and equal property of both companies. Alexander Gibb was to supply a statement of costs so that the accounts could be properly calculated, and interest on expenditure by the Strathspey would be allowed by the Keith & Dufftown at 5% a year. Parliamentary sanction for these adjustments would be obtained "on the first suitable occasion"[14]. Robert Milne had visited iron workings in the neighbourhood of Tomintoul and supplied the Speyside board with a six-year old report on on the deposits. Still hopeful about ore traffic, the board expressed its willingness to share the cost of a thorough survey and ore analysis with the Duke of Richmond and Lennox[15].

The Morayshire company opened the connection between Strathspey Junction and its own line on the same day, completing the new route from Keith to Elgin, and the GNS took over working the trains. An Act of 21 July renamed the Banff Portsoy & Strathisla simply as the Banffshire Railway, reviving the title of a venture wound up in April 1846[16], and authorised it to make a 14-mile extension from Portsoy past Buckie to Portgordon, to the east of the Spey Estuary, raising additional capital of £100,000 plus borrowing powers of £33,000 for the purpose, also authorising the Great North to contribute up to £80,000. On the east side of the Deveron the Banff, Macduff & Turriff Extension Railway obtained powers for a short extension to a new terminus, with a goods tramway continuing to Macduff Harbour. Beyond the Great North's borders, the Scottish North Eastern finally absorbed the Dundee & Arbroath Railway, and, of more concern to the Aberdonians, the Inverness & Perth Junction Railway was opened throughout its length on 9 September 1863.

The impact of the Inverness & Perth Junction Railway

With the advent of the Inverness & Perth Junction Railway a contest began for the mail contract to the northern counties, against strong lobbying from Inverness. A general proposal was made in September to the Post Office for a new service, comprising a Special Mail train daily each way betweeen Keith and Aberdeen, taking two hours, another daily (including Sunday) each way between Aberdeen and Peterhead, to arrive at Peterhead not later than 9 am and at Aberdeen by 11.50 am. A train from Inveramsay to Banff would connect with the Special Mail. On the Strathspey line the company would give a stop of 25 minutes at Craigellachie on one train each way, to allow for sorting of post. Cars would connect with the trains to carry mail at 7 mph between Udny and

Newburgh, Ellon and Cruden Bay, and Mintlaw and Fraserburgh. In addition the Post Office could have use of all trains. The proposed rate was £6,000 a year for three or five years. Part of the package was that the Scottish North Eastern Railway, equally concerned to keep the contract, would guarantee to run the mail between Perth and Aberdeen in three hours[17].

The Scottish North Eastern Railway offer to accelerate the Perth-Aberdeen mail was conditional on the GNS joining the Clearing House for all traffic and giving through rates to and from all its stations. To compete with the Inverness & Perth Junction Railway, the Great North could no longer resist this in any case, and by 23 September it had agreed to join the Clearing House "unreservedly"[18]. John S. Stuart, later assistant to the general manager, said at the 'railway bazaar' of 1893 (see Chapter 19) that the GNS joined the Railway Clearing House in 1859 and he was sent to London to learn its workings and adapt the company's system to its methods. The GNS certainly needed to know how the Clearing House worked, but it did not join at that time. John Stewart admitted at the Formartine & Buchan annual meeting in November 1863 that joining the Clearing House was in "self-defence" against the Inverness & Perth Junction Railway. While goods rates on through traffic went down as a result, passenger fares went up: the GNS charged $1\frac{1}{4}d$ per mile (apart from the daily parliamentary train) for third class, in carriages equivalent to other companies' seconds, and $1\frac{3}{4}d$ a mile for first. "… what we gained by an extra charge on the goods, we gave up by making a much lower charge for passengers"[19]. The era of isolationism was ending.

By now the GNSR was working a main line of $53\frac{1}{2}$ miles and branches totalling 173 miles. It had 30 engines, 124 passenger carriages, and 863 wagons, excluding the rolling stock taken over from the Morayshire Railway. Working expenses remained low, at 38% of gross revenue, and in September 1863, a 7% dividend was again paid on the ordinary shares[20]. At the half-yearly meeting on 25 September, Sir James Elphinstone touched on a few key topics, remarking of the Inverness & Perth Junction Railway "We entertain towards the Highland line the most cordial feelings of amity" and hoping for mutual co-operation. On the Denburn line he observed that "… if our opponents may claim the victory … we have the satisfaction of knowing to a shilling what we will pay." Again suggestions of the desirability of a GNS-SNER merger were in the air, prompted by an assiduous commentator on the railway scene, John McGavin: John Stewart said that the board was willing to consider it[21].

The Post Office's Inspector-General of Mails informed the company in December 1863 that the Inverness & Perth Junction Railway could get the overnight London mail to Inverness by 10 am, a performance which could not be matched by the Aberdeen-Keith route. Prompted by reports that the Inverness & Perth had made a reduced offer to the Post Office for the north mails, Robert Milne was instructed in January 1864 to offer £5,000 including a "free of charge" additional train from Aberdeen at 3 or 4 am, having picked up the mail from the south (due to arrive at 3 am), and connecting at Keith with the 7.45 am train to Inverness. He also offered to match any lower offer made by the Inverness company. A heavyweight deputation led by the Earl of Kintore went to see the Postmaster General, Lord Stanley of Alderley, in February to press the Great North's case. All this was to no avail: the contract went to the Inverness & Perth, and the Great North was left to negotiate a reduced contract for mail carriage within its own system limits[22]. This led to the immediate withdrawal of the Sunday trains between Aberdeen and Keith, and the only Sunday trains on the system were in connection with work on the permanent way. A memorial from the Aberdeen and North of Scotland Trade Protection Society to the Postmaster General reminded him that the city's postal revenue in 1862 was £16,2326, third-biggest in the country after Glasgow and Edinburgh[23]. The setback did not deter the Great North from seeking co-operation with the Inverness companies and the Scottish North Eastern Railway, on selling tourist tickets, at less than the ordinary fares and valid on adjacent lines, during the holiday season. This marked the start of the company's long and successful exploitation of the scenic country it traversed[24].

More branch matters

In the autumn of 1863, once again branch company results did not reflect those of the Great North. The Aberdeeen & Turriff made a loss, the Alford Valley's receipts had fallen by £753. Things were hardly better on the Formartine & Buchan, with an increase in gross revenue of £4,000 but a net revenue of only £686, though a dividend of $\frac{1}{2}$% was paid. Gross revenue of the Banff, Macduff & Turriff Extension had gone up by only £21 in the year. Under pressure from residents of Macduff to have the harbour tramway made into a passenger line, the directors promised to consider it[25]. On the Strathspey Railway, whose capital account had reached £252,400 and was still rising, working expenses and interest rates were exceeding the revenue – still, Sir James Elphinstone felt able to say, "This line appears to me to turn out very well"[26]. With the Deeside Railway lease and working agreement still in limbo, the Great North board decided to buy up the Deeside and Deeside Extension shares held by John Duncan and Patrick Davidson of Inchmarlo – between 5,000 and 6,000 ordinary shares at £15; 1,300-1,400 preference and 600 Extension at par – agreed to be "highly advantageous as giving a majority of votes in the Deeside Railway and enables them [GNSR] to protect their poroperty". This was ratified by a special board meeting on 9 November, and Alexander Anderson as law agent approved a motion to reimburse the directors for any personal loss they incurred in the transaction, whose value was £86,982. Neither shareholder nor parliamentary approval was sought[27].

At the Keith & Dufftown Railway's board meeting on 6 November 1863, the three local directors who had signed for £25,000 of Strathspey shares stated that they had understood this payment was to entitle the Keith & Dufftown to ownership of the Balvenie extension. The GNS however said that was not the case; it was an additional payment. With a view to keeping the matter entirely open, the meeting resolved that an entry on the capital account of £25,000 (Strathspey subscription) remain on the Draft Account, and that with regard to the Balvenie extension, the following entry be made in the General Balance: "By balance on Capital Account £28,329 9s 2½d. Amount expended on Balvenie extension of Strathspey Railway to Dufftown Railway (repayable by Strathspey Railway) £16,963 5s 4d. Total £45,292 14s 6½d"[28]. The only way by which the Keith & Dufftown could produce such sums was by borrowing from the Great North. As far as the Strathspey Railway's accounts were concerned, however, the £25,000 looked like real money.

From Banff, James Moir, deputy chairman and secretary of the Banffshire Railway, wrote to the Great North board in January 1864 to inform it that "through dint of great perseverance" the Banffshire directors had raised guarantees of £20,000 towards construction of the coastal line west from Portsoy, though to go only as far as Buckie. The GNS board had agreed to make a start once this sum had been raised. Alexander Gibb's estimate for the total cost was £60,000 and the GNS took no action, despite Moir's complaint that traffic was going from the coast on Wordie's carts to the Inverness & Aberdeen Junction Railway station at Fochabers[29].

A disunited board

A Train & Passenger Superintendent, Forbes Morrison, was appointed from 1 October 1863, lightening the burden on Robert Milne. The Inspector of Stations, whose job was to keep the station-masters on their toes, was on long-term sick leave and an interim inspector was appointed at £80 per annum, with a list of duties 24 items

Winter scene at Rothienorman on the Turriff line, January 1907. *(Stenlake collection)*

long. Disputes over cartage in Aberdeen arose with the termination of Pickfords' contract in October and the appointment of the rival Mutter Howey company. Pickfords put in a legal claim to have the same access to the station as Mutter Howey, based on the Railway & Canal Traffic Act of 1854, which stated that "every company shall afford reasonable facilities for transfer and forwarding". If the consigner specified that Pickfords should collect, then Pickfords were entitled to access. It was suspected that Pickford agents at departure stations were labelling goods "Care of Pickford & Co." without the consigners' knowledge. For such service Pickfords charged an arbitrary rate well above their (rejected) tender. The Scottish North Eastern Railway, who had sacked Pickfords in favour of Wordies, had the same problem[30]. In December the traffic manager reported that the Inverness & Perth Junction Railway was trying to get the carriage of salmon from the Duke of Richmond's estates from Fochabers to London, and was authorised to "allow such deduction for the gross rate of cartage Fochabers-Keith as will command it via Aberdeen, this Company and the SNER sharing the rebate beyond 1s 6d a ton." Some goods rates to Glasgow and Edinburgh were also reduced because of Inverness & Perth Junction Railway competition[31]. The Great North's board was not a united body, with two directors, John Stewart (still vice-chairman) and his associate Joseph Rowell (their wives were sisters) making a vocal and critical minority of two. Having stood up on numerous occasions to support the branch line policy, Stewart now reversed his stance, complaining that the company continued to throw money away on lines that would never pay. Angry exchanges with Robert Milne erupted at a meeting of the traffic and finance committee on 22 November when Stewart accused Milne of doctoring the minutes, and he hotly opposed the company's proposed Bill which among other things sought retrospective authorisation for the GNS's investment in the Strathspey Railway. Elphinstone in turn attacked Stewart, in a letter claiming that Stewart's influence had prevented an agreement with the Scottish North Eastern and Inverness & Aberdeen Junction Railway in 1860-61. If it was not for Stewart, the expense of opposing the Limpet Mill scheme would have been saved, and "we would not now have to compete with the Highland Line". Only three months earlier, at the ordinary general meeting in September, Elphinstone had said "I have always thought that the Highland Line will operate to the advantage of the lines in which we are interested," adding that the GNS's position in the North of Scotland was impregnable[32]. Stewart now wanted an absolute stop on branch expenditure, but a board motion to that effect was defeated in December by an amendment which provided that no further engagements for branch lines should be undertaken without the sanction of the shareholders, *beyond what the board determines to be absolutely necessary*[33] [author's italics].

On 8 March 1864 an "unseemly scene" was recorded at a special board meeting chaired by Stewart, at which he refused to put forward a motion on the company's proposed Bill, claiming it was unlawful, and was voted out of the chair. Again he accused Milne of doctoring the minutes. Still at odds with the rest of the board, Stewart and Rowell, the former presiding on 18 March in the chairman's absence, proposed a 6¼% half-year dividend, which was voted down by the majority in favour of 5%, prompting Stewart to stand down from the chair. At the next meeting, not attended by the two dissidents, three new directors were appointed, including John Duncan[34].

In March 1864 the half-yearly ordinary general meeting, chaired by Elphinstone, was more contentious than previous ones. The ordinary dividend was reduced to 5% as a result of lower revenues from through goods traffic, though tonnage had risen slightly.

	1863	1862
Passenger numbers	307,512	338,406
Goods tonnage	107,115	106,803
Gross receipts	£40,246	£44,352

The "self defence" purchase of Deeside Railway stock was questioned at the meeting. Further awkward questions came from Stephen Youden of Stonehaven, a persistent critic of the board, who queried the inclusion in the capital account of £7,994 14s 8d as parliamentary expenses on the Montrose & Bervie Bill, and £5,500 for shares in the Montrose & Bervie company, pointing out that these were incurred by individuals and not by the company. Extending his argument, he compared the minimal return of the branch lines with the very large capital invested by the GNS – Elphinstone responded with the claim that the branches contributed £34,000 of traffic to the main line in 1863. Youden's personal shareholding of only £60 was seized on by the chairman to belittle his criticisms, but like the small boy in *The Emperor's New Clothes*, he had pointed out what others did not wish to see. A special meeting followed, which approved the company's Bill giving it permissive powers to contribute further sums to the Strathspey, Keith & Dufftown, and Morayshire Railways, to enable them to complete their undertakings[35].

John Stewart's attempt to get all resolutions of the shareholders' meeting overturned except for the appointment of the new directors, was rejected by a board majority[36]. With Elphinstone almost always away, meetings continued to be chaired by a vice-chairman at odds with the majority of his fellow-directors and with the secretary/manager.

The Denburn Valley Act

Popular opinion in Aberdeen might want to have the Denburn link up and running, but that did not mean a trouble-free passage for the Scottish North Eastern Railway's Bill, which proposed a line of 1 mile 5½ furlongs, with two tunnels of 244 and 269 yards. The Great North board was in the comfortable position of being able to take sides with objectors if it wanted to, as well as make its own comments and demands. Many of the properties along the proposed line were in a run-down state and it was hoped that the railway would bring improvement. A major issue arose with the managers of the Royal Infirmary, who objected to having a tunnel pass beneath their building. The Great North did not consider a tunnel necessary, and was suspected of encouraging the Infirmary's opposition, which was ultimately withdrawn after a maximum speed through the tunnel of 6 mph, and no whistling by engines, were agreed. William Cowan, the locomotive superintendent, protested that trains coming up-hill needed to reach at least 15-20 mph to avoid stalling, and that whistling was an essential safety precaution, and he wrote to Milne, "Don't agree to less than 15 miles coming up and ten going down." During parliamentary scrutiny of the Bill, the 6 mph limit was removed[37]. The Denburn Valley Railway Act was given the royal assent on 23 June, automatically repealing the 'Circumbendibus' Act, and providing for a line beginning 440 yards from the south end of Guild Street Station and ending 110 yards north of the passenger shed at Kittybrewster Station, with a joint passenger station at Guild Street.

The blacksmith's shop at Inverurie Works in the 1900s. The extensive facilities there were never fully utilised, although they could easily have coped with the enlarged company if the amalgamation with the Highland had gone ahead. (*Great North of Scotland Railway Association*)

CHAPTER 8
Collapse, 1864 – 65

A busy board

In the management of a railway company, the constant stream of details and calls for decisions might well deflect attention from longer-term considerations. Items from GNS board and committee minutes at this time reveal a typical range of issues large and small. Four months of haggling with the Post Office produced a mail contract at £3,850 a year for seven years from 1 June 1864, with no Sunday services. The Great North was still working in concert with the Aberdeen Steam Navigation Company: Mr Brand, miller at Inverugie, agreed to send all his southbound meal and grain by rail to Aberdeen and onwards by sea, providing he got a rate of 16s 6d per ton to London. The Morayshire Railway was in financial difficulties and a letter from James Grant asked for a loan of £10,000, which was refused. Grant kept up the pressure, annoyed that the GNS was charging 5½% interest on previous loans to his company while it had itself borrowed the money at 4 or 4½%, but the Great North was making a loss on the working agreement with the Morayshire Railway, and remained obdurate. Alexander Fraser, the engineer, complained to the board about his salary, asking why Gibb received £170 a year for the Strathspey lines while the work and responsibility were Fraser's alone, and threatened to leave unless his salary was raised to £350. Eventually he accepted £300[1].

A special finance committee meeting on 30 August set out probable liabilities over the next three or four years[2]:

Denburn Junction	£125,000
Banffshire Railway	£82,000
Banffshire Extension to Macduff:	£7,500
Montrose & Bervie Railway:	£9,500
Strathspey Railway:	£15,000
New plant:	£50,000
Total:	£289,000

Robert Milne identified the plant required: six engines (Cowan had wanted twelve), 100 open wagons, three first, two composite and six third class carriages, and two brake vans. Buildings were needed at Kittybrewster where much work was being done in the open air, and a shed for mending wagon covers was needed at Waterloo.

Banffshire lines

The interlinked affairs of the Strathspey and Keith & Dufftown companies took up a good deal of time in the second half of 1864 and into the following year. In August 1864 the GNS board resolved that the Strathspey

Railway, in view of its "intimate relation" with the GNS, would be worked at 40% of gross earnings, which promised an annual loss even on a minimal service. The Strathspey board had recorded in July that the company was still without present means of meeting its obligations, which included a debt to the Great North of £37,933 1s 3d for materials supplied and works executed, plus interest. It covenanted to repay this sum by 20 December[3], but meanwhile needed a further £15,000 to pay claims from Charles Brand and others, which the Great North reluctantly agreed to provide. Responsibility for the Balvenie extension and its cost was batted between the Keith & Dufftown and Strathspey companies, but ended with £20,000 being entered on the Strathspey's accounts and the Keith & Dufftown paying a toll of £1,205 a year for use of the extension[4]. Actual cost of the extension and Dufftown Station was established by Gibb as £18,463 5s 4d.

When the Strathspey line was first proposed, mention was made of ore deposits in the mountains around Tomintoul, with two main veins, one of iron ore, the other of manganese. Iron ore had been worked sporadically in the region since 1730, and in 1864 trials of ore mined at Arndilly, on Ben Aigan, were carried out, with the specimen loads carried free by the GNS to Aberdeen Harbour. Hopes of future ore traffic were among the few positive aspects of the Great North's half-year report in September 1864, which recorded a further drop in traffic receipts, but eventually tests indicated that the extraction of the metal from the rock would not be an economic proposition.

It was in this context that the Keith & Dufftown's non-GNS directors proposed that their company's obligation towards the costs of the Balvenie extension and Dufftown Station, and the subscription to the Strathspey Railway, be limited to £30,000, against which they should receive £10,000-worth of Strathspey Railway stock, the rights to the Balvenie extension, and half-ownership of Dufftown Station[5]. They were aggrieved men: the opening of the Strathspey line had done nothing for the Keith & Dufftown, whose gross revenue in 1864 was £3,085 12s 6d, a mere £194 11s 2d more than that of 1863. Working expenses charged by the Great North amounted to 80% of revenue (while the Strathspey was being worked for only 40%), and total expenses exceeded revenue by almost 50%, yet the £25,000 subscription to the Strathspey company still sat among "Sundries on Account" on the Keith & Dufftown balance sheet. W.R. Gordon, a shareholder, noted that the Keith & Dufftown's Act gave the GNS

The railway in the landscape: Craigellachie Junction. In the foreground the line from Dufftown crosses the Fiddich. Beyond the station the Elgin line continues over the viaduct and the Grantown line bends left to follow the east bank of the Spey. *(Stenlake collection)*

power to invest £26,000 in stock, instead of which it had made loans. When he asked if the Great North was legally empowered to lend money at interest, Secretary Milne had to admit "I am not very sure about that." The Keith & Dufftown ordinary general meeting was adjourned for three months, while its accounts were referred to the accountant Robert Fletcher, for scrutiny[6].

The reaction of the Great North board to this behaviour by their satellite was to condemn the Keith & Dufftown's resolutions as incompetent and unnecessary. They refused to submit any question to Fletcher regarding their rights as creditors or shareholders. As law agents, Adam & Anderson sent a copy of the relevant minutes to the Keith & Dufftown directors. Huffing and posturing came also from the GNS auditor, Walker: "I am unwilling to submit to such treatment from such a quarter." At the Keith & Dufftown's adjourned ordinary general meeting in February 1865, Fletcher's report was read out, noting that the company had 196 local subscribers with 497 shares, and that they were highly reluctant to meet their obligations: the £2 share call payable on 21 June 1858 should have raised £994 from them but only £168 was forthcoming. Fletcher found a letter from Robert Milne, written on 7 October 1859, which said that the GNS would take £8,000 of shares in the Dufftown company plus £17,000 in debentures – no mention of loans. Of the £25,000 subscription to the Strathspey Railway, seen by the Keith & Dufftown proprietors' meeting of 30 November 1861 as purchasing 2,500 5% preference shares, only 585 shares had been issued and paid for as of 31 August 1864. But the full £25,000 had been handed over to the Strathspey, with the balance of £19,150 covered by "advances" from the GNS, which by 31 August 1864 had passed more than £38,000 to the Keith & Dufftown – £12,000 in excess of the amount authorised by Parliament. The Keith & Dufftown itself had no legal authority to raise more than its original capital of £50,000 plus borrowings of £16,600.

In the period before the adjourned meeting, the GNS had smartly converted its cash "advances" to the Keith & Dufftown into purchases of 2,687 shares, deducting the price of £26,870 from what it said the Keith & Dufftown owed it. The tone of the adjourned meeting was brittle and hostile, not least from Robert Milne. Duncan, in heartiest style, glossed over the "loans" – after all, what the Dufftown directors wanted was for the GNS to buy shares, and now it had, so why should they complain? The large new shareholding ensured majority votes approving the GNS actions[7].

Despite its parlous financial situation the Strathspey board resolved in December 1864 to proceed with a Bill for a line between Abernethy and the Inverness & Perth Railway[8]. This was dictated by GNS policy (Stewart and Rowell dissenting). With the assistance of Thomas Elliot Harrison, agreement was made for a junction two miles north of Boat of Garten, with a double line to the latter place. By March 1865 the Strathspey's balance due to the GNS was £64,159 16s 2¼d, which it was wholly unable to pay, and its board resolved to allocate 5,000 shares to the GNS on a *pro tanto* basis [i.e. to cover as much of the debt as possible]. The nominal value of the shares was £50,000, their market value was a fraction of that[9]. John Duncan was appointed a Strathspey director on 23 June 1865 and chaired an extraordinary general meeting of the company on the same day, which approved the extension from Abernethy, noting that the Inverness & Perth Junction Railway was now insisting on locating the junction at Boat of Garten, which would actually save the Strathspey around £10,000. The Junction Act received the royal assent on 5 July 1865.

The dividend for the half-year remained at 5%. Passenger traffic earned £15,703 12s 5¼d; mails £2,804 2s 6d, and goods (after cartage costs) £26,084, 1s 4¼d. Sums charged to other companies, plus interest on loans to them, amounted to £14,276 7s 9d. Total expenditure, including interest on the GNS's own borrowings, amounted to £29,100 17s 4½d, though actual working expenses remained a modest £16,166[10].

SNER merger

Possible saving on the cost of the Denburn Valley line arose when John Stirling proposed a "single-sided" station on the east side of the line, rather than the double station set out on the parliamentary plan. The GNS was willing, if £17,000 of the estimated saving of £26,000 was deducted from its total payment, and this was agreed. The Scottish North Eastern Railway described the £17,000 as a "drawback", i.e. a discount[11]. Amalgamation possibility edged forward with the appointment of Thomas Elliot Harrison to advise both companies on how far their mutual interests might be promoted by a working agreement or merger. Stirling was the driver of the scheme: in a letter of 5 September to Elphinstone he proposed they "amalgamate in traffic for the year ending August 1865, with a Joint Committee for rates and Trains, but each Company working its own lines", as a base for full merging. A joint meeting convened by Harrison in Edinburgh to discuss amalgamation had to be suspended when the Scottish North Eastern Railway said it wished to amalgamate only with the Great North itself and to exclude the

Glassel Station, on the Deeside line. The stationmaster's house is built of granite blocks, the station building of bricks. *(Stenlake collection)*

branch companies. Aware that the Great North's involvement with these made such an arrangement impossible, Harrison suggested that the GNS should take upon itself all the liabilities of the branches, so that it might be viewed as a single undertaking[12].

John Stewart disagreed with the merger plan. With the September ordinary general meeting approaching, it was found that he had refused to sign off the minutes of 55 board and committee meetings chaired by him, and a similar number of branch meeting minutes. Asked to do this before the o.g.m, he signed some, but other directors present at the meetings had to sign the rest in order to authenticate them[13]. At this meeeting, Stewart lost his position as vice-chairman, with John Duncan elected in his stead, but remained on the board, a dissenting voice on virtually every decision. He had fallen out with almost everyone including his former associate Anderson (now Sir Alexander), but his motion to stop Anderson's regular attendance at board meetings, except when specifically required as Law Agent, failed to gain support[14].

The Aboyne & Braemar Railway

Given the current state of the branch companies, it seems surprising that a further extension of the Deeside line, the 27-mile Aboyne & Braemar Railway, with a capital set at £150,000, should have been promoted in late 1864. It was a nominally independent enterprise, though its Bill makes clear that it was a dependency of the Deeside Railway, which was still technically independent, though in the control of the Great North. The moving spirits were Col. Farquharson of Invercauld, whose large timber resources in the district were difficult to exploit without transport, and John Duncan. Ironstone workings, though over the hills at Allargue in Upper Strathdon, were cited as adding to the line's commercial potential. The proposed route skirted the policies of Balmoral Castle and hardly had its Bill been published when it was made clear that Queen Victoria did not want a railway bringing trippers to her gates. The royal objection was not publicly admitted until much later, and the Marquis of Huntly employed the engineer Thomas Bouch to criticise the line on technical grounds. The promoters quickly backed off, adapting the proposal to a royally-acceptable 11-mile line ending for passengers at Ballater (population in 1871 691), with a goods-only tramway extending a further mile and a half to Bridge of Gairn, from where Farquharson planned a private access line into his forests; and capital reduced to £66,000, with borrowings of £22,000. The route was an easy one, following the river, with a rise of only 100 feet between Aboyne and Ballater. On this basis the railway's Act got the royal assent on 5 July 1865[15].

Stationmaster, porters and junior clerk at Ballater, *c*.1907. (*Stenlake collection*)

Work began promptly on the line (still calling itself the Aboyne & Braemar Railway) and John Duncan, chairing its first ordinary general meeting in May 1866, hoped it would open by 1 August. Very favourable terms had been granted by local proprietors: land was acquired under feu with either nothing to be paid in the first year, or nothing until the company achieved a 2% dividend; and the Deeside Railway was going to bear the cost of running the trains until a 4 ½% dividend was reached. This remarkably generous arrangement must have caused envy in places like Banff and Dufftown[16]. Opening was delayed by some weeks because of what was described as "a hitch", though the Queen and the Prince of Wales travelled on it. Public opening was on 17 October[17]. The contractor was Kenneth Matheson of Dunfermline (later a director of the company) and engineer was J.W. Stewart of Edinburgh. The station at Ballater was built to allow for a continuation of the rails towards Braemar, and there was talk of a further extension via tunnel to Glen Tilt and the Highland line at Blair Atholl, but these schemes remained unrealised, though the roadbed of the short extension to Bridge of Gairn was prepared[18].

Financial collapse

While employees were preparing for seasonal gatherings, including the annual supper party of the Aberdeen branch of the Enginemen and Firemen's Universal Friendly Society: "a happier party never met to encircle a supper table", and a joint soirée of Great North and Deeside Railway staff at the beginning of February 1865 (the board agreed to contribute £15 towards it), the Great North's management had to confront stark realities. A National Bank loan of £50,000, due for repayment with interest in November was, with some difficulty, extended for a year and £30,000 was borrowed from the Commercial Bank on stiff terms, 7% interest for the first three months and a minimum of 5 ½% thereafter, with £35,000 of Deeside Railway stock placed with it as security.

In February 1865, the directors found that the bottom had fallen out of the Great North's tub. In the half-year from August 1864 to January 1865, gross revenue was £48,849 16*s* 10 ¾ *d*, and gross expenditure was £29,671 17*s* 1 ½ *d*. While that might seem a comfortable margin, it ignored the fact that the GNS had total debts of £504,458[19], not shown in the trading figures. At 4% interest this required servicing of £20,000 a year. Also, revenue on the main line had fallen again, and it was evident that northern traffic, now diverted to the Inverness-Perth railway, had been sustaining the Great North. The worst news was that the Strathspey, Keith

& Dufftown, and Morayshire traffic amounted to no more than £7,000 – the annual loss in working these lines, plus the interest on the capital invested in them, came to more than £14,000. No money was available for a dividend on the ordinary shares, and only $\frac{1}{2}$% could be found for the new $4\frac{1}{2}$% preference shares. Regretting the "temporary suspension" of the dividend and expressing "great disappointment" at the results of the new lines, the directors still expressed "sanguine expectations" of the nearly-finished Fraserburgh line and even of the Strathspey Railway's extension to meet the Perth line near Boat of Garten, and looked forward to a "speedy recovery". To maintain services they had also to proceed with an order for six new locomotives from Neilsons, at £2,885 each[20].

Commenting on the company's half-yearly report, the *Aberdeen Journal* on 29 March 1865 observed that, "We had been accustomed to look on this line as one of the few fortunate enterprises of the kind which, having been constructed after the economics of railway making were understood, had not to suffer from unnecessary and extravagant outlay." Great North share prices had slipped rapidly; down to £60 on £100 of ordinary shares on 22 March and still falling[21]. John Duncan presided at an anxious half-yearly meeting on 7 April. With the advantage of being a newcomer to the board, he gave the shareholders a candid review of the company's past history, including the practice of crediting interest on capital invested in new lines, letting it accumulate – undisclosed – within the capital account and paying dividends against it. But the new lines failed dismally to generate enough revenue to balance these payments. The practice had now stopped. Belying previous board statements, he described the Strathspey Railway as a "military line" against aggression from the Highland side. Equally dismal was a comparison of GNS half-year passenger train revenues between August 1862-January 1863 and August 1864-January 1865.

	To January 1863	To January 1865
Passenger revenue	£19,500	£16,000
Mail revenue	£3,371	£1,187

The committee of investigation

Appealing for a "kind and liberal spirit all round", Duncan noted that amalgamation talks were still going on with the Scottish North Eastern Railway, which now accepted that the entire GNS system had to be involved. Anticipating the demand, he said the board would welcome a shareholders' committee to examine the company's affairs. Preliminary fixing had already produced a list of names – William Graham, Glasgow, David Burgess, Helensburgh, Bailie David McHardy, Aberdeen, John Pullar, Perth (who did not serve), Thomas Irvine, Liverpool, and Samuel Hargreaves, Manchester[22]. The two Lancastrians indicate the continuing importance of shareholdings in that region.

The committee acted swiftly, and its report was presented at a special meeting on 26 April, with Duncan, clearly now the company's front man, presiding. It noted the sums spent without parliamentary or shareholders' sanction: £86,982 2s 0d on acquiring Deeside Railway shares, but accepted the purchase as "protective"; £7,450 invested in the Montrose & Bervie Railway with a further £5,000 due to be called in (though the purchase was condemned as inexcusable there was no comment on the roles of Anderson and Stewart) plus £9,423 to clear the Montrose & Bervie Bill's parliamentary costs. It regretted that the shareholders should have given the board authority to spend over £684,000 on branch lines when "the character of the country" did not justify such an outlay. No blame was ascribed to individuals, and only two practical recommendations were made, that the Banffshire Railway's Portsoy-Portgordon line, on which the GNS was committed to spend £78,500, be put on hold, and the link from Abernethy to the Highland line be completed. In the adjourned ordinary general meeting which followed, Duncan reviewed the report. "In the abstract," he remarked somewhat loftily, the committee was quite right to criticise the Montrose & Bervie actions, "But gentlemen, railway companies must go beyond the purely legal limits at times … in the creation of means for protection," and the Great North board still thought the Montrose & Bervie was an outpost worth maintaining for the time being. All in all, Duncan praised it as "a very good, sensible, harmless Report", mock-chiding it for not telling the directors how to proceed, and adding that they had anyway planned to delay the Portgordon line. He looked forward to an early meeting with Inverness directors for a "free interchange" of traffic. The company was still under "a sort of arrangement at the moment about this amalgamation question with the Scottish North Eastern Company" but this was to be deferred. The SNER can hardly have been in a hurry to merge until the full picture of the Great North's financial position was clear, but there was also a disagreement over cartage in Aberdeen. The GNS wanted its new carter, Mutter, Howey to have the combined company's business, while the SNER wanted to keep its contract with Wordie & Co[23]. Within a year, though, William Walker had had so many complaints about Mutter, Howey's service that the contract was terminated from the end of June 1866, and Wordies became the Great North's carters.

Duncan's confident, authoritative style was intended to deflect criticism but did not entirely succeed. Professor Fuller of Aberdeen University (Mathematics) accused the committeee of being too chummy with the board. In his view the directors had mismanaged the company and should resign. Another shareholder, John Jamieson, was angered by the attempt to place ultimate responsibility on the shareholders, noting how in the past critical or inquiring shareholders had always been "borne down by the large men who ruled the roost then". But approval of the report was overwhelming and the board carried on[24].

The committee of inquiry recorded the various working agreements made by the Great North: the Aberdeen & Turriff was worked at actual cost, as were the Banff Macduff & Turriff Extension, the Alford Valley, the Formartine & Buchan, and the Keith & Dufftown (without any formal agreement in the last case); the Strathspey was worked at 40% of gross revenue (a loss to the GNS), the Morayshire at 45 % (a loss of £988 in the past half-year), and the Banffshire Railway at 65%. Protests from the Banffshire company about the deferring of the Portgordon line had no effect.

Meanwhile the normal stream of routine or unexpected events went on. At Alford the wooden carriage shed was burned down and two carriages were destroyed. Traffic returns for the week ending 29 April showed no improvement – all lines were down on the same week in 1864. Board interest was focused on London, where a parliamentary committee was examining the Bill for amalgamation of the Inverness & Aberdeen Junction Railway and the Inverness & Perth Junction Railway, to which the Great North was seeking to add clauses to protect its position regarding exchange of traffic and through carriage rates. Argument was strenuous and James Loch, for the Inverness companies, claimed that the clauses would effectively transfer management of the Perth line to the GNSR and denounced its "outrageous pretensions". The Bill for the Strathspey-Highland junction was unopposed[25]. By then the Strathspey's prospects had been dealt a blow by abandonment of the Arndilly mine, whose ore proved of insufficient quality to justify the cost of extraction and transport.

Opening to Fraserburgh, and not quite the last of the Montrose & Bervie

The Formartine & Buchan Railway had issued preference shares and the warnings made by "Investigator" in January 1863 were borne out: its ordinary general meeting on 29 November 1864 was told that after expenses and interest payments, only £76 12s 5½d was left and there would be no ordinary dividend[26]. But Peterhead's harbour branch was given the go-ahead. Skirting north of the town, it was to cost £5,000 excluding land purchase, with "interested parties" subscribing two thirds of the amount, and the Great North finding the rest.

Revelations of the company's financial straits were politely ignored by speakers at the celebration on 22 April 1865 of the Fraserburgh line's completion. With the town *en fête*, Sir James Elphinstone informed the guests at a

Fraserburgh's original station in 1865, with three typical GNS buildings, engine shed, train shed and goods shed. A rare photograph included for its historical interest despite poor quality.
(From Cranna, Fraserburgh Past & Present)

dinner in the harbour commissioners' hall that he he believed the Great North system now to be complete, after 13 years, 250 miles, and £2,000,000 of expenditure. He hoped that the company's difficulties were at an end and that it was now on a firm basis. Lord Saltoun, toasting the directors, brandished the spade with which the first turf had been cut on 25 November 1852, and which had been used at all subsequent ceremonies. The $16\frac{1}{4}$-mile line diverged from the Peterhead line at Brucklay – now renamed as New Maud Junction (simply Maud from 1866), with Brucklay Station moved two miles to the north. At Fraserburgh the terminus was close to the harbour, and was described as "most elegant … a more complete and commodious general terminus is not on the Great North." Regular services began on 24 April, which was made a public holiday in Fraserburgh[27]. Peterhead's harbour branch came into use from 9 August, with horse haulage[28]; the Working Timetable for 2 September shows three trains each way daily, eight minutes to the harbour, ten minutes back. At this time most of the two ports' fishery catch was being exported by sea to the Baltic ports, particularly herrings, for which there was huge demand in east central Europe.

In May 1865 the Montrose & Bervie board, on which the GNS still had a director (formerly Stewart, now Duncan) appealed for help in acquiring plant. The GNS declined to work the line but offered to supply plant at cost, including the Morayshire Railway's two tank engines. In the end the Montrose & Bervie turned to the Scottish North Eastern Railway, which invested £15,000 and worked it from its inception on 1 November. Two months earlier the Great North had disposed of its Montrose & Bervie stake, "their purpose having been achieved", for £12,000, payable in Montrose & Bervie debenture bonds in equal instalments over the next three, five and eight years, at 3% interest[29].

Waterloo Station

Store
Coal Store
Lamp Room

Guards' Room

Ladies' Waiting Room

Gentlemens' Waiting Room

Ladies' Waiting Room

Berry's Hotel

P.H.

Telegraph Office | Refreshment Room

Booking Office

Parcel Office

Superintendent's Room

Permanent Way Office

Audit Clerks Room

Store

Traffic Manager's Room

Inspector of Agents Room

Audit Office

Auditors' Room

Corridor

Accountant Cashier's Room

Secretary's Room

Accountant Cashiers Room

B.M. 13.6

Fountain

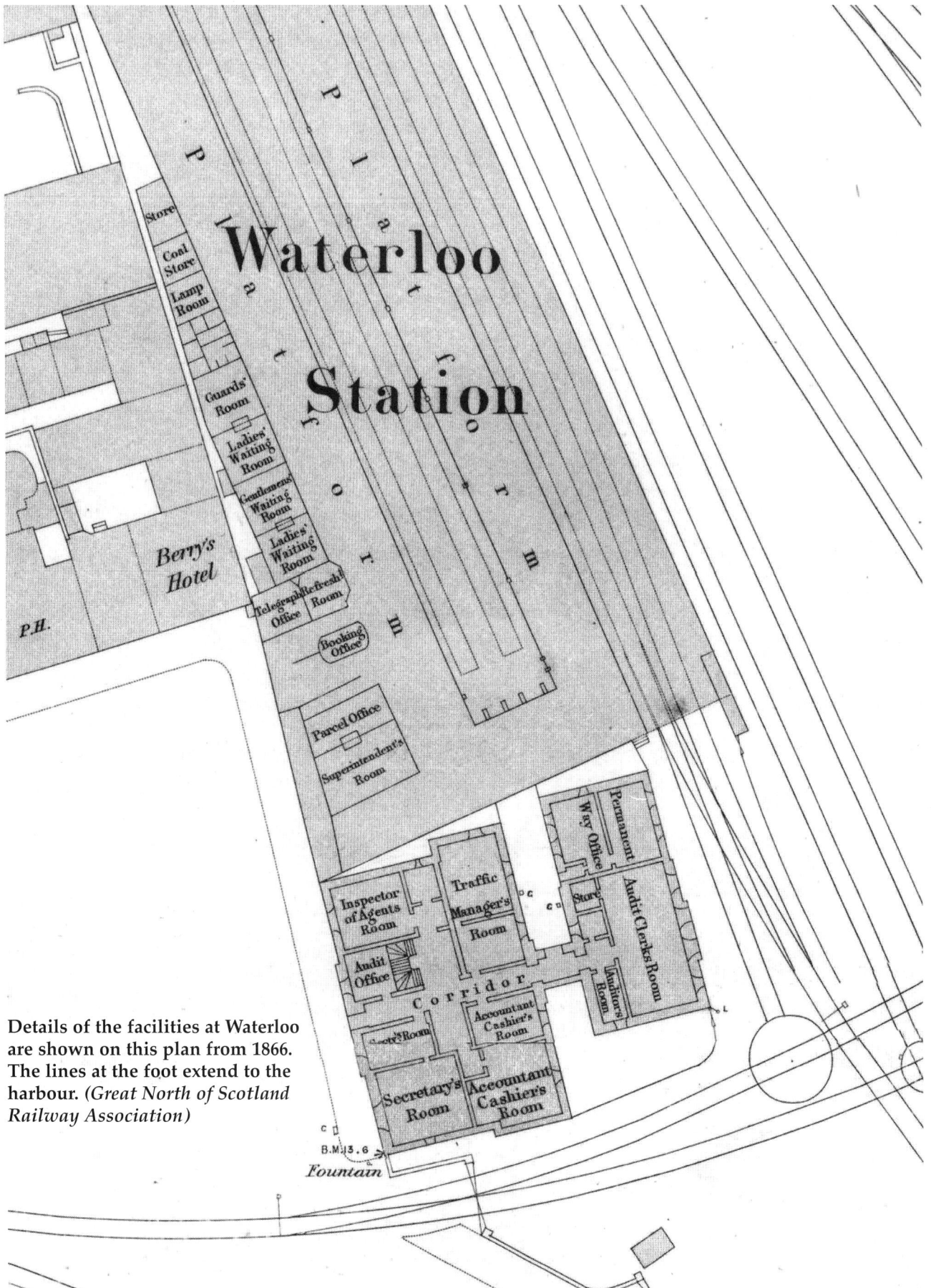

Details of the facilities at Waterloo are shown on this plan from 1866. The lines at the foot extend to the harbour. *(Great North of Scotland Railway Association)*

CHAPTER 9
Remedial Measures, 1865 – 1867

The Highland Railway Company

Letters exchanged in January 1865 between William Walker, GNS traffic manager, and Andrew Dougall, secretary of the Inverness & Aberdeen Junction Railway, give an indication of relations with Inverness. Walker had applied to Dougall for carriage rates between Tain and Fearn, on the Ross-shire Railway, to Aberdeen for onward transport by ship. Dougall replied, "If we give you these rates will you be prepared to give us Rates from Huntly, Banff and Portsoy via the Highland Line to the South?" To Walker's answer that the GNS had always been prepared to do that if the Inverness & Aberdeen Junction Railway would give through rates via Aberdeen, he wrote, " … if you do not have rates from [Tain and Fearn] via the Aberdeen steamer it is your own fault." He did not see that equal rates should be made between two routes when one was 60 miles shorter: "I must say that your request for equal rates, after what has passed, is remarkably cool, to say the least of it." Dougall's attitude to the GNSR would remain consistently negative and hostile[1].

From 29 June 1865, the two Inverness companies were formally united as the Highland Railway. Its Bill had been modified to secure certain rights and arrangements with the Great North. "The Company shall be bound to accept from the Great North of Scotland Company the same mileage rate in respect of competitive traffic passing via Aberdeen as the Company are for the time charging in respect of similar traffic passing via Dunkeld". Inter-company traffic was to be exchanged at Keith (the GNS had wanted Elgin as well) and the GNS was to have booking clerks at Inverness Station, paying an agreed rent for their accommodation[2]. During the committee stage a copy of the elusive agreement of 1854 between the GNS and the Inverness & Nairn company, was produced, on 4 May, but Thomas Bruce, for the Highland, denied its validity, since although it bore the GNS seal and had been signed by the chairman of the Inverness & Nairn, it had no Highland Railway seal, the attestation clause had not been filled in, and it bore no date[3]. Relations between the Highland and Great North were not going to be easy: the GNS had been badly hit by the Forres-Perth main line, and the Highland Railway rejected the Great North's claims to share in its north-south traffic. The Strathspey was still absorbing large amounts of money, and at an extraordinary general meeting of the GNS on 23 June a further subscription of £40,000 was approved[4]. The Great North held virtually all the Strathspey stock, £170,000. The new junction at Boat of Garten was not universally popular in Aberdeen; the *Aberdeen Journal* noted that it would not be to the city's advantage if the GNS diverted through traffic from its more northerly districts on to the Strathspey line in order to gain a greater mileage charge, and to go on via Dunkeld. Aberdeen's harbour commissioners feared loss of trade to the Strathspey line, and a concession had to be made, putting them on the same basis as the company's "most favoured ports": Banff, Macduff, Fraserburgh, Peterhead and Portsoy[5].

Taking stock of a bad situation

An ordinary dividend was again passed over in September 1865, and $4\frac{1}{2}\%$ preference shares received only $1\frac{1}{2}\%$. Gross revenue was rising again, at £52,483 11s 1d for the February-August half-year, though an increase of $\frac{1}{7}$th on first class and $\frac{1}{5}$th on third class fares had to be revoked when the revenue dropped by a greater amount than the increase would have earned[6]. With Duncan effectively in charge, the board and officers were assessing the situation. Burdened with branch lines which were losing money, with a heavy commitment to the Denburn Valley line, on which £61,000 had been paid by October 1865 with a further £64,000 due over the next 18 months, and with bank advances at £230,000, the company needed a radical new policy. John Stewart resigned from the board in October. He would nowadays be considered a 'control freak', struggling to keep all activity in his own hands, and unable to accept that the GNS's future was inseparable from that of other railways[7]. His comb-works was prospering, making Aberdeen the comb-making centre of the Empire (in 1894 it would produce nine million combs in around 2,000 different designs). His seat was taken by William Leslie, architect and contractor of Aberdeen, a future chairman of the company.

The Denburn line contractor, Adam Mitchell, also tendered successfully for the joint station, at £10,488 14s 5d. In the meantime, a Mr Campbell was running the omnibus service between Waterloo and Guild Street for £16 a month, shared by the two companies, who took and shared the fares[8]. The prospect of a joint station might have warmed up merger talks, but in the Great North's current state, amalgamation with the Scottish North Eastern was impossible, and the Scottish North Eastern Railway began much more positive talks with the Caledonian Railway, which had already taken over the Scottish Central in July. Terms were agreed on 31 October, to come into effect from 1 August 1866. Holders of original Aberdeen Railway stock (£830,000) were to receive, as a minimum, guaranteed dividends as follows: from 31 July 1866 to 31 January 1867, 3%, with an extra $\frac{1}{4}\%$ in each successive half-year until 4% was reached, to be maintained thereafter unless the Caledonian dividend exceeded 7%, in which case they would receive a corresponding increase, though always 3% below the Caledonian dividend[9].

In 1902 a football team was started at Inverurie Works, inevitably known as The Locos. It is still playing today in the Highland League. (*Great North of Scotland Railway Association*)

Amalgamation of the branches

The imminent presence of the mighty Caledonian at Aberdeen certainly changed the game for the Great North, not least because the Caledonian Railway and the Highland were close allies, and an amalgamation of these two seemed quite likely, leaving the GNS as a morsel in the jaws of a powerful company that would take advantage of its weakness to force down its value and snap it up at a knockdown price. Even without this stimulus, urgent action was needed, and an important step was taken with the decision to seek amalgamation with seven branch companies into a single enterprise, with a Bill drafted for the 1866 session of Parliament. As of 31 November 1865, when the various companies held their annual meetings, their affairs remained in a very poor way. The Alford Valley's report, with a free surplus of £443 24s 7d, was "not very encouraging", the Aberdeen & Turriff had £32,900 of floating debt, at interest rates up to 9%, which it was seeking to convert into preference stock[10]. The Formartine & Buchan directors' report noted gross revenue at £25,915, expenses at £13,960, and interest charges at £7,009. The free revenue of £5,216 allowed an ordinary dividend of $1\frac{1}{4}$% after the 5% preference dividend[11]. At the Keith & Dufftown meeting, an attempt by the Banff lawyer, W.R. Gordon, to contest the "illegal appropriation" by the GNS of £26,870 of Keith & Dufftown stock found no backers. The prospect of receiving £13 10s in amalgamated stock for every £10 of their Keith & Dufftown stock was sufficient to ensure acceptance. The Strathspey Railway had "scarcely any receipts" but John Duncan held out the prospect of its being "part of a great trunk system" when the junction line was finished. Its revenue for the year was £5,815 15s 6$\frac{3}{4}$d, including £1,128 14s 4d for the Keith & Dufftown's use of the Balvenie extension. The amount due to the Great North as "sundries on accounts" was £68,791 8s 11$\frac{1}{4}$d, with a further £13,430 11s 11d owing to contractors. A third call of £3 a share was to be made on its shareholders, but 14,255 shares were declared forfeited because of failure to pay previous instalments. Contracts for the extension from Abernethy were awarded to McDonald & Grieve, of Alness, who had just finished the Ross-shire Railway, at £4,092 18s 11d, and William Henderson of Aberdeen, for the Spey Viaduct, at £2,878. The Strathspey's ordinary general meeting welcomed the GNS Bill for "permissive amalgamation", hoping it would afford the chance of amicable settlement of points of difference with the Keith & Dufftown company[12].

A Bill was duly lodged for amalgamation of the Alford Valley, Inverury & Old Meldrum Junction, Aberdeen & Turriff, Banff Macduff & Turriff Extension, Formartine & Buchan, Keith & Dufftown, and Strathspey Railways with the GNS. In each case their ordinary shares would be cancelled and replaced with GNSR ordinary. The proportion of GNS and others shareholdings was:

	GNS	Other holders
Aberdeen & Turriff	£40,020	£42,780
Alford Valley	£59,920	£18,140
Banff Macduff & Turriff Extension	£30,456	£28,220
Keith & Dufftown	£40,135	£31,980
Strathspey	£192,700	£12,360 *

* (including £11,000 from the Keith & Dufftown)

For the Formartine & Buchan company the Great North proposed to guarantee payment of dividend on the original shares from 60% of the proceeds of the "Formartine & Buchan line proper" (Dyce-Fraserburgh and Peterhead), after payment of the Formartine & Buchan 5% preference shares, the amounts to be $1\frac{1}{2}$% for the year ending 31 August 1867, 2% for the next year, $2\frac{1}{2}$% for the next, and 3% thereafter, plus the right of participation with the GNS ordinary shares of any surplus above 3%. The Inverury & Old Meldrum line's annual rent of £650 was to be converted into a dividend on £13,810 of new GNSR Old Meldrum preference stock. (Inverury's town council, tired of the mis-delivery of much of the burgh's mail to Inveraray, had informed the Great North in April that it was henceforth to be known as Inverurie, and nameboards and timetables were duly altered[13]). Two other companies were also due to be merged: the Morayshire Railway, on terms to be agreed, and the Banffshire Railway, which obtained an Act on 30 July 1866 allowing a year's extension on finishing the Portgordon line – not yet started – and giving powers for an optional amalgamation with the Great North. The Banffshire company was struggling: with the Great North taking 60% of its gross revenue, it had difficulty in meetings its expenses and interest payments, and though it saw the Portgordon line as a potential revenue earner, it could not hope to build it without the Great North's investment.

The GNS capital account was to be reduced by the cancellation of £463,305 in unsubscribed shares, and the combined company's capital would stand at £2,461,881, plus £726,986 of debenture loans. Support for the amalgamation from GNS ordinary shareholders was assisted by the allocation of £142 of converted branch stock for every £100 of current holdings: the Great North's first venture into 'stock watering'. Further clauses in the lengthy Bill provided for abandonment of the Macduff Harbour Tramway, though the terminal station was to be moved from Gellymill ¾ mile closer to the town, at a cost of £5-6,000. A series of shareholders' meetings' of the branch companies, held on 23 June, approved the Amalgamation Bill either unanimously or by large majorities. The Alford Valley's meeting approved the distribution of £59,920 of unallocated stock among GNS shareholders in proportion to their existing holdings. Keith & Dufftown shareholders noted that they would receive £13 10s in Amalgamated stock for every £10 share[14]. In all cases the expectation was that the combined company would soon resume dividend payments.

Since the dispute with the Scottish North Eastern Railway, under interdict from the Court of Session against the Great North's lease arrangement, the Deeside Railway had continued to operate on its own until its status was confirmed by Parliament. Now the GNS was proposing to regularise the situation by a 999-year lease, from 1 September 1867. The Deeside rolling stock was to be kept up, and to carry the Deeside Railway initials, and a joint committee, three each from the GNS and the Deeside, were to fix the services and charges. Deeside shareholders were to receive a guaranteed 7½% annual dividend, and the Extension shareholders were to get 3½% in the first year, then 3½% in perpetuity. Should the Deeside line's total revenue exceed £27,000 in any year, the excesss was to be evenly divided between it and the GNSR. The arrangement was of course accepted at a formal shareholders' meeting and incorporated in the amalgamation Bill, which became an Act of Parliament on 30 July[15].

A completion and a closure

Captain Tyler approved the Strathspey extension on 27 July and the directors travelled along it to Boat of Garten on the 28th. The Highland's Up, or southbound, platform at Boat of Garten was made an island, with GNS trains using the east face, and the Highland Railway charged £171 11s 4d a year for the use of the station. A two-road engine shed and a turntable were provided by the GNS for its own use and it also installed a large notice-board encouraging passengers to change here for Aberdeen and the South. This was the Great North's longest-distance route, with a train from Aberdeen leaving at 7 am and reaching Boat of Garten at 12 noon; departing again at 5 pm and reaching Waterloo at 10 pm[16], though the service did not last long, and a change of train was needed at Craigellachie. In 1876 three trains ran daily each way between Craigellachie and Boat of Garten, with a fourth from Ballindalloch to Craigellachie. One of the Strathspey's original stations, Dalvey, was closed on 1 September 1868 when the station at Advie was moved ¾ mile south to the location of a new road 0bridge across the Spey[17].

Forty miles to the north-east, services on the line between Rothes and Orton had dwindled to nothing since the opening of the direct line from Elgin, and the Board of Trade wrote to inquire about this in September 1866, as the railway had not been formally abandoned. Milne replied that a limited service had operated until 1 August but the receipts for a year were only £180 (passengers accounting for £40), resulting in a loss. While the directors had no wish to deprive the public, they had no wish to run useless trains. The line could still be used on request, on a toll basis[18].

Searching for a solution

On 2 October 1866 the GNS held its first half-yearly meeting after the amalgamation, with Duncan presiding. Though he claimed to detect "gleams of hope", there was clearly more pain to be endured before the company's position improved. Net revenue at £13,270 3s 1d, was down, due to agricultural depression, worsened by cattle plague, and "excessive rates of interest" on the floating debt [sums requiring payment but held outside the main capital and revenue accounts]. No dividend was declared on ordinary shares, and 5% preference shareholders were given deferred payment warrants. The 4½% preference shares got nothing, as their dividend was based on each half-year's results and was not carried forward. Great North ordinary shares were currently worth £14 against a nominal £100[19], and would stay at that level, or lower, for the next three years. The board was hoping to raise cash by selling the company's holdings in the Deeside and Formartine & Buchan companies, amounting to £203,270, on offer to its shareholders in the first instance, with a dividend of 5% a year secured as a first charge against 60% of the gross revenue of the Formartine & Buchan, and a 7½% dividend from the Deeside. If the shareholders did not take up the whole issue, the shares would be offered on public sale. Finally Duncan announced that all the directors were to resign, to allow election of a new board (or re-election of the old) – asserting that this was not because of financial problems but due to the amalgamation[20].

The railway in the landscape: Dalbeallie (Knockando from 1905), looking east,
with Tamdhu-Glenlivet Distillery, and Knockando Distillery beyond. *(Stenlake collection)*

Unfortunately for the board's plans, 1866 was anything but a good year for large-scale share sales. The London banking firm of Overend, Gurney had collapsed in May, triggering a financial crisis which resulted in the Bank of England raising its base lending rate to 10% later in the year. For the GNS, which owed £345,972 to various banks at the end of 1866, this exacerbated an already-dire situation. The national economic squeeze hurt everyone. Alexander Fraser passed on a petition from the surfacemen requesting a pay rise. For six months of the year they received 2s 4d a day, and for the other six, 2s 0d, and pleaded that two shillings a day was "totally inadequate to obtain for us and our families the common necessities of life". As they were employed all year, they could not supplement their pay by working at the harvest or the herring fishing. Having checked what other companies paid (Highland Railway a flat 13s 2½d a week; Scottish North Eastern Railway 14s a week in summer, 13s in winter) the board conceded an extra one shilling a week for the winter half[21].

On 13 November 1866 the Strathspey Railway, already amalgamated with the Great North from 31 July, held its sixth and final ordinary general meeting. Total expenditure on the line at the date of amalgamation was £305,920 12s 1½d, and receipts for its last 11 months were £4,203. John Duncan pronounced its epitaph: "This line is the most severe calamity to the Great North of any of those branches which are now consolidated with it"[22]. The calamity was entirely self-inflicted. A greater disaster was threatening as banks up and down the country, fearing the worst, called in their debts. In its extremity, the board turned to Robert Fletcher for advice. His recommendation was to issue 4½% pre-preference shares which would take precedence for payment over everything but debenture interest. This was a practice recently imported from the USA, and the board took it up, though it was not welcome to existing shareholders, and an Arrangement Bill was put in hand[23].

The board resigns

Other solutions were also being explored. In November, with the Bank of Scotland demanding £10,670 in immediate payment of interest, and the National Bank of Scotland already selling off Deeside shares (the only currently saleable ones) deposited with it as securities, Duncan and Milne led a deputation of directors to Glasgow to ask the Caledonian to work their line, at a suggested 38% of gross revenue, though its current working expenses were 44%. The Caledonian Railway did not refuse but said many details would need to be worked out, and on 1 December Milne wrote to Christopher Johnstone, the Caledonian Railway general manager, with further information, describing the GNS rolling stock as being "in full average order"[24]. At that time the Caledonian was sending its locomotive coal to Aberdeen by sea, presumably to avoid paying carriage from the Fife mines to the North British; Milne suggested it could use returning empty GNS wagons for the purpose, estimating the annual saving at £5,000. In January, however, the Caledonian declined, though hoping for a more harmonious working arrangement in future. At the same time its secretary, Archibald Gibson, requested further money to be paid on account against the Denburn line. Consideration of this was deferred to the new board[25].

In an atmosphere of crisis, on 4 December an extraordinary general meeting was held, at which Elphinstone offered the resignation of himself and his board: "we place ourselves entirely in the hands of the shareholders". Leading the shareholders was Robert Lumsden of the North of Scotland Bank (he had succeeded Westland in 1864), who secured agreement that they should stay on for two months because of the negotiations with the Caledonian, and the meeting was adjourned to 5 February 1867. Much effort was being spent in staving off creditors, pressing debtors and securing loans. Some creditor banks threatened to appoint a Judicial Factor to manage the company's finances on their behalf. The Railway Clearing House was demanding an unpaid balance of £3,800 9s 11d, an unusual proceeding which suggests it expected imminent bankruptcy. Persons who had given guarantees against the share issues of the Formartine & Buchan, the Alford Valley and Banff Extension Railways were in turn pursued by the Great North with summonses[26]. The Montrose & Bervie company was also chased, having failed to pay interest on its debentures.

Duncan addressed a special meeting of shareholders in Glasgow on 12 March 1867, seeking support for the Bill to convert the company's very large floating debt into new pre-preference stock. The Bill provided for £378,000 though it was proposed to issue £330,000 at first, enough to cover the Great North's obligations incurred for new works and rolling stock, and payments to banks against moneys advanced, including £86,882 due or overdue for the Denburn line and the joint station. Clauses for the abandonment of the Buckie extension were included, and the GNS had also agreed to take on the Banffshire Railway's debts of £45,000: this was the Banffshire's price for accepting the Buckie abandonment and agreeing on amalgamation with the Great North. Its ordinary stock was to merged with the GNS ordinary stock (neither yielding a penny of dividend at present). The Bill also provided for altering the Denburn Valley Act of 1864 to enable the GNS to borrow £41,000 even though half the capital of the DVR had not yet been paid up. Questioned about previous practices, Milne told the meeting that prior to 1863 £2,600 of dividend was paid out of capital, and £7,000 in the year ending 31 January 1864, but nothing since then. Duncan affirmed that no new lines would be proposed after completion of the Denburn link[27].

Aboyne Station after it was rebuilt in 1900, with a train from Aberdeen arriving. *(Stenlake collection)*

Needing new loans to repay and replace old ones, the GNS used friendly brokers like John Walker, general manager of the North British Railway, to negotiate with lenders, but its failure to repay on the due dates caused friction. Walker arranged a one-month delay on a loan of £10,000 from Messrs Woods of Newcastle but warned W.B. Ferguson, who sought a further extension, that the lenders would sell off the shares deposited with them as security. This would damage the proposed new share issue. In February Robert Milne went to Edinburgh to see Walker and reported that "the necessities of the North British Company themselves were the real reason for the urgency". Whether this was the case or not, Walker finally became exasperated and threatened to "leave the Bankers to act as they think fit". Things were finally resolved by the immediate paying of £2,300 and an assurance of the balance by 21 March[28].

At the adjourned shareholders' meeting on 5 February, the resignations of Elphinstone and four other long-serving directors were accepted; of the original directors only Newell Burnett remained on the board. Duncan and four more recent members were re-elected, with six new directors, including William Ferguson of Kinmundy, a future chairman of the company[29]. Sir James was not present (he had wanted to delay the meeting in order to make a statement but this was refused) and Duncan's references to him were not of the kindest: "Sir James, indeed, rendered essential service to the Company in its earlier days … " identifying him firmly with the policies which had led to the present crisis. Duncan himself, elected as new chairman, received many compliments and hopeful comments about his achievement in "turning round" the Caledonian company as its chairman between 1850 and 1852. Sir James, who had lost his parliamentary seat of Portsmouth in 1865, sent in a substantial account for travelling and other expenses prior to his removal from the board and was most indignant to receive a solitary £1 note against his claims. Pursuing the matter, he was curtly informed that he could bring it before a general meeting of shareholders "if he shall so elect"[30].

The interior of the original station at Elgin, with wooden platforms, showing a train of early 4-wheeled coaches. *(Northern Scot)*

CHAPTER 10
A Slow Recovery, 1867 – 1875

'Enemies before and enemies behind'

With a Caledonian merger rejected, the reconstituted board had a company to pull up by its own bootlaces. There were only two committees, Finance and Works, and Traffic. W.B. Ferguson, formerly the Deeside manager, was secretary, and Robert Milne's position was defined as "Manager of Traffic". The pre-preference shares scheme found few friends among the shareholders and a parliamentary committee threw out the clauses in the Bill relating to these on 24 July 1867, but passed those for the Banffshire amalgamation and the £41,000 borrowing rights. Some shareholders also criticised the investment in the Banffshire Railway, but Duncan feared that if they did not take it over, "the Highland Company would walk into it … we have enemies before and enemies behind"[1].

Failure of the pre-preference shares scheme blew a hole in Duncan's refinancing policy, and by April 1867 the floating debt had reached £410,000. The difficulties were only slightly eased by sales of Deeside shares, and a better half-year result, showing gross revenue of £79,112 17s 7³/₄d for August 1866-February 1867, with a net revenue of £32,5165s 2¹/₂d, though after interest payments, only £4,671 15s 8d of disposable revenue remained[2]. 1867 was a miserable year for the Great North, with no end in sight to the problems and a constant need to keep down costs. The annual subsidy of £137 3s 2d paid to the operator of the omnibus between Ellon Station and Newburgh was queried, but the board voted to retain it. It also voted an annual payment of £400 a year to John Duncan for his services. Concessions to customers were cut – the GNS and Caledonian jointly announced that containers such as milk churns being returned empty would no longer be carried free of charge[3].

New plans for a railway beyond Ballater were discussed in August between Robert Milne and Colonel Farquharson of Invercauld. It was agreed that the Aboyne & Braemar Railway would abandon its proposed line between Ballater and Bridge of Gairn, on Farquharson's undertaking to complete a ¹/₂-mile standard-gauge tramway between these locations, with a terminus suitable for handling the timber traffic of Ballochbuie Forest. Railway company wagons would be supplied free of charge, and the GNS and Deeside Railways would have running powers to Bridge of Gairn[4]. The Great North's lease of the Deeside Railway came into operation on 1 September, and a toll of £743 2s 6d for use of the Caledonian line and Guild Street station was recorded in the GNS half-yearly report[5].

An early view of the original joint station at Aberdeen showing the south end with a Scottish North Eastern train in the through platform, beneath the lofty arched roof. Deeside line trains used one of the bay platforms on the right. *(Great North of Scotland Railway Association)*

Opening of the joint station

From 4th November 1867 the Denburn Valley line and Aberdeen's new joint station were opened to traffic, and passenger trains no longer used the stations at Waterloo and Guild Street. Rails in the 245-yard Woolmanhill tunnel were laid not on sleepers but on 27 ft longitudinal baulks, intended to reduce train noise for the benefit of patients in the Infirmary above. The height of the tunnel was 15ft, while that of the 270-yard Hutcheon Street tunnel was 17 ft, and both were excavated from above in "cut and cover" style. The Den Burn itself was piped in a long culvert. At Kittybrewster the new station, like its predecessor, was a wooden building. Signalling arrangements were described as "on the newest principle recommended by the Board of Trade" with a "pointsman's house" fitted with 21 levers at each end of the joint station, and eight levers within the station, and a 22-lever cabin at the Kittybrewster junction. The joint station was "admitted to be unsurpassed, except in size, by any other in the three Kingdoms"[6]. The building, of granite masonry, was designed by William Smith, Aberdeen's City Architect, and the arched roof of the train-shed – 500 feet long, topped by a glassed louvre forming an apex 70ft above the rails, modelled on that of London's Victoria Station – by John Willett, now engineer of the Caledonian's northern division. Each end was partly closed in by glass screens, and over 30 tons of Hartley's patent rolled plate-glass was used, giving a much-admired lightness of appearance. Three tracks passed through, with a single long through platform, and two outside on the west side, and a double-track dock at each end accommodated north and south trains. An external platform for excursion traffic was to be added. Public access was from the east, with ticket offices for both companies inside a lofty booking hall, and separate parcels offices to north and south. James Abernethy & Co. supplied the ironwork for the roof and Messrs Blaikie (their ironworks still going strong) the plumbing work and the iron road and foot-bridges[7]. Completion of the Denburn Valley line made passenger transfers and exchange of goods traffic far easier, and if there were delays for passengers between Caledonian arrivals and GNS departures, or vice versa, at least there was no longer a trek between stations. The opening was not accompanied by ceremony, neither of the owning companies having cash to spare for junkets. Great North services were not speeded up or improved, there were no through carriage services northwards or southwards, and co-operation with coastal steamer companies continued[8].

Alexander Fraser asked the board in October to make the permanent way men's winter pay up to 14s a week because of the high cost of provisions and the failure of the year's potato crop (many of his men had lineside plots), but the directors refused any further increase⁹. Fraser resigned as engineer towards the end of the year and was replaced by Patrick Moir Barnett, who would hold the post for 38 years

A long, hard slog

If the shareholders had expected John Duncan to achieve rapid results, they were to be disappointed. His five years of chairmanship were a long, hard slog, with progress very slow at first, marked by court cases brought both by and against the company, and by efforts to persuade the creditor banks to convert their loans into shareholdings. Economy was the watchword. Free passes for cattle dealers were dropped, and special rates for drovers accompanying livestock were increased.

As of January 1868 the GNS had authorised capital of £3,419,362, of which £867,123 was in ordinary shares. £396,873 was held as security by lenders, almost all of it in a range of 5% and 4½% preference shares. Total capital expended was £3,535,293. Including unpaid calls on share instalments, the company had powers to raise a further £247,809, though the likelihood of attracting investors was forlorn. Revenue was rising, with an increase of £7,595 in the half-year just ended, and net revenue after working costs was £33,274 6s 4d. But interest on debentures, plus guaranteed dividends, amounted to £27,074 0s 10d. Duncan explained to the ordinary general meeting on 19 March that the company had lost £18,950 3s 10d on the sale of Deeside and Deeside Extension shares, which would be added to the capital account since the shares had originally been purchased using that account. The sum of £140,657 9s 3d expended by the Banffshire company was also added to the GNS capital account, in anticipation of amalgamation.

Unsurprisingly, the drive for economies brought the company's standard of service under attack. Robert Milne wrote to the Aberdeen papers in June defending the passenger train arrangements, informing readers that the five junctions between Aberdeen and Keith made timetabling difficult, and with a typical touch of truculence

The view from Windmill Brae to the north of Peterhead Station, around 1905. The locomotive shed is in the centre, and the passenger station, now with train shed, to its left behind the row of cattle wagons. (*Great North of Scotland Railway Association*)

answered a complaint that the Buchan line had only two connections a day with main line trains by declaring "further connections are not required by the traffic," adding that the only doubts the directors had were about over-provision of trains. On the positive side, he pointed out that "a comfortable second class [sic] carriage" was provided on the Deeside line for school pupils, with a quarterly ticket from Banchory to Aberdeen costing 16s, or 2½d a day for under-14s, 3d a day for older pupils – this was "given as a boon to parties desiring to send their children to Aberdeen for school"[10].

The company's pursuit of tardy or defaulting shareholders and share guarantors was not always successful. Milne, describing himself as "civil engineer, Aberdeen", brought a case in the Court of Session against certain parties in Peterhead who had signed a letter in 1858 guaranteeing subscriptions in the Formartine & Buchan Railway to the amount of £20,000 and also guaranteeing Milne against loss on a certain number of shares to be allotted to him if he should not be able to dispose of them at or above par. The signatories were to be entitled to relieve themselves at any time by payment, with interest, of the sums advanced by Milne; and on their doing so, he was to transfer the shares to such persons as the signatories might direct. Milne of course was acting on behalf of the GNS. He now claimed that he held the shares on behalf of the signatories and they should be compelled to pay him the amount of the calls made on the shares which had been allotted to him and remained unsold. The judge dismissed the case, on the ground that the nature of the guarantee was an obligation to relieve any loss on sale of the shares below the par price, and as the shares remained unsold, there was no such loss[11]. This sheds some light on the method of financing the Formartine & Buchan, ten years before – the guarantors had been persuaded to underwrite the nominal value of shares without any money actually changing hands, but with the option of paying later, when the line would be prospering, if the shares had not been sold to a third party in the meantime. Meanwhile the £20,000 showed as paid-up capital. Unfortunately the Formartine & Buchan's dividends of ½% or 1½%, and its well-below par share price, did not encourage third-party sales, nor did it tempt the Peterhead citizens into parting with their cash. Milne was more successful with guarantors of the Banff Macduff & Turriff Extension company, as his arrangement with them guaranteed him against any loss on the shares if he should not have been able to sell them at or above par within two years of the line being opened (from 4 June 1860) – the Banff Macduff & Turriff Extension shares never reached the nominal £10 price[12].

Holders of GNS 4½% preference A shares were simultaneously suing the company in the Court of Session. The Great North's Consolidation Act of 1859 had provided for a 5% preference stock, entitled in perpetuity to payment ahead of any ordinary dividend. It also created the 4½% preference A stock, whose dividend was to rank on an equal footing with the 5% stock, but only payable out of the current half-year's profits – no profit, no dividend, whereas the 5% dividend, if unpaid, was carried forward, accumulating until payment was finally made. The 4½% holders claimed that the company was paying the arrears of the 5% dividends out of half-yearly profits that should be used to pay their 4½%. The Court found for them[13]. In another court, the Sheriff-Substitute of Aberdeen ruled that the Great North's charge to cattle shippers of one shilling per truck for disinfecting treatment (cattle plague was raging across the country) was illegal – the company appealed and the Sheriff reversed the decision[14].

Recovery continued with painful slowness. No ordinary dividend would be paid until 1874, and arrears of the 5% preference shares remained unpaid. Support from the North of Scotland and National banks was vital in keeping the company solvent through 1868, by purchasing large parcels of Formartine & Buchan and Aberdeen & Turriff preference shares at full price, and returning to the GNS £136,010 of 4½% preference B shares held as security against loans. Peter Fletcher notes this as "… risky for the banks, but it offered some chance to recover their advances[15]. By April 1869 the company's debenture debt stood at £842,946, but with new debentures having an interest rate of 4% rather than the 7% or 8% of previous years. Annual interest on the floating debt was down from around £15,000 to £8,000, and the debt itself had been reduced by £310,000.

The struggle continues

The Aboyne & Braemar company had followed a familiar financial path since its opening in 1866: downhill. Of its authorised share capital, £66,000, only £33,620 had been taken up, and the company had debts of £11,322 in January 1869. Its stock was unsaleable at par, but advantage was taken of a provision in the Railway Companies (Scotland) Act of 1867, which allowed companies to sell unissued stock at a discount, if the shareholders approved. The Aboyne & Braemar shareholders did approve. Their company had free revenue of £1,756 4s 11½d for the August 1868-February 1869 half-year, and declared a 2% dividend[16]. The line was still worked by the Great North at the Deeside Railway's expense, and only this saved it from a gross loss. Its half-yearly meeting on 15 September 1868 noted that "the locomotive tram line is at present being proceeded with as far as Bridge of

Torphins Station, with two wooden footbridges of standard GNS pattern. By the 1930s, these started to rot and had to be replaced. The cost-conscious LNER used old rails as their main members. *(Stenlake collection)*

Gairn"[17]. If this tramway was ever fully laid, it did not last long. Large-scale timber traffic never materialised. In 1871, Ballater's new water supply was to be "laid along the tramway"; by 1873, when it was inaugurated, the pipe was described as following "the rut of that abandoned line" down to the village[18]. The Deeside Railway was doing well. Its revenue for the August 1870-February 1871 half-year, plus that of the Deeside Extension, was £26,433 7s 6d, just a whisker short of the £27,000 after which excess profits were divisible between it and the Great North, and leaving a comfortable margin for the working company after lease and operating costs[19].

From 1869 to 1873 a through carriage ran between Elgin and London (Euston) via Rothes, Craigellachie, Aberdeen, and the West Coast route, taking 21 hours 17 minutes for the 620-mile southbound journey and 22 hours coming north[20]. Early in that year the Elgin-Rothes line was under threat of closure, with discussions between Robert Lumsden, the GNS's paymaster, and Thomas Bruce, vice-chairman of the Highland, about consolidation of services and a joint purse arrangement between the Highland Railway and the Great North. Milne was instructed by the board to seek advice on this from T.E. Harrison, who felt that Parliament would be unlikely to authorise the arrangement, and that it would transfer traffic to the Highland's Mulben route which would not be regained if the joint purse arrangement were to break down – he thought the Highland might renege once it had the traffic, and the idea was dropped[21].

Four employees, a driver, two firemen and the chief permanent way inspector, died in an accident near Huntly in the early hours of 28 December, when a snow-clearing train went over an embankment close to the Water of Bogie Bridge. It was formed of two engines, the leading one fitted with "a small wooden snowplough", 32 inches high, and a brake van. Digging out snowdrifts was the usual remedy on the GNS, and this was "the first expedition of the kind for several years." The Board of Trade investigator, Lieutenant-Colonel Hutchinson, concluded that the probable causes were excessive speed at around 30 mph, and breakage of the plough through hitting frozen snow, with parts going under the wheels and derailing the lead engine[22].

The continuing absence of dividend payments was sharpening impatience among shareholders. In April 1870 the Great North's ordinary share price reached its nadir, with £100-worth selling, if anyone wanted to buy, for £7 10s[23], and management costs became an increasing focus of attention. Whilst Duncan defended the company's constant efforts to economise, shareholders from the south stressed the need to cut back working expenses. Did a small company need a secretary and a manager? Could not fares be put up? And fewer trains run? It was noted that the GNSR's working expenses, once famously low, were 52% of gross revenue in the August 1869-January 1870 half-year, compared with the Highland Railway's 34%; also that the Highland Railway directors' allowance was only £250 while the Great North allowed its board £800 a year. Duncan fended off all suggestions except for this, announcing that he was willing to forgo his £400 payment altogether. By October 1870 some dividend payments were being made: 5% preference received 2 $\frac{1}{2}$% and 4 $\frac{1}{2}$% preference A got 2 $\frac{1}{4}$%. The directors' emolument was reduced and the salaries of Milne and W.B. Ferguson were "modified" along with other office reductions to make a £1,000 reduction in general charges. Reduced train mileage upped receipts per train-mile to 57.48d, against 51.45d in the corresponding previous half-year, and working expenses had been brought down from 46.56% of gross revenue to 43.53%. Gross revenue at £95,214 4s 3 $\frac{1}{2}$d for February-August 1870 was the Great North's highest yet, helped by a good harvest and good herring catches. At the end of the year the company introduced a Bill for a small expansion, the first since 1866: the $\frac{3}{4}$-mile extension to the outskirts of Macduff, with an intermediate halt at Banff Bridge, at an estimated cost of £5,356[24].

Smaller sums formed the topic at the 16th annual meeting of the GNS Workmen's Friendly Society. Its income for the year was £320 14s 9 $\frac{1}{2}$d, and expenditure £318 17s 6d. Sickness and funeral money was paid out to members or dependents, the smallest sum £0 3s 6d, the largest £16 13s 4d[25].

Most railway companies were doing well in the early 1870s. The Great North's progress was noticed approvingly in the railway press, and at the half-yearly meeting on 30 March 1871 Duncan was able to point to a "great rise" in the stock, now up to £24 for £100 of ordinary shares; and to the fact that all but ten miles of the main line had been relaid with new heavier rails in the previous few years, the cost charged to revenue. Four new 50-seater carriages had been added to the well-worn rolling stock, at £300 each, along with 50 new wagons. The board was proposing to pay 3% on the 5% stock and £2 14s on the 4 $\frac{1}{2}$% preference A shares. Revenue per train-mile stood at 57.14d, comfortably ahead of the Caledonian, North British and Glasgow & South Western[26]. A bid was under way to regain the northern mail contract – the route via Aberdeen could not compete with the Highland line on timing but Milne proposed to run the Inverness mails, plus the GNS's own local mail service, for £5,000 a year, only £1,000 more than the current contract, on condition that the London mail arrived in Aberdeen 40 minutes earlier than at present, and that the Highland Railway averaged 27 mph between Keith and Inverness, to match the GNS's timing from Keith to Aberdeen. The northern mails stayed with the Highland, but a new contract from 1 June 1871 gave the Great North £5,000 for five years, with the option of re-negotiation if the Post Office should decide to re-route the northern mails via Aberdeen. By 1870, the annual revenue of Aberdeen's post office had risen to £25,000, from £3,000 in 1842[27].

Duncan dethroned

William Leslie, chairman of the GNSR, 1871-1879. (*Aberdeen City Libraries*)

John Duncan had made a visit to the United States in 1871 and was impressed by that country's railway operations: "they beat us hollow in the mechanical appliances for carrying on railways", and he also favoured the American practice of using steel rather than iron rails. Elements of divergence between the chairman and the board emerged at the October half-yearly meeting, when the vice-chairman, Lord Provost William Leslie of Aberdeen, implied that (cheaper) iron rails were quite adequate for the GNS. In Duncan's absence the board had also proposed to issue "debenture stock" at a fixed 4 $\frac{1}{2}$% rate of interest rather than new debentures, which though currently attracting 4% were liable to fluctuate with the money market. Duncan was critical of this proposal. At a directors' meeting on 19 October, he was replaced as chairman by Leslie, and although a company statement said he had "retired" as chairman, he had evidently lost the confidence of his colleagues, who may have tired of his insistence on the "pain before gain" policy. His own affairs were rocky – he had sent a letter of resignation as chairman and director in June because he faced bankruptcy proceedings, due to a "problem with the Commercial Bank", but then withdrew it, giving the board a verbal explanation of the matter[28]. He retained his seat on the board and also the chairmanship of the Deeside and Aboyne Railways. It fell to Leslie to present the most encouraging GNS report for years at the end of

March 1872. "Irregular loans" from banks had been completely paid off, and the company was again paying the full dividend on the 5% and 4 ½% preference A shares (though the arrears on the 5% remained unpaid). Leslie noted that the working expenses in 1871, at £86,369, were almost the same as in 1868, but in that year they had been 47.11% of gross revenue and in 1871 were only 40.67%. Train miles were also almost the same, at 820,000 miles in the year[29]. Ongoing improvements to the line's infrastructure included the rebuilding of the Culter Burn Viaduct, which would leave only two wooden viaducts on the system. A further 150 goods wagons had been acquired. In the half-year between February and August 1872 revenue for the first time went into six figures, at £105,548 18s 8 ½ d, with gross expenses at £50,948 3s 8d, though Leslie warned that costs were increasing and working expenses would rise rather than fall. The accrued unpaid 5% dividends remained a problem, which the directors hoped to resolve by conversion into a new 4% preference stock. With goods traffic rising year by year, another 150 wagons were ordered. During the year the company also received a payment of £26,000 from the Treasury, for purchase of its telegraph system by the government, as provided for in the Telegraphs Act of 1868. The Great North had asked for £66,248, but arbitration confirmed the Post Office's original valuation. In addition, an annual wayleave rent of £525 was to be paid, for up to 600 miles of wires[30].

Signs of improvement

During the lean years, wage rises were out of the question, but in 1872 there was a clamour for increases. In January a "round robin" petition from the station agents for a general salary increase was refused, but Milne was authorised to grant rises in individual cases. After discussion with the Caledonian, a petition from the joint station employees for a pay rise was refused in February. Renewed in July, asking for 3s extra per week, it was remitted to a director, J.B. Nicolson, and the secretary, with instructions to arrange a proportionate increase, not to exceed 2s a week in any case. In August, selective increases were awarded to telegraph inspectors and linesmen and to permanent way inspectors north of Aberdeen, and in October, Cowan, having passed on a petition from engine drivers, was instructed to report on whether any increase for the signatories was necessary, and if so, how much[31]. In May the board accepted the proposal for a general Superannuation Fund for salaried staff, to be managed by the Railway Clearing House, subject to the approval of its own salaried employees, though it took no action in the matter for several years[32]. Easing of the financial position was reflected in a pay rise awarded to W.B. Ferguson in October 1872. Five years

BANFF FROM HILL O' DOUNE

Banff Bridge Station on the Macduff extension, opened 1872. *(Stenlake collection)*

before, he had accepted a drop from £600 to £350 – now his salary was raised to £500. As a wider indication of an improved economic outlook, the Duke of Richmond was having new tests carried out on the Tomintoul iron deposits, though the results were again negative. The company did not improve its train services, however, and at the October ordinary general meeting Mr Robertson of Peterhead claimed that the Buchan line trains were the slowest in the world. Leslie advised him to petition the Post Office for an improved mail service[33]. The Great North would speed up only if someone else paid.

On 27 June Colonel Rich inspected and approved the Macduff extension. Banff's town clerk had written to suggest that the harbour station, on the line from Cairnie, be renamed Banff North and the new station on the extension be Banff South: the Great North opted not to change the harbour station's name and to call the new station Banff Bridge[34].

The effect of railways on Scottish coastal fisheries was stressed with some envy in the 1872 report of the inspectors of Irish fisheries: before the arrival of the Aberdeen and Great North railways there was no outlet for sales of other than cured fish. Prior to 1850, 15,000 barrels of smoked haddock were produced each year in Scotland, at a price of 18s-£1 a barrel, but with the advent of the railways, "fisheries rapidly improved, curing houses erected in almost every fishing village, with more boats, more men, better gear", and the quantity was now some 250,000 barrels a year at around £1 15s a barrel. Crab and lobster fishing had also come on; crabs once fetching $1/2d$ were now worth 2d or 3d apiece to the fishermen – all this "wholly attributable to railways"[35]. Despite this, the railways were only picking up a fraction of the total catch, most of which was exported by sea.

The need for wagons

Aberdeen's urban transport took a step forward in February 1873 with the laying of its first tram line, horse-drawn, across the city centre from Castle Street to Queen's Cross. The line opened in August 1874. Formation of the tramways company by a syndicate of local businessmen in 1871 had been opposed by the Great North.

Wordies' cartage contract was renewed in June 1873 at 1s 2d per ton, and 7s 6d per horse and man per day. To an enquiry from the Post Office (prompted perhaps by Mr Robertson) about the minimum charge for a mail train to Peterhead connecting with the arrival of the 'limited mail' at 10.45 am, the finance works & traffic committee offered to run, not a train, but a light engine to Peterhead and Fraserburgh for a minimum payment of £1,000 a year[36]. Complaints about too many 'newsboys' on trains were dealt with by the same committee – the lads competed, no doubt forcefully, to sell rival newspapers. Milne was instructed to fix the dues to be paid by each newspaper for permission to sell, with only one boy allowed on each train. The annual rate was £60[37]. A more serious issue was the lack of goods wagons, which prompted numerous complaints from customers. Two Aberdeen companies, the Northern Agricultural Co. and the Aberdeen Commercial Co., were regular critics. Faced with a refusal by the Caledonian Railway to transport fish in standard goods wagons, the Great North ordered 50 fish trucks in a hurry. Fish went by passenger train and fish trucks had to be capable of running at speed, coupled to passenger carriages. Delays could be expensive: the GNS was ordered by Elgin Sheriff Court in March 1875 to pay damages to a Lossiemouth fishcurer for fish despatched to Glasgow by the first train on 23 September 1873 and not delivered until the 26th. Another consignment of 29 barrels, despatched on 22 September, did not arrive until 27 December[38].

Recovery continues: Cowan disciplined, Duncan's death

A special meeting of shareholders in February 1873 approved the plan to convert the arrears of 5% preference dividends, now around £40,000, into a new stock at a perpetual dividend of 4% a year. Preference B shareholders, of whom a large proportion were said to be widows and orphans, were to receive a 3% dividend for five years The company's Bill allowing for conversion of arrears of dividends into a new preference stock was given the royal assent on 7 July 1873. The Act also gave voting rights to holders of preference B stock, and authorised increased accommodation for the locomotive works at Kittybrewster, where better facilities had long been needed. Tenders for a new engine shed were accepted in August 1873, totalling £5,246 7s 5d[39]. This was a half-roundhouse, capable of stabling 22 engines, built on the west side of the workshops.

Fatal injuries to passengers were rare on the Great North, and a newspaper report in March 1874 called it "one of the slowest and safest in the kingdom"[40]. Most deaths of non-employees were due to trespassers being hit by trains. Replying to a circular from the President of the Board of Trade, William Leslie wrote that only one passenger had ever been killed in an accident on the GNS (in 1854) and that the system now

The cramped nature of the site at Kittybrewster is apparent from this view over Powis Terrace. The main line is to the right and the roundhouse upper left, with Great Northern Road above.
(Great North of Scotland Railway Association)

covered 283 miles of single and seven of double track. On punctuality, the company believed in "slow speeds and keeping time". Most journeys on the line were short-distance. Describing timekeeping as "generally good" he (like all other railway managers) blamed delays on other companies[41]. Among the GNS staff, however, injuries and deaths were regularly reported, with permanent way workers, as on all railways, being the most vulnerable. Footplatemen too were at risk, and three men died on 12 March when the 1.20 pm Aberdeen-Peterhead mixed train, pulled by two engines coupled tender-to-tender, collided head-on with a light engine between Ellon and Arnage stations. The driver of the light engine had failed to stop at Arnage to wait for the oncoming train[42].

The Aberdeen Steamship company had been sharing the use of a traffic canvasser at Inverness Station but in March 1874 it decided to stop paying, and the Great North paid the whole cost, considering the traffic to be important enough[43]. The 5% preference and 4½% preference (A) dividends were paid in full for the August-January half-year (though not the arrears) and, after a 9-year gap, ½% on the ordinary shares. Pay rates remained comparatively low but selective increases were awarded through 1873-76. Firemen received a pay rise varying from 10-15% after a petition[44]. Forbes Morrison, traffic superintendent, got a rise to £250 in March 1874 and £300 from December 1875; in May 1874 goods clerks earning from £50 to £80, according to their grade, went up by £5 or £10 from £55 to £90. Some station agents got increases at the same time: Kintore went from £70 to £75, Kittybrewster £80 to £85, Dyce £65 (plus a house) to £70, Craigellachie £65 to £70. John S. Stuart, assistant to the general manager, received £260 a year from the end of December 1875, and Samuel Paterson, company accountant, was paid £400 from April 1876. Late in 1875 the price of GNS ordinary shares climbed to £89 10s[45].

Troops, regular and reserve, were regularly carried to and from depots and training camps, but only once for potential action in the north-east, when at the end of July 1874 destructive rioting broke out among the large contingent of Hebrideans and Highlanders in Fraserburgh for the herring season. A special train brought a detachment of Gordon Highlanders from Aberdeen to help restore law and order. There were no fatalities[46].

William Cowan had ruled at Kittybrewster as locomotive superintendent for almost 20 years by 1875, with little in the way of directorial interference. Early in 1875 it was found that when an order for new engines had been authorised in February 1873, Cowan had taken it upon himself to order six rather than four, and had accepted Neilsons' price without reference to the board. His report on this action was considered unsatisfactory and further explanation was demanded. When received, this was accepted only "under the circumstances" – the engines were badly needed and it was felt inadvisable to "disturb" the contract. The board noted that "Mr Cowan misapprehends his position as Locomotive Engineer of the Company and the rights and duties pertaining thereto", and drew up a new code of instruction for his future guidance. A month later the directors were still surprised at the lack of answers from Cowan. The new code, apart from setting out the obvious responsibility to keep locomotives and rolling stock in a proper state of repair, stipulated that "He shall see that all requirements for new Plant and all Tenders are submitted to the Board and no contract of any kind made without express approval of the Board." It was made clear that all buildings were the responsibility of the chief engineer, and any difference between the locomotive and permanent way departments were to be reported to the general manager[47].

At the half-yearly meeting on 30 March 1875 condolences were expressed to John Duncan's family following his death in December 1874. Duncan's great achievement was the Deeside Railway, though his ambition to get it to Braemar was not realised. He had come into the Great North in a controversial way, but his period as chairman ensured the company's survival at a time when it might easily have gone into liquidation. In such a situation the trains would have gone on running, under different ownership, but the shareholders would have lost heavily. They had reason to be grateful to him, in a year when the Great North's ordinary dividend at last regained a meaningful level, at 3%, and the ordinary share price had recovered to £91 by December. Between February and July 1875 the company recorded its greatest traffic increase in any half-year, with passenger revenue at £60,843 and goods at £69,316, compared to £55,953 and £61,151 in the corresponding period of 1874. Receipts per train-mile were up from 67.16d to 69.31d. Manures of various kinds, natural and artifical, were an important item in the goods traffic and Leslie noted that the company had carried 32,421 tons of it, at a value of £389,052, "equivalent to half the rental of Aberdeenshire". He could not predict that manure carriage would give the Great North an unwanted notoriety within a few years[48].

Inland stations on the coast line had little traffic. Barry was closed in 1863 but reopened as Glenbarry in 1872. A proposal in August 1875 to close the station at Knock aroused local protests and was abandoned. A siding at Millegin Bridge between Grange and Knock, serving a sawmill, was closed at that time[49]. Passenger numbers on the Great North were a little short of two million in 1875, at 1,900,579, of whom 241,091 bought first class tickets. In addition, 7,928 season tickets were issued. Gross passenger receipts were £131,994. The tonnage of minerals carried was 258,463, and general merchandise accounted for 354,649 tons, with a total goods revenue of £140,176. Passenger train miles were noted at 543,807, and goods train mileage at 453,816 – as many of the trains were mixed, considerable goods mileage may be included in the passenger figures. The Highland Railway, in the same year, simply gave a combined figure for passenger and goods miles, of 1,372,706. As the two companies were of broadly similar size, it is interesting to see where other differences lay. The Highland carried fewer passengers, 1,427,494 in all, but its gross passenger revenue was £192,457; and a smaller tonnage of goods: 113,127 tons of minerals and 258,668 tons of general merchandise, but its goods revenue was more than the Great North's, at £154,223. These differences reflect the greater distances and longer journeys made on the Highland system, with 402 route miles compared to 286. The Highland Railway had 67 locomotives compared to the GNS's 53, and its working expenses amounted to 47% of gross income, compared to the Great North's 33%, so that the latter's net receipts were only a little lower, at £148,214 against the Highland's £161,806[50].

CHAPTER 11 New Departures, 1875 – 1880

A regional metropolis

Aberdeen, metropolis of a primarily agricultural region, had a population of 88,198 in 1871 and was growing steadily (163,891 people in 1911). Its industrial base was diverse: though the textile industry had greatly declined – in the 1850s some 12,000 people had worked in linen, wool and cotton – it still had tweed and woollen mills, and paper-making, established in the area since the 1750s, was expanding rapidly in the Don Valley between Inverurie and the city. Still based on plenteous water supplies, the industry's dependence on water-power to drive its machinery was now largely replaced by steam. Blaikie Bros. was only one of several foundries and ironworks producing fabricated ironware of all kinds but also making machinery, mostly for milling and grinding. Other factories produced clay pipes, soap and of course combs. Brewing and whisky distilling drew on farm produce, as did the slaughterhouses: it was estimated in 1865 that the equivalent of 33,800 cattle left Aberdeen as dead meat, and another 9,000 live, all by rail, with a further 4,450 live cattle by sea. Meat was also preserved by salting and tinning, as were fruit and vegetables, all shipped to far-off markets from Aberdeen canneries[1]. Granite extraction, cutting and polishing employed many workers. The enormous and deepening pit of the Rubislaw Quarry, owned by the Gibb engineering family, was right in the city, and granite was also brought from Kemnay and other places for outward shipment. Ship- and boat-building were expanding, and ancillary maritime industries including ropeworks and sailmakers were also located close to the harbour, as were large lime and artificial manure works. Service activities were important, with markets for agricultural products as well as fish. Public health, with Asylum, Infirmary and other hospitals, employed large numbers, as did the university and schools, law offices, and shops supplying a wide range of household goods to better-off inhabitants of the country districts as well as the city bourgeoisie. Such a spread of activities helped compensate for Aberdeen's comparative remoteness from sources of coal and from iron and steel producers, and while the city's manufacturing businesses were subject to fluctuations in the wider economy, its broad base of service industries provided a substantial cushion in hard times.

Problems of improvement

Shipment of cattle for the London Christmas market, as ever, was seen as an indicator of farming's condition, and it was noted that on 9 December 1875 almost 900 head of cattle were transported by rail from Aberdeen, in five special trains of 30 trucks, and in addition 134 were sent by steamer. This was one traffic where the railway was definitely well ahead. Between 6 and 9 December 2,075 cattle were received at Aberdeen stations, compared to 1,439 in the equivalent days of 1874[2]. On the Deeside Railway, too, traffic was going up, and considerable expenditure was needed to increase facilities at stations for both passengers and goods. At many stations the

The forecourt of Aberdeen Joint Station in 1923. Harbour rails in foreground. (*Stenlake collection*)

platforms were too short to accommodate the longer trains of summer services. The lease agreement with the Great North did not cover the question of payment for station improvement or enlargement, and the issue was before the joint committee. At the October 1875 half-yearly meeting complaints were raised about the late opening of booking offices before train departures. In the rush for tickets, it was claimed that the weak were pushed aside. The joint station that had seemed so spacious when opened was now liable to become overcrowded at busy times. Conscious that many passengers on the line were "pleasure seekers" who might return if their experience had been enjoyable, the Deeside remitted the matter to the Great North for action[3], and through the winter of 1875-76 discussions went on between the Great North and Deeside boards, culminating in a proposal from the Great North that the two Deeside companies should amalgamate with it, with retrospective effect, as from 31 August 1875. Deeside stock was to be guaranteed dividends as follows: £9 5s on every £100 for the year ending 31 August 1876, rising by five shillings each year to £10 at 31 August 1879. Extension shares would be guaranteed £6 on every £100, rising in smaller increments to £6 10s at 31 August 1879. From 1 September 1879 onwards, these stocks would be replaced by new Great North of Scotland (Deeside Rent-charge) stock, of which £250 would be issued for every £100 of Deeside, and £166 for every £100 of Extension stock, with a perpetual guaranteed dividend of 4% a year, payable half-yearly. In addition a Deferred stock would be issued, of £25 for every £100 of the new Rent-charge stock, which would participate on an equal basis with GNS ordinary stock in any dividend payment by the GNS in excess of 5% a year. The Aboyne & Braemar company, whose working agreement with the Deeside was due to expire in October, could not be left out at the extremity, and obtained an amalgamation offer of £60 GNS ordinary shares for every £100 of fully paid-up Aboyne shares, to take effect from 31 January 1876. Despite a few protests at the inadequacy of the Great North's service, especially in winter, these favourable terms were unanimously accepted at shareholders' meetings of all the companies on 17 February. While the necessary Bill was before Parliament, and the Great North somewhat more vulnerable to public pressure than usual, public meetings at Aboyne and Ballater put forward requests for service improvements and reductions in carriage costs. In particular, the GNS did not offer a Railway Clearing House through rate for coal and other goods on the Deeside line coming from or going outside its own system, applying the full local charge to and from Aberdeen[4]. The amalgamation Bill received the royal assent on 13 July.

A new five-year mail contract was in force from 1 June 1876. Its value of £7,750 a year, 50% more than the previous contract, was an indicator of the dramatic rise in commercial and personal communications. To facilitate two-hour running between Aberdeen and Keith, the Post Office was to instal exchange apparatus at certain stations. A further £875 was added in 1877 to cover provision of a new mail train to Peterhead[5].

Between 1866 and 1876 the annual revenue of the Great North had risen from £164,000 to £278,000, but the combined effect of the lean years and the long-established policy of holding down operating costs meant that the company was in a poor state, in the 1870s, to cope with increased traffic and the travelling public's expectation of higher standards of service. Most of the stations, wooden buildings or stone cottages, had not been enlarged since they were built. Platforms were low and short, built to a height of 18 inches for the original trains of four-wheel carriages, whereas 2ft 6in was now standard and trains were longer. Low speeds were compounded by delays due to the lack of crossing loops both on the main and Deeside lines. Most of the rolling stock was elderly, and repair facilities at Kittybrewster were primitive and even more so at Banchory. Now in a state of comparative prosperity, borne along by an expanding national economy in which manufacturing played a very large part, the company needed a modernisation plan. William Leslie, aged 78 in 1876, was a steady-as-she-goes chairman, and Robert Milne, with the company since 1851, was wholly identified with its traditional management style, harking back to a time when railway travel was considered a privilege and the public meekly accepted the officious attitudes of station staff. Times were changing, however: railways had become a basic service and even lines which had minimal competition, like the GNS, were expected to have the same concern for passengers' convenience that companies competing for traffic had learned to show.

An Act was obtained on 28 June 1877 authorising enlargement of stations on the main line as far as Inveramsay, and the Deeside line as far as Culter, also enlargement of the joint station, and Kittybrewster Works. In November, Leslie asked for reports from Barnett and Cowan on their departments' future requirements and costs, and gave his own report to the board on 6 December. The list was lengthy and its estimated costs came to £135,037, while the company had only £31,968 available. Priorities, and a time-scale, had to be decided. Congestion was naturally worst around Aberdeen. In 1877 the GNS was earning an average of £20 5s per mile per week, but on the section between Inveramsay and Kittybrewster it was £60-plus, comparable to the Glasgow & South Western's £61 10s and even the Caledonian's £71 10s (both of these with heavy coal and ore traffic). The single-track line was full to capacity, and accommodation at Kittybrewster could not cope with the traffic. Doubling of the track as far as Kintore was decided on, with the expansion of yards at Kittybrewster, and the provision of more crossing loops

Cowan class M engine No. 58 of 1878 (rebuilt 1903) at Boat of Garten. *(Stenlake collection)*

and longer platforms on the Deeside line. Improvements were to be made at Kittybrewster Works, where nothing had been done since 1856, when the company had fourteen engines compared to the current 56, and the Banchory works were to be closed. Cowan had also asked for twelve additional engines, and it was resolved to renew the locomotive stock at the rate of two engines a year, drawing on the revenue account. The Denburn Act and the 1877 Act authorised the company to raise a maximum of £225,000 in preference shares but Leslie, confident in increasing revenue, preferred to raise funds by borrowing[6].

Farming, fishing and what constitutes manure?

At the end of a long drawn-out process, the GNS had been brought back to a state of financial health just at the beginning of the period known to economic historians as the 'Great Depression', which lasted until the early 1890s. It was a time of contradictory economic indicators: industrial production was rising rapidly but commodity prices and producers' profits were falling. Railways were in a better position than most industries, especially as far as passenger services were concerned, as falling prices gave millions of low-paid people a little bit of extra latitude in their spending. But agriculture was badly hit by falling prices, and anxiety in the farming community and its suppliers was to make trouble for the Great North.

Fishing was a success story from the 1850s through to the mid-1870s. This was the era of the astonishing rise of the herring catch off eastern Scotland. The landed catch was measured in crans (a cran equivalent to around 750 fish), and in 1874, the peak year between 1853 (338,740 cran) and 1876 (327,284 cran), 524,450 cran were landed at ports between Aberdeen and Wick: approximately 393,337,500 fish. Herring boat crews travelling to and from home pushed up passenger numbers on the Buchan lines. The number of herring boats operating from GNS ports soared, with 736 at Fraserburgh, 621 at Peterhead and 440 at Aberdeen while smaller harbours like Rosehearty, Boddam and Port Erroll had 90, 73 and 18 respectively, in 1877. In all there were 3,359 herring boats working between Aberdeen and Wick in that year, well over half of them at GNS ports[7]. Although a very large proportion of the catch went back to sea, salted in barrels, to the Baltic ports, the prosperity of the fishing industry led to the expansion of harbours and the increasing industrialisation of techniques. In 1882 Aberdeen had its first steam trawler. On the Moray Firth coast, Portessie, Buckie, and Portgordon, still with no railway access, had hardly any share in the herring boom.

What could be called the Great Manure Dispute erupted in February 1878, though its origins went back much earlier. The pricing schedule attached to the Great North's original Act had only one classification for "all sorts of manure, lime, etc.", permitting a maximum carriage rate of 2d per ton-mile (the Deeside line's rate was 1½d). But from 1854 the company had been charging the rate specified by the Railway Clearing House (of which it was not then a member), which accorded artificial and packed manures, including guano, the same rate as grain, 3d per ton-mile. In 1876 the Aberdeen Commercial Company, manufacturers and distributors of fertilisers, also grain and coal merchants, challenged this practice. A letter to Robert Milne received an unsatisfactory answer and in May 1877 the Commercial Company refused to pay its bills. With no resolution to the dispute, it brought a case against the Great North before the Railway Commissioners, a body with judicial powers, set up in 1873, who compelled the Great North to reduce its rates and repay past overcharges to the Commercial Company. "Manures" ranged from loose-shovelled horse dung to processed and bagged artificial fertiliser, with an according price range for the end-buyer. It went against the Great North's, or Robert Milne's, instincts to have to charge the same rate for two items that hardly resembled each other and one of which was worth five or six times the other, and someone came up with a clever idea. On 4 February 1878 the GNS notified the manufacturers and distributors of artificial manures that "the Company do not profess to act, and do not act, as carriers of dung, compost, manure, bones, guano, phosphates etc., but will upon certain conditions and agreed rates provide waggons and locomotive power for the purpose, as of 1 March 1878." The intention was to remove these items from the standard range of goods carried, and instead to convey them on a toll basis that went right back to the inception of public railways, as if the shippers were hiring their own train. For this the company believed it could charge what it liked, or at least what it thought the traffic would bear. It was believed that the Aberdeen-Banchory charge (17 miles) for artificial manures would go up from 2s 2½d to 5s 8d per ton. The company refused to carry manures except on this basis, and the Caledonian colluded, refusing to carry artificial manures from Montrose to Aberdeen except on a toll basis. Compelled to sign a "requisition" agreeing to pay the toll, the Commercial Company lost no time in bringing these "excessive and illegal rates" before the Railway Commissioners, who ruled that the Great North was not entitled to pick and choose between which goods it transported as a common carrier, and which goods it wished to convey on a tollage basis, and that in any case it could not charge more for tollage than the normal maximum. They did allow the company to charge a penny per ton for allowing their wagons into the premises of the Aberdeen Lime Co. and other works for loading, but the Great North failed in another bid to charge the fertiliser companies for moving loaded wagons on the harbour rail tracks – the rails belonged to the harbour commissioners and though the Great North paid 7½% a year on the cost of the rails, it had no right to recoup this by a subsidiary charge. When the GNS appealed to the Court of Session, the Commissioners' verdict was upheld, on 25 October 1878, and the railway had to pay the pursuers' costs[8]. The case aroused great interest in railway and commercial circles, since victory for the Great North would certainly have encouraged other railways to take similar action. It also left the GNS board determined to get its own way in the matter.

Hazards of mixed trains, and a new chairman

An accident occurred ¾ of a mile north of Plaidy, on the Macduff line, on 3 May 1878. Three carriages of the 3.45 pm mixed train from Macduff to Aberdeen fell from a 30ft embankment, and eight people were injured. Reporting to the Board of Trade, Major F.A. Marindin observed that the train was travelling at 30 mph though its required average speed was only 17 mph. Six loaded goods wagons were between the engine and the passenger carriages and he ascribed the cause to a broken axle in the fourth wagon. The train was "improperly made up" with the goods wagons next to the engine – a practice which the Board of Trade was anxious to stamp out but which was kept up by the railways because it made shunting at intermediate stations much more convenient and quick[9].

William Leslie died on 18 February 1879, aged 80. Self-educated, he was both architect and engineer, and had been involved with the construction of the Deeside and Formartine & Buchan lines. He had been a sensible and steady though not proactive chairman, with a humorous touch – when a shareholder complained about the inadequacy of Kintore Station in bad weather, he offered, "If Mr Farquharson lays on a storm I will send a deputation of directors to try it out"[10]. William Ferguson of Kinmundy was elected as his successor, and announced that there would be no ordinary dividend, "however small" for the August 1878-January 1879 half-year. Also, noting that the Court of Session had backed the judgement of the Railway Commissioners in the manure case: "we simply have to face this"[11]. In March Robert Fletcher, for long the company's auditor, resigned through ill health.

For Queen Victoria, her regular journeys, twice a year, between Windsor and Balmoral, were a routine that had to be endured. For the Great North, which took charge of the Royal Train at Ferryhill Junction, it was also a routine. A typical journey, recorded in May 1879, reported that Ferguson, Robert Milne and W.B. Ferguson joined the train there. It took five minutes to change engines, "during which time Her Majesty looked out of the saloon window", then at 12.01 pm the train went on, arriving at Ballater at 2.25. The Queen, like the Great North, preferred low speeds[12].

At Ferguson's second ordinary general meeting as chairman, in September, the report was hardly better. Revenue had fallen again on both passenger and goods trains. The number of first class passengers had fallen by 11½%, and third class was down by 4¾%. An ordinary dividend of 1% was announced. At this meeting, as at the previous one, there was criticism of the goods rates as being too high. Mr Farquharson of Whitehouse, on the Alford line, asked why a wagonload of coal could be taken from Airdrie to Aberdeen for 8s 9d, while it cost 5s 6d for the much shorter distance from Aberdeen to Whitehouse: the chairman replied that there was sea competition for the coal traffic to Aberdeen, and also pointed out that a trainload of coal wagons was cheaper to work, per wagon, than a single wagon from Aberdeen to Whitehouse[13].

The Earl of Aberdeen's Railway

All railway results were depressed at this time, but the young Earl of Aberdeen, a railway enthusiast from boyhood, chose it to propose a new branch line from Udny to Methlick. In turn this prompted a local meeting in Oldmeldrum to propose an alternative, by extending their branch to Methlick. William Ferguson was anxious to dissociate the GNS from both schemes, writing to Oldmeldrum to say that Lord

William Ferguson of Kinmundy, chairman of the GNSR, 1879-1904.

William Moffatt, secretary and general manager, 1880-1906: portrait from an illustrated interview in *Railway Magazine*, October 1899.

Aberdeen was proposing to bear the cost of his line, with the GNS contributing nothing, but meanwhile the Earl suspended his plan for a year, to see whether the Oldmeldrum proposal came to fruition. A voice from the past, Sir James Elphinstone, wrote to the Oldmeldrum promoters to call the Earl's scheme a white elephant[14], and in the event, no more was heard of it.

Ownership of the Great North company of course rested with its shareholders, and the share register of 1 December 1879 sheds some light on who the proprietors were, though it does not indicate the size of their holdings, most of which were doubtless quite small. They included Lord Aberdeen, John Adam, the pointsman at Maud (the only waged employee on the list) the trustees of the late George Baird, also of William Baird, John Baird (via his agent William Taylor), William Cruickshank, station agent at Elgin, Robert Milne, and Aeneas Mackintosh (a director of the Highland Railway) – in all around 3,000 names, mostly from the north-east, their trade or status including farmers, ministers, landowners, grocers, sailmakers, fish-sellers and merchants. Institutional shareholders included the National Bank, the North of Scotland Bank, the North & South Wales Bank of Liverpool, the Northern Assurance Company, and the Union Bank[15].

William Moffatt starts the speed-up

The two senior managers retired in 1880, Robert Milne in March, and W.B. Ferguson later in the year. Ferguson was appointed a GNS director but he died in 1881. Milne was not offered a seat on the board, though the directors' report said "he continues his connection as a consulting officer". He was awarded £400 a year "at the Board's pleasure", to cease if his Railway Clearing House superannuation exceeded £760 a year. His departure, ascribed to poor health, was a significant moment. Though not the architect of the Great North's almost-fatal branch line policy, he applied himself consistently and earnestly to the daily practice of economy, occasionally defending it in replies to complaints. It is easy to be unfair to his regime, which in essence was like that of many other railways, and Milne deserves credit for his part in ensuring that the company survived intact. The impression left by his official persona is at variance with what is said on good authority to be a portrait of Milne in a novel by the (male) writer Shirley Brooks, as the railway contractor Robert Urquhart. Physically a giant, of a "stern and resolute nature" who once threw a mutinous navvy off a viaduct, he is also frank, generous and open-hearted: "I never do things by halves[16]." Nevertheless, a case like the manure dispute suggests a combination of high-handedness and obstinacy even when the company was clearly in the wrong. Even after the legal ruling, the GNS continued to charge the excessive manure rate from country stations, though not from Aberdeen[17]. Milne's approach and style were those of an earlier generation, and William Ferguson seized the opportunity to make a change of policy. The new general manager was an Englishman[18], William Moffatt, manager of the North Eastern Railway's Tyne Dock at Newcastle. Energetic, forward-looking, he and his chairman complemented each other's qualities. Ferguson was an intellectual type, with a long business career in Liverpool and London[19] and a strategic cast of mind. Both men shared the aim of making the Great North a successful and respected, if necessarily modest-sized, section of the national railway network. On W.B. Ferguson's retirement, Moffatt also assumed the role of secretary, saving a salary but also concentrating executive authority in his hands. Very much on the look-out for extra traffic, he noted from the 1879 fishery reports that Fraserburgh and Peterhead were exporting large amounts of fish to Baltic ports, and promptly made arrangements to charter a steamer at Aberdeen and quote the fish-sellers a through rate by rail from the Buchan ports to Aberdeen and thence to Stettin, which would undercut the smaller vessels[20].

By 1 June 1880 the main line was doubled between Dyce and Kintore, and work was in hand on Kintore-Inveramsay. Additional services began to appear in the timetable, an early train from Macduff to Aberdeen, leaving at 7.20 am and arriving at 9.50, with a return service departing at 3.30 pm and reaching Macduff at 6.05. Fifteen minutes were pruned from timings on the Buchan line. Through trains were between Aberdeen and Peterhead, with connections to Fraserburgh from Maud. Here too extra trains were put on, a mixed train from Maud to Fraserburgh at 3.20 pm, and Maud-Peterhead at 7.00 pm[21].

**Maud Junction, looking north. With three auction marts, Maud was a
centre of livestock traffic. (*Stenlake collection*)**

The timing of these improvements did not seem auspicious. Gross revenue between February and July 1880 dipped slightly while working expenses rose from 42.75% of total revenue to 45.15%, and only preference dividends were paid in September. To pay for ongoing and future works the ordinary general meeting on 23 September approved the issuing of £225,000 worth of stock as 5% preference, and a debenture stock of £33,000 at $4\frac{1}{4}\%$[22]. The new dynamism in the Waterloo Quay offices resulted in an omnibus Bill for the 1881 session of Parliament, embracing the takeover of the Morayshire Railway, revival of the Banffshire coast line, re-classification of artifical manure, use of locomotives at Aberdeen Harbour, and the application of 'terminal' charges in addition to goods rates. A loan of £10,000 was obtained from the North of Scotland Bank, at 1% above the Bank of England rate, to pay the necessary deposit on the coast line's capital[23].

Absorption of the Morayshire Railway

Back in 1866 the Amalgamation Act had allowed for the merging of the Morayshire Railway with the Great North, but the Elgin-based company, its line worked since 1863 by the GNS, had kept a somewhat precarious independence, engaging in sporadic and inconclusive negotiations on amalgamation with the Highland as well as the Great North. James Grant had died in 1872 and Bailie Alexander Urquhart of Elgin was chairman, with an unusual deputy in W.J. Wainwright, general manager of the Glasgow & South Western Railway. Wainwright was a non-attender at Morayshire Railway meetings though his advice to the company was said to be of great help. Now in 1880 the Morayshire was under pressure from the Great North – Moffatt wanted to run fast trains between Aberdeen, Dufftown and Elgin, which would require it to spend £10,000 on necessary improvements. Cash-strapped as ever, encumbered by a large floating debt, the Morayshire Railway could not provide this, and the Great North pushed for amalgamation. Talks went on through the summer and autumn, variously in Aberdeen, Glasgow and Perth, with Wainwright setting out the conditions required by the Morayshire. By December terms had been agreed: the GNS would create a Morayshire Railway rent-charge stock of £39,274 to cover the smaller company's floating debt (£12,620 of which was owed to the Great North). The Morayshire had an issue of 1860 5% preference stock which was to be exchanged for an equivalent amount of GNS 5% preference stock, and its £53,000 of paid-up ordinary stock was also to be exchanged at par for GNS ordinary stock (this was generous to Morayshire Railway shareholders since their company had never paid a dividend on its ordinary stock – admittedly GNS stock was currently paying nothing either, but no-one expected that state of affairs to continue). Dispute flared up in Elgin over the Morayshire's 1856 £10 preference shares. Worth £10,000, the issue had flopped and most remained unsold and forgotten, until, with the merger negotiations already under way, chairman Urquhart and some others bought them up at highly discounted prices (Urquhart paid £310 for 100 in October 1880) and then claimed that the shares were due arrears of dividend at 5% a year since 1856. Legal advice quashed that piece of opportunism but the Morayshire board still managed to extract £15 from the Great North for every £10 1856 preference share[24]. Bailie Urquhart, seizing the chance to make a bit of a killing after a good many years of unremunerative attention to the Morayshire Railway's affairs (£1,200 of its floating debt was owed to him) was doing what many others did, or would have done, in other spheres as well as railways. The Morayshire's secretary, Alex Watt, who had effectively held the struggling concern together, was appointed district superintendent of the GNS northern section, at a salary of £250 a year[25].

The coast line revived, and a controversial Bill

Construction of a large new fishing harbour at Buckie from 1874 had revived the Great North's interest in a coast line from Portsoy as far as Portgordon, and the Bill provided for rail access to the Buckie quays. Preliminary plans had included a southwards continuation from Portgordon via Fochabers to meet the Highland Railway at Orton, but this was quashed by the Duke of Richmond, who refused any railway past Gordon Castle. In a public statement the company referred only to "difficulties which have arisen[26]. A certain dogged quality that the Ferguson-Moffatt duo were to show in other issues first became apparent in the Bill's "manure clauses" which specified that "'dung, compost and all sorts of manures' shall be deemed not to include guano, bones, artificial and packed manures", to be carried at the higher rate applying to coal and coke. The Bill also dealt with terminal charges, which the Great North had long wanted to apply but had so far refrained from taking action, as its original Act did not clearly specify its ability to do so (a serious omission, for which both Adam & Anderson and the parliamentary solicitors bore responsibility). Now it sought authority to make "reasonable charges" for sleeping carriages, saloon carriages, refreshment carriages, but with the real focus on "receiving offices for parcels or goods, and for collecting, unloading and delivering traffic, and for use of covers, tarpaulins, warehouses, storehouses or sheds," covering all other options with "any other service not incidental to conveyance." The rates proposed went from 6d a ton on bulk goods, to 8d a ton on grain, sugar etc., and 1s a ton on general merchandise. As the board had known they would be, the rates and terminals clauses were hotly contested, with a committee of railway users formed to co-ordinate opposition, but as Ferguson said to the shareholders' meeting which approved the Bill, "we must have more revenue". The company's plant and facilities were insufficient for the present level of demand, quite apart from future requirements. On terminals, every other railway exercised such powers: "we are not quite sure but that even with our present Act, we might make them too, but the clause is not very clear." It was perfectly clear to the board that the same customers who complained about "a starved and unsatisfactory railway service" should be prepared to pay a little more for a better one, rather than raise a howl whenever the company tried to increase its charges. The clauses relating to Aberdeen Harbour, including the use of locomotives, the reduction or ending of line rental, and authorisation for the GNS to charge a penny per animal or per ton of goods for conveyance on the harbour rails had been at first opposed by the commissioners, but arrangements were in hand for an amicable agreement. A new five-year postal contract raised the annual rate to £9,750[27].

There had been several bad winters, with snow blocks and consequent loss of revenue, in the late 1870s, but that of 1880-81 was the worst in living memory, and even in March, gale-blown snow blocked every line. Three hundred men were digging out drifts on the main line, 200 on the Buchan lines, and 110 on the Turriff line, and the cost of hiring extra labour was £2,387 in February-March[28]. Terrible weather added to economic recession brought another decrease in revenue, and the ordinary dividend was passed over again. In London, the 53 clauses of the GNS Bill were being savaged by opponents. Alexander Copland, joint manager of the Aberdeen Commercial Company, testified both to the committee dealing with the Bill and to the select committee on railways, sitting at the same time. He described how he had found the GNS overcharging for carrying his products in 1876; he had obtained a judgement against the company from the Railway Commissioners in 1878 and that was when the attempt to levy a toll was made. Counsel for the Great North pointed out that the large sums which the company had had to pay back to the Commercial Co. and other shippers had not been passed on to these companies' own customers, but that was hardly a defence of their client. Moffatt, as the Great North's prime witness, at least could not have the company's former practices held against him, and in reply to one question he denied that Robert Milne had ever been consulted about the Bill. Ferguson gave Moffatt a ringing commendation: "… our new manager has already infused a spirit of life and activity into our affairs"[29]. He too was intensely busy behind the scenes, writing to, and arranging meetings with, opponents of the Bill as well as potential supporters. Seeking support from a former Liverpool business connection, John Cropper, Liberal MP for Kendal, he wrote that the Bill was coming up for a third reading on

30 May, "which is opposed as dealing with Rates and so should await the Select Committee which will not be available for a year or two, and in the meantime my railway is starving"[30]. The committee moved on to the Portgordon Railway, opposed by Lord Seafield as injuring the amenities of Cullen House (the company tried to placate him with a 1,280-yard tunnel[31]). Seafield was a director of the Highland Railway, which had produced a proposal to serve Buckie by a line to Keith: by 1880 Buckie had 627 first class fishing boats and 3,815 fishermen and was no longer a Cinderella location to railway companies. Thomas Bruce, vice-chairman of the Highland Railway, told the committee that a Bill for this line would be lodged if the GNS line were refused. The Highland Railway's attack effectively torpedoed the section of the Bill dealing with the Portgordon Railway, which was thrown out by the Commons committee. The second Commons reading of the truncated Bill was unusually controversial because of the manure rate clause – described as "unparalleled audacity" by Lord Randolph Churchill – and the opposition of the farming lobby to any increase at all in charges to farmers[32]. Clauses allowing terminals payments were included, but were thrown out by the House of Commons, and Ferguson tried in vain to get Lord Kintore (appointed a director in September) and Henry Cripps the parliamentary solicitor, to overcome the Duke of Richmond's hostility and have them restored in the Lords. The remnant of the Bill duly received the royal assent on 11 August, and the Morayshire Railway was merged with the Great North with retrospective effect from 1 October 1880.

It had been a bruising season for the Great North, but the board resolved to bring back the Portgordon proposal in a new Bill, this time to go all the way to Elgin. The Highland Railway was still proposing its line from Keith, and though a compromise solution, a Highland Railway line from Elgin to Buckie meeting a GNS line from Buckie to Portsoy, was canvassed[33], the rival schemes remained. Ferguson told the half-yearly meeting on 22 September that the company was working hard to improve passenger services and revenues under "the active and enlightened management" of another new senior official, the passenger superintendent, A.G. Reid, and also praised the "indefatigable" goods manager, Alexander Ross[34]. Universal praise did not come Ross's way: in March 1881 the Royal Commission on Agriculture heard from J.W. Barclay, Conservative MP for Forfarshire, who also farmed in Aberdeenshire: "there is no doubt that that farmers in this country may suffer considerably from the excessive and in many cases illegal rates which are charged by railway companies for the conveyance of their produce, as well as for the preferential rates which they give to foreign agricultural produce." He cited the Great North's failure to alter the manure rates at wayside stations, though it had done so for Aberdeen: "These excessive rates affect the price of produce very considerably." The company's classification of turnips and carrots along with grain, while having nothing like the same value per ton, had held back the production of these vegetables in Aberdeenshire[35]. Barclay's statements should be seen in the context of his role as a spokesman for agricultural interests: he was not a friend to the GNS and was trying hard at the time to prevent the passage of its Bill.

Medium and large snowploughs in action on the Peterhead line. From a postcard dated 22 February 1909, recording that no trains ran for nearly a week, and mail was delivered by boat. *(Stenlake collection)*

CHAPTER 12 Northern Rivalries, 1881 – 1885

A busy year for the Great North

In 1881 *The Great North of Scotland Railway: A Guide* was published in Edinburgh. Its author was the chairman, whose keen interest in history, antiquities and local lore is evident in its pages. Ferguson was an honorary LL.D. of Aberdeen University and enjoyed using the title of 'Doctor'. Very little is included about the railway company or himself. We learn that Aberdeen in 1880 had 158 sailing vessels, total tonnage 92,217, and 53 steam ships, total tonnage 25,965 (not including fishing boats), and that efforts were in hand to mine silver and lead in Coulart Hill, by Lossiemouth. Fraserburgh Harbour was being enlarged and he calls it "the greatest herring fishing station on the East coast ", with around 800 boats[1]. (This appears to have been Ferguson's second book; see Appendix 3.)

It was to be a very busy year. In March a self-appointed committee of shareholders had submitted to the board a scheme for consolidation of preferred and guaranteed stock. The directors expressed approval but wished to defer the matter. The committee however, pushed ahead, circulating its proposal to all shareholders on 6 June. A powerful interest behind the scheme was the Baird family and the Baird Trust, who had large investments in all the Scottish railway companies[2] The GNS had around £2,000,000 of capital in preferred and guaranteed shares, in eleven separate stocks and at four separate dividend rates, and the new scheme would reduce this to four stocks all at 4%. In proposing consolidation the committee was less interested in tidying up the company's stocks than in increasing their value, by an estimated £89,656. Though the directors still felt it was a premature move, they agreed at an e.g.m. on 22 September to put forward a Bill to enable it[3], and stock consolidation was included in the Various Powers Bill which gained the royal assent on 19 May 1882. Up to fifteen separate GNS stocks had been quoted on the Aberdeen exchange, and this was reduced to ten, formed by the end of October 1883 (all stocks at £100 par unless otherwise noted) comprising[4]:

GNS ordinary	£48 15s
GNS 4% Lien	£101
GNS 4% Guaranteed	£98
GNS 4% Preference A	unpriced
GNS 4% Preference B	£90
GNS 4% Redeemable	£94
GNS £10 5% Preference C	£10
GNS Deferred Ordinary 1	£11
GNS Deferred Ordinary 2	£3
GNS 4½% Debenture	£113

The Bill was a multiple-purpose one, and power to increase the goods rates was again included at first, but negotiations with customers were also going on, and in view of the distressed state of agriculture, the board agreed to withhold its reapplication for a year. Also the parliamentary select committee on rates was still at work and no alterations were likely to be approved until it had reported. Though he must have been highly conscious of the fact that he had embarked the company on an expansion programme without obtaining the instruments for increasing revenue, Ferguson remained confident for the future, assuring a shareholders' meeting on the Bill that once the coast line to Elgin was finished, a link would be made between the termini at Banff and Macduff, and a new east-west line would be made between New Maud and Turriff. Actual work was slowing down, though, and a time extension had to be applied for to complete doubling to Inveramsay and on the Deeside line as far as Park[5].

Battling for the coast line, and exchange at Elgin

In March 1882 the coast line – now 25 miles 247 yards, including a lengthy Spey Viaduct – was again before a parliamentary committee, this time in contention with the Highland's proposed line from Keith to Portessie. William Ferguson blamed the Highland Railway for refusing to entertain a joint or compromise line. Ferocious arguments were going on, and tempers were being lost. A battle arose with Buckie Harbour Trustees over the space provided for the station – "you are strangling us" wrote Ferguson, and another with Lord Seafield and his thuggish factor W.G. Bryson over survey access to the Seafield grounds[6]. In the event the committee approved both lines, with the coast line receiving the royal assent on 12 July. Known as the Buckie Extension Railway, it was to be a separate venture, with capital of £220,000 in £10 shares, and a guaranteed dividend of 4% a year, based on the line's own revenues. The line passed Cullen on embankments and viaducts, Lord Seafield's request for the tunnel plan to be revived having been politely declined[7]. Work began on 24 April 1883 when Lady Gordon Cathcart of Cluny cut the first sod at Buckie, and the towns on the line proclaimed a general holiday. Fishermen, fisher lasses, schoolchildren, Oddfellows, Freemasons and Volunteers paraded through Buckie, and two field guns were fired, with bonfires in the evening. There were three contracts, Portsoy-Spey Bridge, let to Messrs Adam of Callander, Spey Bridge-Elgin, to Grainger of Coupar Angus, and for the ironwork of the Spey Viaduct, to Blaikie Brothers of Aberdeen[8].

Shunting at Rothienorman, a view looking north. (*Stenlake collection*)

The immediate economic scene remained depressing. Despite service improvements, traffic had fallen off and there was still no ordinary dividend[9]. A small boost was given to the Dufftown line with the approval of a siding to a lime quarry at Drummuir, at a cost of £500. Its owner, Mr Kemp, would pay £30 a year for a signalman, but would be relieved of that if he agreed to route all the coal for his works at Drummuir and Keith via the GNS from Boat of Garten[10]. Cattle shipments from Aberdeen to the London Christmas market in December 1882, though down on the previous year, included 34 truck-loads from Easter Ross where a group of farmers were at odds with the Highland Railway. Highland Railway officials did their best to prevent it, but failed, in a tactical victory for the GNS goods manager, Alexander Ross[11].

Revenue was beginning to rise again, but so were costs. Between August 1882 and January 1883 the company earned £151,931 2s 10d but working expenses were £81,721 8s 8d, and interest costs on top ensured that an ordinary dividend was again passed. At the ordinary general meeting on 22 March 1883 it was noted that the stock consolidation had been completed, but that the expected benefits of higher premiums on the shares had not as yet been achieved[12].

Acquisition of the Morayshire line and the authorisation of the coast line gave the Great North two routes between Aberdeen and Elgin. Under present agreements, however, the only station for interchange between Aberdeen and Inverness was Keith. The GNS management felt it was only reasonable that passenger and goods traffic should also be handed over at Elgin. If traffic that had formerly gone via Keith were exchanged at Elgin, the Highland Railway would lose revenue on its line via Mulben (still the shortest route between Aberdeen and Elgin), and the Highland Railway refused to make any concession. When concession was forced on it, with the parliamentary committee on the coast line project giving the GNS running rights between Elgin and Forres, in return for Highland running rights between Elgin and Portsoy, the Highland Railway still kept the Great North at bay by refusing to take up its powers, which meant that the other company could not do so either. This dispute exacerbated the two companies' already-difficult relationship all through the 1880s and into the 1890s.

The Inverythan accident

On the evening of 27 November 1882 news reached Aberdeen that an iron bridge at Inverythan, between Fyvie and Auchterless, had collapsed while the 4 pm Macduff-Aberdeen mixed train was passing over it. Five people were killed, two seriously injured and eight or nine others had minor injuries. Five or six fish or meat wagons were immediately behind the engine, then a luggage-brake van, two third class and one first class carriages, and a brake van. A 36ft cast iron beam had snapped, and three box wagons, the luggage van and the two third class carriages were destroyed. Ever since the collapse of Robert Stephenson's Dee Bridge at Chester in 1857, cast iron

Remains of wagons and coaches destroyed in the accident at Inverythan in November 1882. The cause was failure of a cast-iron girder. *(Douglas McRae collection, Great North of Scotland Railway Association)*

bridges had been a source of concern, and Major Marindin of the Board of Trade was on the scene by the 30th with a posse of directors and officials, including the Caledonian Railway's chief engineer, George Graham. A temporary timber bridge was in place within 48 hours. Marindin ascertained that the girder, in place since 1857, had an internal flaw which could not have been identified by normal inspection. The nature of the accident absolved the Great North from blame, but the company was reported to have "stretched the point", giving financial assistance to victims though resisting "extravagant" claims – altogether under £1,000 was paid out. Following the accident report and a letter from the Board of Trade, the GNS gave assurance that the new coast line would have wrought iron bridges, and resolved that the superstructure of all new and renewed bridges with straight girders of more than 25ft span would be of wrought iron. The company paid £50 and £25 to two local residents who gave "accommodation, board and attendance" after the smash, also £10 10s to Fyvie Hospital where five of the injured were taken[13].

All trains stop at Crathes; and a short-lived peace with the Highland

When Crathes Station, on the original Deeside Railway to Banchory, was built, among the terms on which its land was feued to the railway company was one which specified that all passenger trains, including expresses, should stop there. Finding that this was no longer happening, the landowner, Sir Robert Burnett of Leys, took the Great North to court. Since 1865, so-called Queen's Messenger trains had run on the Deeside line to bring official messages to and from Balmoral Castle while Queen Victoria was in residence there. The Treasury paid the GNS £9 2s a day for these trains, inclusive of £1 11s 6d for the Ballater-Balmoral section, and the trains also carried passengers, stopping at stations to let passengers dismount as requested to the guard. Burnett demanded that they all stop at his wayside station, along with all other trains. The Court of Session dismissed his case, but an appeal to the House of Lords reversed the ruling. Finally in 1914 the claim was given up[14].

In 1882 a prospectus was launched for a Glasgow & North Western Railway, to Fort William and up through the Great Glen to Inverness. This was considered by the Highland Railway as a deadly threat, and in order both to prevent the GNSR from supporting the upstart scheme, and to avoid war on two fronts, the Highland's attitude to Aberdeen became more emollient. After much discussion, an agreement was reached in London on 7 May 1883 between Moffatt and Andrew Dougall on the exchange of goods, mineral and livestock traffic:

1. Traffic from the GNS, except Aberdeen, for stations north and west of Elgin (except stations south of Forres on the Perth line) to be exchanged at Elgin.
2. Traffic from Aberdeen, including off steamers, to Highland Railway stations north and west of Elgin to be equally divided between Elgin and Keith, week or month about, as agreed.
3. Traffic between Highland Railway stations south of Forres, and GNS stations, may be exchanged at Boat of Garten, Keith or Elgin.
4. Through traffic coming via Aberdeen from the Caledonian line to be exchanged at Keith.
5. Through traffic coming via Aberdeen from the North British to be exchanged at Elgin.
6. All traffic from former Scottish North Eastern Railway stations to be exchanged at Keith.
7. Provided that traffic from and to GNS stations at Keith or west of Keith may be exchanged at any junction, the GNS will give the Highland Railway the same through rates from the Highland stations at Grantown, Broomhill and Boat of Garten to all stations on the GNS line as the GNS charges for its own stations at Grantown, Nethy Bridge and Boat of Garten.
8. Receipts for all traffic to be divided according to Railway Clearing House rules.
9. The Railway Clearing House to be authorised to divide receipts on all traffic now in abeyance.
10. The same through rates to apply whatever the exchange junction.
11. Agreement to be effective from 1 June 1883, determinable on three months' notice.

The Great North board approved the terms, though it felt they did not give the company as much as it was entitled to receive[15]. In May 1883, as part of its campaign to prevent the Glasgow & North Western Railway, the Highland company announced that it was considering the construction of a direct line between Aviemore and Inverness, making a considerable shortening of the direct route between Inverness and Perth. A knock-on effect of this would be to reduce the importance of Boat of Garten as an exchange point for passengers, since the best trains would obviously take the new line from Aviemore, a station to which the GNS had no access. The Great North responded with its own alternative plan for a railway from Nethy Bridge to Inverness, to be a joint venture with the Highland (which had not been consulted), and this was set out in a 'New Lines' Bill for the parliamentary session of 1884. Benjamin Blyth's firm of Blyth & Cunningham had already made a survey between Nethy Bridge and Carr Bridge and now were to survey the entire line. It was on the advice of its parliamentary solicitors, Dyson & Co., that the Great North proposed to make a line between Nethy Bridge and Inverness; its original plan had been to apply for a junction with the Highland Railway at Carr Bridge, but Dysons advised that this would not indicate enough "necessity"[16] to a parliamentary committee. Also included in the Bill was a much shorter and uncontentious line, of 2 1/2 miles between Fraserburgh and Rosehearty.

As a result of these moves, and of Parliament's rejection of the Glasgow & North Western, the agreement of 7 May did not last even until the end of the year – in December Dougall gave the requisite three months' notice, citing delays and irregularities, dissatisfaction among his customers, and the whole thing as "the reverse of convenient"; adding "That it has not accomplished its object is only too apparent from the intended Great North of Scotland Bill next session, which includes repeal of the clauses of the 1865 [Highland Railway] Act regulating exchange of traffic." Moffatt replied that he had had no indications of complaint, and pointed out that the agreement had been made rather than have the GNS resort to the Railway Commissioners for satisfaction of its claims. Suggesting that Dougall might have waited for the publication of the GNS Bill rather than make assumptions about it, he added that perhaps a parliamentary committee should be asked to "determine the questions between us"[17]. In March 1884 Dougall wrote to complain that the GNS was still sending goods for exchange at Elgin though the agreement had been terminated.

The Highland company was also considering a new line from Stanley to Dundee, and this, with the Nethy Bridge scheme, prompted an ambitious proposal from the Marquis of Huntly, circulated in September 1883 but already known to the GNS board, for a new railway branching off the Deeside line at Dinnet, traversing the Cairngorms to meet the GNS at Nethy Bridge, and turning north via Grantown to Inverness. A southern arm through Glentanar to Forfar and Dundee was also mooted, and it was hoped that the East Coast companies might route London-Inverness trains this way[18]. The Marquis's argument was that the Highland Railway's proposals would retard the development of railways to the east of the Highland main line, and the Great North board, while refraining from full backing – Moffatt wrote to Ferguson, " … I don't see it as a scheme we can touch"[19] – was willing to work this 'Strathspey, Strathdon & Deeside Railway' and agreed to give £1,000 towards the costs of its Bill, subject to approval of the wording[20]. Ferguson said nothing about these matters to the GNS ordinary general meeting on 20 September.

The parliamentary committee dealing in April 1884 with the Highland Railway's Bill for amalgamation with the Sutherland and Caithness lines decided that the GNS had no grounds for declaring an interest, but

**Cowan class C engine No. 1 of 1879 (rebuilt 1897). This was the GNS's
last outside-cylinder 4-4-0 type.** *(Stenlake collection)*

The new station at Fraserburgh, in the 1900s, with the St. Combs train. *(Stenlake collection)*

allowed the Highland to oppose the Strathspey, Strathdon & Deeside Junction Railway Bill, on the ground of its connection with the Great North's proposed Nethy Bridge-Inverness railway. When the Strathdon's counsel denied any such connection, claiming that it was "purely local and independent", the scepticism of his Highland Railway counterpart was undisguised. The Strathdon and Nethy Bridge-Inverness lines were rejected, but strenuous efforts by the Great North to get its position at Inverness strengthened by clauses in the Highland Railway Amalgamation Act met with some success. Despite the plea that only running powers from Elgin would prevent the Highland Railway from obstructive tactics, the committee would not go quite as far, but through bookings, through carriages and wagons, and through rates between both systems were confirmed, and exchange facilities were to be provided at all frontier junctions[21]. At one point the GNS requested that the Highland be made to provide a connection for every train at Keith and Elgin; Mr Pope, the Highland Railway counsel, suggested that in such a case the GNS, "in a spirit of what he might call devilment" might run trains which were not reasonable. He withdrew the word "devilment" as "Mr Ferguson looked at him so reproachingly", but still suggested that he would not put a bit of devilment past Mr Moffatt. The Bill for a railway between Fraserburgh and Rosehearty received the royal assent on 28 July.

Restive shareholders, and the North British at Aberdeen

Lack of any ordinary dividend was making shareholders restive by mid-1883, and the value of £100 ordinary was down to a little more than £40. A letter to the *Aberdeen Journal* hoped the "astute and esteemed chairman" would explain why a total of almost £18,000 had been carried forward in the half-yearly accounts since 1880, and also shed light on the "operations" at Kittybrewster and their cost. At the half-yearly meeting on 20 September, Ferguson again defended the withholding of an ordinary dividend, saying it was preferable to hold funds against possible further Inverythan claims rather than pay a "trifling" ½% dividend, and reminding shareholders that there was still a great deal to do by way of station improvement, new rolling stock, steel rails, etc. He was not prepared to prophesy when an ordinary dividend would resume, and gave nothing away about the cost of extending the yards at Kittybrewster, though describing the work as "an immense advantage". At this time, Moffatt and Ferguson were anxious about the possible reduction of goods rates on through traffic, wanted by some of the large railway companies, and Moffatt went to meetings of general managers at the Railway Clearing House to defend the position: "… some companies are unsympathetic to smaller companies' requirements … If we were to have our tolls reduced it would be a calamity"[22].

From 28 April 1883 a new presence appeared at Aberdeen Joint Station when the North British company, on completion of its rebuilt viaduct at Montrose, began to use the running powers for passenger trains it had long ago acquired over the Caledonian line. It had been running goods trains to Aberdeen since March 1881 but these did not impinge on GNS or joint tracks. Aberdeen now had passenger services via both West and East Coast routes. In February a diplomatic agreement had confirmed the exchange of directors' silver passes for free travel between the North British and GNS directors, but the North British Railway's right to use the station was immediately raised at the Great North board, and the question was remitted to Moffat, to discuss with the Caledonian and the company's parliamentary counsel, Henry Cripps[23].

Cowan's departure, and coast line progress

In August 1883 the general manager received an anonymous letter from an employee in the locomotive department, about wastage and misuse of materials, drinking on duty, and avoidance of work. Among the claims was that "young Mr Cowan", the superintendent's son who was also employed at the works, was removing expensive teak wood to break up as firewood. Moffatt interviewed the writer and believed him to be sincere and without personal motives, and also thought it possible that Cowan senior did not know what was going on[24]. It can be no coincidence that William Cowan's retirement was announced in October, and his son resigned at the same time. Cowan received an illuminated address from his own department, but refused any "more tangible" gift. He had run the locomotive department for 26 years and if he had had his difficult moments with the board, his word had been law with his men and there had never been a strike among them – some had been with the Great North since its opening in 1854. In his farewell remarks, he described himself as the first engineer in the country to introduce bogie engines, and the first to use steel tyres on driving wheels[25]. His relations with Krupps were such that he was promptly appointed their agent for steel locomotive tyres in Great Britain and the USA. He was succeeded by James Manson, assistant locomotive superintendent on the Glasgow & South Western Railway.

Passenger fares on the GNS were 2d a mile for first class (1.87d on the Deeside line) and 1 1/4d for third – the other Scottish companies charged 1d[26]. The 'Cheap Trains Act' of 1883, remitting government duty on fares of 1d a mile, prompted the company to reduce its third class fares to this level from 1 February 1884. The figures were carefully worked out, with the calculated loss on fares, assuming the same number of journeys, as £4,818, the gain on tax relief as £2,833, and the net loss as £1,985. Ferguson hailed it as a "gift" of £5,000 a year to users, though the company expected greater custom. It certainly worked: in the first year of reduced fares, third class numbers went up from 1,073,391 to 1,280,845[27]. Further doubling of the Deeside line, two miles 1,202 yards, as far as Cults, was ordered in December 1883, at an estimated cost of £6,600, and numerous small increases of staff numbers and wages were approved, suggesting some easing of financial stringency. An ordinary dividend of 1% was announced in March 1884, and would be repeated in the next two half-years.

On 1 April the first section of the coast line opened as far as Tochieneal, from a new station at Portsoy, with a wooden building (all the coast line stations were of wooden construction), and a footbridge linking its two platforms, one of the first to be put up on the GNS system. Horse buses from Buckie and Cullen met the four daily trains, which ran to and from Banff. A modest traffic of fish carted from Buckie began at Tochieneal – at this time the GNS was carrying around 9,000 tons of fresh fish a year, about a third of the total coming from Fraserburgh, which averaged 3,576 tons a year between 1880 and 1885[28]. The western section, between Elgin and Garmouth, was opened on 12 August: 8 3/4 miles long, its construction had been quite straightforward, with a single-span lattice girder bridge over the Lossie being the only important engineering feature. Garmouth had sawmills cutting up logs into sleepers and pit-props and the adjacent village of Kingston was still engaged in shipbuilding: the industry, though in decline, lasted until 1914.

James Manson, locomotive superintendent, 1883-1890. (©CSG CIC Glasgow Museums Collection)

The railway in the landscape: The coast line at Cullen, completed in 1886. *(Stenlake collection)*

Progress on the central section was very slow and in October 1884 £5,000 had to be advanced to the contractors, W.&T. Adams, against their accumulated debts. A year later Blyth and the law agents were instructed to press for more men to be employed on the work. The most difficult section was at Cullen, where cuttings, embankments and viaducts were required. At the end of March 1886 the line was finally completed, and opened for traffic on 5 April[29]. For the bridge at Seafield Street Cullen Town Council wanted something "ornamental as well as useful" and the main arch was modelled on London's Temple Bar. Lower Castle Street now ran below a viaduct of six arches, and another of eight arches, 75 feet high and 610 feet long, crossed the Cullen Burn. Its piers were of blue limestone with freestone corners and strengtheners, and arches of red bricks in an unusually large size, 12 by 6 by 4 inches. Without naming names, at the September 1885 half-yearly meeting Ferguson criticised the late Earl of Seafield, through whose intransigence "Instead of a picturesque and graceful viaduct across a small part of the park … we have had to make an enormous cutting of 223,740 cubic yards through a hill east of the town, with a station outside the town and away from the harbour, cross the town by two expensive and unsightly viaducts, and then make another huge cutting through the links". He called it "a blot on the fair face of nature", adding that "Future generations will be baffled"[30].

The Spey was crossed between Garmouth and Fochabers (Spey Bay from 1 January 1918) stations by the GNS's longest bridge, 947 feet, with a main span of 347 ft and three 100ft spans on each side, all of lattice girder construction. No rock foundations had been found and the bridge is mounted on cylindrical pillars sunk 50 feet into the ground; the main ones of 15-feet diameter, the others of 9-feet. When full the Spey here ran in three channels and the main course was intended to pass under the central span, requiring a diversion about half a mile upstream and the excavation of some 50,000 cubic yards of earth and gravel, used to make the flood banks. Estimated at £25,000, the viaduct's actual cost was £40,000, helping to push the coast line's capital cost up to £270,000. Adams' contract price was £52,286 19s 7d but they claimed a total payment of £77,742 2s 7d and the Great North made a counter-claim, alleging unreasonable delays of 837 days at £20 a day. The matter went all the way to the House of Lords and was not fully resolved until December 1891, though the Lords had dismissed Adams' appeal a year earlier. It is not clear whether Adams ever paid up. Their cautioner – a guarantor against default – settled with a payment of £500[31].

The Spey Viaduct: inside view of the bowstring girder span. *(Stenlake collection)*

Other issues, 1884 – 86

A top-level Great North of Scotland - Highland Railway meeting was convened by William Ferguson at Elgin on 15 October 1884 to discuss the possibility of a new joint station at Elgin. Thomas Bruce, leading the Highland delegation, said his company was quite willing to acquiesce, and the two engineers, Patrick Barnett and Murdoch Paterson, were instructed to draw up plans, using ground already owned by the Highland. The Great North was to lay sidings and platforms at its own expense, aligned with the present Highland Railway station. All passenger and parcel traffic would be managed by the Highland Railway and the revenue split according to the proportion going by each line. The GNS was at liberty to appoint an inspector to make sure that things were properly done. Subsequently the Great North board decided to have its own staff, but like other initiatives with the Highland, the project languished in a climate of suspicion and hostility[32].

In December 1884 the finance committee decided to allow passengers to travel in the brake vans of goods trains, if they paid the first class fare and signed an indemnity relieving the company of responsibility in case of accidents[33]. In 1883-84 the company for the first time carried more than two million passengers: 1,801,972½ third class (half-fares were counted as half a passenger) and 195, 215½ first class[34].

From its beginning, the Great North had used the electric telegraph to control its services along the single track, and it introduced what was first called the "telegraph speaking instrument" (not a telephone but a needle telegraph) from the autumn of 1882, at Logierieve, Brucklay, Tillyfourie, Wartle, Knock, Auchindachy and Cromdale. John Fyfe of the Kemnay granite quarries was allowed to use a company line for communication between his quarry sites. By the end of 1884 an agreement with the National Telephone Co. provided for telephone lines between the superintendent's office at the joint station, the head office at Waterloo Quay, Moffatt's house in Union Place, Reid's house in Eldon Terrace, and three ticket sales points in the city centre, at a cost of £60 a year. The ticket sellers paid half of their cost. They received 2½% commission on the sale of tickets to stations within the GNS system: passengers to further destinations had to go to the station[35].

The gas works railway

Aberdeen had had coal-gas works since 1824. By 1883 they were owned by the town council and had been operating at Sandilands, near the harbour, since 1846. Growing demand for gas led to growing coal requirements – around 30,000 tons a year – and the council decided to instal a short railway from the harbour to the gasworks.

The subsequent four-year mini-saga is quite revelatory of how affairs between the town authorities and the railway companies were conducted. The Aberdeen Extension & Improvement Act, 1883, provided for a line through the streets from Waterloo Quay. The Great North had initially opposed the measure, for tactical reasons, and during the passage of the Bill the council made a seven-year agreement with the company to carry coal to the gasworks, and residues away, at 6d a ton. Integral to the agreement was that the railway company would sell to the council properties it owned on the east side of Cotton Street, required for widening of the street, for £1,180 8s 11d, the price it had originally paid for them; it was also specified that the GNS would make the junction with the harbour sidings and supply two 20-ton tank engines, at an estimated cost of £800 each[36]. As a cheaper alternative, the Great North also offered to build a branch from the Waterloo line into the gasworks, crossing Cotton Street, but the council preferred the option of a railway through the streets, a decision severely criticised by Alexander Copland, of the Aberdeen Commercial Company, a harbour commissioner and Conservative political opponent of the Liberal-dominated town council. Copland pointed out that 21,500 tons of gasworks coal came via the Caledonian Railway and only 6,500 tons by sea to Waterloo Quay, and suggested that pressure from the Caledonian, which would lose its terminal charges at Guild Street if the coal went straight through to Kittybrewster and down the GNS Waterloo Branch, had influenced the council's decision[37]. Strong opposition was also mounted by residents in the Footdee area, who held an "indignation meeting" in January 1885. The Improvement Act required the harbour commissioners' consent to the use of locomotives along the quays (as the council had a majority of seats on the commission, this consent was taken for granted), and in June 1885 William Moffatt duly wrote to the commissioners requesting permission to use a locomotive on the harbour rails, stressing that with upwards of 100,000 tons of goods being handled each year, horse haulage was no longer sufficient. The harbour commissioners now balked at this, claiming that the rails would not support the weight of an engine. Unwilling to bear the cost of replacing the rails, they remitted the matter to their Maintenance of Works committee, where it languished. Denied the possibility of using locomotives, the Great North repudiated the haulage agreement. Arbitration by the Sheriff had been provided for in the event of dispute, and with its railway under construction from December 1885, the council resorted to this process on two counts, to compel the GNS to undertake the haulage, and to sell the Cotton Street properties for only £464 17s 3d, the valuation put on them by the City Chamberlain[38]. The gasworks line was completed on 24 November 1886, with no-one to work it. In December Sheriff Guthrie Smith, as arbitrator, ruled that it was up to the harbour commissioners to make their lines fit for use by locomotives, and that the GNS was within its rights to withdraw from the haulage agreement; and in May 1887, following arbitration by Sheriff-Substitute Brown, the town council finally agreed to pay £1,300 for the Cotton Street properties[39], and later in that year the town council purchased its own locomotive to work between the harbour and the gasworks. The Great North, which had set out to be helpful, found itself completely excluded from the gasworks traffic, and also had to continue with horse haulage for its harbour traffic while the council's engine puffed up the 1 in 40 slope of Church Street with the coal wagons[40].

A less contentious goods branch, a tramway from Carron on the Strathspey line to Mackenzie & Co.'s Dailuaine Distillery, was approved in March 1885. Patrick Barnett estimated its cost at £3,100, of which the GNS would bear around £500 for the junction, signals and a siding at Carron[41]. In June an agreement for a minimum of Fifteen years was made with the Culter Paper Co., for extended sidings and a fixed carriage rate for goods, and a draft arrangement was made for a siding off the Lossiemouth line to the Spynie Hill quarry, but this was never put into effect. The whisky industry was beginning on a boom, and other distillery connections approved included the mile-plus tramway from Longmorn Station to the Glenlossie Distillery, where the GNS paid for the junction[42].

CHAPTER 13
A Service Reformed, 1885 – 1889

Highland connections and disconnections

Despite the many pious words uttered by the Highland Railway counsel in the parliamentary hearings of 1884, efforts in 1885 to dovetail services with those of the Highland got no co-operation. Proofs of the Highland Railway timetable from 1 July showed various alterations and discontinuations of trains to the detriment of the Great North. The 12.25 pm Keith-Inverness was now to depart from Elgin at 12.50, just ten minutes before the arrival of the GNS express from Aberdeen via Dufftown. The Highland Railway also refused to accept through carriages at Elgin, forcing passengers to change trains there, with a lengthy wait. The Great North board sought a court interdict on these vexatious practices and resolved to apply to the Railway Commissioners to determine what exchange facilities the Highland should offer, once the coast line was opened. Meantime rapid rearrangements were made to minimise inconvenience to travellers, with an extra train from Aberdeen at 10.10 am to connect with the Highland Railway's 12.25 pm at Keith. Speeding-up of some trains made the Dufftown route to Elgin quicker than the shorter route via Mulben: the 11.00 am from Aberdeen reached Elgin at 2.45 pm, while passengers changing at Keith would not reach Elgin until 3.14. On 16 July the GNS lodged a case with the Railway Commissioners to compel the Highland to run two express passenger trains each way daily between Inverness and Elgin, so as to provide a fast service via Dufftown to Aberdeen using through carriages of the GNS; also to get improved goods exchange facilities at Elgin, and to make the Highland Railway give longer advance notice of changes to timetables and carriage rates[1].

Plainly the Highland was not going to co-operate except under compulsion, and though litigation was expensive, there was no other option. The Great North was getting by financially with a series of relatively modest-sized short-term loans: £25,000 from the trustees of the estate of the late William Baird, of Elie, in December 1884, £50,000 from the North of Scotland Bank renewed for three months, and a new loan of £30,000 from the National Bank, both in July 1885, and a further renewal, of £20,000 from the National Bank, in August. As one loan was paid off, another would be taken out. But the Railway Commissioners' judgement, in September, was a disappointment. The present arrangements were described as unsatisfactory to both companies, each practising delaying tactics on the other's trains. The Highland was ordered to provide proper connecting services, but for the Aberdeen-Inverness route Keith was decreed as the exchange point, because the Mulben line to Elgin was nine miles shorter, and no order was made for exchange facilities at Elgin. In 1884 26,884 through passengers were booked via Keith; while the number at Elgin was unconfirmed, Andrew Dougall said it was only two or three thousand, while Moffatt claimed over 26,000. Nor would the commissioners compel the Highland Railway to run the desired two expresses to Elgin[2]. At this time there was no Board of Trade sanction for passenger trains to use the connecting line between the stations at Elgin, and the commissioners suggested that the Great North should make an application. A hint of exasperation with both companies comes through in Sir Frederick Peel's remarks: it was impossible not to notice how any initiative put forward by company A invariably had a snag as far as company-B was concerned. The Highland wanted the Great North to run two connecting trains from Boat of Garten daily, rather than a single mixed train; William Moffatt was willing, so long as one of these trains had GNS through carriages to and from Perth. But here the commissioners as well as the Highland demurred, since coupling and uncoupling would cause delays to the Highland's fast trains. In a judgement delivered on 19 December, the commissioners accepted a Highland offer to run two trains daily between Inverness and Keith that did not stop at Forres, if the GNS would provide close-timed connections with Aberdeen. With an almost detectable groan the commissioners noted that "the Great North of Scotland are of opinion it would cause them great inconvenience to run these trains…" Despite the potential for delay at Forres, the Great North wanted to tap the Perth line's traffic.

Comparison of some key statistics from both companies in 1885[3] shows some changes compared with the picture ten years earlier.

	Great North of Scotland	Highland Railway
Authorised capital	£4,090,480	£3,973,113
Authorised loans	£1,103,354	£1,656,413
Route miles	298	418
Total passenger journeys	2,065,845*	1,468,373
Total passenger train receipts	£153,058	£232,135
Total minerals tonnage	316,616	114,825
Total merchandise tonnage	345,562	236,888
Total goods receipts	£154,753	£143,678
Total train miles	1,473,713**	1,673,580
Total net receipts	£152,394	£182,309
Proportion of expenses to revenue	52%	53%
Number of locomotives	71	75

*The GNS carried 169,160 first class passengers.
**The GNS recorded 809,249 passenger train miles and 664,464 goods train miles; the Highland Railway as before gave a combined figure.

The Great North's figures reveal the extent to which service improvements had raised operating costs without – as yet at least – yielding significant improvements in revenue. In October 1885 the ordinary share price, which had been falling gradually for ten years, reached a low of £48 2s 6d against a par price of £100, but a modest rise, to the £57 - £60 level, followed[4]. By February 1886 the Aberdeen Chamber of Commerce was noting "the prospect of better feeling" between the two northern railway companies, with the fastest train to Inverness down to 3 hours 20 minutes, but the commissioners had made an unsatisfactory judgement, and would soon be hearing from the Great North again.

The draft of a new traffic agreement with the Highland Railway was submitted to the board on 1 April 1886, approved a fortnight later, and on 18 June was signed by both companies at a meeting in London. In all there were 27 clauses, intended to cater for all eventualities relating to through traffic on all routes. Both companies committed themselves, in good faith, to establish a complete system of through communications between their various lines. Gross receipts of through traffic were to be evenly divided after deduction of charges, and through fares were agreed. Fares and rates were as far as possible to be arranged in concert, but any fare set by one company without prior agreement was also to be charged by the other company. Complete facilities for interchange by exchange of rolling stock and forwarding of through vehicles were to be afforded by each company to the other. A joint committee was to meet regularly to manage the relationship, and William Ferguson, Thomas Adam (vice-chairman) and two other directors were appointed as GNS members[5].

A schedule set out four trains in each direction:

DOWN		MAIL		
Aberdeen dep.	7.00 am	10.10 am	1.15 pm	4.55 pm
Keith arr.	9.33 am	11.46 am	3.30 pm	7.25 pm
Elgin arr. (via Dufftown)		12.48 pm		
Elgin arr. (via Portsoy)		12.52 pm		
Keith dep.	9.40 am		3.35 pm	7.35 pm
Elgin arr. (via Mulben)		1.00 pm		8.33 pm
Inverness arr.	11.50 am	2.15 pm	6.05 pm	10.05 pm
UP				
Inverness dep.	10.10 am	12.00 pm	3.00 pm	4.00 pm
Elgin arr.	11.33 am	1.25 pm	5.30 pm	
Keith arr. (via Mulben)	12.10 am		4.50 pm	6.20 pm
Elgin dep. (via Portsoy)		1.35 pm		5.35 pm
Elgin dep. (via Dufftown)	11.40 am	1.40 pm		5.40 pm
Keith dep.	12.55 pm	2.40 pm	5.00 pm	7.05 pm
Aberdeen arr.	3.15 pm	4.20 pm	7.00 pm	9.30 pm

Various stipulations were made about maximum permissible waiting times at Forres and Elgin. An addendum to the agreement on 25 June allowed return ticket holders to come back by a different route[6].

For the main agreement the arbitrators were James Grierson of the Great Western Railway, and W.J. Wainwright of the Glasgow & South Western, both of whom died in 1888, when Henry Tennant of the North Eastern was appointed sole arbitrator. Even at the start one issue required clarification. The Highland contended that rates and charges should be calculated as if the traffic passed over the shortest distance possible (viz. its route via Mulben, as provided for in Section 82 of its Act of 1865) while the GNS pointed out that since the agreement of 1 August 1884, the rates had been calculated on the basis of the route mileage actually travelled. The issue was referred to James Beale, a London solicitor, who ruled on 9 July 1886 that "… the proviso of Section 82 of the Highland Railway Act 1865 … does not apply to traffic exchanged under the Great North of Scotland Act of 1884 between the two companies at Elgin … receipts of such traffic are to be divided between the two companies in accordance with their respective mileage and under the rules of the Clearing House." This pleased the Great North but not the Highland, and argument continued, with Dougall claiming that proceeds of through traffic on any route between Grange South and Elgin should be halved, and Moffatt contending that the actual mileage basis should be used. It was 1899 before this was resolved. Soon Dougall was submitting other issues for arbitration, but the Great North always had a longer list of grievances: a typical Highland Railway action reported at a Finance committee meeting in Elgin on 5 May 1888 was to divert five double vans of sheep and six trucks of cattle, booked at Inverness to go via the GNS, on to its own Dunkeld line. Reviewing its armoury, the Great North board instructed the law agents to examine the running powers agreement made with the Inverness & Nairn Railway in 1854 and prepare a case for counsel's opinion[7].

Speeding up the mail

While the Highland negotiations were going on, the company was working on a revised mail contract, which would take account of the completed coast line. Aberdeen's Chamber of Commerce was pressuring the Post Office for better service, in a co-ordinated campaign, informing Postmaster-General Shaw-Lefevre that the Great North was prepared to lay on additional trains including one to Buckie (whose mail currently came via the Highland Railway from Keith) for "a very moderate sum"; and the Duke of Richmond and Gordon (title of the Duke of Richmond & Lennox from 1876) led a large delegation from north-eastern towns to meet him. Unfortunately the postal officials did not regard the Great North's demands as at all moderate and deprecated its claim for equal payment with the Highland Railway, which covered a greater distance and ran mail trains on Sundays[8]. Following a meeting between Ferguson and the Postmaster-General, however, improvements were agreed and revenue got a boost, with the mail contract raised to £7,500 for the first six months of 1886 and £17,500 a year from 1 July, subject to the provision of certain new trains. Converted third class compartments had been

Grange Station, opened in 1856; junction for the Banff Portsoy & Strathisla line from 2 August 1865. *(Stenlake collection)*

used for sorting mail, but on 29 October 1885 the Caledonian agreed to extend the run of its London-Aberdeen sorting van to Keith, from 1 January 1886. From that date exchange apparatus was in use at Pitcaple, Oyne, Kennethmont and Rothiemay, with three worked on the Down, and four on the Up journeys[9]. From 3 May the sorting carriage would run to Elgin, taken forward from Grange via the coast line by a train due in Elgin at 8.30, and exchange posts were set up at Portsoy and Cullen[10], while places between Keith and Elgin via Dufftown received mail from a train due in Elgin at 9.00. As part of a general speeding-up of the 'Scotch mails' from 1 July, a 'New Special Post Office Train' left Euston at 8.30 pm, carrying mails only, arriving in Perth by 7.35 am. Four passenger carriages were added at Perth for Aberdeen, leaving at 7.40 am and arriving at 9.55. From the same date an early mail train left Aberdeen at 3.45 am, arriving at Keith at 5.45 and Banff at 6.45. Connections for Banff, Fraserburgh and Peterhead then left, bringing mail to the Buchan ports 35 minutes earlier. A new train on the Strathspey line advanced the district's postal deliveries by 5 1/2 hours: leaving Boat of Garten at 10.25 am, it reached Craigellachie at 11.45, returning from there at 3.05 pm to reach Boat of Garten at 4.25. While the Queen was at Balmoral, an additional mail train ran on the Deeside line, from Aberdeen at 10.10 am, reaching Ballater at 12.00, leaving again at 2.40 pm and in Aberdeen at 4.25. A contract was signed on 22 June and the new services ran from 1 July[11]. This greatly improved the exchange of mail between the Banffshire and Moray towns and the south, and the GNS built two six-wheeled sorting vans at Kittybrewster and first hired, then bought an ex-London & North Western Railway van, all of them in service before the end of November 1886. By 1896 other stations were equipped with mail pick-up apparatus, including Gartly, Kintore, Kinaldie, Bucksburn and Woodside. Insch followed in 1898 and Cornhill at the same time or later[12].

To allow trains to run directly from Aberdeen on to the coast line, a connection to the Banff Branch was laid from Grange on land given by the Duke of Richmond, completing a triangle between Grange, Grange South, and Grange North Junctions on 3 May 1886. Parliamentary authorisation was given retrospectively in the company's Act of 19 July 1887, in order that charges for its use could be legally made.

Revenue for the half year August 1885-January 1886 was £158,642 4s 4d compared with £164,897 10s 6d in the corresponding previous period, and the ordinary dividend was cut to 1/2%. Bad weather was partly held to blame, though economic downturn was chiefly responsible, with a "severe and long-continued depresssion" still affecting trade and commerce on a national basis[13].

Fish, beef, whisky, and curling

Fresh fish was a popular item on London dinner tables, and fishmongers charged premium prices for it. The herring catch off Scotland's east coast in the 1886 season was worth £1 ½ million, with huge catches in the southern part of the Moray Firth. By mid-August, around 1,300 boats had landed 30,100 cran at Aberdeen, 40,000 at Peterhead, and 58,000 at Fraserburgh. Excess could be a problem as well as dearth, and despite good railway connections, newspapers carried stories about difficulties in despatching large amounts of fish. William Ferguson denied that the GNS carriage rates were any part of the problem, pointing out that the open market arrangement saw prices per cran fluctuate between 6s and £1. Providing enough fish trucks must have been difficult, however. Fish traffic helped to push up revenue, and a 1% dividend was restored for the February-July half-year[14].

Fish transport brought another deputation from Fraserburgh in 1886 about the Rosehearty railway, on which there had been no action. Rosehearty had 28 white fish and 37 herring boats, and also crab and lobster boats. An estimated 12,000 barrels of cured herring had been carted from there and Sandhaven to Fraserburgh in 1885. The board was cautious, advising the deputation that the £40,000 capital needed would have to be raised locally, though the GNS would work the line and guarantee a minimum annual dividend of 2 ½ %[15].

In early 1888 a Private Member's Bill sought to impose a uniform carriage rate for fish across all railways, something William Ferguson strongly opposed. In 1887 the GNS had carried its greatest tonnage of fish yet: 20,431 tons, up from 14,173 tons in 1886 and more than double the 1885 figure. Fish was sent from Peterhead to London at two fifths of a penny per pound weight, or 3/10d if the consignment exceeded three tons – a fraction of the final price. A large cod (26 lbs plus) fetched 4d on the quay but was sold to the consumer at 4d a pound, giving the fish merchant and the fishmonger a very handsome profit[16]. Though the Bill failed, the fish salesmen, "a greedy cartel" as Ferguson described them, continued to campaign against carriage rates.

The advent of steam trawlers from 1882 had greatly increased the white fish catch, and Aberdeen's much-needed new covered fish market opened in May 1889 on Albert Quay, close to the joint station. The north-east fish merchants were reliant on the Caledonian or the North British and their West and East Coast associates to get the

Buckie Station and harbour, with steam drifters (introduced around 1900) and 'Zulu' sailing boats. *(Stenlake collection)*

catch to London in good condition, but the Great North had to carry it from ports north of Aberdeen, almost always by passenger train or by special express. William Acworth wrote in 1890:

"I left Peterhead for London one day last Spring by the 2.45 pm train. A few miles outside Aberdeen we were stopped, and learned that the fish special, which had started in front of us, had broken down … The fish train and the passenger train were amalgamated, and we ended in reaching Aberdeen only about twenty minutes late. Meeting there the superintendent of the line, who was on the look-out for our arrival, I expressed my regret that the London express would be delayed. 'Oh, never mind the express,' was his reply; 'what I want to do is to get the fish special away to Perth in front of you'"[17]. Buckie's new harbour and rail links made it a significant fishing port, with the Great North getting the bulk of the traffic, as the table below shows[18]:

Fish by rail (tons)	1888	1889	1890	1891	1892	1893
Buckie (GNS)	2,236	3,196	2,738	2,380	2,179	1,998
Buckie (HR)	690	769	748	619	447	585
Fraserburgh (GNS only)	4,050	4,970	5,129	3,870	4,358	5,085
Peterhead (GNS only)	4,172	5,679	6,731	5,981	6,465	6,782

Aberdeen beef cattle regularly commanded the prizes and best prices at the London Christmas stock markets, though not all of it originated in the county. Of 668 truckloads sent between 5 and 11 December 1886, 49 came via the Highland line, 210 from the Buchan line, 185 from the Turriff line, and 145 from the main line and the coast[19].

Alfred Barnard published his account of the whisky distilling industry in 1887, recording visits to 28 distilleries in the GNS region, mostly between Elgin and Dufftown. Naturally he travelled by rail wherever possible, but makes almost no comment on the Great North, which suggests he found it satisfactory, and he frequently enthuses over the view from the carriage window: "such pictures of rocky ridges, wooded plantations, miniature waterfalls, river and mountain, that it all seemed like magic"[20]. He made his first tour just as the whisky boom was getting under way, noting that the Balmenach tramway was about to be laid and that arrangements were in hand for the line to Dailuaine. Some distilleries already had sidings, including Banff (Boyndie siding) and Tamdhu, where on a subsequent visit he notes a station (the future Knockando) was due to be opened in a few months[21]. At Tamdhu barley wagons unloaded straight on to the granary floor, and draff was discharged into wagons through an archimedean screw machine. Distilleries did their own delivery and collection, with Miltonduff keeping twelve cart-horses for the Elgin Station traffic. Between Ballindalloch Station and the Glenlivet Distillery Barnard passed sixteen carts, which shows that the proponents of a branch line really had a case. Much of the product was destined for England, where Scotch whisky had supplanted French brandy among spirits drinkers.

Very cold winters were a regular occurrence and like the other Scottish railway companies, the Great North made provision for curling, at that time a popular outdoor sport which attracted large crowds. Most localities had a curling pond, and the company agreed in November 1887 to allow the Pitfour Curling Club to put up a temporary platform near Mintlaw, at its own expense[22]. Such transient halts, used on only a few days in a year, were unstaffed and unsignalled, and working was by special instruction to train crews and staff issuing tickets. The most ephemeral was Rothiebrisbane, between Rothienorman and Fyvie, used as a station site on one day, 11 October 1918, for a cattle sale[23].

The cost of the coast line

Service improvements continued, with a new 3.35 pm express train from Aberdeen, stopping only at Inveramsay, Insch, Huntly, and Grange, where it divided, with one portion going by the coast line to Elgin, arriving at 7.10 pm, and the other via Craigellachie to Elgin, arriving at 6.40. There was a connection to Boat of Garten, arriving at 8.25. Passengers from Glasgow and Edinburgh could comfortably reach Strathspey or the Moray coast within a day[24]. Finance was still a problem, and the company had a Bill in to raise its capital by £50,000 in shares and £100,000 by borrowing. At an e.g.m. on the Bill on 17 February it was revealed that expenditure on the coast line had reached £305,000, as a result of the Cullen deviation and the Spey Viaduct. The cost of land bought from the Seafield and Fife estates had also been "very much larger than we could possibly have anticipated"; but Ferguson assured the meeting that the revenue coming in was more than twice what was needed to ensure payment of a dividend on the capital investment. The Bill also provided for raising £28,000 of stock to enable cancellation of the outstanding redeemable stock currently being charged to the revenue account at £1,000 a year,

Official invitation to the opening of the Coast line on Saturday 1 May 1886.
Regular services started on the same day. *(Great North of Scotland Railway Association)*

and for authorising the "little cut off the main line" to Grange North[25]. The ordinary general meeting, held on 17 March, could look at some encouraging figures and achievements: increased mail revenue, large fish traffic; of the system's 315½ miles, only 70 miles did not have steel rails.

Banff found that the opening of the coast line marked the end of its time as terminus of a railway from Aberdeen, leaving it on a branch from Tillynaught, while the coast line trains went on to Buckie and Elgin. It had no connection for the 3.35 am mail or the 3.30 pm express. A letter of complaint from the town council went unanswered for six weeks until John Stuart, assistant general manager, came down, and candidly admitted that the running of the trains was designed to favour Aberdeen-Elgin services. The only concession was to equalise the fares between Banff and Banff Bridge stations and Aberdeen. No more was ever heard of the connecting line between the two Banff stations. Two years later Banff was still protesting, but William Moffat refused to accept the town council's proposal for an improved service, as too costly for the likely number of passengers[26]. The coast line suffered its first accident on 16 May when the 10.10 am Aberdeen-Elgin was derailed at 40 mph on a low embankment between Buckpool (briefly known as Nether Buckie on opening) and Portgordon. It had four vehicles, a PO sorting carriage, a composite carriage, a third class brake and a guard's van. One passenger was seriously injured, and the cause was ascribed to the rails – of new steel type – expanding out of gauge because of extreme heat[27].

As if to underline the ongoing dispute with the contractor, in late December 1888 the embankment east of the six-arched Cullen Viaduct collapsed, pulling down two arches and partly demolishing a third. Rapid repair works ensured that the line was reopened in fifteen days, with the embankment extended to replace the fallen arches, and the third filled in with concrete, at a total cost of around £5,000. The Spey Viaduct had problems of a different sort: much work had been done to control the flow of the country's fastest river, but it was not easily tamed. In 1889 the Duke of Richmond raised a court case against the railway company after the river broke through its embankments and resumed its main course through the eastern channel. The Great North denied it had any responsibility to direct the flow under any particular span and refused to raise the sills beneath the side spans because of the danger of flooding. The Fishery Board added its complaints, blaming the viaduct for a diminution in the salmon catch. The Duke also claimed £21,000 damages from the GNS for loss of fishing income through delays to the bridge, but the Court of Session dismissed his case in December 1889[28].

Developments in Aberdeen: the suburban service

An e.g.m. on 10 August 1887 approved the current Bill: £100,000 was to be raised in debentures and 13,405 £10 redeeemable (C) preference shares of 1882 were to be converted into £134,050 of preference (C) stock, at a guaranteed dividend of $4\frac{1}{2}\%$ for five years and 4% thereafter. Revenue was rising again, faster than operating costs, and the ordinary dividend for February-July was edged up to $1\frac{3}{4}\%$. The new suburban services had lifted third class passenger numbers over the two million mark for the year 1886-87, and despite running 52,992 more train miles than in February-July 1887, all on passenger trains, working expenses were down on the previous comparable half-year, at 49.73d per mile compared to 50.7d. Double-tracking was now in progress on the main line between Inveramsay and Insch, seven miles at a cost of £25,000. Additional houses were being built for staff, and a programme of footbridges for stations was in hand[29].

Paper making was also booming in the late 1880s with new mills set up and old ones enlarged to supply ever-increasing demand. Aberdeen's industrial suburbs now stretched up the Don Valley, and in the course of 1886 the company planned a more intensive train service. The concept of the suburban railway, as distinct from the country railway, was well established and encouraged by the reduction that year of passenger duty from 5% to 2% on trains serving a designated suburban district. A plan for "omnibus trains" was presented to the Finance committee in September, and a service began from 1 November, though it was not until mid-1887 that the suburban service between Aberdeen and Dyce, immediately known as the "subbies", really got under way, with the opening of new intermediate stations at Bankhead and Stoneywood (1 July) and Don Street (1 August). A station at Hutcheon Street was opened on 1 December. Third class fares were one penny from Aberdeen to Kittybrewster, and $4\frac{1}{2}d$ to Dyce, with first class at double the rate. The returns over six months showed a leap in terms of numbers, 109,771 $\frac{1}{2}$ fares sold; though only a modest rise in receipts: £115 19s 1 1/d, but the subbies were popular, and definitely to be regarded as a success. Twenty trains ran to Dyce on weekdays, with 21 coming the other way, with 23 and 26 respectively on Saturdays (and no Sunday service). The Aberdeen Tramway Company, its vehicles still horse-drawn, had to cut its fares to compete with the subbies[30], and their popularity created demand for a similar service on the Deeside line, but this was deferred, as substantial alteration would be needed at the south end of the joint station to accommodate the extra trains.

Union Terrace, Aberdeen, looking towards Rosemount from Union Bridge. The terrace bank was undercut to make space for the turntable in 1893. *(Stenlake collection)*

Civic improvement was a big theme in Aberdeen in the 1880s, and the City Improvement Act of 1883, in addition to the gasworks railway heralded a phase of development centred on the construction of a raised street linking Schoolhill with the Rosemount area, bridging the Denburn Valley and the railway line. In 1887 the Great North sought to acquire a slice of Union Terrace Gardens to increase capacity at the north end of the station, something made necessary by the success of the suburban trains. The gardens had been pledged as a public recreation area, and a stand-off resulted between the town council and the company[31]. Under the terms of the Improvement Act the Great North had to approve the Rosemount Viaduct over its line, which it declined to do unless ground were given to fit in the planned Schoolhill commuter station, partly under the arch.

At Kittybrewster, a big change was planned. As a considerable achievement in a cramped and under-equipped site, the works had just completed the first locomotive entirely built by the Great North, designed by James Manson, with a second under construction[32]. Since the 1850s the city's expansion had transformed the semi-rural site into suburbia, making extension impossible, and finally in May 1887 the board decided that the locomotive works should be transferred to a new site. Port Elphinstone and Dyce were both considered but in November the question was deferred[33]. In August the board recorded agreement with the Aberdeen Harbour Commissioners for a steam locomotive to run on the harbour rails, and the decision to build a new carriage shed at Kittybrewster, capable of holding 50 vehicles. The contract, worth £1,509, was given to McKinnon & Co.[34]

Two men died in an accident at Kintore on 11 September. The 7.29 pm Kintore-Alford goods was at Ratchill Quarry siding, near Kemnay, with its engine detached, shunting wagons into the siding. Two young men from Kemnay were in the brake van, as legitimate passengers. They had been drinking but were "perfectly sober" according to the guard. It appears, though, that they tampered with the brake wheel, and the train began to run backwards down the 1/70 gradient. Passing the junction, it ran into the Alford siding at Kintore at around 60 mph, smashing the buffers and demolishing the granite ticket office. The van was crushed and the men killed[35]. On the same day a goods train collided with a mineral train at Inveramsay, carrying materials and workmen's carriages for the line doubling, and several men were injured. The Board of Trade inquiry into the Kintore crash revealed that quite often wagons were bumped off the line on to the road leading to the station, and a local petition was got up to have safer access provided[36].

Stations, old and new

With the prospect of a joint station at Elgin looking very remote, the finance committee met there in May 1888 and looked at plans for a new GNS-only station, though no action followed. Inverurie sent a deputation in November 1888 requesting a new station to replace the original and now decrepit structure, and the board promised early and favourable consideration.

North British trains were adding to the congestion at the south end of the joint station and on the line to Ferryhill. No agreement had been reached on the terms on which the North British Railway was using the station, though "out of regard for the public convenience" the Great North had been allowing it to do so, in the hope of an amicable arrangement. Moffat reported to the finance committee in June 1888 that North British Railway engines had been using the GNS turntable at the north end of the joint station without permission, and he had put a stop to this[37]. The North British was basing its free use of the station on the running powers granted in the Caledonian-SNER Amalgamation Act of 1866, which accorded it "accommodation at Aberdeen Joint Station", and the GNS and joint station committee lodged a court action in December, intended to determine the rights of parties. This was dismissed on 25 July 1889 because the Caledonian company, as joint owners, were not a party to the action, and an appeal followed immediately[38]. A spat with the Caledonian over its aquisition of land to enlarge its goods station was resolved when the GNS was given free access to the depot[39].

The goods rates dispute

Railway rates for goods traffic, always a fruitful source of dispute, were to become a major public issue in 1889. Ever since the 1860s, Parliament had been making sporadic efforts to exercise some control in the matter of railway rates for carrying goods. Two mutually contradictory concepts were involved. One was the freedom of railway companies to run their business as it suited them, within the provisions of their founding and any subsequent Acts of Parliament. The other was the monopolistic status of most railway companies within their own regions. While there was competition in some places – the prime Scottish example being the Glasgow-Edinburgh routes – great extents of the country, including the north-east, were served by a single company, which dictated the scale and standard of its own service. Passenger train fares were secured at the lower end by the provisions of 'Gladstone's Act' of 1844 and the Cheap Trains Act of 1883. Goods carriage rates were fixed at the top end, with each company required to set out its maximum rate for different classes of goods, in schedules attached to the founding or amending Acts (in the Great North's case that of 1859). These *maximum* rates were rarely applied, and all companies operated an *ad hoc* system of discounts or rebates (known as 'drawbacks') in their dealings with larger customers. In the eyes of its customers, the Great North had always charged a relatively high rate for goods traffic, and it had already provoked controversy in the artifical manure dispute. A parliamentary select committee on railways sat in 1881-82, and on 12 May 1881 it was informed by Alexander Copland that the Great North had not altered the excessive manure charge in the rate books of its country stations, and the company was compelled to pay further reparations[40]. In 1888 a new Railway & Canal Traffic Act required a complete listing of all goods classifications and carriage rates and charges for goods. All companies were given six months to review their scale of maximum charges and deposit them with the Board of Trade, to be scrutinised. The railways were also required to set out their charges for 'terminals', and the GNS took the opportunity both to increase its maximum carriage rates and to impose terminal charges.

Publication of the companies' rates resulted in a storm of protest from bodies representing the traders, and in the hope of achieving a balance, the Board of Trade was instructed to produce its own set of goods classifications and a proposed scale of maximum charges. In the late Spring of 1890, the board issued its report, in the form of Provisional Order Bills, separate ones for major companies, with smaller companies grouped together: the GNS being included with the Ayrshire & Wigtownshire, Callander & Oban, and Highland companies[41]. Railway companies and their customers found much to complain of in the Board's proposals, and it was found necessary to appoint a joint committee of both Houses to consider the principal objections (and counter-objections). Alex Copland, of the Aberdeen Commercial Company, had led the opposition to the GNS in the manure dispute and remained vigilant on the issue of carriage rates. In February 1889 he warned against higher maximum rates to be introduced for hauling coal on the Deeside line, and within a month the Aberdeen Railway Traders' Defence Association was set up. Its secretary, T.R. Gillies, widened the attack by denying the Great North's legal right to

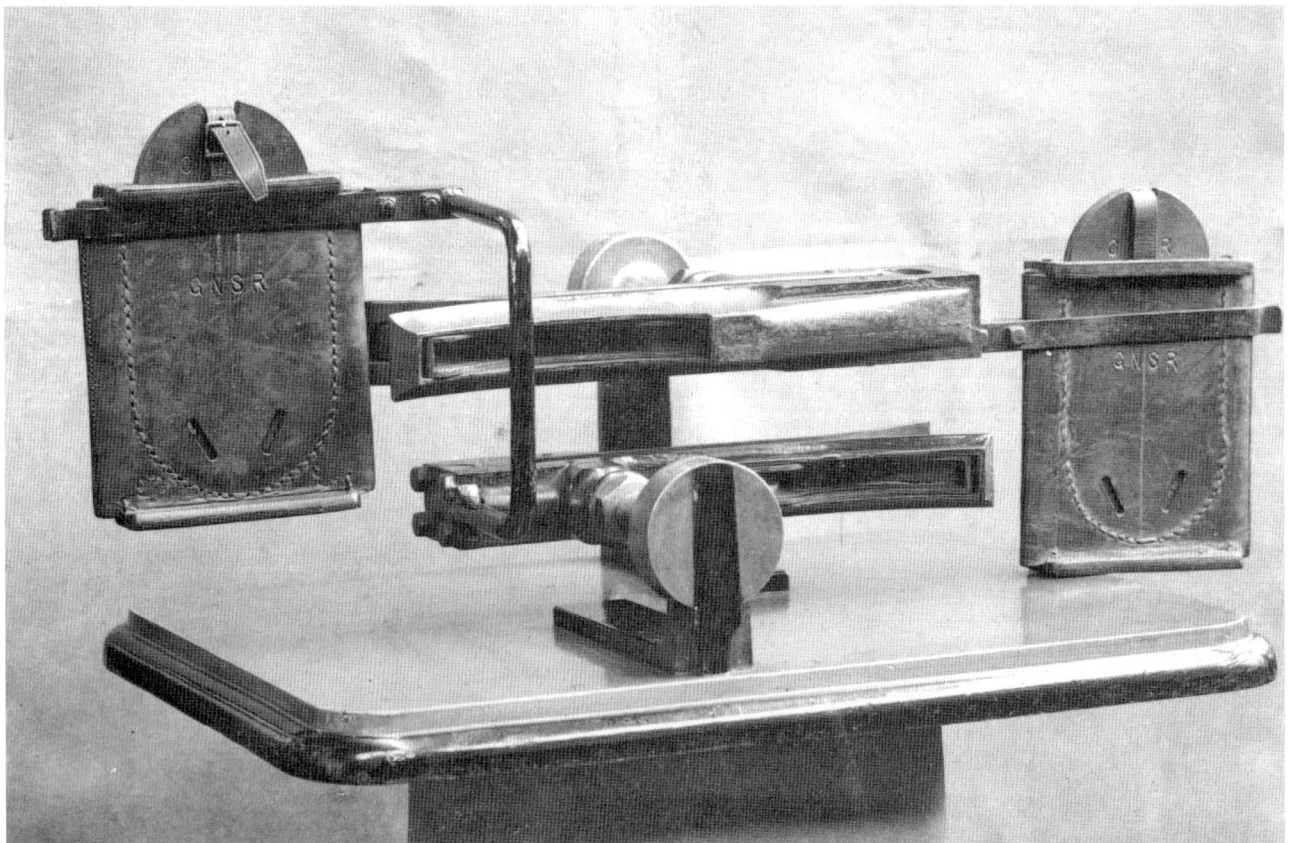

This display model shows how the automatic tablet exchange apparatus worked. The tablets were carried in stout leather pouches. The one on the left is held in the clip on the lineside stand and is about to be grabbed by the jaws of the locomotive-mounted exchanger. The pouch on the right is about to be caught by the lineside catcher. *(Great North of Scotland Railway Association)*

charge terminals, citing a clause in the company's Act of 1859 which said that it could charge for the use of warehouses, or for collections and deliveries, "only when such services shall be performed otherwise than on the premises of the railway". By the end of March the company faced a united chorus of hostility, with "the whole country up in arms" and exaggerated prophecies of doom, "the fish trade will be extinct". At the half-yearly meeting on 28 March, Ferguson defended the new rates as reasonable, and said that many would actually be reduced. The dividend on ordinary shares was 1½% which hardly indicated a company bloated by profiteering. By June, 172 objections to the Great North's new rates had been lodged[42].

The tablet exchanger, and working conditions

At the same meeting, the chairman noted the invention by James Manson of an automatic tablet exchanger, a device which simultaneously improved speed, safety and efficiency on a single track railway line. Interconnecting apparatus between the locomotive cab-side and a stout lineside post neatly switched pouches containing the token controlling entry to each section of single line. They were first introduced on the coast line. Seeing his invention as a humanitarian device – the manual exchange of hooped tablet pouches between locomotive firemen and station staff was a frequent source of injuries – Manson did not take out a patent, enabling other railway companies to copy it freely[43]. Barclay-Harvey states that Manson was aided by John Duncan, a blacksmith at Kittybrewster Works, who had previously been employed at the Broadford Sewing Mills, Aberdeen, and had seen apparatus that transferred cotton between machines[44]. On some Great North lines, however, neither train staff not tablet was in use at this time, with train movements still controlled by telegraph between stations. On 25 July 1889 the 2.40 pm mixed train from Fraserburgh to Aberdeen was mistakenly diverted into a siding at Brucklay and collided with six standing wagons. The train was formed of three open and two covered wagons, a composite carriage, two thirds with brake compartments, a first class and two third class carriages, and a brake van. A carter in the station yard was killed, and seven passengers were injured. Investigating, Colonel Rich of the Board of Trade noted that the pointsman had only been in the company's employment for 23 days and had been on duty for 10 hours when the accident happened. He placed the main blame on the company – if the facing points had been interlocked with the signals the mistake would not have happened; the operator was young and inexperienced; there was no tablet or train staff. Interlocking of points and signals had been possible for 30 years, and though at shareholders' meetings the chairman made a regular point about the extension of steel rails, it is clear that in many ways the Great North's older lines were in need of modernisation[45].

Mention of the Brucklay pointsman's hours on duty touched on another hot issue. Working hours were set by the company and often exceeded a twelve-hour day: some GNS guards were noted as having to work sixteen-hour shifts. Both within the railway industry, and among the general public, excessive working hours were heavily criticised as a frequent contributory cause to accidents. The Amalgamated Society of Railway Servants (Scotland) had recently organised a well-attended mass meeting of railwaymen in Aberdeen, at which its secretary Henry Tait announced that as soon as the union had a majority of railway staff as members, it would approach the companies directly, for a maximum ten-hour day and for uniformity of pay scales. The pressure was kept up and at another mass meeting in Aberdeen on 15 December there were hisses when a letter from Moffatt was read out, stating that the GNS dealt directly with its own staff, had had no trouble in the past and anticipated none in the future. A resolution for an all-out strike was proposed, but only a third of those attending supported it. Working hours were in the local news at the time: fourteen people had been injured at Huntly Station on 21 November when the 7 pm from Aberdeen was run into by the 5.45 pm from Elgin: the pointsman who had failed to set the points for the Up platform was tried at Aberdeen Sheriff Court in December. His working hours were 4.30 pm to 4.30 am. The Sheriff said he had made "an honest mistake" and gave a verdict of Not Proven, which was greeted by applause. Compensation to victims cost £2,430. Henry Tait used the case to criticise the signalling at Huntly as "of the most obsolete character." Claiming that the union now had 470 members in Aberdeen and "substantial numbers" in Keith and Elgin, he insisted that "nothing short of a ten-hour day, time and a quarter for overtime, and time and a half on Sunday duty would satisfy them". Commenting that some employees had had wage rises and others had not, he said the company was deliberately trying to create divisions among its men. A strike seemed a real possibility and James Manson confronted the issue in his address to the locomotive department's annual social gathering in the Northern Friendly Society's hall. Other managers were there as guests, but no directors. He said he did not believe that a universal strike would take place, as the union did not represent the majority of servants, and drew attention to the fact that in May 1884, soon after his appointment, and without any prior agitation, he had made "a great reform" of wages and hours, cutting from 18 to 25 hours a fortnight from enginemen's working time. Manson also stressed the ease of driving an engine in the present times, compared to the arduous task of earlier days[46].

CHAPTER 14
Pushing at the Frontier, 1890 – 1892

The expansive spirit of the 90s

William Moffatt's sustained efforts to improve the Great North's standards of speed and efficiency were publicly acknowledged by the late 1880s, with newspaper comments like that of the *Dundee Courier*, noting approvingly that the company was run on business principles, and "there is not a train on the GN system that does not run to time"[1], and the already-mentioned accolade of the economist William Acworth. Compliments continued through the 1890s, often on the smartness of station procedures, with some stops lasting only 29 seconds: "In smartness of actual working it outdoes them all" wrote W.J. Scott[2]. The commercial and industrial boom of the 1890s fostered the spirit of expansion and optimism which had already begun in the later 1880s. New initiatives and new opportunities were looked for, and seized.

Palace Buildings, a granite pile housing Mann's Palace Hotel and the household goods emporium of Pratt & Keith, above the north end of the joint station at the corner of Union and Bridge Streets in Aberdeen, was put up for sale in April 1889 and the Great North made a rapid offer of £30,000, payable at Whitsunday 1890. This was accepted, with the vendors to settle all claims relating to the hotel, including sanitary repairs at £400, and to secure a rent to the GNS of £750 a year until its lease came to an end. Pratt & Keith were to have their space altered and pay a rent of £800 a year on a 15 year lease. Parliamentary approval was needed for this – hotel-keeping was not mentioned in the Great North's various Acts – and it was agreed that the sale would be cancelled if this was not forthcoming. On the north side of Union Street there was still no agreement in January 1890 with the town council over the company's proposal to extend the platforms and place an engine shed, coaling bench and turntable by Union Terrace Gardens; and the board was becoming impatient. A top-level delegation from the company waited on the city's Bills & Law Committee to impress on it the urgency of the matter. At an e.g.m. on the current Bill, which included a provision for acquiring the extra space, Ferguson criticised the council's opposition as "jeopardising an enormous advantage to the community … for the sake of a paltry little bit of ugly ground," and claimed the amenity of the area would be improved by the work. But a report commissioned by the council from an independent engineer, John Strain, encouraged it to resist the full scale of the Great North's demands[3].

Relations with the Highland were not improved when the Great North embarked on the experimental chartering of a steamboat between 15 May and 30 June 1889 to carry fresh fish from Stornoway to Strome Ferry under a contract with the fish merchants that specified consignment south via Aberdeen[4]. Though the Great North had a legal right to promote its traffic, the Highland Railway considered this as invasive of its domain. In the Court of Session on 7 June, Lord Traynor "closed the record" in an action brought by the Highland against the Great

The Palace Hotel at Aberdeen occupied a favoured spot on Union Street, as well as being beside the station, to which it had its own footbridge connection. The hotel was destroyed by fire in 1941 and the site sold. (*Great North of Scotland Railway Association*)

North, requiring the latter to implement an arbitration made by James Grierson of the Great Western, and to accept the division of around £10,000 held in suspense by the Railway Clearing House in connection with a dispute over interpretation of the agreement of 1886 for traffic between places south of Grange South Junction and west or north of Elgin, or south of Forres. The imminent opening of the Forth Bridge meant that soon the East Coast route would be able to operate through carriages, and fish trucks, on faster trains from Aberdeen to London via Edinburgh. Ferguson pointed out at the Great North's ordinary general meeting in September that the East Coast could now get a train to Aberdeen at 7.30 am, the same time that the Highland Mail left Perth for Inverness; and with only 124 rather than 144 miles to travel, passengers from the south could have breakfast in Aberdeen and still reach Inverness before the Highland train. "But," he added, "these are speculations"[5]. Still, such speculations, combined with the Highland Railway's lack of action on its direct line from Aviemore to Inverness, prompted a new scheme from the Great North. Prepared with care, it embraced a separate railway between Elgin and Inverness, a line on the Black Isle from Muir of Ord to Fortrose, and a branch from Elgin to Burghead. Burghead (population in 1881 1,428), once part of the Great North's original scheme of things, had been terminus of a Highland Railway branch since 1862, but the Highland's standard of service was much criticised locally. In May a deputation from Burghead, Hopeman and Duffus proposing the line to Elgin had been favourably received by the GNS board, and a prompt survey was commissioned[6]. Patrick Barnett reported that a tramway link to Hopeman Harbour would cost £1,200, and the board agreed to pay half of this, if guaranteed free use. The Highland Railway immediately proposed a counter-scheme, with a line from Burghead through Hopeman to Lossiemouth, and the competition generated much local excitement. Though the Black Isle railway would have no physical connection with the Great North system, the board made an agreement with Fortrose Town Council for the use of the pier there for a train-ferry service to Ardersier, terminus of a branch of the GNS's proposed new line. The ferry would be capable of holding twelve trucks[7]. It was a bold plan, and of course was vigorously opposed by the Highland. Even as these rival plans were maturing, the two companies were still privately holding talks about a potential amalgamation: when the GNS board discussed a letter on the subject from Andrew Dougall on 1 November 1889, one of the directors, Mr Edmonds, "stated the history of the steps which had been taken in the last three months." Dougall's letter offered a meeting with the Highland Railway board to discuss a merger, on the understanding that all hostile schemes be withdrawn in the meantime. An exchange of letters over the next five weeks established that the Great North had no intention of withdrawing its Bill for the new lines unless the Highland agreed to give joint notice of an Amalgamation Bill for 1890. Dougall, however, had proposed 1891 for this, and refused to bring it forward. With that, the GNS new lines Bill went ahead, and the scene was set for another parliamentary confrontation[8]. Two companies that could not even agree on the rent to be paid by the GNS for its booking office in Inverness Station were clearly not in a fit state for amalgamation; in December 1890 the Highland Railway also applied to the Railway Commissioners for the right to receive half the revenue of the refreshment rooms and bookstall at Keith, forcing the Great North to assert its ownership of the station[9]. The Highland's response to speeding-up of the East Coast route was make a unilateral change to the arrival time of the first train from Aberdeen at Inverness: the joint committee had altered its departure time to 6.50 am which should have made the arrival earlier but instead the Highland contrived to delay this to 12.15 pm, by which time the morning train to Wick had gone (having picked up the passengers coming from the south via Forres)[10].

Ferguson suggested that "a new solution" might be found to the difficulties between the companies if the GNS were given running powers for certain through services between Aberdeen and Inverness[11]. This prompted a renewal, from the Highland end, of the notion of an amalgamation, with "all hostile schemes" to be withdrawn in the meantime, but the Great North refused to withdraw its Bill and the Highland mounted forceful opposition, including its own Bill for a Burghead-Hopeman Extension, a line to Ardersier, and a Black Isle line extending beyond Fortrose to Rosemarkie. Public interest in the competing Bills was high, especially in Elgin, where William Ferguson and a party from the GNS, in the town to promote their Bill, were thanked for the great improvement of Elgin as a business centre since the opening of the coast railway. Opinion generally was in favour of the Great North, which offered the benefits of competition, whereas the Highland, as a petition from Elgin against its Bill pointed out, was trying to stifle competition. Normally the GNS kept aloof from investment in harbours, but it did guarantee £200 a year as collateral security for a loan raised by the Lossiemouth Harbour trustees, who needed to deepen their harbour to keep it competitive[12]. This may have been partly to keep Lossiemouth on side while the Highland Railway was offering a Burghead-Lossiemouth railway, but the old Morayshire company had had close connections with the harbour trust.

A set-back in Parliament

The approaching parliamentary battle loomed over the half-yearly directors' report and the ordinary general meeting of March 1890. The Great North maintained the small ordinary dividend of $1\frac{3}{4}\%$, noting various cost commitments, apart from the Huntly crash. Work had to continue on the interlocking of points and signals, the improvement of signalling, the installation of automatic brakes on trains and the phasing out of mixed trains. The company had chosen to use the Westinghouse air-brake system, which its engineers regarded as more dependable than the vacuum system in frosty weather (though the Highland Railway opted for vacuum brakes). Whether or not Henry Tait was right in his assumptions about selective wage rises, the locomotive and traffic departments' wage bill rose by almost £2,000 in 1889-90.

William Acworth's *Railways of Scotland* was published while the Bills were being examined by a committee headed by Sir Richard Paget, MP for Wells, in Somerset. Looking back on GNS history, in a comparison with the Highland, Acworth wrote of the need to live down a reputation "acquired by long and patient continuance in ill-doing," with "despotic treatment" of passengers and a refusal to time its trains to correspond with arrivals from the south, before stressing the great improvement that the Ferguson-Moffatt regime had brought about – ten years before, the 86-mile journey from Aberdeen to Elgin took a minimum of $4\frac{1}{4}$ hours; now it was done in just over $2\frac{1}{2}$ hours by a route that was seven miles longer[13]. Perhaps reminders of the bad old days encouraged a misleading perception of the Great North, putting it at something of a disadvantage in the latest contest with the Highland Railway. Ferguson, Moffatt, and Benjamin Blyth spoke up for the GNS Bill, with Moffatt affirming that if the Great North had a free hand, traffic between Aberdeen and Inverness could be tripled. But on 29 April the committee refused a second Elgin-Inverness railway, and Ferguson then withdrew the Black Isle proposal. The Great North's Elgin-Burghead line was also thrown out, while the Highland's Bill was passed[14].

At the end of several months of intensive and expensive campaigning, the Great North was left exactly where it was at the beginning. Ferguson reported to his colleagues that the Committee "from the first stopped their evidence, declined to hear anything to do with the difficulties with the Highland Railway Company and gave their decision without hearing the other [GNS] side at all[15]." Witnesses for the Highland had emphasised the "invasive" nature of the Great North's scheme. If the Invernessians had 'won', however, it was by burdening themselves with additional lines which they had not planned.

Keeping the Great North busy

The board had much else to deal with. On 14 August 1890 the company's Various Powers Bill, including the Palace Buildings purchase, was given the royal assent. The board received local petitions for a branch line from Peterhead to Port Errol, and for an extension to Newburgh, without enthusiasm, and on 8 October deferred any decision. Exploitation of the granite south of Peterhead was the prime reason for the proposal, though at this time Newburgh was importing 12,755 tons of goods and shipping out around 5,000 tons a year[16]. Sparring with the Highland continued – it had applied to the Board of Trade for arbitration on alleged differences under Section 55 of the Highland Railway Act, 1865; the board resolved to oppose the move, and the Highland Railway's case was dismissed. Three directors went to Elgin to

Schoolhill Station, with high-level and low-level entries, shortly before its demolition in 1973.

attend a meeting of the Great North of Scotland-Highland Railway joint committee on the 25th, but no-one from the Highland turned up[17]. The resignation of James Manson had been regretfully accepted by the board: he was returning to Kilmarnock to become locomotive superintendent of the Glasgow & South Western Railway. From nine applicants, James Johnson, of the Midland Railway, was appointed as his successor, at £500 a year, and took up the post on 25 August[18]. Agreement was reached in October with Aberdeen town council's Improvements Committee on acquiring ground at Rosemount Viaduct for erection of Schoolhill Station, opened on 1 September 1893, with access both from ground and viaduct level, and of 136 ½ square yards on the north side of Union Terrace for a turntable, at a total cost of £1,252 14s 9d.

After many complaints, improvements to Banff services were finally conceded. Passengers to Keith on the 10.55 am from Banff could change at Rothiemay on to the 9.40 express from Aberdeen to Keith, and additional trains were put on to Tillynaught, for coast line, and Grange, for Strathspey, connections, to run as an experiment until the end of April 1891[19]. If Banff was temporarily placated, it was Fraserburgh's turn to complain. Letters in December from the town council and harbour commissioners criticised the inadequacy of the station both for passengers and goods, with fish traffic often delayed; the once-praised station now was seen as badly situated and "not nearly so comfortable and well-appointed as a town like Fraserburgh has a right to expect". Better carriages were also requested. Furthermore, the mail service was unsatisfactory: the 4.30 am mail train from Aberdeen did not reach Fraserburgh until 9.10, whereas the mail was at Keith by 5.15, Buckie by 6.25, and Elgin by 8.30[20]. For almost all visitors, a town's railway station was its gateway and civic pride wanted to make a worthy impression. Goods facilities were also improved where demand existed. Extensive limestone quarries were close to the Glendullan-Mortlach distilleries branch at Dufftown, and a siding to the Parkmore Limeworks was approved in September[21].

After more than ten years of pressing for a reduction in working hours, consistently rebuffed by the railway companies, the first real test of strength between the Amalgamated Society of Railway Servants (Scotland) and the employers came on 21 December 1890, when thousands of men walked out on the two largest companies, the North British and Caledonian. At a mass meeting in Aberdeen, GNS men expressed support for the North British

Railway and Caledonian Railway men, offered to give them financial help, and promised their "utmost influence" to prevent men from filling strikers' jobs. But they continued to work. On the 31st, James Black, a GNS director and ex-Provost of Elgin, adressed the annual joint festival of GNS and Highland staff there. Backing the call for a ten-hour day, he also claimed that the railway companies had been striving to make it possible, and forecast that it would happen in a short time[22]. The impact of the strike on Aberdeen was relatively limited, though the two southern companies ran restricted and delayed services. Great North trains were running virtually as normal, though an aid committee was formed to raise money to help "married men with large families" among the strikers[23]. By the end of January the strikers had returned to work.

A return made under the Licensed Premises (Scotland) Act in 1891 recorded that the GNS owned the Station Inn at Udny, the Station Hotel at Lossiemouth, refreshment rooms at Dyce and Ballater, and a pub at 3 Garvock Street, Aberdeen[24]. All these were tenant-run. The company was due to take over the Palace Hotel in December 1890, and a hotel committee was set up, four strong, including the chairman and deputy chairman, its expenses to be remunerated from hotel funds. A manageress, Miss McKilliam, was appointed for the Palace, at an annual salary of £120 plus board and lodging, and a complete refurbishment began, including electric lighting and four hydraulic lifts from the American Elevator Co. in London. A chef was employed at £150, kitchen maids at £20 and scullery maids at £15 a year. New furniture was purchased, mostly from J.&A. Ogilvie of Aberdeen[25]. In June the company obtained an interdict on the hotel's former owner, Charles Mann, from naming his new establishment in Bath Street as the 'Palace' or 'Mann's Palace' Hotel[26]. After thorough renovation, the Palace reopened on 28 August, advertising air conditioning: "a mechanical process of ventilation and warming", first of its kind in the country, with purified air. There was also a "first class sanatorium." The Great North's new role as hotel proprietor was resented by the city's established hoteliers, especially when it built a footbridge to give direct access from the station to the hotel, and unofficial warfare intensified among the 'boots' of the central hotels, one of whose jobs was to lure visitors arriving at the station to their own establishments. The Palace Hotel's boots was given a privileged position inside the platform barrier while the others were not allowed to pass it. In reply to a protest forwarded via the North British chairman G.B. Wieland, Moffatt replied that "… to admit your servants within the Barrier would unquestionably lead to inconvenience and confusion. No undue influence shall be used to to get any of the travelling Public to go to the Palace Hotel in preference to the other Hotels in the city"[27]. In the joint station itself, the Great North's campaign to make the North British Railway pay for its

Lossiemouth Station opened in 1852 as terminus of the Morayshire Railway.
Its buildings are dominated by the GNS-owned hotel. (*Stenlake collection*)

usage had met a setback when Lord Kinnear, required by the senior judges of the Court of Session to withdraw his dismissal of the case, now ruled in favour of the North British Railway's freedom to use the station. The joint station committee agreed to appeal to the House of Lords[28].

The Garve & Ullapool Railway

In the spring of 1891 the Railway & Canal Commissioners yet again had to deal with issues between the Great North and the Highland. The dispute revolved around the rent payable by the GNS for its booking office at Inverness Station. In Aberdeen the Highland Railway had a rent-free booking office at the joint station which, according to Moffatt, took "vastly more" than his company did at Inverness. Andrew Dougall claimed that of the 40 daily trains at Inverness – twelve each way on the south line, eight on the north line – 34 carried traffic for the Great North. Terminals also came into the argument. The Highland Railway kept all the terminal charges at Inverness to itself, whatever route the goods had come by: Moffatt insisted that if the Great North paid rent, it was entitled to a proportion of the terminals on its traffic[29].

In April Ferguson and Moffatt seized a new opportunity to extend Great North services to Inverness and even far beyond. On 14 August 1890 an Act had been obtained authorising the Garve & Ullapool Railway, a line of 33-plus miles from Garve, on the Highland Railway's Dingwall & Skye line, to the fishing village of Ullapool on Loch Broom. The share capital was £240,000, with loans of £80,000, a huge amount for a thinly-populated district to raise, but Government money was currently available for improving communications in the north-west Highlands[30] and the Garve & Ullapool committee were informed by the Treasury that the scheme would only receive a subsidy if an established railway company agreed to take responsibility for building and working the line. Though the Highland had made an agreement to work the Ullapool line, it was offering no financial support and had a preferred candidate for any subsidy in its own proposed extension from Strome Ferry to Kyle of Lochalsh. The Great North's ambition to extend its system was well-known, and the Garve & Ullapool directors began secret negotiations with it in April 1891. On the 25th, the board met to approve an agreement made by Moffatt "to construct, maintain and work in perpetuity" the line, in consideration of receiving a Government guarantee of not less than £6,000 a year for 25 years from opening. William Ferguson had met W.L. Jackson, Secretary to the Treasury, and asked for an undertaking that the GNS would be given running powers from Elgin to Garve, but Jackson had said only Parliament could grant this. Moffatt was ill and an adjourned board meeting was held at his house, where a majority of seven to three approved the agreement. The minority wanted a guarantee of running powers before commitment[31]. Unfortunately for the GNS, secrecy could not be maintained in an intensely political atmosphere with different ministers supporting competing projects, and in May the Highland Railway blandly announced that it was willing to build and work the Ullapool line on the same basis as proposed by the Great North. With both offers on the table, local opinion in Wester Ross and Lewis was very much in favour of the Great North, suspecting with good reason that the Highland Railway was more interested in blocking the line than building it.

Further misfortune came for the Garve & Ullapool company just at the time it got its Act, when a Royal Commission set up to review transport in the western Highlands decided that Ullapool's location made it unsuitable for development as a fishing station, a view which was maintained by a special commission set up in 1891 with a brief to pick a single railway scheme for subsidy. The commission nevertheless recommended support for two – the proposed West Highland extension from Fort William to Mallaig, and the Highland Railway's Kyle extension. In December 1891 the Garve & Ullapool directors were informed that a government subsidy was no longer available to them[32]. It is not clear whether they passed on this news to the Great North, which was preparing a Bill for a complete takeover of their company, assuming the subsidy to be in built. In March 1892, Dr Robert Farquharson, Liberal MP for Aberdeenshire West, inquired why negotiations between the Treasury and the GNS had not been completed and was informed that "the proposed arrangement was attended with difficulties for which a solution could not be found." Opposed by the Government, the GNS Bill never got beyond a second reading in the Commons[33]. With no prospect of raising capital, the Garve & Ullapool company kept a tenuous existence until 4 August 1893, when an Act of Abandonment was passed. Though the Highland Railway and the Treasury were bitterly blamed, it was the two commissions' rejection of Ullapool as a fishing port that scuppered the Garve & Ullapool project. Of course for the GNS it was primarily an opportunity to get better access to Inverness, but it was not a cynical scheme: the company knew something about the west coast fishery traffic and had strong support on Lewis[34]. Other hopeful projects beyond Inverness were offered to it, including lines in Caithness from Wick to Lybster, and Wick to Gills Bay, but the board regretted that though "very anxious to get a footing in the Northern Districts, they cannot see their way to take active steps in the meantime"[35]. Wick Town Council had never liked the Highland Railway, and sent a letter of commiseration to the GNS after failure of the 1890 Bill, urging it to keep up its efforts.

New offices and old issues

Successive board reports had described the coast line as a financial success, despite the ongoing dispute with the contractors. The line had been established as a separate undertaking with its own capital of £270,000, and the GNS was paying 4% on this sum each year. Now the company wanted to convert the 'Buckie' stock into GNS Lien Stock (i.e. stock whose dividend was secured as a first charge against the earnings of a specified line or company), which would have preference for dividend payment over GNS guaranteed stock and the 4% A,B,C and D preferred stocks. The proposal was attacked by a group of Edinburgh-based shareholders led by the lawyer Lewis Bilton, who pointed out that the company had not published a separate revenue account for the coast railway, and claimed that the line's working cost was as much as its revenue, that it was failing to earn the dividend, and that the true value of a £100 coast line share was only £33, compared to the £121 of GNS lien stock being offered – this would make the holders a gift of £237,000. An interdict against the conversion was sought at the Court of Session and at the hearing the board stated that a separate revenue account had been kept, though not published, and "was always available for shareholders to look at," though the shareholders had never been told of its existence. Gross revenue on the line in 1890 was stated to be £28,000, of which £10,800 was available for dividend: exactly the sum required to meet the 4% on capital. Interdict was refused and the scheme was approved at a special meeting of shareholders[36]. The episode showed a spirit of resistance among shareholders, especially ordinary shareholders, and although their dividend reached 2% again for August 1890-January 1891, their votes at the ordinary general meeting of 25 March 1891 forced a sum of £35,219, debited to permanent way reconstruction, to be charged to capital rather than to revenue, against the board's recommendation[37].

Other important decisions were made in 1891 about the company's operations in Aberdeen. In July a conference with the harbour commissioners approved a draft fourteen-year agreement for the introduction of steam locomotives at the harbour: three engines weighing around 22 tons were to be built, two for use and one as reserve[38]. At Waterloo Quay, office accommodation had become increasingly cramped, and the building itself perhaps rather too modest in appearance for a company which despite the parliamentary setbacks had grown in

The cliff-edge location of Macduff Station is very apparent in this shot of a train leaving for the South. The locomotive appears to be No. 63, Manson's first design for the GNSR. Engine shed on the right.
(Stenlake collection)

size and confidence, and in October the decision was taken to erect new offices in Guild Street, by the joint station, replacing the spinning and dyeing works of Hadden & Son, who had demanded £42,890 for the site, reduced by arbitration to £32,000. Ellis & Wilson of Aberdeen were chosen as architects, at a fee of 4% of accepted building tenders, though, if the company rejected their plan, only £100 was to be paid. The new offices were to have electric lighting[39].

Operating systems were criticised in the wake of an accident on 28 August, when the 3.40 pm suburban train from Dyce to Aberdeen ran into the 3.40 Aberdeen-Kintore goods, about 500 yards north of Kittybrewster, injuring several people. The passenger train had passed two signals at danger and it was said that heaped-up coal in the engine's bunker had obscured the view. Major Marindin, for the Board of Trade, condemned the company's regulations for block working as "far from satisfactory"[40]. Henry Tait, of the Amalgamated Society of Railway Servants (Scotland) kept up his intermittent attempts to obtain some recognition for the union from the Great North. Following an accident at Kinaldie on 18 November, when the 2.25 pm Up mail from Elgin to Aberdeen ran into the 1.15 Up goods from Keith, which was crossing on to the Down line to let it pass, Tait applied for permission, as representative of the engine crews, to travel to the Board of Trade inquiry in the special train laid on for the inspector. The company's answer was studiously non-committal: "if the Board of Trade intimate a desire that any person be accommodated in the special train they will give effect thereto"[41].

New representations from Peterhead about a southwards coast line were made in 1891, not to the unresponsive Great North but the North British Railway[42], without result. In the Gardenstown area, agitation continued for a railway to 'open up' the district, either by a line to Macduff, seen as commercially most useful, or to a junction at Plaidy, the cheaper option. There was also still talk about a complete coast line between Macduff and Fraserburgh, though the Rosehearty Branch remained stalled through inability to raise capital. Pressure for better services also increased. Ballater wanted an early goods and mail train, an improved station, and a crane. Banff was enraged by the withdrawal of its 8.50 pm train from Tillynaught, and there were suggestions of a "policy of revenge" by the GNS against previous complaints. Moffatt replied that the number of people using the train was "so exceedingly few" that he could not understand the reaction. Banff's spokesman, the solicitor Francis George, responded with a lengthy criticism of the Great North – the coast line had been built purely to be a thorn in the side of the Highland Railway, and "every consideration must give way for the gratification of this suicidal impulse." Instead of trying to push beyond Inverness, the Great North should improve its inadequate local services, and if the 8.50 pm were not restored, Banff should use Highland Railway services whenever possible[43]. But Banff was a long way from any Highland Railway station. Demands for improvement came also from Strathspey line users, for whom mixed trains were still the standard, with consequent shunting delays made worse by increasing traffic to and from the distilleries[44]. Through 1891 Moffatt and postal officials were arguing over a new contract, with Moffatt demanding a 60% jump to £32,000 a year and the PO men seeing no reason for any increase at all. The Highland was receiving £55,526 a year and Moffatt pointed out that the Great North's train mileage was not much less: 917,344 miles in the last half-year compared to the Highland Railway's 994,815, but the officials saw the GNS as "essentially a local line" and the Postmaster-General commented testily that "The GNS are the most close-fisted of their species", though it was acknowledged that the company performed its services satisfactorily "and in a very good spirit". In November the Post Office, fearing it might do worse under arbitration, agreed to a rate of £22,250 for five years[45].

CHAPTER 15
A Model Line, 1892 – 94

Goods rates – controversy renewed

Since September 1891, Great North shareholders' meetings had been held at the Palace Hotel. At the March 1892 gathering, Ferguson noted that the ordinary dividend was now 3%, partly due to the new deal with the Post Office. Shareholders' meetings of all railways usually had at least one regular attender who rose to criticise board actions, and at this time Lewis Bilton was the dissenting voice. Clearly seeing the Great North board as a self-perpetuating oligopoly, he attacked its standard procedure of appointing new directors between ordinary general meetings, suggesting that retiring directors deliberately timed their departures to make this possible. Ferguson responded that the directors were only "exercising their powers and responsibilities"; and the board had no difficulty in getting its way. Capital was increased by the issue of £200,000 of 4% preference stock, largely taken up by existing shareholders[1].

The issue of goods rates had not been settled by the Board of Trade's efforts to impose a scale of charges, and a new parliamentary joint committee was appointed in 1891-92 to consider objections both from the railways and the traders. These encounters were affected, though few people registered the fact at the time, by the fact that the country was passing through a phase of economic expansion, which led to some misapprehensions about long-term railway profitability. On 4 and 5 May 1892, William Moffatt appeared before the joint committee to represent the Great North's petition to have some of the Board's charges increased. Moffatt stressed the difficulties of the company's goods operations: small loads conveyed for relatively short distances over steeply-graded lines, with average earnings of £559 per mile on merchandise, compared to the Caledonian Railway's £2,438. Much of the cross-examination centred on the wealth of the Great North: its capital resources and the size of its dividends. Quizzed about the company's capital and its dividend payments, he had to explain that the company's ordinary stock was £920,000, of which £404,753 was a nominal addition made in 1866, leaving the true ordinary stock – "solid money" as one committee-man described it – at £513,379. Moffatt gave an explanation of the circumstances of 1866 to the committee – the absorption of unproductive branches into the company: "The reason why it [the additional ordinary share issue of 1866] was given was that ... at the time of the amalgamation in 1866, their stocks went down as low as £9, and it was thought they were entitled to this isssue ... "[2].

His questioner was the counsel representing the Aberdeen Harbour Commissioners, who wished to imply that the company was favouring its shareholders at the expense of its customers. Also present for the commissioners was Alex Copland, backed up by John Smith of the Aberdeen Agricultural Company. Discussion on actual rates centred on coal – the GNS carried 176,429 tons in 1891 and expected to lose £2,949 a year if the new charges were imposed. It wanted to increase the proposed maximum rate. Copland had two complaints against the railway company: firstly it charged too much for transport from the harbour to inland places; secondly it charged too little in through rates direct by rail from the collieries, undercutting the seaborne rate to Aberdeen. Counsel for the GNS pointed out that the harbour commissioners were simply trying to keep their traffic and their high dues: shore dues at Aberdeen were 4*d* per ton compared to 1*d* at Leith and 1 ½*d* at Dundee. The traffic at stake was large: in the year ended September 1891 the harbour had handled 354,700 tons of English, and 62,246 tons of Scotch, coal. It emerged that neither the GNS nor the harbour commissioners made any money out of coal to Buckie – it was much cheaper to send a coalboat direct to Buckie from the Firth of Forth ports, but there was real rivalry in short-haul traffic (up to 30 miles or so) from Aberdeen. Again the high usage of road engines is evidenced: Copland could send coal to Dess by road at five shillings a ton, inclusive of delivery "to the gentleman's cellars" and take back a return load; while the GNS charged 4*s* 6*d* per ton, for minimum 6-ton lots, to Dess Station and would apply further terminal and cartage charges[3]. Copland's evidence to the committee gave further details of Aberdeen Harbour's traffic: 7,000 tons of lime, 30,000 tons of paving stones, 24,800 tons of bones and manufactured manures, 2,500 tons of oil cake, 27,200 tons of wheat and oat flour, 14,400 tons of esparto grass imported and 12,900 tons of paper exported, 286,000 tons of grain, and 14,000 tons of oatmeal. He did not include any figures for fish. The harbour's total income from dues was around £52,000 a year. In his final remarks, counsel for the Harbour Commissioners pointed out that the Great North got a mileage bonus (payment for more miles than actually run) on coal both from the Caledonian and the North British, and also that the Board of Trade was allowing it to make terminal charges, adding "As to their pleading poverty, I think what we showed about them watering their capital proves there is no poverty to plead." For the Board of Trade, Lord Balfour of Burleigh admitted that the losses claimed by the GNS from the new rates were greater than the Board had intended, and the committee allowed a modest increase on the mileage rates for Class A goods (primarily coal) , and some minor modifications on Class C (chiefly grain and timber) to avert a claimed loss of around £1,200 a year. The company's main gain was in the re-classification of artificial manure as Class C, and permission to incorporate terminals in its charges[4]. That the new charges were not harmful to the company is shown in figures quoted in Chapter 23. Having got a schedule of charges, it remained for the company to incorporate these into its own rate books: every station needed one, setting out its charges for the various classes of goods to all other stations in Britain. With some 7,000 stations, and with any kind of goods liable to be sent between any two, this was a huge task for the railway companies, including the GNS, which, though it had only a hundred or so stations of its own, had to calculate rates to all the others. Innumerable adjustments, particularly for "smalls" and special deals within the maxima had to be made, and a completion date of the end of 1892 was imposed by the Board of Trade.

The railway in the landscape: Lumphanan Station and village, *c*.1900. *(Stenlake collection)*

Progress and expansion

In September 1892 the ordinary dividend was up to 3½% and for the first time a dividend was paid on the Deferred No. 1 shares, of ½%. Double tracking to Culter was opened on 24 September, and among new works reported were new crossing loops at Lumphanan, Dinnet, Lonmay, Brucklay, Strichen and Crathes[5]. Rolling stock, which had always been kept below the company's peak requirement, was now admitted to be inadequate for the traffic. In the February-July half-year 60 new wagons, fourteen meat vans and three third class carriages had been added, but from 1 October, the company had to borrow 100 vehicles from "our friends in the south". Shareholders at the ordinary general meeting were also informed that the board had decided to transfer the locomotive works to a new site at Inverurie. A team of directors had visited railway works at Swindon, Stratford, Doncaster, Wolverton and Kilmarnock, and had been impressed by the range of labour-saving machinery now available, also by the facilities for staff at Wolverton, with recreation grounds and a railwaymen's institute. William Dean, locomotive superintendent of the Great Western Railway, had been retained as a consultant on the new works. Raising of the directors' own emolument to £1,000 a year was unanimously approved[6]. In the following month an array of new schemes was unveiled, with a Bill providing for a fifteen-mile branch line from Ellon to Boddam, further doubling of the Deeside line as far as Park, and a reservoir and waterworks at Elrick, near Newmachar – this last to avoid Aberdeen Corporation's heavy charge for water. Seventy acres of land for the locomotive works at Inverurie were to be purchased, and the cost of these developments was estimated at £200,000[7]. Also included was the purchase of ground for a new resort-hotel at Port Errol, on the Boddam line. There was nothing new in a railway company owning hotels, but so far, they had been in city centres, adjacent to the station. The concept of the resort hotel, usually a 'hydropathic', was fashionable: Moffat had one since 1878, Peebles since 1881. For railway companies the great exemplar was the Banff Springs Hotel in Canada, opened by the Canadian Pacific Railway in 1888, and the Great North pioneered the idea of the Scottish railway hotel as a destination in its own right, with golf course, spa, sea bathing and other attractions.

An e.g.m. on 25 January 1893 approved the Bill, which also included a proposal to establish a savings bank. Although a "large and prosperous" savings bank was already connected with the company, there was no power to make it "part and parcel" of the Great North's concern. Depositors would now have the entire undertaking as security. The board also proposed to join the Railway Clearing House's superannuation fund for salaried staff; benefit funds already existed but now it was felt a properly established fund was necessary[8]. At the Palace Hotel, where Miss McKilliam was evidently a very effective manager, additional floors had been added on the east and south sides and her salary was increased to £200 a year in August 1892 and then £300 in January 1893[9].

Improved services from Inverness via Aberdeen to Edinburgh and Glasgow were introduced in January 1893. A new train left Inverness at 9.00 am, reaching Aberdeen at 12.55 pm, with onward connections to Glasgow, arriving at 6.00 pm by the Caledonian Railway and 6.25 by the North British Railway, and to Edinburgh, arriving at 5.55 (CR) and 5.20 (NBR). The Down trains left Edinburgh at 1.55 and 1.50 pm, and Glasgow at 1.20 and 2.00 pm, by the North British and Caledonian respectively. The North British train reached Aberdeen at 6.00 pm and the Caledonian at 6.20, and an Inverness connection left at 6.40, arriving in Inverness at 10.40[10]. Though it took over an hour more from Inverness than the Highland's Limited Mail, for any traveller starting east of Forres it was a preferable way, and even from Inverness it offered a change of scenery and (via the North British) the excitement of crossing the two great bridges.

"A little adhesive" – goods rates again

The Board of Trade refused to extend the deadline for fixing the new goods rates from 1 January 1893 and was taken by surprise when the railway companies, having had insufficient time to work out the details, simply applied the Board's own maximum rates from that date. Like most companies, the Great North failed to complete the exercise within what Ferguson called an "utterly inadequate" time. From January till March, the officers were engaged "night and day" in making revisions and adjustments, and meanwhile the GNS charged everyone the full permitted rate, to a chorus of indignation. A meeting at Banchory protested against a 50% increase on mixed goods and smaller items. The GNS now charged any consignment of bagged oats under two tons as if it were two tons. The customer saw this as exploitation, since seed was often sold in quantities much less than two tons; the company, carrying less than two tons in a truck built to carry six or eight, saw it as a reasonable compromise[11]. The government appointed yet another select committee on railway rates in May 1893. Many companies had reverted to their 1892 rates in the face of customer protests, but it was noted that the Great North was not among them, sticking to the rates of 1 January 1893. Sir James Whitehead MP commented that "They are a little adhesive sometimes in the Great North of Scotland"[12]. Its deliberations resulted in the Railway & Canal Traffic Act of 1894, which compelled all railways to prove that "special circumstances" required any increase in goods carriage rates made after 1 January 1893, if challenged by a customer. The virtual impossibility of proving such circumstances with the statistics and systems available ruled out any increase which a customer chose to dispute[13]. On 5 July 1894, in a typical challenge before the Act became law, questions were asked in Parliament about the GNS and Highland companies making a large increase in the rates for carrying flour, rice, grain, barley, pease, etc., to and from Lossiemouth Harbour, which had recently been deepened at a cost of £20,000 but was losing trade because of these increases. The GNS disputed the figures and denied any intention to put Lossiemouth Harbour at a disadvantage. But the select committee had already noted how both companies had colluded in raising the rates for carrying grain, oil cake and manure to some of the smaller ports, with the aim of discouraging onward transport by sea[14] (here the Great North's policy had turned a full circle since John Stewart's time).

Demand for new lines, and the Deeside Suburban

At the March 1893 half-yearly meeting, the question of a railway from Turriff to Maud was raised. The route of this Central Buchan Railway, if ever built, was hotly contested among villages which felt they must be on it, with Cairnbanno and New Deer against New Pitsligo. Three different possibilities were proposed, and the coastal line from Macduff to Fraserburgh also still had its advocates. The GNS kept largely aloof, though willing to work the line. Ferguson had said that land for it should be given gratis, later claiming it had been by way of a joke, but soon it became company policy. By September another new scheme was proposed by Colonel Innes of Learney, a branch off the Deeside line to the agricultural area of Echt and Skene. Ferguson remained non-committal and Colonel Innes praised his diplomacy, combining "the necessary reticence and caution of a chairman with the urbanity and courtesy that are agreeable to the shareholders"[15]. Campaigning went on into the new year. The Macduff & Fraserburgh committee sent a deputation to the GNS in January: 315 boats were working between the two ports and over 4,000 tons of fish a year were being landed at the small but newly deepened harbour of Gardenstown (population 1,120 in 1891); and another group came to interest the directors in a line from Tillynaught via Aberchirder to Rothienorman, taking in the Glendronach Distillery en route. William Ferguson noted somewhat wryly that five lines were now being proposed: the Great North would make rough surveys in all cases and endeavour to ascertain the likely costs[16].

James Johnson's handsome class R 0-4-4T showed a striking similarity to engines on the Midland Railway where he had trained under his father S. W. Johnson. With accelerative power matched by the quick-acting Westinghouse brake, the class proved ideal for the sprightly Aberdeen suburban services.

Bieldside, opened on 1 June 1897, was a passenger-only station, for Deeside suburban trains. The engine appears to be fitted with a snowplough. *(Stenlake collection)*

The multi-proposal Bill for new projects became an Act on 24 August 1893. A senior Liberal figure, Lord Morley, had queried the issue of new preference stock by a company which already had three times as much preference as ordinary stock, to which Moffatt replied that "the circumstances of the Company were peculiar" and they could not see their way to increasing the ordinary stock[17]. Its recently-attained 3% level of dividend was unlikely to enthuse investors. A new 'Further Powers' Bill was lodged for 1894, for a deviation on the Boddam line, and a further assault on Highland territory. The seven-year agreement between the two companies had expired in July 1893 and the Highland company had declined to renew it and withdrawn any facilities which the GNS could not claim under an Act of Parliament. Once again the GNS was seeking running powers between Elgin and Inverness, with a branch of its own to the Caledonian Canal at Muirtown. It sought loading and unloading facilities at Kyleakin and Strome Ferry, and authority to place its own officers and company servants at Wick, Thurso, Muir of Ord, Inverness, Nairn, Forres, Dalnaspidal, Newtonmore and Kingussie; and for Great North of Scotland and Highland Railway tickets to be interchangeable. By March 1894 a somewhat more reasonable attitude prevailed at Inverness, and the GNS withdrew its application for running powers and an extended presence at Highland Railway stations, though still "far from satisfied" at the extent to which their trains were held up by delays on the Highland Railway line between Perth and Forres[18].

At the end of 1893, 29 December, the 9.10 am train from Keith to Dufftown was diverted into a siding at Drummuir and collided with standing wagons. One man, jumping from the engine, was killed and several people slightly injured, including two fishwives from Buckie. The pointsman, James Blackie, was prosecuted at Banff Sheriff Court in February and pleaded Not Guilty. The jury agreed and he was acquitted, to applause. Westinghouse automatic brakes were fitted to both engine and carriages, but could not function because three goods wagons had been placed behind the engine. A more unusual type of accident occurred to the 1.45 pm goods train from Aberdeen to Ballater on 4 January 1894 when the coupling between the first and second wagons parted. The engine continued with the crew apparently unaware of the lightening of its load until the driver, applying the brake for the tunnel west of Aboyne Station, saw the wagons coming down the incline behind him, and put on steam again, to lessen the impact. The wagons collided with the rump of the train, and the guard was killed[19].

Since the completion of double track as far as Culter, capacity existed for the intended suburban service on the Deeside line, but plans had been in suspension for two years because of difficulties in acquiring land for enlarged and additional stations. At the ordinary general meeting on 22 March 1894, Ferguson announced that £4,500 had been charged to the capital account for land acquisition, in addition to £26,854 spent on improved signalling and new sidings, access roads and bridges. From 2 July the Deeside suburban service began, with new stations at Holburn Street, Pitfodels, and West Cults. Bieldside was added in June 1897. Eight trains each way formed the initial service, taking 22 minutes into Aberdeen and 21 to Culter. By 1900 the number of trains had doubled, and congestion on the line from Ferryhill to the joint station was a constant problem.

The joint station, Boddam Branch and light railways

Certain parties, notably Aberdeen's town council and chamber of commerce, had felt for some time that a comprehensive approach to modernisation of the station was needed. Lord Provost David Stewart (son of John Stewart, and a director of the GNS since 1891) had to declare his interest and remain on the sideline as a council committee debated how to overcome the Great North's "obdurate resistance" to enlargement, deciding in the end to make an approach to the Board of Trade or the Railway Commissioners[20]. One reason for the Great North's apparent laggardliness was the protracted dispute with the North British company over its use of the station. In November 1893 the House of Lords had upheld the appeal made by the joint station committee against the Court of Session's judgement in favour of the North British, on the basis that the Scottish North Eastern Railway in 1866 had had no right to make an agreement involving property partly owned by the GNS without that company's consent, and costs were awarded against the North British Railway[21]. The North British now had a Bill in Parliament with clauses relating to this, following an agreement made with the Great North, the Caledonian, and the joint committee, allowing it to use the station on payment of £1,500 yearly to the joint committee from 14 November 1893, subject to revision depending on traffic levels and if the station were enlarged. It would also pay the Great North £7,500 in settlement of all previous claims. This ruling finally cleared the way for action in enlarging the joint station, as neither the Great North nor the Caledonian Railway were inclined to spend large sums on this work until it was confirmed that the North British would have to pay to use it[22]. Keeping up to date with technical developments, the engineer's department was reorganised, with Patrick Barnett as engineer-in-chief, supported by Mr Mann as permanent way engineer and Mr Horn as electrical engineer. It had already been decided by the joint committee that Aberdeen Station should be lit by electricity[23].

Charles Brand, the contractor for the Boddam Branch, began work on 8 September, when the Countess of Errol cut the first sod, at Ellon. Lunch followed for 550 guests, in a marquee in the grounds of Ellon Castle. With granite quarries to be served, the Boddam fishery, and the Cruden Bay brickworks, as well as the proposed hotel, the 15-mile line was regarded as a safe project. Land was being provided at a very moderate feu duty, around 10s per acre, and several proprietors had consented to give limited guarantees against an operating loss. The branch was designed to normal standards, but light railways were forecast as the next generation of rural development. The concept was not new: back in 1868 an Act had allowed for the construction of light railways, with a maximum speed of 25 mph, and "signals, interlocking etc. may be dispensed with", and another Act of 1874 allowed the Board of Trade to authorise certain railways, but very little advantage had been taken of them. Now legislation to further simplify the procedure was under discussion, stimulating the already lively interest in new local lines in the north-east. A line from Ballindalloch to Tomintoul was proposed, also to serve the Glenlivet Distillery, where the furnaces beneath the whisky stills burned several thousand tons of coal each year; and the iron and manganese deposits in the Lecht Hills were once again cited as justification for a railway. The five schemes for railways across Buchan remained in competition with one another. At the Ellon Castle lunch William Ferguson informed the guests that it was very much in the minds of the GNS directors to consider how far the districts now unserved might be opened up by means of light railways[24].

Mixed trains, and another attempt on Inverness

In the half-year between February and July 1894, the company's gross revenue for the first time exceeded £200,000. The ordinary dividend was $3\frac{1}{2}\%$ and for the second time a dividend on deferred ordinary shares was paid, a slender $\frac{1}{4}\%$. Total revenue was £200,675, equivalent to 50.22d per train mile, up from 48.66d in the previous comparable half-year. Cost per train mile had risen too, but to a lesser degree, 25.27d against 24.39d, but Ferguson forecast a further rise. The Board of Trade, empowered by the Regulation of Railways Act (1889) to compel railways to use automatic brakes on passenger trains, had circulated all companies to this effect on 24 October 1889. The Great North, like the Highland, ignored it, as far as mixed trains were concerned. Mixed trains were seen as the most cost-effective way of providing a service on lines with limited traffic, and operational efficiency required the goods vehicles to be next to the engine, which precluded use of the automatic brake since the GNS had no goods trucks (except fish trucks to run with fast passenger trains) fitted either with the brake or the brake pipe to carry compressed air. Now the Board of Trade was toughening its stance and insisting that the passenger carriages be marshalled in front of the goods trucks, and Ferguson warned that this meant no more mixed trains, with a "serious reduction of travelling facilities to the public"[25]. James Johnson resigned in August and was replaced by another Englishman, William Pickersgill, aged 33, a district locomotive superintendent on the Great Eastern Railway, at £500 plus a house. The company's policy of employing relatively young locomotive superintendents, in their first top job, reflected both its relatively small locomotive stock, 123 in 1894, and the fact that established engineers usually earned a lot more than the GNS paid its senior managers.

Late 1894 saw the outbreak of railway warfare in the Great Glen, when the West Highland and Highland companies both lodged Bills for railways to link Inverness with the newly-opened West Highland line. The Great North, seeing the threat of a new Inverness-Glasgow route, renewed its application for running powers between Elgin and Inverness, with a Bill providing for double track between Elgin and Dalcross, except for the Findhorn Viaduct, to be laid at the GNS's expense (the road-bed already allowed for a double line). The Highland had reverted to an obstructive and frequently provocative attitude, with consequent delays and disputes. A court case, brought by the GNS over apportionment of through rates between Aberdeen and Inverness, concluded with an award in favour of the Great North, confirming the division set by arbitration in 1886. About £5,000 was to be re-apportioned, plus "a considerable accumulation since July last year." An article in the *Aberdeen Journal* entitled 'Aberdeen and the Impending Railway Fight' noted the Great North's five attempts to get running powers through to Inverness, and the likelihood that if a Great Glen line were made, "a large portion of the northern traffic which legitimately belongs to Aberdeen as the chief northern port and business centre, would be carried away south"[26]. In February the two Great Glen Bills were withdrawn but the Great North maintained its Bill, and as much support as possible was mustered, from the traders of Nairn to the Aberdeen Branch of the United Kingdom Commercial Travellers' Association – its members being intensive railway users – though the latter had complaints about both companies, the Highland's delays and the "rudeness" of Great North staff. Aberdeen Town Council resolved to send a deputation to London to support the Bill, and a total of 75 petitions in favour were sent to Westminster. At this time James Bryce, Liberal MP for Aberdeen South, was President of the Board of Trade (1894-95) but pronounced himself impartial in the matter[27].

The GNSR offices constructed next to the Station Hotel in Aberdeen in 1894: a contrast to the original modest premises at Waterloo. Included was a palatial board room, one of the finest which the LNER inherited. *(Keith Fenwick)*

CHAPTER 16
Diversification, 1895 – 1897

Another disappointment

William Ferguson was always capable of saying unusual things for a railway chairman, and presiding at the company's annual staff reunion at the Albert Hall, Aberdeen, on 15 February 1895, he said he was pleased to note the recent increases in the wage bill – "a fair and good day's pay for a fair and good day's work" – and that he had long felt the workers should share in the company's success. The half-yearly meeting on 20 March was held in the boardroom of the new "splendid offices" in Guild Street, and the chairman noted that (despite his previous remarks on the subject) the abandonment of some mixed trains had added 54,394 train miles in the August-January half-year, taking the total for the first time into seven figures, at 1,006,178 miles. The company was still running a few mixed trains, by agreement with the Board of Trade, but this was on a temporary basis. On the running powers Bill, he was confident that "the time had come" and that the Highland Railway would benefit rather than lose out as a result[1]. In the last weeks of May, supporters and opponents were heard by a parliamentary committee under Sir John Kennaway, MP for Honiton. Moffatt, as the Great North's chief witness, said that the facility clauses granted to the GNS in the Act of 1884 had failed to meet the realities of the situation and that only full powers to reach Inverness would enable it to provide a reliable service. For the Highland Railway, Dougall suggested that the Bill was unnecessary – in 1894 only 28,881 passengers had been transferred between the two companies, with 905 parcels. Goods from Highland to Great North stations amounted to 17,221 tons. Such traffic, already shared, did not justify running powers. Possibly this argument impressed the committee, as the Bill was thrown out on 30 May[2]. As with many previous committees and commissions, Kennaway's committee seemed to think that the two companies should simply stop sparring and settle down to peaceful co-existence. This was a superficial appreciation of a long and deep-seated antagonism which, though nourished especially in Inverness, existed on both sides, with long memories of broken promises and attempts to steal a march on each other. Though disappointed again, the Great North made a quick approach to the Highland for a meeting, in order to follow up the committee's recommendation about co-operation.

Railways international and local

In July 1895 the company played host for a day to the delegates who had been attending the International Railway Conference in London, taking them on a special train to Ballater and coach to Braemar. In a speech to the visitors from Russia, Germany, France, the USA and other countries, Ferguson said that "It was now recognised that the leading men in the railway services of the world were the biggest men of the age"[3]. During that summer, overnight 'racing' between the East and West Coast routes from London to Aberdeen flowered briefly. The Great North was not involved and passengers from the south, deposited at the joint station shortly after 5 am, had a lengthy wait before the GNS's morning departures[4].

In the limited sphere of north-eastern Scotland, railway development remained a preoccupation. A GNS survey between Ballindalloch and Glen Livet was excitedly assumed to be the active planning of a line[5]. In September, news of a revived scheme for extending the Alford line into upper Strathdon led to a meeting in Rhynie, to promote an alternative line from Kennethmont past Rhynie to Mossat and Kildrummy, and the merits of both schemes were hotly debated. An alternative line to Tomintoul from Dufftown was proposed, and a committee formed[6]. The Great North made no commitments, though it announced plans to build new stations at Aboyne and Elgin. There was much to evaluate, including the fact that around 200 steam traction engines were at work on Aberdeenshire roads, more than in any other county in Great Britain apart from Kent. "Road trains" coming into Aberdeen were regarded as a public nuisance[7]. The weight of a traction engine with two loaded wagons was greater than many bridges over the railway could safely bear.

Money to spend

At the time of the Scottish railwaymen's strike in January 1891, placatory remarks had been made by the GNS about a ten-hour working day, but in the expansionary years that had followed, nothing had been done to reduce working hours. Some 50 to 60 locomotive men gathered in Aberdeen on 20 October 1895 to protest about excessive hours and agreed to seek a maximum twelve-hour day. Complaints were also made that the eight-hour gap between shifts was often shortened, and that eye tests were used as an excuse for sacking men. The GNS had a stricter test for vision and colour recognition than the other companies, with eyesight tests imposed every five years up to the age of 60, and two-yearly thereafter, with additional tests in the event of an accident or serious illness. William Pickersgill, the new locomotive superintendent, and his assistant McCombie, were blamed: a memorial [memorandum of appeal] to Pickersgill was said to be a waste of paper and ink, and the meeting resolved to approach the Board of Trade directly. The Amalgamated Society of Railway Servants (Scotland) became involved, and took charge of the issue[8]. Genuine as the grievances were, there is also a hint here of the way in which the 590 close-knit locomotive department workers might test the mettle of a new chief from another company – eventually Pickersgill established a good relationship with his men. Still, it was obvious to the staff that the company had money to spend: in December it announced further doubling of the main line, from Gartly to Insch, and with the aim of having a permanent way "second to none", a new system of ballasting was used: "a heavy load of rough granite blocks is first laid, on which the sleepers are placed for carrying the steel rails of

Banchory Station, after rebuilding in 1902. The Aberdeen Commercial and Lime companies' premises are in the background. (*Stenlake collection*)

exceptionally heavy calibre, and between the sleepers and over the stone is spread a layer of small broken metal. The rails consequently rest on what is practically a macadamised road …" Fifteen new engines were to be purchased from Neilsons of Glasgow, and it proposed to build 40-50 new, fully up-to-date corridor carriages at Kittybrewster, with electric lighting and lavatories. A "commodious" new station was to built at Banchory and another at Tillynaught, with a covered platform. The possibility of a hotel at Ballater was still being considered[9], and several sites south of the Dee were examined by the hotels committee, with the thought of piping the mineral waters from Pananich Wells to a "hydro", or alternatively purchasing the Invercauld Arms Hotel in the town. Plans for the resort hotel at Port Errol were well in hand by now, with a 55-bedroom design selected in January, amended in November, to cost £15,000[10].

This substantial programme prompted a deputation from Fraserburgh, reiterating the demand for a better station than the present "wretched affair". As modernisation gradually proceeded, the difference between the new and the old must have seemed ever more stark. There were still bad old practices at many stations, deprecated by the Board of Trade and often resulting in injuries. The stationmaster at Murtle, William Craib, caught by a steel wire against a post while a wagon was being "roped", in the dark, from a siding, had both legs almost severed, and died[11].

Fifty years from the company's incorporation, a "jubilee" ordinary general meeting was held on 18 March 1896. The ordinary dividend was $3^{3}/_{4}\%$. In 20 years, the Great North's annual revenue had risen from £265,211 (1875-6) to £416,597 in the year ending 31 January 1896. With virtually no mixed trains now operating, train miles had risen to 1,099,061 in the August-January half-year, but despite this, working expenses at 45.8% of gross revenue were among the lowest in the country. Referring to the current agricultural depression, which had brought renewed complaints about goods carriage charges, Ferguson pointed out that railways helped to alleviate rural distress by their large contribution to local rates. He advised farmers to make better use both of the company's scale of bulk charges by combining loads, and of its special rates for small consignments of items such as butter and poultry. To calls for rate reductions, he had to say that "a railway is not a charitable institution." As far as further new lines were concerned, the directors were waiting for the forthcoming Light Railways Act before taking action.

Inverness – battle resumed

The resignation of Andrew Dougall as general manager of the Highland Railway, in February 1896, removed a dedicated adversary, and the *Aberdeen Journal* hoped that an "intelligent, conciliating and enterprising policy will be pursued"[12], but old issues still prevailed. In July 1896 the House of Lords was considering an appeal from the Highland Railway against a judgement of the Railway Commissioners relating to how charges on inter-company traffic should be implemented. The Highland argued that James Beale's arbitration of 1886 expired with the seven-year agreement made in June 1893, and that the proviso made in 1865, that rates and charges were to be calculated as if the traffic had passed over the shortest distance the lines of both companies could give (viz., via Mulben rather than either of the GNS routes to Elgin), should be applied. The Great North claimed that the 1884 Act, which provided that each company should charge by actual mileage, overrode the 1865 statute. The Lords agreed, and dismissed the appeal[13]. In August the Highland went to the Court of Session to seek an interdict against Great North servants working on the platforms at Inverness. On 14 July, Mr David Beddie, "ostentatiously dressed in the uniform of an assistant stationmaster" had been seen helping passengers into the two GNS through carriages for Aberdeen. The Great North claimed that the Highland Railway staff were not attending properly to its passengers. After an exchange of letters the Highland Railway withdrew its application and the GNS withdrew Mr Beddie, on the understanding that it "will have no ground for complaint regarding passenger accommodation"[14]. An Aberdeen historian claimed that the Great North's best train from Aberdeen to Elgin in the summer of 1896, covering $80^{3}/_{4}$ miles in 118 minutes, was "one of the fastest in the kingdom"[15].

Rumours in autumn 1896 that the Great North was about to make another attempt on Inverness were borne out in November when the Railway & Canal Commissioners began to consider cross-petitions from the Great North of Scotland and Highland Railway on traffic between Aberdeen and Inverness. The commissioners might have felt rather wearily that they had been here before, but it was obvious that they had failed to resolve the situation. The Highland was still holding trains at Forres if there were delays on the Perth line, and so missing southbound connection at Aberdeen, and Moffatt also made a cogent case for exchange at Elgin. In 1885 the GNS had nine trains a day to Elgin via Craigellachie; now with the Buckie route as well, there were 25, and the fastest service between Aberdeen and Inverness went via the coast line. Passengers were deserting the Keith connection – in

**The railway in the landscape: Buckie, looking westwards. The confined space
for railway lines is apparent. (*Stenlake collection*)**

July-August that summer, 1,566 transferred from the 6.45 am train from Aberdeen at Elgin, and only 175 at Keith. Only two trains each way carried through carriages (GNS stock) between Aberdeen and Inverness and both companies were resisting more, the GNS refusing to take on Highland Railway carriages at Keith from the Mulben route, and the Highland Railway refusing to take carriages off the 6.45 am express at Elgin. The Highland still wanted exchange at Keith only, on the grounds that there was a single station there, part-leased by the Highland Railway, while at Elgin there were two separate stations. After July 1893 it no longer had a booking office at Aberdeen, and its counsel suggested that the Great North booking clerks were deliberately steering passengers on to their own line. Both companies made proposals for revised schedules, though the Highland scheme would increase Great North train mileage by 60,000, and its own not all, while the GNS proposal would impose 37,481 additional miles on itself, and 23,162 on the Highland[16].

While awaiting the commissioners' verdict, the GNS lodged a new Bill for running powers through to Inverness, double track (at its expense) between Elgin and Dalcross, and a joint station at Elgin. At Inverness, the Great North was to have its own terminus on Longman Road, north of the Highland station, and branches to the River Ness (Thornbush Quay) and the Caledonian Canal at Muirtown. Establishment of a hotel at Ballater was also included. There was a wider context to the Inverness scheme: once again a railway through the Great Glen was being actively promoted, with three rival Bills[17], and the Great North would certainly have felt a need to protect its own position. Also the Highland Railway was at last building its cut-off line between Aviemore and Inverness, with completion anticipated in 1898. The resultant speeding-up could be expected to siphon off a large proportion of traffic from the line to Aberdeen. In December the commissioners gave their decisions. The number of trains inter-connecting at Keith and Elgin should be equal as far as possible, with connection times of ten minutes desirable. Through carriages were to be exchanged at both places, with the Highland to take them from its station to the GNSR at Elgin, and vice versa. The Great North was to be allowed to have an attendant in its through carriages to Inverness. A Highland request for two additional Great North trains on the Strathspey line to Boat of Garten was refused, and the two companies were given six weeks to come up with an agreed schedule. No order was made as to costs, which with the Dean of Faculty representing the Highland Railway and the Lord Advocate for the GNS, would not be small[18].

Fun, fish and Fraserburgh

Dr David Stewart (Hon. LL.D of Aberdeen University), who had been Lord Provost between 1891 and 1895, was knighted by Queen Victoria in June 1896. For his next arrival in Aberdeen Mr Duguid, superintendent of the joint station, arranged for detonators to be set off as the train approached. July saw the annual conference of railway general managers and superintendents held in Aberdeen, and the delegates were treated to a trip to Elgin and back in a train of four new corridor carriages, one composite, and a Caledonian Railway saloon[19].

The notoriously fickle herring shoals had moved to the waters off Orkney in 1894, when the GNS chartered a steamer to carry fish from Stromness to Lossiemouth for onward carriage by train[20]. In May 1896 they were prolific off the north west coast, and every evening great quantities from Stornoway merchants were unloaded at Strome Ferry and shipped on by the Highland, both via Keith and the GNS, and directly south on the Perth line. The Great North accelerated its Keith-Aberdeen train so that the East Coast timing to London matched that of the West Coast lines. A fish train, drawn by an engine "of the ordinary stock" driven by Driver Pearson of Keith, ran the 53¾ miles from Keith to Aberdeen in 53 minutes, with the 21¼ miles between Insch and Dyce covered in 19 minutes, at speeds up to 70 mph. Despite higher catches, Peterhead's harbour branch was not seeing much activity and the seaward end was truncated to help extension of the Port Henry Harbour[21].

Fraserburgh, with harbour extensions being planned, and still agitating for a new station and better carriages, at least got an improved mail service from 1 August. Early-morning mail left Aberdeen at 4.45 am on a goods train, arriving at around 8.00, but the London mail, having arrived at Aberdeen at 7.35 am, was not taken forward until 9.25, and reached the town after eleven o' clock. Now a new train left Aberdeen at 8.00 am and was in Peterhead at 9.35 and Fraserburgh at 9.45. And the directors came to Fraserburgh to look at a possible site for a new station, on reclaimed ground adjacent to the south pier[22].

Manson's class P of 1890, along with his slightly larger class Q of the same year, had eight-wheeled tenders to carry an additional one ton of coal and 900 gallons of water compared with the six-wheeled version. Three of each class were built, including no. 13 illustrated here. *(Keith Fenwick collection)*

Trams above, trains below. Union Bridge, Aberdeen, after its widening in 1908. *(Stenlake collection)*

The Light Railways Act

On 14 August the Light Railways Act became law. Among its provisions were that new schemes must be published in October and lodged with a new body, the Light Railway Commissioners, by 1 November, with 1 May and 1 November as the lodging dates in future years. The commissioners would assess the proposal and make recommendation to the Board of Trade. It was now time for the backers of the various schemes to produce their plans, and a meeting at Forgue in April had hoped to put the Rothienorman-Aberchirder line at the head of the region's queue. A deputation sent to meet the GNS board was told that for any light railway to be worked by the company, local interests would have to provide "material support" and land would have to be given free. Meanwhile, a party of directors was going to visit the Continent, to look at light railway development[23]. A large and influential deputation came to see the directors on 30 September about a Central Buchan Railway, though its route remained in dispute. Ferguson put forward his own preference for a railway branching from the Fraserburgh line between Strichen and Brucklay, running via New Pitsligo and Cuminestown to Turriff and on to Huntly – he had not forgotten his promise to a parliamentary committee in 1882 of an east-west line between Turriff and New Maud. The estimated cost was £185,000, but he said the board needed more time to discuss the matter (an indication that the board was by no means of one mind). Two separate deputations for light railways into Glen Livet followed, one for a line from Dufftown, the other for a line from Ballindalloch. Ferguson promised that the board would give them serious consideration[24].

The Tramways bid

Two other issues in Aberdeen engaged the company in August, one quite minor, the other causing a degree of national interest as well as a noisy local controversy. The lesser one followed a case at Perth Station, where that town's hotelkeepers won the right to send their boot-boys into the station to compete with the railway-owned Station Hotel. The Douglas and Imperial hotels in Aberdeen attempted to send their men past the barrier at Aberdeen, only to be resisted by the station staff, at the orders of A.G. Reid[25]. Far more important was the Great North's attempt to take over the Aberdeen Tramway Company. In every city in the land, street tramways had been opposed by railway companies, on the grounds of being unnecessary, or offering unfair competition, but the opposition had rarely been successful. Aberdeen had had horse-trams since 1874, and by 1896 the network of routes extended out to Kittybrewster and Bridge of Dee, but the tramway company had been only a modest commercial success and was now faced with the need to raise capital to electrify its system, as other cities were doing. The Great North's proposal to take over the enterprise, the first action of the kind by a railway company, was hailed by some parliamentarians as "novel and important" and William Moffatt as a pioneer[26]. It was indeed a forward-looking plan, with an eye on possible links with light railways out into the countryside; and if successful would have given Aberdeen an integrated transport system unique in Great Britain.

A letter from Moffatt informed the town council that subject to its approval, the GNS had made a provisional arrangement to acquire the Aberdeen Tramways Company. This would facilitate the construction of light railways out into the countryside, especially the proposed line to Skene and Echt. Electric traction would be used. The price was £90,384: £16 per share on the Aberdeen Tramway Company's 5,649 shares, plus relief of its mortgage and debts. Immediately the council was sharply divided, with a substantial number of councillors arguing for a takeover of the tramways by the council itself. The hotly-debated merits of public and private ownership of an urban transport system prefigured an issue that still resounds in the 21st century. Council approval of the GNS purchase was needed because the tramway company's lease would revert to it on termination. Though the city by now had a bloc of "socialist" councillors brought into office by a much-widened electorate, the argument was financial as much as political, revolving around whether the ratepayers (householders and businesses liable to pay local taxes) would have to subsidise a cheap municipal tram service, or whether it would bring profits to the city coffers and reduce the rates. A majority voted for municipal takeover and the council would not even meet the Great North directors to discuss the matter; its stated position being "no party trading for profit to shareholders to come between the ratepayers and the acquisition of the tramways"[27].

At the same time, the town council was still pressing the Great North about the need to enlarge the joint station and provide "a station worthy of the city as a great railway terminus." A deputation from the council and other local bodies was told by William Ferguson that there were "difficulties which he cannot explain"[28]. These may have related to the Caledonian Railway, which felt no urgency about enlarging the joint station largely for the benefit of the Great North's Deeside suburban service.

The forward looking Great North purchased some hopper ballast wagons and a plough brake van in the mid-1890s, to a design used by the Great Western Railway, to speed up the job of spreading ballast. Some were derailed near Strichen, to the diversion of local boys. *(Great North of Scotland Railway Association)*

Elgin's third engine shed was this four-road structure built by the GNS in 1902, replacing the Morayshire Railway's second shed, of 1863, which still stands nearby. (*Stenlake collection*)

Only about a dozen shareholders came to the Great North's ordinary general meeting on 16 September to hear Ferguson's review of the past six months' activities. The ordinary dividend was $3\frac{1}{2}\%$ and $\frac{5}{8}\%$ was paid on the deferred ordinary shares. Now only a handful of mixed trains were being run, and train mileage had climbed to 1,118,405. Among other statistics, the company had carried 101 funerals. He expressed disappointment at slow progress on the Boddam line and regret at the council's decision on the tramways, and was not encouraging about the economic prospects of light railways following a report from the general manager, chief engineer and locomotive superintendent, who had been sent to inspect various continental systems[29].

Four men were injured in the cab of engine No. 52 in an accident at Knock in the small hours of 29 July. It was pulling a ballast train of twelve loaded wagons, a brake van, and two carriages holding 36 workmen, and had left Portknockie at 10.30 pm, bound for Grange. At 12.50 am it was diverted into a siding at Knock, hit the buffers, and the engine was derailed. The stationmaster at Knock knew of the train but misread the staff circular specifying its route: he expected it to be using the Rothes line via Keith. There was a ballast quarry and siding at Glen of Rothes and the train actually had originated there. On the day, the stationmaster had been on duty for 18 hours, due to the Banff annual holiday, and a Sheriff's inquiry at Banff, with a jury, accepted that the circular was open to misconstruction and exonerated him. The train had passed a danger signal, but the driver in evidence stated that "in ballast trains they did not take account of signals"[30].

Defeated in the tramways contest, the company was still confronted with the various proposals and demands for light railways. At this time the only one of serious interest to the board appears to have been that to Skene and Echt, west of Aberdeen. It was intended to link it to the tramway network[31], with running powers through the city centre to Waterloo. Features of Bavarian, Saxon, Dutch and Belgian cross-country light railway systems were proposed, with stopping places instead of stations. In the application to the Light Railway Commissioners it was set out as two lines, one from the western terminus of the Aberdeen District Tramways at the junction of Bayview Road and Queen's Road West (at that time almost in open country) to Kirkton of Echt ($13\frac{3}{4}$ miles); and a short link from a junction with the GNS Waterloo line at the bridge under Nelson Street to a south-facing junction with the tramline on King street. Estimated cost was £60,000. A rival scheme, of very similar nature, including a branch to Waterton of Echt, was simultaneously put forward by a group of local businessmen, with an estimated cost of £103,571[32]. No other project was formally proposed, though in December Lonmay Parish Council set up a committeee to discuss with adjacent parishes the possibility of a light railway from Fraserburgh to St. Combs. Ideas for Aberdeen were still fluid, and at an e.g.m. of Great North shareholders on 30 December, the chairman unveiled a wider scheme, reminiscent of the "circumbendibus", a suburban line diverging westwards just north of Kittybrewster, to meet the Deeside line around Holburn Street, with trains operating a circular service from the joint station, and a connection to the proposed Echt tramway for goods and livestock. "Circular suburban lines are being built in all our great cities," he proclaimed, and expressed the hope that at agreed hours, goods wagons might be carried along the city tramways[33]. Curiously, however, the Bill introduced for this line took it no further than a terminus at Oldmill, just west of the Rubislaw Quarry[34]. In the event, the proposal was withdrawn.

Rising revenues, and splitting the stock

From 1 May 1896 the mail contract rate was raised to £26,000 a year, and in March 1897 a new four-year contract was signed[35]. The continuing boom in the whisky industry led to new distilleries, increased revenue and improved rail access. A branch from Carron to Dailuaine was again under negotiation in April, with an estimated cost of £5,000 and an annual cost of £1,165 including 6% on the initial cost. The distillery company would pay 6*d* per ton on draff, and 9*d* per ton on other traffic, in addition to the rate charged to Carron, on a total annual tonnage of around 15,000. This would leave a probable deficiency of 10 $\frac{1}{2}$ *d* per ton on working the branch. The line was not laid until May 1906[36]. At Balmenach, a new siding was installed at the end of a two-mile tramway from Cromdale laid in 1897, so that the distillery's branch engine could be utilised to drive machinery. Sidings were also agreed for a new distillery at Towiemore, two miles north of Drummuir in Strathisla, and an additional loop line was laid at the Ben Riach Distillery, Longmorn, from where there was also a two-mile line to the Glen Lossie Distillery (built 1894). At Dufftown the goods branch was extended from Parkmore to Mortlach, at a cost of £6,200, and the distillery company agreed to pay an additional 10*d* per ton on the Dufftown goods rates, on a traffic of 7,500 tons a year. The line, which necessitated diversion of the Dullan Stream for some 400 yards, and the building of new dams, dikes and water intake for the Crachie woollen mills, was completed in autumn 1899[37]. On the Speyside line, the new station of Dalbeallie was opened on 1 July 1899 (renamed Knockando on 1 May 1905[38]).

Other provisions in the Great North's Bill for the 1897 session included arrangements to reorganise the ordinary stocks, to purchase or erect a hotel at Ballater, and to raise additional capital of £300,000. The existing ordinary stock was to be duplicated into two equal amounts, one to be known as Preferred Converted Ordinary, the other as Deferred Converted Ordinary, which would be issued free of charge to holders of the Preferred Converted Ordinary, to match their holding. Any dividend on the Preferred Converted Ordinary would not exceed 3%; if there were funds available for further distribution then the excess between 3% and 5% would be shared equally between holders of Deferred Ordinary stock and holders of the existing Deferred Ordinary Stock No. 1. Any excess over 5% would be shared on an equal basis among holders of Deferred Converted Ordinary and the existing Deferred Ordinary Nos 1 and 2 stocks. The new Preferred and Deferred Ordinary shares would each have half the voting rights of the original ordinary stock. A director's minimum stock-holding qualification was £1,000 of preferred ordinary shares[39]. The effect was to double the nominal ordinary capital of the company without adding anything to its actual resources, but establishing a higher and more stable value for (preferred) ordinary shares, though these were behind other preferred stocks in the dividend queue. To critics, this was more "watering the stock", inflating the company's apparent value without providing a pennyworth of real additional capital. The Bill received the royal assent on 15 July but the directors did not take immediate action with regard to the stocks.

**Dalbeallie Station. The whisky cask is from Cardow (now Cardhu) Distillery,
a mile from the station.** *(Stenlake collection)*

CHAPTER 17
A Spirit of Expansion, 1897 – 1899

The Boddam Branch, and new services

The Boddam Branch, already well behind schedule, was further delayed by heavy snow in February, but Brands took a party of directors and guests as far as Port Errol later in the month, using their own engine and two open goods wagons, with packed straw to keep the travellers' feet warm. The completed line opened for all traffic on 2 August, without ceremony. A *Glasgow Herald* article noted that the bridges were of red or grey granite, some faced with concrete, and the ballast was of granite chips from Crathes and gravel from Kintore. Cruden Bay station, for the hotel, though of wood like all others on the line, was described as extremely handsome, with ornamental gables and panel work, separate first class waiting rooms for ladies and gentlemen, a refreshment buffet, and a carriage verandah outside. The hotel was still being built, and there was some adverse comment that Port Errol's name had been omitted in favour of Cruden Bay[1]. Boddam's station was much less elaborate but "will by no means be ineffective"[2]. It had a one-road locomotive shed, with a turntable alongside.

In April 1897 the Light Railway Commissioners came to Aberdeen to review the competing proposals for the Skene-Echt district, and the GNS slipped in a supplementary application for the western section of the "circular" line. The local syndicate withdrew its proposal, in return for a "reparation" of £1,500 from the GNS. Access to the city tramlines had been refused by the town council, reducing the overall usefulness of the scheme, but the Commissioners agreed to recommend it[3]. The Railway & Canal Commissioners issued an order confirming through carriages between Aberdeen and Inverness, with equal numbers to be exchanged at Keith and Elgin, while the Great North's application to run its engines between Elgin and Inverness was held over pending a decision on the Great Glen schemes.

Deeside services were improved from 1 May, with a new fast train from Ballater at 8.30 am, calling only at Aboyne, Torphins, Banchory and Crathes, arriving in Aberdeen at 9.40. A return train left at 4.35 pm, calling at the same stations, and reaching Ballater at 5.50. On the main line, a new morning express left Aberdeen at 8.05, detaching carriages for the Macduff line at Inveramsay and dividing at Grange South, reaching Elgin at 10.35 via Craigellachie and 11.10 via Buckie. At Craigellachie there was a ten-minute connection with a Strathspey line train, and a seven-minute interval at Elgin enabled arrival at Inverness by 12.00. At last there was progress, though the Highland company was dragging its heels about a joint station at Elgin, for which the GNS had drawn up plans[4].

William Moffatt was often in poor health and was allowed leave of absence for a recuperative trip to Europe in the spring of 1897. Back "with renewed vigour" in July, he was granted £100 by the board towards his costs. There

"Ellon Junction for Cruden Bay" – an Aberdeen train enters the station, with the Cruden line train waiting. (*Stenlake collection*)

was much for him to attend to. Items at the finance committee meeting in August included light railways: all schemes were still being pressed, but the Fraserburgh-St. Combs line had jumped to the head of the queue, having secured a special advance of £5,000 from the Treasury. Its promoters were offering free land but no cash, and they asked the GNS to provide £9,000 and to construct and work the line. The company agreed, providing that the terms of the required Light Railway Order were acceptable. That summer, the east coast herring fishing failed, and the Fraserburgh fishcurers applied to the Great North for reduced rates to enable fishermen and women whom they had hired from west coast districts to return home; the company agreed to carry those who were "really destitute" free of charge (it was typical that the fishcurers should unload responsibility to the railway). It was agreed to lease an office in Inverness, close to the station, for £110 a year, and to construct more wooden footbridges for stations, at £95 each[5].

At the September half-yearly meeting, Ferguson made some cautionary comments about costs. Revenue was up but so were operating expenses because of more and faster trains, higher wages and more employees – required because of reduced working hours – and he expected the Workmen's Compensation Act, due to come into force on 1 July 1898, to increase costs further. Preparations were going ahead for the new locomotive works at Inverurie, which would radically change the character of the town, whose population was around 3,000. The company was proposing to build houses only for foremen, with private builders putting up houses for other staff, though initially many would come by train from Kittybrewster. A capacious new station was also announced for Inverurie[6].

In Aberdeen, the double line between Ferryhill Junction and the joint station, serving also the Caledonian and North British goods stations, could no longer cope adequately with the traffic. The Caledonian had been slow to respond to repeated Great North requests for a quadruple line, and only when a draft Bill was prepared for an separate GNS line from Ferryhill to the joint station did it agree to lay the extra tracks[7].

Although the Great North might be considered a northwards extension of the East Coast route, it joined with the Caledonian and Highland companies in October to oppose the Forth Bridge Railway (a conglomerate of the Midland Railway and the East Coast companies) in its attempt to have the through carriage rates apportioned so as to give it an additional 19 miles on top of its actual length. In January 1898 the Forth Bridge and North British

The railway in the landscape: train passing Torphins. *(Stenlake collection)*

Railways applied to the Railway & Canal Commissioners for an order compelling the GNS and Caledonian to apply this additional mileage, and in the North British Railway's case, also an additional ten miles for the Tay Bridge. The Railway & Canal Commissioners dismissed the applications in 1899, only to allow them when re-presented in 1900. The GNS and Caledonian Railway appealed against the Forth Bridge ruling, but on 4 December 1900 the Court of Session upheld the commissioners' final decision, though it was to apply only from the date of the judgement and not have retrospective force[8].

More protests than compliments normally greeted the Great North's goods rates, so Moffatt must have been pleased in February 1898 when Strathbogie Farmers' Club saluted his reduction of rates for small parcels of farm produce as the action of "an enlightened company"[9]. He must also have hoped they would make good use of it, as otherwise it would simply reduce the operating surplus. Higher wages were already doing that. A sub-committee on applications for increases in salaries and wages approved rises for the 131 signalmen. The men at Aberdeen North, treated as Special class, now earned £1 4s a week, and others earned sums between 17s and 24s. First class boxes were: Kittybrewster North & South, Dyce South, and Elgin East. Second class were Buxburn, Kintore, Inverurie, Inveramsay, Tillynaught Junction, Elgin Joint, Ellon (from opening of junction) and Maud. All other boxes were third class. Other increases were also awarded: at Kittybrewster twelve yard staff got from 1s to 2s 6d extra; five men at the cattle truck department got from 1s to 1s 6d and three at the sack department got 1s. At Waterloo 44 men got 1s - 1s 6d, while six men at the covers shop there got 1s. Eight Deeside line goods staff got between 1s and 1s 6d, and three at Denburn Junction Goods Department, by the passenger station, got 1s. Moffatt himself was allowed by the board to take on the additional role of Joint Manager and Receiver of the bankrupt Mersey Railway, whose tunnel linked Birkenhead and Liverpool[10].

A unique gesture – the staff receptions

Railway directors in other companies regularly paid tribute to the quality, spirit and loyalty of their employees, usually at annual staff soirées, but the Great North board made a unique gesture in early 1898 by inviting the entire staff of 2,300 and their families to four large receptions in Aberdeen: two in January and two in March, held in the Music Hall and overflowing into the adjacent YMCA building, with approximately a quarter of the total each time. Retired as well as current staff were invited, along with guests from the city, the North British Railway and the Caledonian Railway, and altogether some 8,000 people were entertained, with catering done by the Palace Hotel. Directors and officials attended each one. William Ferguson is perhaps the only railway chairman,

This possibly posed photograph shows a class S or T locomotive hauling a rake of six-wheelers on the main down line beside Kittybrewster North signal box. The likely date is 1896, when the two-colour carriage livery was introduced. New signals were provided in 1901 to replace those shown.
(Great North of Scotland Railway Association)

other than of very small companies, to have shaken hands with virtually every employee of his company. At the January gatherings he observed that since 1867 the company's revenue had gone up by 159% but its wage bill had gone up by 226% – it was "trying not to neglect the interests of those by whose labour, address and skill the great work is accomplished"[11]. Apart from an organ recital and dancing, among the attractions was a cinema show by Walker & Co., of Bridge Street, which included moving film of a GNS train stopping at a station, which no-one could identify. This was only two years after the Lumière brothers' pioneering film of a train entering the station at La Ciotat in France. The receptions were suggested by Lord Aberdeen, the vice-chairman[12], and did not preclude the usual departmental and local gatherings; the locomotive running department's reunion on 22 January was its largest yet. At one of the big receptions the chairman had referred to the Great North as "Little and Good" and Pickersgill, presiding, suggested GNSR might stand for "Great Notoriety for Safe Running"[13].

Town councillors were guests at the receptions, but harmony was limited by the council's opposition to expansion of the goods station at Waterloo Quay, and the company's opposition to a council Bill for acquisition of the tramways and the right to assess ratepayers for any discrepancy between revenue and costs. To the Great North, as one of the city's largest ratepayers, to have lost the tramways and then be compelled to subsidise their losses, was a large pill to swallow. News that the council was getting the Aberdeen Tramway Company for £1 less per share than the GNS offer caused some public protest, though supporters of the council's Bill claimed that the railway company was orchestrating it. A trade-off between company and council on the Waterloo enlargement came in July when GNS land by the gasworks on Cotton Street was exchanged for council land wanted by the railway, and the GNS agreed to pay £1,000 towards the widening of Miller Street, along which the gasworks tramway ran[14]. Ferguson also criticised the council's demands for expensive features like overbridges on the proposed western lines; in his view, public bodies were preventing the development of light railways by seeking to inflict excessive costs[15]. The board was having second thoughts about the western light railway scheme even as shareholders approved it, along with the elements of a new Bill, providing for double track between Keith and Dufftown, and Park and Banchory, and the improvements at Elgin. Pressure from shareholders in Liverpool, Edinburgh and Glasgow also pushed the board, reluctantly, into splitting £920,000 of ordinary stock into preferred and deferred as set out in the scheme of 1896. Preferred and deferred converted ordinary first appeared in the Aberdeen stock exchange's listing on 9 March 1898[16].

The half-year report to 31 January 1898 announced the ordinary dividend at 4%, and noted that the entire line from Aberdeen to Huntly was now doubled, except for one mile near Rothiemay, where the work was in hand. At the subsequent ordinary general meeting Lord Saltoun complained about the timing and condition of Fraserburgh trains, and also wanted a Sunday service, but Ferguson replied that a majority of the board, including himself, were opposed to Sunday trains[17]. Saltoun was against the St. Combs railway, believing that the fisherfolk should gravitate from their villages to the towns, and saying the line was "virtually doing mischief", but the meeting gave the plan its approval[18]. Fish remained a very important item for the company though the quantity indicated a slight decline: 15,299 tons in 1897, 17,748 tons in 1896, 17,440 tons in 1895, 15,875 tons in 1894, 19,236 tons in 1893, 19,347 in 1890. The Great North's tonnage was slightly ahead of that of the Highland, which carried 13,543 tons in 1897 and 12,257 tons in 1896. South of Aberdeen the Caledonian had the larger share, carrying 19,614 tons from Aberdeen compared to 12,259 tons on the North British[19].

Other enlargements and improvements were in hand, including plans for a new GNS-only Elgin Station, in "baronial style", both companies having rejected the other's plan for a joint station[20]. On 1 June an exchange platform came into use at Grange South Junction, renamed Cairnie Junction, enabling trains on the Keith and Banff lines to exchange passengers here rather than at Huntly: the island platform had no public road access. Four new passenger services were introduced between Keith and the coast line, three of them also connecting with Banff. A crossing loop was provided at Glassaugh and it was suggested that a "coast suburban service" was about to be introduced. The Alford line was also improved, with a new station and crossing loop at Kemnay – previously the only crossing station was Tillyfourie – and better facilities at Alford were promised. From 1 July weekend fares and single journey fares were also reduced[21]. Discussions had been going on between Moffatt and Farquharson of Invercauld, successor of the Gairn Branch builder, about relaying the Gairn Branch in connection with the long-held notion of a hotel at Ballater, but while the laird was willing to feu the old rail line, he did not want a hotel to compete with his own, and the scheme was not pursued. Tenders for building work at Inverurie were accepted in April, to a total of £36,570[22].

Light Railway Investigations

Pressed by yet another deputation from Ballindalloch, Ferguson said in September 1897 that the board had not yet been able to decide between a line from there or from Dufftown into Glen Livet[23]. By November, a strategy for dealing with the various light railway schemes had been worked out. Most importantly, the Great North now required guarantees from the promoters against any loss incurred in working their lines, additionally to the ground being given free. This was a discouragement to the local committees, but hopes of government and council funding kept the proposals alive.

The Great North was certainly diligent in its examination of light railway systems. In spring 1897 a party of directors had visited Ireland to look at light railways there, and in September Moffatt and Pickersgill led a group to inspect the Isle of Man's electric tramways and light railways, and held a dinner for the Manx directors and officials[24]. Tough conditions were set out to a meeting of the Turriff-Brucklay line proposers on 1 October: land for a double line and all stations was to be given gratis, no fencing to be erected by the railway company, and the GNS was to be either supplied with half the capital interest-free, or with a guarantee against annual loss beyond a certain proportion, for a specified period. The backers found these conditions "onerous". In 1899 Moffatt met with representatives of Colonel J.G. Smith, the Glenlivet whisky supremo, about a line from Dufftown, and agreed a loan of £10,000 over ten years at 3½% interest, to cover half the interest on the necessary capital of £40,000, and to cover half of any annual loss on working, up to £600[25]. New lines were still being proposed, and in late 1898 both the GNS and the Caledonian were approached about a line between Aboyne and Laurencekirk, via Strachan and Glenbervie[26].

In December 1898 the GNS lodged an application for the "Echt extension", a line of 3¼ miles, described as completing the western light railway scheme by connecting it with the GNS at Kittybrewster, though in fact it appears rather to have been a continuation of the line from Oldmill into the joint station, bypassing Ferryhill and the Caledonian line, since it was noted as very expensive, being mainly in tunnel or deep cuttings; and would increase the cost of the whole Echt scheme to £131,691[27]. The St. Combs Light Railway Order was confirmed on 8 September 1899. Five years were given for completion of the 4 miles 514 yards, and as it was to be unfenced, American-style cowcatchers had to be fitted to front and rear of any engine working the line[28]. It was to be the Great North's only light railway – in November the company withdrew its application for the Echt line[29]. No public explanation was given, but construction costs and lack of local financial backing undoubtedly played important parts. The exuberance of the 1890s was slipping away.

The terminus at Boddam, opened in August 1897, with R-Class 0-4-4T No. 89. *(Stenlake collection)*

The Cruden line

The Cruden railway was not operating profitably and the company was seeking payment from local figures who had guaranteed certain sums in the event of an operating loss. The Rev. George Brown of Longhaven was sued for £50: he had guaranteed £500 over ten years against its losses. The Sheriff of Aberdeen ordered him to pay but was overruled on appeal to the Court of Session, the minister claiming successfully that he had made only a conditional pledge, subject to the siting of Longhaven Station to his satisfaction and to a guarantee from the company against damage by the railway to his tenants' property, which the company had not provided. To improve the line's appeal to excursionists, the company decided to put up a request-stop platform at the Bullers o' Buchan, at a cost of £50. Six years later an old carriage body was placed there as a shelter, at a cost of £3 5s[30]. There was no hotel traffic, as "due to adverse circumstances" its opening was put off until 1899, though the golf course had been laid out and was in use[31]. In late December a special train of "luxurious bogie saloons" built at Kittybrewster had taken directors and guests to view the almost-finished hotel. William Ferguson, described as a keen golfer, acknowledged that the venture was "something in the nature of a speculation", and the company promoted it vigorously, with advertisements for its "New Seaside and Golfing Resort". Miss Kate Campbell was appointed manager, at £100 a year, though Miss McKilliam was in overall charge, and a golf professional, Alex Weir, was appointed, at £70 a year. On opening day, 1 March, the Port Errol schoolchildren got a holiday and Ferguson, saying he was *not* a golfer himself, referred to Moffatt, who was absent through illness, as the mainspring of the project. The building, of pink granite, was a mile from the railway and an electric tramway was laid to bring guests from the station. This line, of 3ft 6in gauge and operating on 500-volt DC current from the hotel's generator, opened in June, and though it may appear a rather extravagant provision, it should perhaps be seen both as a test and as a demonstration of what the Great North could do[32]. It would have been easy to run a branch into Port Errol, which was further from the station than the hotel was, but this does not seem to have been considered. A laundry was built on the site, serving the needs of the Palace Hotel as well. The tariff for August-September was 15s per day on the first floor, 14s on the second floor, 12s on the third floor and 10s 6d on the fourth, inclusive of breakfast, lunch, afternoon tea and dinner, though a fire in the room cost extra. After five months of operation the results were described as "most encouraging" and the hotel committee decided to keep it open though the winter, at a reduced rate of £2 10s per week[33].

Aberdeen Station and workmen's services

Aberdeen Station had long ceased to be admired. A public meeting on 7 October 1898 deplored its cramped and overcrowded conditions, though it was accepted that the Caledonian, not the Great North, was responsible for the delay in improving it, and a civic deputation went to see the joint committee. Action was taken in late 1898 with a Bill lodged by both companies for an enlarged station on the same site, with a new layout at Ferryhill Junction, and quadruple track from there into the station. The Caledonian was to raise £300,000 towards the cost and the GNS £100,000[34]. Despite its often-expressed desire for a new station, Aberdeen Town Council, to the GNS's "shock and surprise" made numerous objections to the Bill, which had to be adjusted. Two English companies, the North Eastern and Great Northern, asserted a right, based on an agreement with the Scottish North Eastern Railway but never put into practice, to use the station but this was refused by Parliament, and the Aberdeen Joint Station Act received the royal assent on 9 August[35].

Even before the Denburn line was opened, the Great North had run a workmen's train between Waterloo and Stoneywood (not a public station until 1887) for Pirie's paper mill, out at 5.30 am, back at 5.25 pm[36]. An 1899 parliamentary enquiry into workmen's trains elicited the information that it now ran two such services, one from Aberdeen to Dyce, departing at 5.25 am, with a return service at 5.55 pm; and one to Culter, at 5.30 am, returning at 5.45 pm. The fares were 1s 6d for six returns to Bankhead (4$\frac{1}{2}$ miles) and 2s for six returns to Culter (7$\frac{3}{8}$ miles), and in 1899 12,595 tickets were issued on the Dyce line, mostly to Bankhead, and 13,397 on the Deeside line[37]. Doubling of the Deeside line between Culter and Park was completed on 28 August, and though authority had been obtained to extend it to Banchory, this was to be as far as it went.

A new relationship with the Highland Railway

From 1898 the Highland Railway had a new director, William Whitelaw, whose family had very large GNS shareholdings, and a new spirit of accord opened between the companies. In May 1899 the Great North directors made a friendly visit to Inverness, for a trip on the new direct line to Aviemore. Travelling in a new saloon built for royalty, special occasions and hires, they returned on the Strathspey line. Soon the GNS was offering a one-day circular tour from Aberdeen, taking the Strathspey line to Aviemore, then the direct line to Inverness, returning via Elgin and the coast line, using new corridor carriages. A new train from Keith to Aberdeen at 5.55 pm for the first time enabled passengers from the Highland's northern termini at Wick and Thurso to reach Aberdeen in time to catch the night trains to the south, by both East and West Coast routes. An inquiry which the GNS might once have jumped at, from Provost Sutherland of Dornoch, as to whether it would be interested in working the proposed Dornoch Light Railway, was turned down in September, and in December both boards dined in Inverness, "in the hope that by a free exchange of views benefits to both companies may result." It was agreed that a committee of five directors from each company should meet regularly to discuss matters of common interest[38].

The railway in the landscape: Insch and its station. Tillymorgan rises beyond. *(Stenlake collection)*

A commemorative group montage of those attending Lord and Lady Aberdeen's dinner for stationmasters in 1904. *(Ferryhill Railway Heritage Trust)*

CHAPTER 18
The Old Order Goes, 1900 – 1907

Expansion gives way to economies

After the almost exuberant expansion of the 1890s, the Great North hit choppier water with the turn of the century. The directors' report for September 1900 recorded the worst results for years. Gross revenue was down by £4,247, expenditure was up by £5,600. Coal prices were rising and though train miles were 89,231 down compared with February-August 1899, the coal bill was £4,000 more. The whisky industry had peaked, and distillery traffic was falling. The dividend on preferred ordinary shares was cut to 2%. At the ordinary general meeting on 12 September, William Ferguson announced that the Great North and Highland companies were considering a closer relationship to secure more economical and improved working, with a formalised joint committee consisting of five directors from each[1]. With revenue slipping back, in common with all other railway companies the GNS was finding that the parliamentary restrictions on rate increases made it virtually impossible to raise charges in the face of increasing costs, even when the existing rates were well below the permissible maximum. Cost-cutting was the only answer. New sidings would be rare, but £821 was authorised to be spent on one about a mile south of New Machar, for the delivery of some 75,000 tons of material for the large new lunatic asylum to be built at Kingseat. Aberdeenshire County Council agreed to pay 6d per ton above the normal rates to New Machar[2]. The summer of 1900 also saw completion of the new two-track girder bridge over the Deveron at Rothiemay, giving two lines of rail all the way between Aberdeen and Keith. An Act of 12 August 1898 had also authorised further double-line sections between Keith and Dufftown, Longmorn and Elgin, Elgin and Lossie Junction, and Park-Banchory, but in the new climate of austerity, these were never started.

The Great North's high reputation gave new opportunities to senior managers. A.G. Reid resigned in February 1900 to go to the Dublin, Wicklow & Wexford Railway as general manager, and the board awarded him 100 guineas as a farewell present. William Deuchar, chief clerk in the general manager's office, became passenger superintendent, at a salary of £550[3]. William Moffatt's status among his peers was further confirmed by his unanimous election as chairman of the General Managers' Conference for 1901. In May 1901 he gave up his role with the Mersey Railway, by which time that company had been reformed, its bankruptcy lifted, and a programme to electrify the Mersey Tunnel was in hand. In his duties with the GNS, vigilance on the Highland Railway's activities was still required: in January 1901 it was found to be giving an abatement of 84lbs per ton, or 3¾% off the agreed rate, to senders of dead meat from Keith. Correspondence ensued with Whitelaw, and the matter went to the joint committee to be resolved[4].

The two-track girder bridge at Rothiemay, built 1899-1900. (Stenlake collection)

Developments at Inverurie

Building work was going on briskly at Inverurie and the directors made a visit of inspection on 12 April. Their intention was to transfer the locomotive, carriage & wagon and paint shops by Whitsunday (26 May) 1901 but later in the year it became clear that delays in the provision of heavy equipment, including electric cranes, would mean postponing the locomotive department's move to Whitsunday 1902. A works committee was set up in March 1901, its first task to obtain tenders for an estimated £12,170-worth of equipment for the new engineering shops, including cranes, rails and electric motors, with a 60-ton crane at £2,420, and 15- and 5-ton cranes both at £880. Also at Inverurie, the Free Church building on Constitution Street was to be converted into a recreation and reading room, at a cost of £310, and at the workmen's request, a cricket pitch was provided. The carriage & wagon, paint and trimming works were the first to be transferred to the new site, during May. William Dean of the Great Western Railway was paid £250 for help and advice on the new works[5].

Inverurie's spacious new station was opened on 10 February 1902, and William Ferguson was made a freeman of the burgh. A company township to the north of the old town, locally known as "the colony", was well advanced, with houses now being built for 124 families, and the former Drill Hall also became a recreation centre. The cost of the works and machinery, originally estimated at £80,000, was now around the £100,000 mark[6]. Locomotive work was transferred to Inverurie early in 1902, and by the end of 1903 the new works were fully established, with five large buildings, steel-framed and granite-clad, housing the offices, the locomotive works, the carriage & wagon works, the paint shop, and the forge. Only the main permanent way depot had not yet been moved: this came in 1905. Apart from steam power, electricity was supplied by the works' own generating plant. The 1904 report of the committee of the Council of Education in Scotland praised the "important step" taken by the GNS in establishing a number of classes at Inverurie in technical subjects, in association with the town's School Board[7]. The initiative was not kept up however, due to the greater appeal of evening classes in Aberdeen.

Directors resign – and rejoin

In March the board set up an Investigation Committee, formed of the chairman, Sir David Stewart, and Andrew Bain (a Glasgow businessman who joined the board in December 1899 on the recommendation of Glasgow shareholders) to examine whether any board members or company officials had been profiting from their positions beyond any legal entitlement. Two issues lay behind this, involving purchase of land and of coal.

The new station at Inverurie, 1902. *(Stenlake collection)*

Thomas Adam, a director, had sold a site in Market Street, Aberdeen to the company and Lord Kintore, also a director, had sold land in Inverurie. It was August before the committee reported. Adam's transaction was cancelled and he repaid the company's money. It was remitted to the works committee to decide whether the ground at Inverurie should be retained or not. The committee found that Adam and Kintore had disqualified themselves as directors "in respect that they have been at a time subsequent to their election … concerned in a contract as to land with the Company" but also "inasmuch as the transactions of purchase of land were entirely *bona fide* on their part, and entered into to no prejudice of the Company, it is proper to [re-] elect them as Directors, Thomas Adam in place of Lord Kintore, Lord Kintore in place of Thomas Adam." Sir David Stewart dissented from this proposal and moved that the seats be held vacant until the next shareholders' meeting, but the proposal was carried by a majority of six to four[8].

The second issue related to the supply of coal, which had been the responsibility of William Moffatt, supervised by Thomas Adam, both for the fuel and its delivery, and he was instructed to produce a copy of his agreement with the Caledonian for coal carriage. Coal supply had never been out to tender and had always come from certain Fife pits and South Hetton in County Durham. Stewart moved that Moffatt's explanation of the coal supply be considered unsatisfactory, but his motion was defeated by six votes to five. It was agreed however that all future coal would be got through competitive tenders. The Caledonian agreement appears to have been a package deal, as in December a sub-committee was appointed to negotiate with the Caledonian company "with the object of obtaining freedom as to the purchase of this Company's locomotive coals"[9]. It seems that Stewart, Bain and two other directors, Jones and Williams, suspected that some old-fashioned and improper practices had been going on; and if such was the case, they were now stopped, though all those concerned retained their positions. From this incident onwards, some dissension on the board was evident. Ferguson and Moffatt had been running the Great North for 20 years and though their double act had transformed the company, their style and methods were viewed increasingly critically by a board minority which felt that a shake-up was needed.

Soon afterwards it emerged in the newspapers that a dispute among GNS directors was developing, with two groups issuing circulars in advance of the ordinary general meeting on 10 September, that produced by Stewart and Bain seeking "economy and efficiency". At the meeting, however, it was announced that the difficulties had been dealt with, and contentious matters were not discussed. Colonel Innes of Learney, a long-time advocate of local branches and light railways, was appointed a director[10]. At this time the company had 1,395 debenture holders, with an average holding of £996, 3,426 preference shareholders, with an average of £994, and 1,384 ordinary shareholders, with an average of £1,404; and the total capital was given as £6,738,656[11].

**Elgin in the August 1915 floods, showing the western front of the GNS station
and the walkway between the stations.** *(Stenlake collection)*

Suburban trams and a new light railway

At this time the company was opposing an application from the Aberdeen Suburban Tramways Company (not owned by the city) to build electrified lines outwards towards Inverurie and Peterculter. The lines were to run almost parallel to the railways, and the GNS claimed they would pass within 100 yards of six or seven stations, and that the town council was going to sell them electricity at a subsidised rate. The convener of the council tramways committee described the Great North's suburban services as unsatisfactory[12]. Elgin's new station was also opened in 1902, at last giving Moray's county town a worthy terminus, gabled and turreted, housing a domed booking hall with "art nouveau" glasswork, with three terminal platforms and a fourth on the linking line to the Highland. There was also a walkway to the Highland station.

At the company's 100th ordinary general meeting on 9 September 1902 a telegram of congratulation from William Whitelaw, now chairman of the Highland Railway, was read out. Ferguson noted that the opposition to the suburban tramways had failed. But he picked out encouraging signs, earnings per train mile had risen from 51.33*d* to 52.77*d*, and operating expenses had fallen from 48.75% of gross revenue to 47.38. Coal prices were, for the moment, falling – down by £2,676 in the half-year. A dividend of 3% of preferred ordinary, and 1% on deferred ordinary was declared. Apart from Inverurie, various developments were in hand. Mrs Duthie of Cairnbulg cut the first sod of the St. Combs light railway on 10 September, a new station was going up at Banchory, and the company had bought the Hadden's Mills building, facing the Guild Street offices, for £32,000[13]. The positive note was maintained at the next ordinary general meeting on 24 March 1903, when the chairman announced the largest annual dividend since 1864 – 3% plus 1½% making "rather more than 4½% on the original ordinary stock." Gross revenue had gone up by £3,132 to £255,032 while expenses had gone up by only £454 to £125,156, a better result than other Scottish railways. A proposal to create £375,000 of new capital and £150,000 of borrowing powers was accepted. This increase in capitalisation was not for new works but to pay off temporary loans and thus save on interest payments, which suggests that the company's general financial position was not as rosy as Ferguson's comments suggested. The chairman also welcomed the advent of the Consolidated Pneumatic Tool Company at Fraserburgh, where a new factory was to be built alongside the railway (it began operations in 1906, with its own siding). He could not avoid stressing the need for economies, however, and suggested that all five Scottish railway companies should merge into a single concern, in order to maximise economic working[14]. The St. Combs Light Railway, speedily laid, was opened on 1 July 1903, with services from Fraserburgh's at last enlarged station[15].

A Maudslay 30/40hp 18 seat bus, built in 1907, at Ballater about to leave for Braemar. A train from Aberdeen has arrived in the bay platform in the distance. Buses left about 15 or 20 minutes after arrival of connecting trains and took 90 minutes for the 19 miles to Braemar, or 105 minutes when the roads were 'heavy'. *(Stenlake collection)*

Motor buses – the Great North takes to the roads

On 19 January 1904 Lord and Lady Aberdeen entertained the company's stationmasters to dinner at the West End Café in Aberdeen; a total of 130 guests were present. It was said to be Lady Aberdeen's idea, because she always found the stationmasters to be so obliging[16]. In 1904 the GNS was maintaining its dividend levels at 3% (ordinary preferred) and $1\frac{1}{2}\%$ (ordinary deferred) though as with other railways at this time, this was achieved only by close attention to operating economies. Nevertheless the management kept up its interest in innovation, ordering two steam-powered railcars early in the year for use on branch lines. Such railcars were something of a fashion at this time, but the GNS broke new ground for a railway company by investing in road motor services, using petrol-engined vehicles. A report from William Moffatt proposed this initiative for suitable districts, and a sub–committee was appointed to look at putting it into effect. News soon got around – a public meeting in Tarves in February 1904 produced a petition to the GNS to start a motor car service between Udny and Methlick, where Lord Aberdeen had once proposed his railway[17]. Following visits to manufacturers, four 18 hp Milnes-Daimler buses, to hold eighteen passengers each, were ordered. A fifth was supplied as a chassis, its body built at Inverurie, and the first service, connecting Ballater Station with Braemar, began on 2 May 1904, at a fare of $1\frac{1}{2}d$ a mile, higher than third class on the trains. The buses were described as painted in crimson lake, like the GNS railway carriages[18]. 'Purple lake' is the more usual description. This was the beginning of a substantial road operation. Road vehicles, though not without problems of reliability, discomfort – solid tyres on bumpy roads[19] – and lack of luggage space, were nevertheless flexible in route operation, cheaper to buy than steam railcars, convertible into lorries if necessary, and used an existing system of roads. A central maintenance depot was set up at Kittybrewster. The Braemar bus, seen as an experiment, was quickly confirmed as a success, and in the autumn two buses were transferred to run between Udny Station and Methlick. Acquisition of up to ten more vehicles was being envisaged by the end of 1904, and six were ordered. Railway ownership of bus services may also have been a pre-emptive move, before someone else set up services that might compete with, rather than feed, the GNS trains. In April 1904 the company reduced train fares and increased services to Culter and Dyce, before the suburban tram lines were opened; but by August the directors' report recorded that the new trams from Deeside Road to Bieldside, and from Great Northern Road to Bankhead, had affected suburban revenues. Total revenue for February-July was almost static, £247,766 8*s* 2*d* compared with £247,680 4*s* 8*d*[20].

District road committees were quick to demand reparation for the impact of bus wheels on road surfaces[21], and both to counteract this and to regularise a practice which was not covered by any Act of Parliament, the Great North sought a Provisional Order in April 1905 entitling it to operate road vehicles. Though initially opposed by various bodies including Aberdeen Town Council, the suburban tramway company, and rural coach operators, the order was granted, the Act of 26 June 1906 also authorising the buses to carry mail and parcels. The company was precluded from running road services within Aberdeen city, except to and from its own stations and hotels. New vehicles were ordered and a Huntly Station-Aberchirder service began. Great North road traffic was expanding each year, as was the vehicle fleet. By April 1907 bus services were also running between Culter, Echt and Midmar (Tillybirloch), also with a lorry service; Schoolhill (Aberdeen)-Cluny; and Schoolhill-Newburgh, though the Udny-Methlick service was withdrawn as unremunerative. In the August 1906-January 1907 half-year, compensation of £157 17s 6d was paid to coach hirers in Ballater and Braemar, and £120 to operators in Aberdeen and Cluny, against loss of revenue; and £150 was paid to Mr Cruickshank of Newburgh to withdraw his motor bus. Profit on the motor services was modest: with a gross revenue of £12,986 in the same half-year, the net earnings were only £380 18s 2d after costs and depreciation[22]. Private cars were also taking to the roads in greater numbers: in February-July 1908 the company carried 200 carriages (horse-drawn), down by half from the corresponding six months of 1907.

William Ferguson dies, Sir David Stewart takes over

William Ferguson of Kinmundy died on 11 September 1904, in the 25th year of his chairmanship, after a short illness. Under his regime the company, emerging from the depths of insolvency, had reached a plateau of modest but steady profitability, acquiring a reputation for efficiency and innovation as a regional railway. If he failed in his dearest aim, to make the line a truly 'Great North' one by gaining powers to run trains to Inverness and even beyond, he had the satisfaction in his final years of seeing a positive attitude replace the long hostility of the Highland company. Sir David Stewart, his deputy, was elected as chairman. William Moffatt remained as general manager and the company's general policy and philosophy did not change. The main themes of the next few years, expansion of road services, proposed amalgamation with the Highland Railway, the enlargement of

Integrated transport, 1905-06. A bus for Echt and Midmar awaits the train at Culter. From 1 November 1906 the service ran directly from the Schoolhill bus terminus. (*Stenlake collection*)

Aberdeen Station, the drive to maintain economies, had all begun in Ferguson's time.

Sir David, addressing the staff's annual social meeting in January 1905, did not maintain Ferguson's optimistic tone, describing the circumstances as "not the brightest" with traffic and revenues dropping. Hopes that post-Ferguson, Sunday services might be introduced, were disappointed – the new chairman did not think that the Deeside residents would like to have their district "turned into a pandemonium" on Sundays, and he thought Sunday running would also be "demoralising" to railway employees. The ordinary general meeting in March confirmed the trends. The whisky trade was still below the peak of the 1890s, fishermen were operating further out in bigger boats and boat-building on the Moray coast was in decline. Coastal steamer services were undercutting railway rates. Revenue from the hotels had also fallen. Economies were still the order of the day.

Amalgamation with the Highland?

In Aberdeen during the autumn of 1905 the prime talking-point in railway matters was the emergence of an amalgamation scheme between the Great North and Highland companies. Backed by both boards, it envisaged a single 'Highland and North of Scotland

Sir David Stewart, chairman of the GNSR, 1904-1919. *(Aberdeen City Libraries)*

Railway', whose headquarters would be in Aberdeen. William Whitelaw, its most ardent advocate, told the Highland's half-yearly meeting in September that the merger was essential: the Highland could not proceed with the development of the North "if we stand on our own feet." On 10 October representatives of both companies met in Perth and signed a Minute of Agreement as to the terms[23], and a Draft Provisional Order was lodged with Parliament for the 1906 session. The new company would have preferred and deferred ordinary stock on the GNS pattern and shareholders in the Highland, which had never split its stock, would receive £50 in preferred and £50 in deferred stock for every £100 of their holding. A management committee of sixteen directors, eight from each of the former companies, would run the new concern. The merger was unopposed in Aberdeen, where it seemed perfectly reasonable that the head office should be in a city four times more populous than Inverness, and the locomotive works in the newly-completed facility at Inverurie. Shareholders in the Great North were assured by a board circular in January 1906 that interest in their lien, debenture and guaranteed GNS stocks would continue at the present levels, but it was hoped that the market value of their shares would increase. It was proposed to cancel Great North deferred ordinary No. 2 shares, which had never received a dividend, paying £8 for every £100[24]. The two companies were of approximately equal size in most respects: the GNSR's preferred converted ordinary shares amounted to £1,063,653 10s 1d, and deferred to £1,166,475 10s 11d, while the Highland's ordinary stock amounted to £2,564,383.

Both boards were taken aback by the vehemence and extent of opposition which arose in Inverness and most other towns (except Wick) in the Highland's area. A letter from D. Forbes Dallas in the *Scotsman* on 25 September 1905 set the tone, condemning the Great North as "a backgoing line" and the whole plan as an Aberdonian scheme for "doing" Inverness. Much of the opposition case was based on the Great North's financial position and its "watered" capital. The hidden hands of the Baird family and its trusts were suspected to be driving the merger. Bairds, Whitelaws and their family trusts were quoted as having £138,609 in lien shares and £98,935 in preference shares in the Great North, while their holdings in the Highland amounted to £29,571[25]. The necessary shareholders' meeting in Inverness, on 7 March 1906, gave approval to the amalgamation, with £2,200,000 of voting power in favour, and £700,000 against, but after consultation with Stewart and his board, the amalgamation Bill was withdrawn, and it was intimated that it would not be reintroduced in 1907. The Great North board minuted that the Bill had "unexpectedly not met with the support necessary under the parliamentary standing orders for the directors of the Highland Railway Company"[26].

Virtually every detail for the merger had been agreed, including which officials would be retained, or not (those departing were to have pensions made up to two-thirds of their average salaries in the previous seven years) and at the GNS half-yearly meeting held on the 21st, Sir David Stewart expressed some chagrin about the failure, "because he held that the line from Aberdeen to Inverness should be in the hands of one company", and estimated that amalgamation would have produced a clear net gain of some £46,000 a year, worth £22,000 to Great North shareholders and £24,000 to those of the Highland Railway. The only drawback to a merger, in his view, was that the North British Railway "might some day creep up Loch Ness" and compete disastrously with the Highland line. On the domestic front, he reported that the new railcars were running successfully on the Lossiemouth and St. Combs lines, and that the bus services were earning 4% on expended capital. Leasing of advertising space inside the buses to Abrahams of London, at £15 per vehicle per year, helped this along[27].

Failure of amalgamation did not reduce the wish of the Great North and Highland boards to smooth out problems of exchange traffic and to co-operate in the interest of cost-saving. New traffic arrangements were under discussion in the summer of 1906 and from 17 September the Highland Railway passed on to the GNS 40% of its receipts from all traffic exchanged at Boat of Garten from or to Great North stations and stations south of Perth. Locomotive coal for certain GNS depots was to come up the Highland line via Boat of Garten, and £700 held in suspense by the Railway Clearing House was to be released to the Highland, on the understanding that statutory rights of both parties regarding traffic exchange at Keith were reserved[28].

William Moffatt retires

In April 1906 William Moffatt retired after 26 years with the company, and the board awarded him a retiring allowance of £625 (three months' salary) and a pension of £700 a year[29]. The Great North's emergence as a notably well-run railway in the 1880s and 1890s was due to his ability, enterprise and energy, backed by Ferguson as chairman. His relations with Sir David Stewart were less assured. John Stuart, the accountant, retired in April after 50 years with the Great North. From 2 April, George Davidson, company solicitor, became general manager at £900 a year and T.S. Mackintosh, assistant to the general manager, became company secretary, at £500. John Morrison, the cashier, now combined the role of accountant with his previous functions. Lord Aberdeen, who had been deputy chairman, resigned on his appointment as Viceroy of Ireland, and was replaced by Andrew Bain, a director since 1889[30].

As often happened with the departure of a top official, a degree of reorganisation and tightening up of procedures followed, accentuated in this case by the ongoing need to find economies. A committee was set up to review the company's organisation. Mr Gray, the stores superintendent, was transferred to the post of travelling traffic agent and the stores department was reorganised, with a sub-committee of directors supervising all purchases (the traffic committee had just approved a tender for 106 dozen assorted brushes, for sweeping, carriage cleaning, whitewashing etc.). A board decision of 1901 not to award retirement allowances to officials in the national superannuation scheme was re-confirmed. A fortnightly record was to be kept of employees absent with leave and receiving pay, whether sick, on holiday, or through accident. The female clerks in the audit office were dispensed with, receiving one month's pay. One cost-cutting move was dropped when 95 stationmasters appealed against the substitution of a plain jacket for their uniform coats, and the board agreed to spend an extra £40 a year for frock coats embroidered with 'Stationmaster'. The coal carriage contract agreed by Moffatt with the Caledonian was terminated[31]. Later in the year, on the retirement of Patrick Barnett, the chief engineer, his department was also reorganised. Although tribute was paid to his long service, it appears that his departure was not voluntary. He was given three months'

Andrew Bain, chairman of the GNSR, 1919-1922.
(Mitchell Library, Glasgow)

notice and a pay-off of half a year's salary, £425. Five members of his staff were dispensed with, in order to cut the payroll down from £2,650 to £1,975 a year. James Parker, of the South Eastern & Chatham Railway, was appointed as chief engineer, at £600 a year[32].

Other important negotiations were also going on with the Caledonian in 1906. For mutual convenience, the goods yards adjoining the joint station were exchanged. In December the GNS placed an order with George Hall, contractors of Kittybrewster, for a new goods yard at Market Street, with nine tracks and around two miles of sidings[33]. Work on quadrupling the track from Ferryhill had been going on since 1902, on new granite arches replacing the old brick ones, and new platforms were being built on the west side of the station, alongside the train shed.

For the Great North the passage of royal persons along the Deeside line was a matter of routine, albeit carefully managed, but when King Edward VII made a formal visit from Balmoral to Aberdeen to open the new university buildings in September 1906, special lengths were gone to, with a new roof to fit the Royal Train at the Holburn Street platform, enlarged waiting rooms, the footpath to the street widened and its gradient reduced. Spending of £25 on decoration for the Palace Hotel, £10 for the head office, and £35 on the joint station was authorised[34]. No doubt even such small expenditures were carefully monitored, for the company was looking for every means to keep its costs down.

The hotels, 1900 – 1905

New attractions were added to Cruden Bay Hotel. Eight "bathing coaches" enabled ladies to enter the sea without having to undress on the beach, the croquet lawn was enlarged, and a ladies' golf course was opened. Company advertisements proclaimed these features, also seeking to extend the hotel's season, announcing that the weather in autumn and early winter was "usually fine," also naming the line as "The Royal Route to the North of Scotland, for Inverness, Strathpeffer, and Wick", with express trains between Aberdeen and Inverness, and carriages provided with lavatories and electric lighting[35]. The tramcar shed was converted to a male staff dormitory during the July-September peak period, freeing ten bedrooms in a new wing added to the hotel. The season remained a short one and there were difficulties with the management. Miss Campbell had resigned in 1900 and her successor, Miss Frater, was dismissed in 1901 for failing to keep provision costs down. A new manager, Mr Trenchard of the Claremont Hydropathic, Rhyl, was appointed in February 1902 at £130[36]. The hotels had a bad year in 1905, with the Palace's net profit falling and Cruden Bay making a loss for the second year in succession: with revenue of £7,480 against costs, including interest payments, of £8,184. Mr Trenchard had gone, and Miss Williams, manager of Bruce's Hotel, Carnoustie, was appointed at £100 a year plus 2½% of net annual profits as an incentive to keep costs down. Indeed, the hotels committee had tried to sell a lease of the Cruden Bay Hotel, but none of the large hotel chains were attracted. To crown it all, the Palace was suffering from rat infestation[37].

CRUDEN BAY HOTEL

CRUDEN BAY STATION

The hotel at Cruden Bay was built in Scottish baronial style on a commanding position looking southwards over the North Sea. The overhead wires of the tramway to the station can be seen on the right. Trams ran to the front door. *(From a carriage print, courtesy John Diffey)*

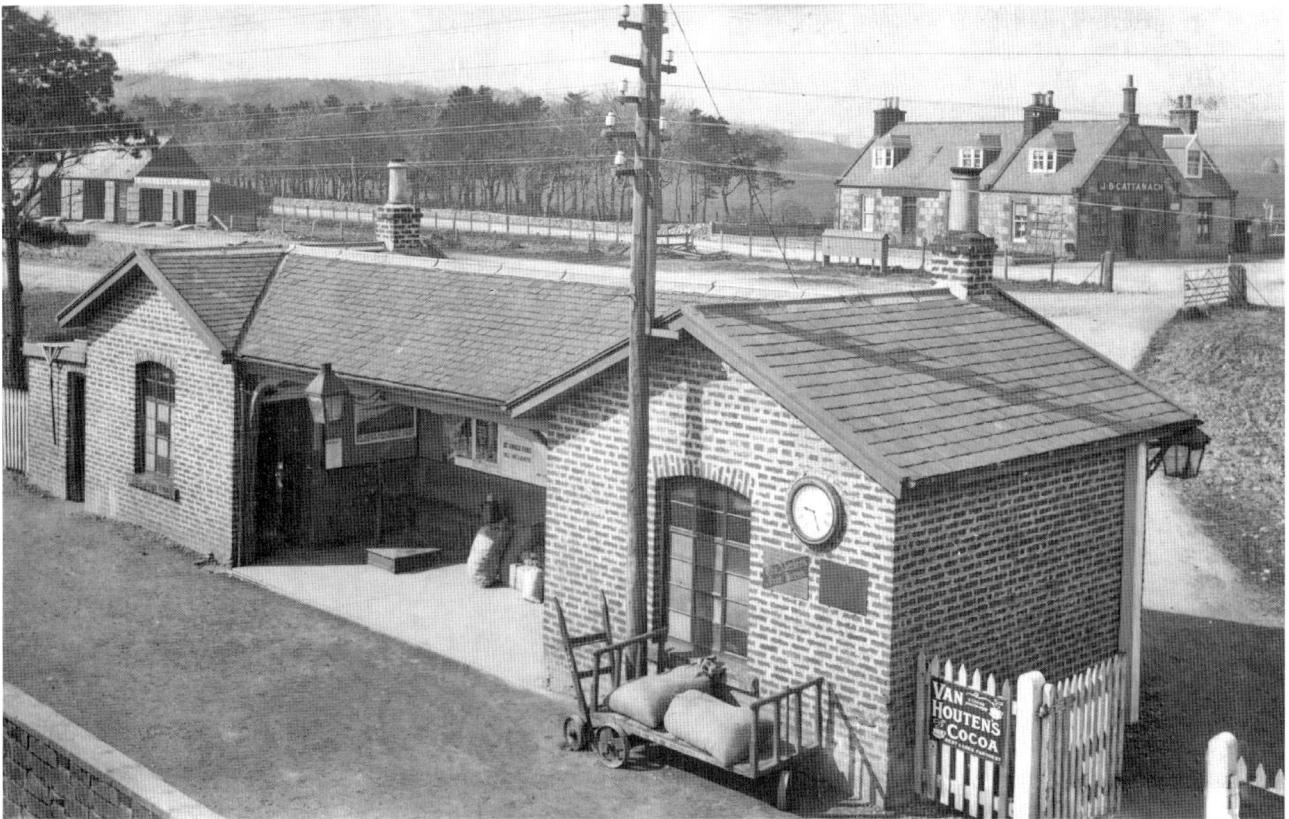

Auchterless Station on the Turriff line, with the village shop, and fertiliser company sheds on the left. *(Stenlake collection)*

To the relief of the guarantors, the ten-year guarantees against loss on the Cruden Bay line expired in July 1907. They had been worth £1,000 a year to the GNS: the line had never covered its costs. Interest alone on the capital of £144,000, at 4%, was £5,760 a year. Three passenger trains each way daily served the line from Ellon, with an additional one on Mondays and Saturdays. The only large goods customer, the Cruden Bay Brick and Tile Works, had negotiated a rate reduction in 1906, bringing the minimum quantity of goods shipped at the special rate of 2s 3d per ton down to 3,000 tons a year[38].

Reparations, snow blocks and new tours

Two old adversaries, the Aberdeen Lime and Aberdeen Commercial Companies, had taken the Great North before the Railway & Canal Commissioners, claiming that the company was failing to provide station accommodation and to provide terminal services for them, and demanding a rebate on past carriage charges. The case was settled before it came to trial, with the Great North to repay to the two companies a discount at the rate of 80% on site rents and on tickets issued in the managers' names; and guaranteeing that if the occupancy of their sites was disturbed, they would get equally suitable sites if the railway company had ground available. To cope with the farming industry's requirements, both had lime depots at many stations[39].

The board also agreed to assist in the introduction of a system of steam haulage round the quays at Aberdeen as soon as the harbour engineer should certify that the rails were of suitable standard for locomotives, and the harbour commissioners should pass a resolution requesting a uniform rate for steam haulage. The company would then provide locomotives and apply a uniform rate for haulage from all parts of the Victoria and Upper Docks[40].

In October 1906 the stores committee sought immediate tenders for 200 foot warmers, which was just as well as it proved to be an exceptionally cold and snowy winter. Heavy snow blocked the Buchan, Alford and Deeside lines at the end of the year. On 29 December the 8.00 am train for Aberdeen left Peterhead on time and reached Aberdeen at 10.25 am on the following day. Only five passengers were on board, and they spent the night in the hotel at Udny. The crew stayed on the train and arrived exhausted. In January 204 shovels were bought, urgently needed for snow clearance work[41]. Snow delays that winter cost the company some £3,000 in lost revenue and £700 in clearing costs. A further £2,700 was lost by the termination of an agreement relating to southbound traffic, "owing to the southern railway companies having come to an agreement among themselves," Sir David Stewart told the shareholders in March. The arrangement, presumably the mileage allowance on through fares and carriage rates to England referred to in the parliamentary hearings of 1892, had been worth £155 a week to the Great North[42].

Plans for increasing revenue went alongside cost cuts. In February 1907 the board approved a new programme of three circular rail/motor tours to operate on Saturdays in June, and from 1 July to 18 September:
Aberdeen-Ballater (train), Ballater-Corgarff (motor), Corgarff-Tomintoul-Ballindalloch (horse coach), Ballindalloch-Aberdeen (train). First class £1, third 15s.
Aberdeen-Alford (train), Alford-Corgarff (motor), Corgarff-Tomintoul-Ballindalloch (horse coach), Ballindalloch-Aberdeen (train). First class 18s 6d, third 14s.
Aberdeen-Ballater (train), Ballater-Strathdon-Alford (motor), Alford-Aberdeen (train). First class 12s, third 9s[43].

In June a party of London and provincial journalists was taken on a promotional trip from Aberdeen by train to Dinnet, GNS charabanc from Dinnet to Corgarff, horse brake to Tomintoul, charabanc again from there to Ballindalloch, and train to Aberdeen. Stewart, Bain, Pickersgill and Deuchar accompanied the party and there were lunches, dinners and civic receptions. Unfortunately it rained incessantly during the three-day trip, with occasional sleet, but the report bravely said that "there was compensation in the pristine freshness it imparted to the leafage and the herbage[44]."

The GNSR owned several steam lorries. Foden M8941 was obtained in 1916. Alongside is a Sentinel from Ellis & McHardy's fleet. (*Great North of Scotland Railway Association*)

CHAPTER 19
New Kinds of Dispute, 1907 – 14

Accidents, unavoidable and otherwise

On the night of 13-14 April 1907, a crane toppled off the Fiddich Viaduct, near Dufftown, while replacing cast iron girders with malleable iron. Two men were killed and three seriously injured, from a team that had been employed over the previous two years on bridge renewal. This was a freak occurrence, but bad working practices were still accounting for deaths among the workforce. In July 1908 guard C. Spark was in charge of horse shunting at Aberdeen Harbour. As two loaded wagons were being drawn forward by three horses, he dodged under the hauling chain to be ready to connect another wagon, fell between the rails, was run over and fatally injured. The Board of Trade inspector noted that Rule 23 (a): shunting poles must always be used when practicable, was routinely ignored by shore guards. Shunting methods were again criticised after the death of pointsman George Stewart at Bucksburn on 15 June 1910. Two loaded timber wagons in No. 8 siding were to be pushed by hand on to the sawmill line, to be propelled up to the sawmill by the shunting engine. Three men were pushing, when the wagons stopped on the points. A plank was used as a prop, with Stewart holding it against the wagon until the engine was brought up, at an angle to the wagons. He was pinned between the drawbar hook of the tender and the buffer of a wagon. Propping was officially banned on the Great North under Rule 113 (d), but it is most unlikely that Bucksburn was the only station where it was still practised. Tow-roping and fly-shunting, also frowned on by the Board of Trade, with the latter said to be prohibited at all GNS stations except one, were also causes of injury[1].

The Great North was receiving favourable mention in the financial columns for its maintenance of a steady if unspectacular dividend, once again 3% and 1% for February-July 1907. In that half-year gross revenue rose by £1,417 10s 4d despite the fact that the corresponding period in 1906 had included £4,028 17s 3d from the now-lost "arrangement". Expenses were up by £5,060, however, including an increase of £2,885 on the locomotive coal bill. Working expenses per train mile rose from 24.81d to 27.72d, and as a percentage of gross receipts from 46.63% to 48.37%. Train mileage was being kept in hand: passenger miles were up by 1,783, and goods by 9,584. On the whole, the results compared well with most British railways. A reminder that a substantial proportion of shares was held in Liverpool came when John Jones, a Liverpool-based director from 1901, died in 1907 and was replaced by another Liverpudlian, David G. Irvine[2].

The almost-strike, 1907

In September 1907 the Amalgamated Society of Railway Servants organised a ballot of its members on the question of whether to strike over the issues of pay and conditions, which resulted in a 90% vote in favour. The union's tactics were criticised by the chairman at the ordinary general meeting on 17 September, as "trying to bring its leaders between the Company and its employees"; Sir David insisted that the Great North was always willing to receive employee deputations through the proper channels (viz. departmental heads) and considered that this was the only way in which discipline could be maintained and the staff controlled. He had every reason to believe that the men were "fairly well contented," citing the benefits of a railway job: steady and permanent employment, free passes, reasonable holiday without loss of pay, in many cases a pension, "in several cases a better and cheaper cottage"… the directors were always willing to pay the best wages the company could afford; and he concluded by saying that the man who dictates wages and conditions of service must be the man who raises capital, answers to the shareholders, deals with the government, and is generally responsible for the wellbeing of the organisation as a whole[3]. This was as clear a statement of the responsibilities of directors in 1907 as anyone could make, but Stewart's position was undercut by the government which, in order to avert the economic disruption of a railway strike, brokered agreement with the railway companies and the Amalgamated Society of Railway Servants for the setting-up of conciliation boards, with both management and staff members, to consider issues relating to pay and conditions. The arrangement turned out to be a four-year stop-gap, but in any case the Great North employees were less militant at this time than those of the Caledonian and North British. Stewart's regime may have been rather more austere than that of William Ferguson, but there is no evidence of serious dissatisfaction, and in March 1908 Sir David remarked that no-one on the GNS had wanted a strike, as far as he knew, and that "as soon as a proper scheme for conciliation and arbitration was drawn up, they should, he hoped, fall in with it." Along with the North British, Glasgow & South Western and Highland companies, the Great North concluded an arrangement with the Board of Trade by the end of March. Three sectional boards, locomotive, traffic, and permanent way, were set up in each district, northern and southern, with a central board in each[4].

Looking after details

Careful management implied looking after details, and the GNS looked out both for economies and small ways of increasing revenue. Passenger tickets supplied by Edmonson's works in Glasgow cost £292 10s in the year to 30 November 1906, while the Bell Punch & Printing Co. of London offered tickets at 1s per thousand, delivered to Aberdeen, giving a total cost of £127 5s for 2,545,000 tickets. George Davidson was instructed to look into the question and the contract stayed with Edmonson, who supplied the ticket machines. Twelve pictorial postcard

Aberdeen Joint Station from the north end with reconstruction in progress. The original roof is still in place. Several new platforms have been built. Hadden's Mill was to the left where new platforms are under construction. *(Great North of Scotland Railway Association)*

A train for Fraserburgh at St. Combs, hauled by class D 0-6-0T No.8, fitted with cowcatchers at both ends to comply with the requirements of the Light Railways Act. (*Great North of Scotland Railway Association*)

dispensers were installed at larger stations, selling ready-stamped postcards for a penny (inland postage being $^1/_2d$). In March 1907 the hotels committee decided to instal refreshment rooms at Craigellachie. It shopped around for whisky supplies, ordering 30 gallons of the local Longmorn product for the Elgin refreshment rooms but opting for 30 gallons from John Walker of Kilmarnock for the Palace Hotel, at 12*s* 11*d* a gallon[5]. Following the service reductions in previous years, in August 1908 deputations from Fraserburgh and Peterhead came to ask for improvements, and, in the latter case, a new station. The original station, out at the west end of town, had been virtually unaltered since the line was opened. Sir David gave a rather vague assurance: the probability was that a new station would be built "in due course"[6].

In April 1908, Great North and Highland engines began hauling trains all the way between Aberdeen and Inverness, with benefits both to timing and to economy, and that summer the GNS half-day Speyside excursion, started in 1905, was experimentally extended to Kingussie, with a GNS engine and crew[7]. A joint meeting on 4 December agreed that the Great North would handle routine maintenance of Highland engines at Keith, and the Highland Railway would do the same for GNS engines at Forres. The fact that Great North engines were at Forres at all was a testimony to how things had changed. It was also agreed that each company could return the other's wagons with loads whenever possible, rather than empty[8]. The GNS participated in a joint conference, held by the Board of Trade, with the North British Railway, Caledonian and English companies, following a North British decision to advance the departure of the night train from Aberdeen to London by half an hour. This was because of morning congestion on lines into London, but it meant earlier postal collections in the north-eastern towns, which caused protests in the business community[9].

Progress at the joint station

By late 1908, with completion of quadruple track from Ferryhill, four new platforms had been opened on the west side of Aberdeen Station, serving the suburban trains, and by mid-1909 were connected by a footbridge to a substantial granite suburban booking office and waiting room at the north-west end of the station, on the corner of Guild Street and Bridge Street[10].

This 20/25hp Milnes-Daimler lorry, SA 158, was delivered in 1905 as part of an order for seven vehicles. The others were fitted as buses, and SA 158 has also been photographed with a bus body. The driver wears waterproof clothing. *(Great North of Scotland Railway Association)*

James Parker gave the board a preview of the completed Aberdeen Station in September 1912, based on his plans. To be of grey granite construction, the two-storey buildings would include a hall for ambulance training, parcels offices, offices for each company, waiting rooms, first and third class refreshment rooms, a tea room and a dining room, and left luggage office. Lavatories, bathrooms and dressing rooms were to be provided for the use of passengers. The estimated cost was £150,000, though the full cost of the works from Ferryhill was expected to be around £800,000. Up to 31 July 1912 the two companies had spent £202,000[11]. Public interest and concern had been focused for many years on the condition of the joint station, and an Aberdeen versifier wrote in 1911[12]:

> *In bonnie Aiberdeen they're kickin' up a soun'*
> *Aboot the station being ower little for the toun …*
>
> *Our present passenger station wad mak' yer een feel sair,*
> *There's hardly room for strangers to be stannin' there,*
> *An' if you tak' shelter frae the stormy blast*
> *The roof is leaky, and the rain fa's fast …*

Addressing the Great North, he says:

> *Ye'll need tae hurry up an' put your contract oot*
> *And lat the public know what ye're aboot:*
> *For I say hurry up, for ye hinna muckle time,*
> *The roof will tummel in an' block the railway line.*

The new station at Portsoy, built 1884. Harbour branch and original
passenger station (converted to a goods depot) on right. *(Stenlake collection)*

Development of the bus services; light railways deferred

The idea of light railways had not been abandoned, especially between New Aberdour and Fraserburgh (though powers granted to the GNS under the Act of 1884 had expired in 1889), but no further extensions to the system were made. With the St. Combs line now ten years old, the Fraserburgh & Rosehearty Light Railway scheme had been under discussion again. The government had expressed a willingness to grant £17,413 towards it, and the GNS was prepared to invest £22,413, making £40,000 available, while the communities along the line were asked to raise £5,000 and provide the necessary ground at no charge. This, however, appeared to be impossible to do, and the project was again stalled. Meanwhile the Great North bus service to New Aberdour via Rosehearty was described as doing fairly well[13]. Somewhat different figures were mentioned in July, when the board informed the railway's promoters that it would accept a permanent interest-free (government) loan not exceeding £12,625 to construct the line, repayable only in the event of the company failing to work the line in a reasonable manner, and even then subject to deduction of debenture and mortgage claims. At the same time the board was being approached by the Scottish Light Railway & Development Syndicate (Ltd), a body which wished to build a line from Strichen or Brucklay to Turriff, with a branch running from New Pitsligo to New Aberdour and Rosehearty. It wondered if the GNS would be willing to advance a portion of the costs, a question which was remitted to the chairman and general manager[14]. Rural development was very much a theme of the time, with a range of organisations on the look-out for government funding. His Majesty's Treasury would not agree to the terms of the loan, and the Great North board minuted that "Having regard to all the various complications that seem to arise, and as there is no inducement of any kind for the GNSR to make the line at all, the Directors think it better to revert to the original conditions on which the free gift was offered by Treasury"[15]

Additions were still being made to the road services. More lorries both petrol and steam-poweredwere acquired. From 1 November 1907 a mail bus ran from Ballater to Braemar on Sundays, also carrying passengers, and so breaking a long GNS tradition. From 18 May 1910 buses on four routes were fitted with letter-boxes, a feature unique at that time, the success of which led to the placing of a letter box on the brake van of the 5.40 pm St. Combs-Fraserburgh train in October[16]. The initiative came from the Post Office, which proposed a charge of £1 per box per annum; the GNS settled for £2. Collections were made from the last bus of the day from Braemar, Cluny, Echt and Newburgh. New GNS bus services were few, but in 1912 it bought the business of Mr Simpson,

Rosehearty, along with his Peugeot bus, and operated the Fraserburgh-Rosehearty route. In 1914 the company put on a lorry service between Aberdeen and Newburgh. Despite continuing coastal shipping traffic in lime, grain and coal, no rail connection was ever laid to the quay at Newburgh, an easy six miles from the Buchan line. Possibly the fact that the Aberdeen Lime Company was a main user of the port had something to do with this: its relations with the GNS appear to have been consistently hostile[17]. The bus services were all-year and protests came from Upper Deeside when the district road committee wanted the Ballater-Braemar bus withdrawn in winter because of damage to the road surface. Sir David stated that the company felt a public responsibility to maintain the service, and offered help in keeping the road clear of snow[18].

As ever, when there was a snowy winter, exposed sections of the Great North suffered blocks, delays and sometimes derailments. Around 20 December 1909 four snowploughs were in continuous operation to keep the Buchan lines clear. December was the month for shipping stock to the London market, and delays meant loss of revenue and reputation. Between 5 and 11 December 1909, 1,705 head of cattle, 1,426 sheep and 707 pigs were passed on to the southern companies: 3,838 in all compared with 3,018 in 1908[19]. Alexander Ross, after 48 years with the company, 32 as goods manager, resigned that month through ill health. The members of the Railway Clearing House Goods Managers' Conference presented him with a silver candelabrum, though the GNS directors seem to have been content merely to describe his work "in laudatory terms". He had not done badly for himself, having purchased the Muiryfold estate, near Grange, about fifteen years previously[20]. Goods managers, with close business contacts, and authority to negotiate deals, were well-placed to receive commercial hints, favours, perhaps gifts, though the watchfulness of rival shippers, as well as accepted standards of ethics, precluded outright bribery. Ross's assistant, S.R. Willox, took over as manager. Short-haul goods traffic had long been competed for by traction engine operators, and by now long-distance goods was being contested: in 1910 the United Yeast Company switched from rail to road transport[21].

Bad new for small harbours; and a second Aberdeen hotel

In the spring of 1910 the rails of Portsoy's harbour branch, unused for around 25 years, were lifted. H.A. Vallance wrote that "the coming of the railway proved the undoing of Portsoy as a seaport", but in fact the construction of extended harbours at Buckie and Macduff, able to take the larger steam-powered boats of the 1890s and later, was responsible. The difficulty of working Portsoy's steeply-graded harbour line did not help, but he notes that the harbour siding at Banff (another harbour which was not enlarged) shared a similar fate[22].

In July the Station Hotel in Aberdeen, next door to the company offices, was put on sale, at an upset price of £13,000, and the Great North bought it for considerably less: capital expenditure in the half-year August 1910-January 1911 was £11,483, and Sir David Stewart remarked that the hotel had been acquired "on very favourable terms". Not only was it conveniently placed, opposite the planned entrance to the enlarged station, but it would end the confusion of travellers who had supposed the 'Station' to be the railway company's hotel[23]. The company now owned and operated two large hotels in Aberdeen. A substantial increase was made in hotel takings in 1912, with the Cruden Bay receipts described as "a record" though not otherwise specified. In the next year, however, Cruden Bay made a "small loss", the Palace only a "modest balance" and the Station Hotel was just about breaking even[24].

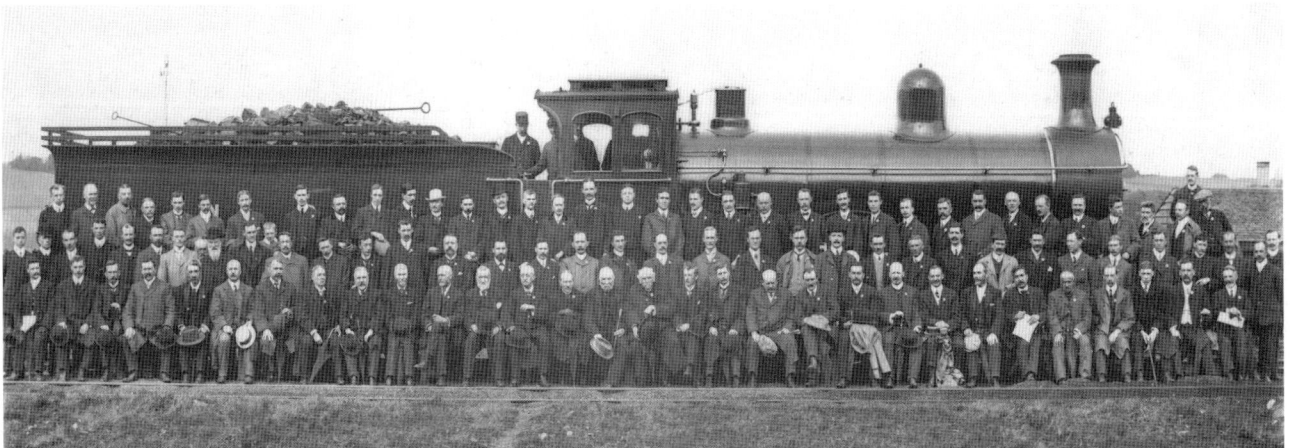

On 30th July 1907, a party from the Institution of Mechanical Engineers visited Inverurie Works and were photographed in front of a gleaming Class T locomotive. *(Great North of Scotland Railway Association)*

Railway pay and national politics

Political issues were unusually intense between 1910 and 1911, and George Davidson issued a circular to the staff in January 1910 requesting them not to take public sides on political matters, as this annoyed the traders. Trade, especially the whisky trade, was depressed, a general election was imminent, and tempers were high. Though the circular did not try to influence what the employees put on their ballot papers, it attracted some adverse comment, with Winston Churchill – home secretary in the Liberal government at the time – calling it "very unusual" and undesirable, though not illegal[25]. One of the main political controversies centred on the railways themselves, where Lloyd George's settlement of 1907, intended to last until 1913, was fast unravelling through discontent among the workers at how the conciliation and arbitration system was being operated. On the Great North there was no evidence of dissatisfaction, with conciliation rarely being resorted to: four deputations went to the management between 1907 and 1911. In November 1910 a conciliation board had considered an application from locomotive department workers for changes in hours and conditions, resulting in "complete and amicable agreement" on all points, to last until 1913[26]. A new crisis arose when railway workers voted for a national strike in August 1911. In common with other railway companies, the Great North had always refused to negotiate directly with trade unions, but the Amalgamated Society of Railway Servants had succeeded in recruiting around three quarters of the company's uniformed staff, and if a strike had taken place, its services would have been seriously disrupted. It was the peak of the fishing season and there was anxiety at the ports – Buckie alone needed 400 tons of coal a week, railed from Aberdeen docks, to supply steam-powered drifters[27]. Once again the government acted rapidly, offering a Royal Commission to examine the working of the 1907 conciliation scheme, and this was accepted by both sides. The Commission got down to work quickly, and an early witness was James Rothney, a Great North signalman for fourteen years, and secretary of both a sectional and a central conciliation board. He had criticisms of the conciliation scheme's prolonged timetable for redressing grievances, and of the company's refusal, in some cases, to honour the conciliation board's decisions. He cited a petition submitted in January 1907, not answered by the management, overtaken by the conciliation scheme, submitted by a conciliation board to the directors on 30 November 1908, resulting in a meeting with directors and officials on 13 March 1909, and finally settled on 28 July 1909, awarding the men about a quarter of what they had asked for. On working hours, the company interpreted a ten-hour day for a signalman to mean 6 am to 6pm with two hours off. He also claimed that men who complained were subject to intimidation and threats of dismissal, if they did not sign counter-petitions against new demands[28]. These

Cruden Bay Station in the days of promise, opened on 2 August 1897. *(Stenlake collection)*

The terminus and branch train, St. Combs Light Railway. *(Stenlake collection)*

allegations were denied when George Davidson gave evidence three weeks later, claiming that the GNS had not really needed the conciliation scheme but had accepted it, found it worked satisfactorily, and neither the company nor the employees were seeking further changes[29].

Meantime the salaried staff, stationmasters and clerks, had submitted a memorial to the board regarding their levels of pay, requirements for Sunday duties at no extra payment, and other issues. Davidson was instructed to personally visit all stations on the system and inquire into the working conditions of the stationmasters and senior clerks, a task he completed in late November. His report resulted in positive action, with an all-round salary increase for the stationmasters from 1 December, and an extra allowance to those not provided with a house. Clerks' pay was also improved, with a new scale from boy clerks upwards. It was also decided to enforce a retiring age of 65 for salaried staff, which resulted in numerous retirements and consequent promotions[30].

At the end of 1911 the Great North's weekly wage bill[31] was:

Way and works (438 men and boys):	£461 4s 8d
Working stock maintenance (452):	£465 19s 3d
Locomotive department (318):	£412 7s 0d
Signalmen, gatemen, pointsmen (192):	£181 5s 5d
Ticket collectors, porters, policemen (368):	£349 3s 8d
Guards, brakesmen, motor vehicle staff (102):	£128 13s 4d

At the 118th ordinary general meeting on 12 September 1911, Sir David reported that the Great North was holding its own after a satisfactory six months, though once again government policy was eroding business margins, this time with the National Insurance Act, which he thought would cost the company £1,625 a year for invalidity pensions alone. Anticipating what Davidson would tell the Royal Commission, he said he did not believe the Great North men would have gone on strike and that the board much appreciated their attitude.

At this time the three larger Scottish railway companies were locked in a commercial and legal dispute with their biggest industrial customers over the question of demurrage charges – penalty charges for holding wagons or using sidings for more than a stated minimum period. On the Great North, like the Highland, this was not an issue, despite the fact that the GNS was perpetually short of goods wagons. This reflected the nature of the traffic: in the north-east there were neither coal mines nor steel works nor any other kind of industry that required goods wagons in large numbers. No doubt there were stations on the system where a local coal merchant might keep a loaded, or part-loaded wagon on a siding for days or even weeks, but the numbers involved were small and no need for a special policy was felt.

In November 1911 the railway unions published a "national programme" setting out their standards for wages and working hours. The Great North did not make any direct response. Industrial trouble in the coal industry cut down supplies and pushed up prices, and services were cut back for a time during March 1912 and again in September. In June a circular from Davidson gave details of concessions made to guards and brakesmen, from 7 July:

> Guards' minimum first year's pay up from 25s to 26s a week
> Guards' maximum pay up from 28s to 30s a week
> Brakesmen's starting pay up from 20s to 21s a week
> Brakesmen's maximum pay up from 23s to 25s a week

Twelve hours to elapse between signing on and signing off, including meal hours, with a minimum of nine hours between shifts, except in emergency. Wages of time plus a quarter payable for overtime above twelve hours, with time plus a half for Sunday work, with a minimum of half a day's pay at the standard rate.

A week's wage was guaranteed to all men whose conditions of service compelled them to devote their whole time to the company, suspendable at one week's notice in the event of services being curtailed. In August J.R. Bell of the Amalgamated Society of Railway Servants noted a "very fair" agreement with the locomotive department staff[32]. By September, the chairman was able to record friendly agreement on wages and conditions with all departments except the signalmen, with whom discussions were still continuing. Under a title of extreme length[33] a parliamentary paper set out a comprehensive scale of hours agreed for GNS employees in the course of 1912. These arrangements were intended to obtain until 30 June 1915.

Goods staff, Waterloo:	Twelve hour day, one hour (usually) for meal.
Porters:	Hours to be fixed by Superintendent; as far as practicable, not to exceed existing booked hours. Sunday work at time plus a half.
Guards and brakesmen:	Twelve hours including meal hours. Sundays: time plus a half, with minimum equivalent to half a day at ordinary rate.
Permanent way men:	60-hour week. Overtime at time plus a quarter.
Drivers and firemen:	Eleven-hour day. As far as possible, men working suburban trains to have a ten-hour day with one meal hour, or to be booked off after 9 hours. Overtime at time plus a quarter; Sunday work at time plus a half. Lodging allowance 2s for the first night each week, then 1s 6d, with a weekly maximum of 9s. Nine hours rest between shifts except in emergencies.
Signalmen:	Hours graded by type of box (six classes). Classes 1 and 2: eight hours; class 3 ten hours (except Inverurie: twelve hours); class 4: ten hours (except Woodside, Peterhead, Fraserburgh, Ellon South, Tillynaught: twelve hours); classes 5 and 6: twelve hours. Overtime at time plus a quarter; Sunday work at time plus a half, with minimum rate as for guards and brakesmen. Minimum nine hours between shifts.

Housekeeping matters, 1911 – 13

The Railway Companies (Accounts and Returns) Act of 1911 altered the timing of railway accounts and substituted annual figures and annual meetings for the long-established half-yearly accounts and gatherings. Consequently a five-month set of accounts was presented for August-December 1912. Sir David had suggested the prospects for this period were "not rosy" but the Great North kept up a relatively steady performance with gross revenue for the five months at £228,197 18s 4d, and working expenses at £116,138 6s 2d; and the dividend

Inverurie in the 1900s, showing the locomotive works and the 'colony' of railway housing. Benachie is on the horizon. *(Stenlake collection)*

of 3% on converted preferred ordinary shares was maintained, with 1% on deferred converted ordinary. Petrol prices had risen by 100% and coal by 30%, and a rise in carriage rates by a maximum of 5%, or "less if possible" was proposed.

Dividends continued to be declared on a half-yearly basis and 3% and 1% were again announced in July 1913. Long agitation for improvements on the Buchan line resulted in a decision to spend £731 on steam heating for the carriages[34]. The board also had to cope with a strike threat by men working at the Waterloo goods station. A change of personnel had resulted in a refusal to be bound by an agreement on wages and conditions made on 6 January 1912 and intended to last until 31 December 1914. The matter was passed to the general manager to resolve, and the current scale for porters and assistant shore guards was raised from 21s-26s a week by 1s a week in the second and third years of employment[35].

A letter from Donald Matheson, general manager of the Caledonian, informed the GNS board in December that his company was offering the post of locomotive superintendent to William Pickersgill, who later in the month presided at his last soirée of the locomotive department staff. His post was offered to John Auld of the Barry Railway, who withdrew, and the second choice, Thomas E. Heywood, assistant locomotive superintendent of the Taff Vale Railway, was appointed in February 1914, at £650 a year, with £50 deducted for his house[36].

Among the range of housekeeping matters and activities of the board and its committees in late 1913 and early 1914 might be noted the sale of two old engines, Nos. 28 and 33 from 1862 and 1863, for scrap at £505; a visit by a party of directors to the Glasgow & South Western's Turnberry Hotel in November 1913 (cost £24 4s 8d) probably to see how it coped with the winter season; a year's agreement with the Pumpherston Oil Company for Scottish-produced fuel oil, 30-35,000 gallons at 11½d a gallon, to be delivered in tank wagons; a note from the finance committee that the company was paying the Aberdeen Steam Navigation Company sums between £39 and £130 a month – the reason unspecified but the fluctuating amounts suggest a traffic-sharing arrangement; the Dailuaine Distillery's own engine to do shunting for all goods traffic at Carron and haul all traffic on the distillery line, with the normal charge of 1s a ton remitted; the abolition of the post of northern district superintendent on John Ross's retirement: northern stations would now be controlled from Aberdeen, with direct telegraphic communication to be set up with stations between Keith and Boat of Garten. This would cost £360 but would result in savings of £195 a year. The directors' own fees and charges for six months amounted to £1,004 15s 9d. The newly-formed National Union of Railwaymen (successor to the Amalgamated Society of Railway Servants from 1913) gave formal notice of its intention to terminate the current conciliation arrangements from December 1914[37].

Careful stewardship brought its rewards. At the 122nd ordinary general meeting on 17 February 1914, Stewart could announce that though operating costs had risen by £25,000, revenue had increased enough to justify a larger dividend, with 2% on the deferred converted ordinary for the July-December 1913 half-year, and he emphasised that additional traffic, not increased rates, had produced the result, describing it as traffic which "should never have been lost". Gross revenue for 1913 was £584,641 2s 9d, and working costs were £323,128 9s 3d. Higher charges had brought in less than £2,000 for the whole of 1913. He looked forward to occupancy of Aberdeen's new joint station buildings between May and July. Extensive alterations to the Palace Hotel were planned, with Pratt & Keith's lease to terminate in May 1915[38].

In the company's first experience of a strike, 30 engine cleaners walked out in June 1914. It lasted only a matter of days, ended by agreement that in future cleaners working a seventh shift in one week would be paid at the rate of time plus a quarter, and the directors promised to consider a pay rise[39]. New conciliation arrangements were under discussion between the committee of railway general managers and the railwaymen's unions, and in July the board was asked to approve suggested changes, including abolition of an independent chairman of central boards, and the appointment of assessors and umpires. Considering that the present arrangements worked well as far as the GNS and its staff were concerned, the board resolved to adhere to them, subject to reasonable adjustment, and to oppose any scheme which did not provide machinery for final settlement of disputes[40]. Less than a week later, all such issues were thrust aside when the British government informed Germany that a state of war existed between the two countries from 11 pm on 4 August.

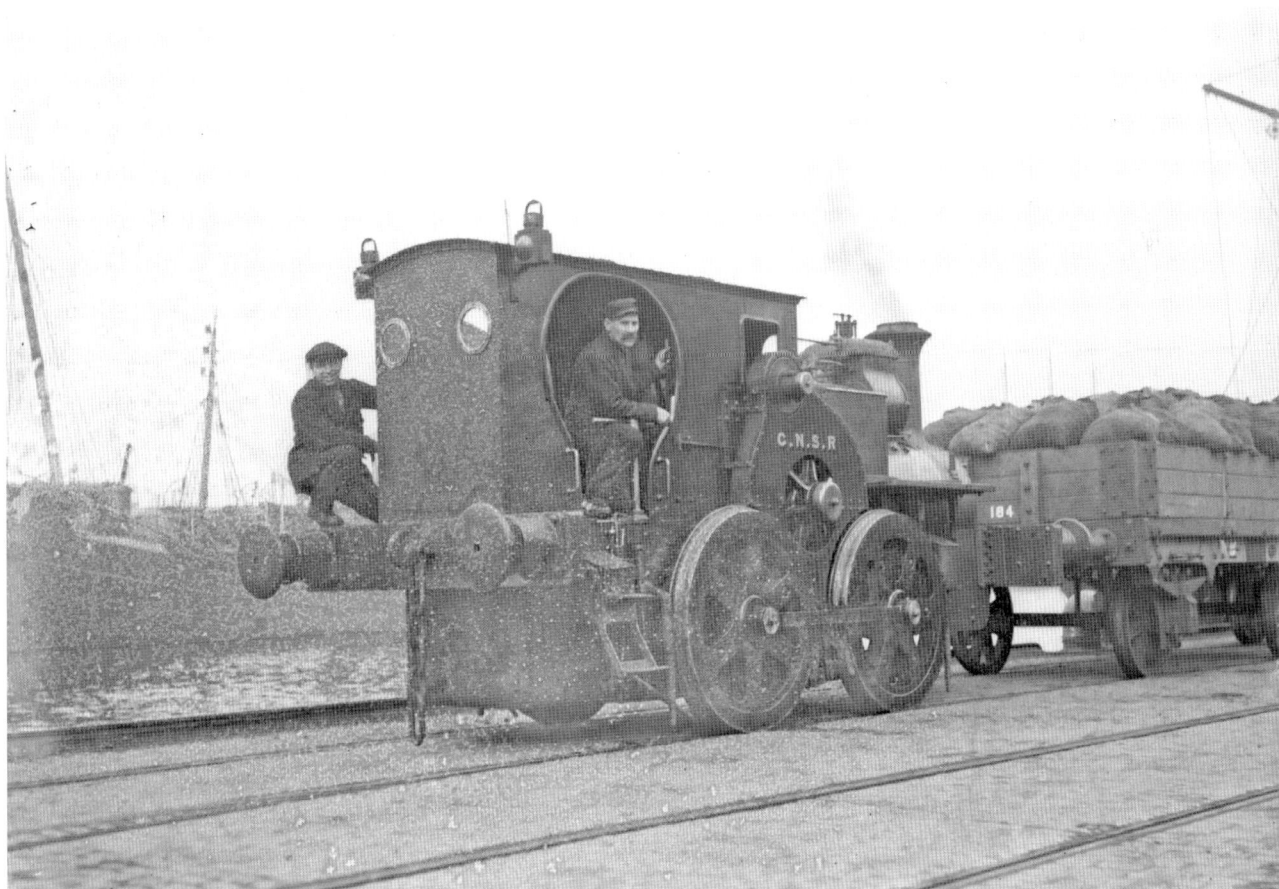

An Aveling & Porter geared locomotive at Aberdeen Harbour. It bears the GNSR letters but no number, and was probably on hire in 1914-15 from either Glenlossie or Dailuaine Distillery prior to use of the Manning, Wardle pugs. (*Aberdeen University Library*)

CHAPTER 20 The Great North at War , 1914 – 1919

Under government control

In common with every other railway company, the Great North was informed that an Order in Council, under the terms of the Regulation of the Forces Act, 1871, had placed the railways under the control of the government from 4 August. Preparations for such an eventuality had long been made, in concert between the War Office and the railway companies: since 1896 an Army Railway Council (renamed War Railway Council in 1903) had existed, its members including six railway general managers. Draft mobilisation timetables had been in existence since 1904, and a Railway Executive Committee had been in being since 1912. This body, formed of the general managers of twelve companies, the only Scottish one being the Caledonian, with the president of the Board of Trade as its titular chairman, was intended to assume overall control of the entire British railway system in the event of a national emergency. A small central office, formed of railway staff – only six people initially – provided a secretariat. Despite the conjunction of mobilisation with the August bank holiday and the territorial troops' training period, the mobilisation was achieved with remarkable speed and smoothness. Action was immediate in the deployment of regular and mobilisation of territorial troops, and the calling-up of naval reservists. Inter-company co-operation was equally prompt – Pratt records that on one Sunday in August, the Great North accepted 21 troop specials off the Highland Railway at Keith[1]. Special trains were provided within the first few days to move territorial units of the Gordon Highlanders from Aberdeen, Banchory, Keith and Peterhead to a camp in Bedfordshire.

At the directors' first formal meeting since the declaration of war, on 25 August, it was recorded that the company was now directly under government control. Already three of the GNS lorries had been commandeered, and their cost was noted as £503 15s each, excluding tyres. In September the Railway Executive ordered 50 general service wagons to be built at Inverurie. Pre-war issues continued, at least for a time. Exchanges between the GNS, the Fraserburgh & Rosehearty Railway promoters, and the Treasury resulted in the board's acceptance of a Treasury loan, interest-free and repayable after mortgage and other debts were cleared, to construct the line. The loan was to be secured by a mortgage on the whole undertaking of the Great North of Scotland Railway. In October it was noted that the existing conciliation scheme would remain in force for the present – but pay and conditions were soon to be taken out of the company's control[2].

Under the terms of government control (though occasionally amended) railway companies would be fully compensated for any losses or damage suffered during the period of state control. The companies would be paid by the government using their 1913 accounts as a basis, unless receipts for the first half of 1914 were less than those for the first half of 1913, in which case the sum payable was to be reduced by the same proportion. Thus the railways were assured of net earnings no less, though also no more, than those of 1913. Consequently, when the Great North's net receipts at the end of October 1914 showed an increase of £2,057 over 1913, that sum had to be remitted to the Railway Executive[3]. All government traffic, of people and goods, had to be carried at no charge and with no accounts rendered.

The final accounting was to be made difficult by the steady increase in costs throughout the war years. Coal cost from 9s to 9s 6d a ton in September 1914 and had risen to between 14s 6d and 16s a ton by February 1915. The war at sea reduced imports and the prices of food and other commodities rose, necessitating the first of a series of "war bonus" payments to all railway staff, waged and salaried, in February 1915, with the companies compelled to absorb 25% of its cost.

Railway works were required to fulfil government orders: the War Office ordered 350 picketing posts and 3,500 picket pegs from the Inverurie works, with payment on the basis of materials at replacement prices, plus wages and ascertained working costs, and 12½% added to the total for management charges. At this time Inverurie had no new locomotives under construction and none were built there by the Great North during the war years, though normal maintenance and repairs were still required and numerous engines were reboilered and fitted for steam heating of trains. Inverurie is recorded as having produced 64,090 adapters for graze fuse No. 100, 12,017 grenade dischargers, 24 regulation ambulance stretchers and four snowploughs for use in France[4].

Decisions and deferments

In November 1914 the Great North lodged an application for a Provisional Order for various projects, including double-track between Dyce and Ellon, extra land at Kittybrewster, alterations to the Palace Hotel, and the authorisation of debenture stock to an amount equal to the feu duties and ground annuals paid by the company. The Order was confirmed on 24 June 1915[5]. Traffic on the line to Inverness became much heavier and the double-tracking to Keith proved a valuable asset. With intense pressure on the Highland lines, it was agreed in December that GNS engines should, for the time being, run all trains between Aberdeen and Inverness, with the Highland paying one shilling per mile. An unusual initiative at this time, either as an economy or to ensure supply, was a proposal from the general manager that the company should set up a poultry farm at Cruden Bay, to provide eggs and table chickens for the hotels, and 5.85 acres at Nethermill Farm were leased for this purpose[6].

A troop train leaves Elgin behind Class V No. 113 during the August 1915 flood. *(Stenlake collection)*

In 1915 and 1916 intermittent discussions went on with the promoters of the Central Buchan Railway, still seeking a link between the Buchan line and Turriff. Having refused to contribute £15,000 towards its cost, the Great North board finally put the whole issue on hold until the end of the war[7]. Despite occasional petrol supply problems, the bus and lorry fleet continued to operate through the war years, with 36 buses and eleven lorries in 1916. Two Coventry-Daimler charabancs, acquired in 1914 for the tourist runs, were regularly loaned to the Red Cross for use with convalescent soldiers.

The new joint station, and new power at the harbour

Aberdeen's rebuilt joint station, when completed in September 1915, was described as "artistically and operatively" adequate. Covering a total of 11 1/2 acres, of which five acres were built upon or roofed over, it had thirteen platforms, with a total length of 3,780 yards, compared to the old station's 1,416 yards. Platform 6, 532 yards long, could comfortably accommodate two full-length trains[8]. The glazed roof over the wide concourse still remains. Though still half-owned by the Caledonian, and administered by the joint committee, the great majority of services were Great North, and it took the lead in matters concerning the station and its running. The Railway Executive's accountancy sub-committee disputed the GNS's claim for compensation made for expenditure on the "displacement" of the joint station during the control period; and for £12,600 to charged to the revenue account in respect of replacement of obsolete carriages. The matter was referred to the general manager, who was able to report by November that the company could make the displacement charge, but the charge on replacement carriages was refused[9].

By this time Aberdeen Harbour had become tremendously busy. Unlike the Firth of Forth ports, it was not wholly taken over by the Admiralty, but from 15 January 1915 it was the prime base for supplying the Grand Fleet, then stationed at Scapa Flow in the Orkney Islands, with virtually everything except bulk ammunition and coal. Victoria Dock was the berthing point for supply ships, alongside the GNS Waterloo goods yard. A two-storey transit shed on the quay, with three 30cwt electric cranes, belonging to the harbour commissioners, was taken over. Though both the Caledonian and GNS lines connected with the harbour tracks, and the great bulk of supplies came up via the southern lines, the Great North handled all traffic on the harbour lines. Apart from fleet supplies, vast amounts of material for shore establishments, including around 50,000 tons of prefabricated concrete, and large amounts of iron and steel, were shipped out. Other equipment and goods included around 50 seaplanes,

Schoolchildren watch as a detachment of Gordon Highlanders are piped on board a troop special at Banchory, on 16 April 1915, bound for camp at Bedford, then France. *(Stenlake collection)*

dismantled and packed in 40-feet crates and delivered on low-loading wagons; ten locomotives, twelve travelling cranes, many cars and lorries, guns up to six-inch calibre, boats up to 60ft long, 600,000 gallons of lubricating oil, 150,000 gallons of petrol, and half a million sacks of potatoes. Incoming wagons were held at the Caledonian yard at Craiginches, and passed on as dockside space became free, in a carefully managed operation which minimised turn-round time. Inevitably there were accidents, with unloaded articles piled on the quay, and the company appealed to the harbour commissioners to ensure that a space of at least 4ft 6in was kept between goods and the railway tracks[10]. Only on one occasion was there serious congestion, with some 500 wagons held waiting when two supply ships were grounded in a storm. Large amounts of goods went the other way, including guns and machinery to be repaired or replaced, empty casks and crates, contractors' plant returning, etc. Admiralty and railway officials conferred constantly to ensure maximum use of wagons in both directions, since the farms of the north-east were working at full stretch to supply grain, potatoes and beef, while forests were being cut down wholesale and the timber sent south for use in the trenches of the western front. Wagon use was a general problem, and the Great North board received a report from a joint committee of the five railway companies on the possibility of placing all open wagons in a joint pool. The three large Scottish railways began operating a pooled wagon scheme on 5 June 1916, and the Great North, along with the Highland, joined it on 2 January 1917.

Ever since 1861 the GNS had been seeking to use locomotives on Aberdeen's dockside lines. Agreement was finally reached with the harbour commissioners in spring 1914 and in May two 28-ton tank engines were ordered from Manning Wardle, of Leeds, at £2,650 each. On arrival in August 1915, they turned out to be two tons over-weight. Two 28-ton replacements were supplied for £2,540 each, and the GNS also bought the original pair at half-price, acquiring four dockyard pugs just at the time when they were most needed[11]. Locomotive haulage on the harbour tracks showed a loss for 1915 of £967 13s 4d, reduced to £466 5s 2d if Admiralty traffic were included, and after an argument with the harbour commissioners about the need for an increase, the rate per ton was raised in July 1916 from 2$\frac{1}{4}$d to 3d. The carting agents' rates were raised in August, to 12$\frac{1}{2}$% over the 1913 level.

The Zeppelin threat, and the price of coal

The line's eastern exposure to Zeppelin and naval raids prompted the board to spend £239 3s 9d on insurance premiums against aircraft and shore bombardment, though no damage was incurred. In the event, defensive precautions were more damaging: the engineer reported in October 1916 that telegraph wires had been cut at several locations by steel cables dangling from derelict anti-aircraft balloons[12]. In December 1916 companies were asked by the Railway Executive to identify permanent way materials that could be sent to France, including branch lines that might be closed down and double lines that might be singled, but no GNS branches were closed and, if anything, it needed more double line capacity for wartime traffic[13].

From December 1917 Aberdeen was also the headquarters of the five-strong American battleship squadron sent to reinforce the Grand Fleet. Their supplies were landed at west coast ports and moved by rail to Aberdeen, joining the queue for quay space. Naval traffic in the final years of the war amounted to an average of almost 6,000 tons each month, reaching its peak in the second half of 1918 with 40,000 tons. The GNS dealt with 67,283 loaded wagons between 15 January 1915 and 28 February 1919, with a total load of around 297,900 tons, in Admiralty traffic (excluding coal to the Pocra Quay coaling depot), quite apart from other commercial usage of the harbour. Fishing activity was severely restricted by the commandeering of trawlers for minesweeping (in 1912 161 steam trawlers were registered at Aberdeen), and part of the fish market was used to store the removed trawl gear as well as a workshop making submarine detection apparatus. With its maritime workshops, Aberdeen was the central depot for stores and sweeping gear for all minesweeping trawlers, with a regular outward flow of parts by rail to other ports.

Coal prices were still going up, and the Fordell Colliery in Fife found it had made an unfortunate deal with the GNS in October 1914, for the supply of 18,000 tons at 8s a ton, to be delivered at the rate of 350 tons a week, over a year. The colliery company asked for an additional 2s per ton, which was refused, and at the end of the contract period, delivery was 6,000 tons short. This too went to Davidson for resolution, and the final 3,000 tons were supplied at an extra 3s per ton[14]. By the end of 1916 coal was at £1 per ton. The company's carting agents received a further 5% rate increase in October, and the general manager reported a further set of war bonus pay rises in the same month. Late in 1915 the "Derby Scheme" of voluntary registration for possible military service was introduced and the board encouraged it by agreeing that married employees who were called up – and "released" by the board, railwaymen being a group whose work was accepted as nationally necessary – could have their pay made up to four fifths of former earnings, after taking into account the army separation allowance and allotment, and the 10s per man paid by the government[15].

Wartime shortages and demands

Creosote, used as a preservative for sleepers, was in very short supply: in mid-1917 the Ministry of Munitions was reserving all stocks for fuel. This was possibly good news for those who lived near the Great North's creosoting plant at Dyce, established in the 1870s, which was notorious for leaking poisonous effluent into the River Don and the Dyce Burn. New attempts had been made to prevent this in 1915. But by December 1917 a licence to purchase 7,500 gallons had been granted[16]. Fuel oil distribution was also strictly controlled, and in August 1916 the Petrol Control Committee allocated purchase licences for only 60% of the fuel requested for lorries, and 50% for buses. By mid-1918 the position was better, with licences granted for 2,600 gallons of motor spirit a month, enough to meet requirements[17]. At every turn, officialdom might block the path. The Great North's booking office in Inverness Station was taken over for military use, despite protest, but the Highland found space for the former enemy in the old parcels office[18]. In September 1917 the company was asked to provide three locomotives for use in France – while no reply can be traced, the GNS had no heavy goods engines and there is no evidence of any being sent. Co-operation had its limits – when the secretary of the Aberdeenshire territorial units wrote to request the use of GNS lorries for Volunteer Motor Transport, he received the stout reply that vehicles would be given only for "the immediate purpose of repelling a German invasion"[19].

William Deuchar, passenger superintendent, gave three months' notice of retirement in February 1918, after 47 years with the company, and was awarded £1,000 to augment what was described as the "comparatively small" allowance of £260 a year from the Superannuation Fund. He was succeeded by William Johnston, chief clerk in the general manager's office, at £500 a year[20].

The Highland was now an ally, and collaboration was also close with the Caledonian and North British companies, though it did not prevent legal disputes. The Caledonian contested an attempt by the Great North to make a mileage supercharge, Forth Bridge style, on the Denburn line between the joint station and Kittybrewster, and the case went through judgement and appeal in the Court of Session through 1915 and 1916 before the Court finally ruled in December 1916 that the principle was inapplicable in this case and nothing in excess of the statutory maximum charge for terminals should be allowed[21]. In return the Caledonian raised a case against the GNS for £9,993 as alleged rent due in the period from 1 August 1911 to 31 December 1916 for use of the line between Ferryhill Junction and the joint station, citing the agreement of 1855 between the Aberdeen and Deeside Railway companies. Someone had evidently been looking through the archives. £13,500 was paid promptly to the joint station committee[22], and soon afterwards the Great North issued a summons against the Caledonian for a payment of £23,919 1s 11d due under the agreements of 1898 and 1911 regarding the enlargement of the joint station. The Great North was also pursuing the North British for an increase in its payment for use of the joint station. In September 1916 the North British Railway offered an addition of £3,000 to its present £1,500 and to pay £10,000 on account for the period up to July 1916, but wanted its share of the station expenses to be reduced from 20% to 17½%, but the Great North refused and by January 1917 it was agreed that the North British Railway would pay an annual rent of £3,250 a year, plus £12,000 for its use up to 30 June 1916; and continue to shoulder 20% of the station's running expenses. In May 1917 Andrew Bain and George Davidson met Henry Allan, deputy chairman, and Donald Matheson, general manager, of the Caledonian Railway at Glasgow, to sort out questions relating to land and works in Aberdeen, which resulted in the Great North paying over £3,369 18s 2d to the Caledonian[23]. By June 1917 the company had closed its Glasgow office, though the Edinburgh office was kept open.

Having made special arrangements for men who registered for service under the Derby scheme, the company was finding itself short of skilled men by February 1916 and the chairman hoped it might be possible to retrieve some from the armed forces[24]. Compulsory conscription was introduced in 1916, but railway work remained a reserved occupation. New war bonus payments were awarded to railway staff in October 1916, something the companies were powerless to resist. The Great North was still paying a regular surplus over the 1913 revenues to the Railway Executive. When 320 stationmasters and senior clerks petitioned for a pay rise in January 1917 they were informed that the war bonus payments (increased again in April 1917) were intended to meet their needs, but the board did grant a "war allowance" of one shilling a week to pensioners, to last for not more than six months after the end of the war[25]. In common with all other railway companies, the Great North could only record and implement central decisions on pay and conditions, though the directors were alarmed by the scale and frequency of increases and stressed their "temporary" nature. After two and a half years of war, with all costs rising, passenger fares were abruptly raised by 50% in January 1917, but goods rates remained unchanged. In August war bonus payments were consolidated into war wages. Anxiety over wage costs, dividends and other aspects of state control brought a Railway Stockholders' Protection Association into being in September, and the Great North board agreed to provide it with "such information … as they consider prudent", which included the names of the 50 largest shareholders and of institutional shareholders. With the other Scottish companies the GNS mounted a successful opposition to the proposed Education (Scotland) Bill, which would have changed the rating basis for education charges from nett to gross valuation of assets, costing the company an additional £1,000 a year[26].

In March 1917 the finance committee authorised spending £270 16s on pictures to hang in the Palace Hotel, but the company's hotels did not do very well during the war years, despite Aberdeen being a strategic transport centre. Train travel was very often irregular, overcrowded and uncomfortable, not encouraging to tourists from the south, even if continental travel was out of the question. Cruden Bay Hotel's exposed North Sea location may have deterred some potential visitors. Unlike some other resort hotels, it was not taken over for military or hospital use. Business travel was much reduced, including the activities of commercial travellers, who had been regular clients and also hired stock rooms in the station hotels for display of merchandise. The hotels became more expensive to stock and operate; in 1916 expenses were £33,981 and revenue £32,572, and the position improved only marginally in 1917, with expenses at £36,636 and revenue at £38,516[27]. The Great North maintained its summer Deeside and Donside tours through the war years until the summer of 1918, along with its guides and handbooks to hotels and holiday homes.

Day-by-day activities

All railway companies were requested by the Railway Executive in July 1918 to provide a quota of urgently-needed coal for Italy and France, Britain's allies in the war, to be secured by a diversion of coal from the pit-heads. The Great North was given a quota of 3,200 tons, at the rate of 800 tons per week. Its stocks of coal were 13,267 tons in November 1918, which explains why it was raided again by an official known as the "Coal Controller", who diverted 1,500 tons of Balgonie coal to the Caledonian in November 1918 and again in January 1919. At this time coal was around 21s 6d a ton, over double the 1913 prices[28]. As ever, the board and committees were also dealing with a variety of matters, large and small, as a selection from June-July 1918 shows. Vacuum cleaning equipment for carriages had been installed at Kittybrewster, and the traffic committee saw regular reports from the carriage cleaning inspector on cleaning activities, as well as regular reports on goods which might have been sent by rail but had gone by other means – this had been a feature for years, but in 1918 road haulage replaced sea as the competitor. In anticipation of the 1918-19 grain crop, 100,000 sacks were required, and licences had to be acquired for their purchase, a first order being 15,000 from Grimond's, Dundee, at 4s 3¾d each, less a 2½% rebate (subject to licence being granted). A small income came from pontage charges: the Durris estate paid £30 a year for the use of Park Bridge over the Deeside railway by all tenants. In the case of the Spey Viaduct at

The Spey Viaduct between Spey Bay and Garmouth, opened in April 1886; river in spate. *(Stenlake collection)*

Garmouth, the company paid the Duke of Richmond & Gordon an annuity of £120 a year, which was compounded in June for a one-off payment of £3012 1s 8d. Horse haulage was still in use at some stations and was costing the company £80 a month. In an unusual gesture, W.F. Jackson, retiring general manager of the North British, was allowed to retain his silver pass over the Great North system. These reciprocal passes were normally handed back on retirement, but Jackson had done considerable work on behalf of all the companies on the question of local rates and taxes. In the summer of 1918 the board noted that the Railway Companies' Association was forming a committee to consider the future working of the railway system, with two Scottish representatives, William Whitelaw (now chairman of the North British) and Donald Matheson of the Caledonian[29].

Working with the Highland

As already noted, a very important part of the Great North's war contribution was in acting as a relief line to the hard-pressed Highland. An 0-4-4 tank engine was temporarily loaned but recalled by December 1915[30]. From August 1914 to August 1919 it took 48,440 loaded and 9,033 empty wagons which would otherwise have gone from Inverness via Dunkeld. An average of 220 wagons a week may not seem very great, but this was around ten extra trains on a line very busy on its own account, and with only 97 tender engines, some of which at any time were out of action for repair or maintenance. In May 1917 the GNS was experimentally working trains on alternate days between its Buckie Station and Rathven, on the Highland Railway line to Keith, but this line, already closed between Rathven and Keith, was lifted entirely at the end of the year[31]. In May 1918 a trainload of locomotive coal ran from Aberdeen to Inverness on every second day, pulled by a GNS engine and manned by a GNS crew. There were also one-off arrangements, as when at the Railway Executive's request the GNS provided an engine, guard's van and crew to work seed potato traffic from Dingwall to Aberdeen on 20 February 1918 – one of the very few instances of a Great North engine travelling beyond Inverness. With the board's agreement George Davidson wrote to the Highland's general manager, Robert Park, proposing a connection to the east of Elgin between the Highland Railway line from Keith and the GNS Craigellachie line, with the object of making the Great North station into a joint one, and the idea was remitted to the Great North/Highland Railway joint committee. But the Highland members politely declined, because of the heavy expenses involved, and "the conditions obtaining at present"[32]. The two stations at Elgin were destined never to become one.

In its own war traffic, the GNS carried 88,105 tons of coal to Peterhead, used as a bunkering point for minesweepers and small naval vessels; and a very large tonnage of timber[33]. In 1913 timber traffic amounted to 56,797 tons; in 1918 it was 238,328 tons, coming mainly from Canadian forestry camps at Kemnay, Knockando and Nethy Bridge. Timber sidings were installed between Garmouth and Urquhart and at Nethy Bridge in 1917[34]. Despite the commandeering of much of the fishing fleet, the remaining boats worked intensively, and with no export market for herring, and increased need for home-produced food, the company's rail-borne fresh fish tonnage rose dramatically, from 7,087 tons in 1913 to 53,302 tons in 1918. While much went by scheduled passenger trains, many specials were also required, putting further strain on the locomotive resources, and also on wagon stocks. In the herring season between June and September 1917 the company ran 406 fish specials, forming 8,830 wagon-loads, with a weight of 22,928 tons of fish. An extended loading area and two extra sidings for 57 wagons were put in at Peterhead in late 1918; the cost of £1,500 to be met by the government, though the company agreed to accept the extra facilities, on valuation, after the control period ended[35]. The soaring cost of sea transport and the lack of shipping also resulted in extra traffic, estimated at 50,000 tons a year of mixed goods[36]. Sudden requirements for fish trucks caused problems, and Sir David Stewart observed that the common user policy for wagons did not work satisfactorily for the Great North, which on 15 February 1918 had 651 wagons due to it from the pool. The company was having to hire wagons, paying around £450 a month to Hurst, Nelson between August and October 1918[37]. The pooling arrangement lasted until 31 May 1921. It was not a free exchange: the GNS paid £909 2s 7d to the Paymaster-General for "hire charges on pool rolling stock" in September 1921[38]. Much of the extra traffic, especially the fish, brought additional income, though much timber was carried free for the government; and the company paid the government a surplus on the 1913 net revenue all through the war years. The fishery companies were prospering and in August 1918 the Great North had £40,000 on loan from four Aberdeen fishing companies[39].

Late in the war, it was decided to establish a naval airship station at Lenabo, in east Aberdeenshire, with the GNS to make a branch line of three miles 800 yards from Longside Station to help in its construction and supply. A three-span timber bridge over the Ugie was the main engineering requirement, and an estimate of £19,042 for railway works was sent to the Admiralty. A contract with William Tawse & Co. of Aberdeen for £23,015 13s 9d was agreed in January 1918. The line opened in mid-1918 and carried 31,913 tons of war material[40].

GNS buses meet at Bellabeg, Strathdon, *c.*1914. On the left is a Milnes-Daimler 18-seater, one of the second set delivered in 1905. On the right with semi-open coachwork is a Milnes-Daimler 18-seater charabanc of 1912, coming up from Ballater on a service mainly run as part of the Three Rivers tour. Tourists would transfer to a horse-drawn coach at Cockbridge for Tomintoul, and thence by bus to Ballindalloch Station. *(Stenlake collection)*

Post-war planning

By August 1918, thoughts were turning to post-war policy, and numerous bodies were set up nationally and locally to consider what needed to be done. In August 1918 the Rural Transport (Scotland) Committee met in Aberdeen to review requirements and proposals. Five light railway schemes were brought forward: Aberdeen to Echt and Skene; Aberdeen to Newburgh; Udny to Methlick; Ballater to Braemar; and Alford to Bellabeg (Strathdon). Following evidence from Great North officials, the committee's view was that while motor omnibuses and steam lorries had improved local transport, "they do not allow of the traffic being fully developed, and probably have only postponed the demand for railways"[41]. The committee also acknowledged that "their policy is not bound by financial considerations." Another line being pressed for was an extension from Boddam to Peterhead, but government control was cited as the reason for no action at that time[42]. At the same time, in London, plans for a centralised Ministry of Transport – originally to be called Ministry of Ways and Communications – were being worked out, which would keep hold of much of the apparatus of control established for the emergency period, and all the purse-strings, and would show no sign of sharing the committee's opinion.

Additional war bonus payments continued to be made after the cessation of hostilities. On 10 December 1918 the board noted that the "war wage" paid on top of the company's own 1913 rates had reached 33*s* a week for male staff over 18 and 21*s* 6*d* for females over 21; 16*s* 6*d* for boys under 18 and 10*s* 3*d* for girls. Salaried male staff aged eighteen-plus whose basic salary was £800 a year or less also got a war bonus of 33*s* a week, with 18*s* a week for junior clerks under eighteen. Increases for senior staff kept pace. Simon Willox, the goods manager, had his salary raised from £600 to £700 and other office staff received increases, totalling £609 14*s*. Clerks and stationmasters on £70 a year were put up to £75. Fraserburgh's stationmaster had his salary increased from £145 to £155 and to £160 from 1 January 1920[43].

During the war 609 members of the staff served in the armed forces, of whom 93 were killed in action. A war memorial tablet to be displayed in the head office was planned, and the shareholders were asked to contribute to a £2,000 fund, the interest on which would be used to help the families of employees who had died on active service[44]. In the aftermath of the war, two GNS men received MBEs, James Knight Mitchell, station agent at Waterloo, and James Sim, chief trains clerk, who had served 50 years with the company. David McNicol, stationmaster at Aberdeen Joint Station, was also awarded an MBE[45].

At the end of 1918 the company was asked to provide passenger carriages for temporary use in France to help in demobilisation, and 31 were despatched south on 17 January 1919, returning at the end of March[46].

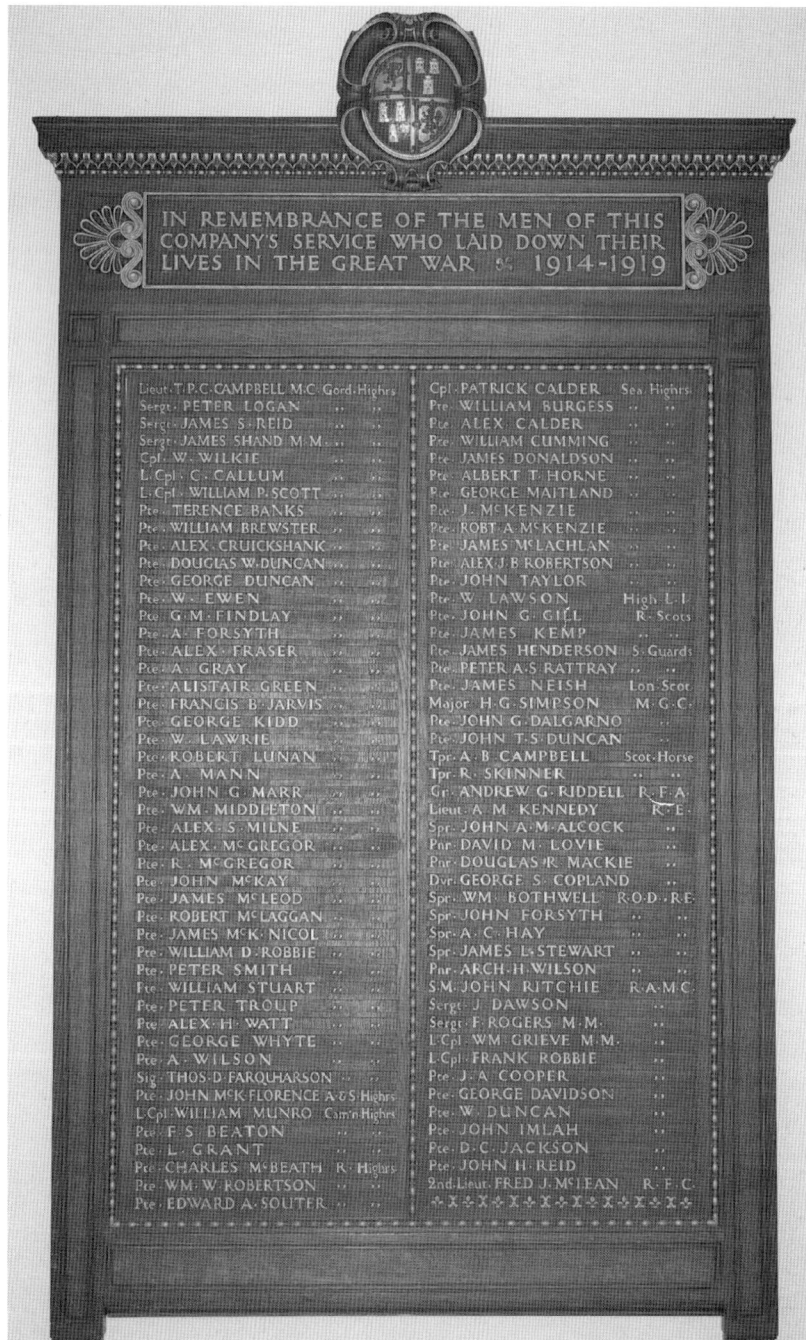

The GNSR memorial tablet, made of oak, with the names in raised gilt letters of the 93 men who gave their lives in the First World War. Housed for many years in the company's offices in Guild Street, after these closed it was moved to the station, again under cover. It now has a permanent place in the passageway from the concourse to the new shopping centre. *(Keith Fenwick)*

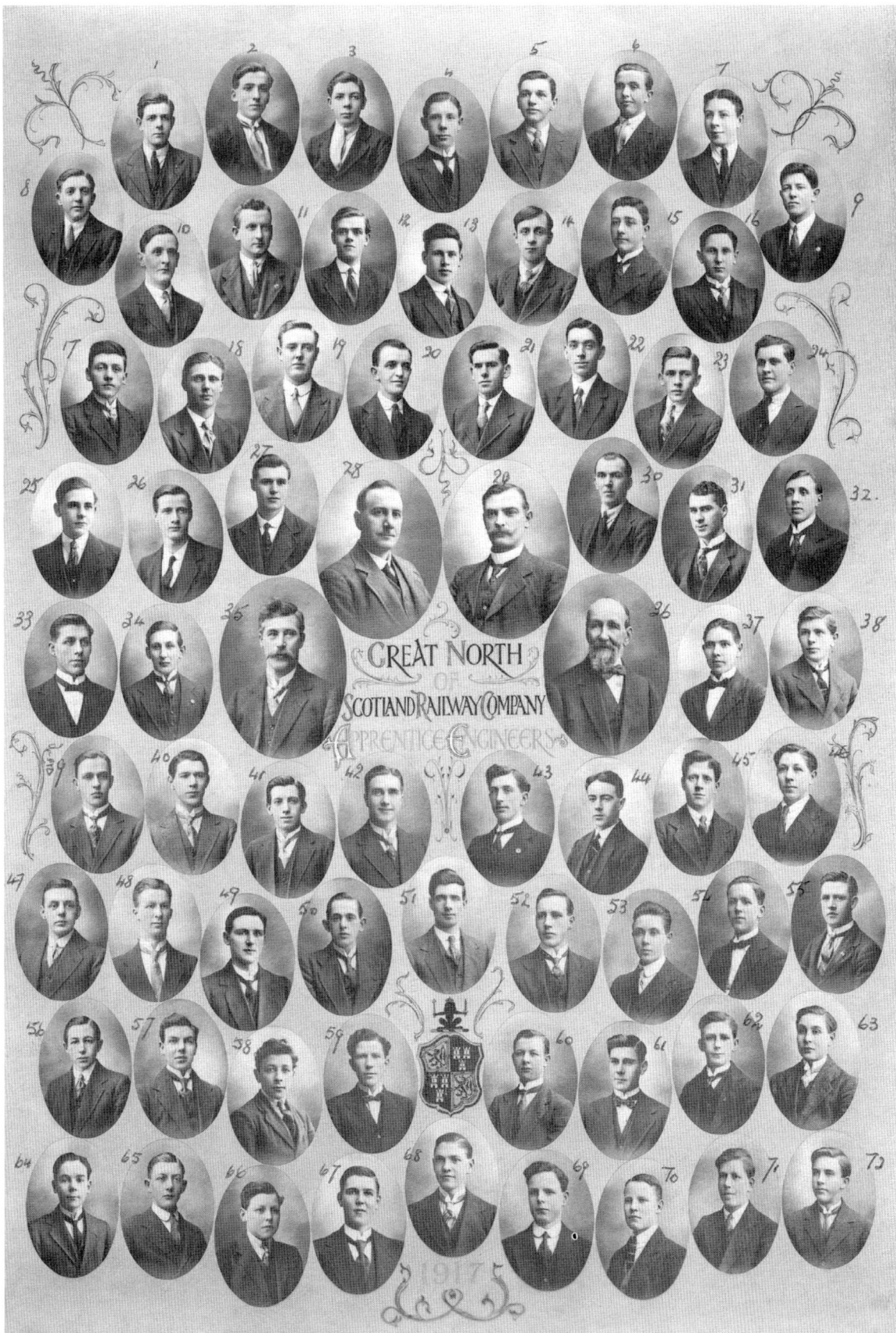

A photo montage showing GNSR apprentice engineers in 1917.
(*Great North of Scotland Railway Association*)

CHAPTER 21
The Final Years, 1919 – 1923

Readjustment, reaction and renewals

The four years immediately following the First World War were a time of re-adjustment in many different ways. The government controls which had been such a feature of life in 1914-18 were gradually and sometimes reluctantly relinquished. Prices of most commodities and services had doubled between 1913 and 1919, and wages had gone up accordingly. In industrial relations the position of trade unions was much stronger, and the mood of the labour force was militant. Millions of men were demobilised from the forces, having been promised a return to a "land fit for heroes". The war economy had to be dismantled, with the need for military supplies back to peacetime level. A period of relative confidence, with increased output and also rising costs in 1919 and 1920 was followed by virtual economic collapse in 1921.

The conventional view of British railway companies in the aftermath of the war is that they were run down, in a state of disrepair if not decrepitude, and badly needing large-scale investment in modernisation after five years of very intensive activity on most lines, during which there were greatly reduced facilities for maintenance and repairs. There had of course been very little material damage, compared to what would happen in the Second World War. In the case of the Great North, which had been in good condition in 1913, there does not seem to have been a marked deterioration. In June 1922 a goods train was derailed in a cutting between Dufftown and Craigellachie, its nineteen wagons were telescoped and the guard seriously injured. The accident was ascribed to a fractured rail on the inside of a curve; the permanent way on the section was in poor condition and scheduled for renewal. It was said that renewal would have taken place except for wartime delays[1]. This was the only instance of serious damage ascribed to wartime conditions, but the war had been over for three years.

The company, as we have seen, had a good and busy war record, and was able both to maintain its dividend payments during the war years and to pay a regular surplus to the government despite carrying very large amounts of goods and many hundreds of thousands of military personnel without receiving any payment at all. In the course of 1914-18 there had been comparatively few changes. Apart from the four small dockyard locomotives, no new engines were acquired, and construction of new rolling stock was for the Railway Executive, not the Great North. Ongoing work, like the completion of the joint station in Aberdeen, was generally completed though no new works were undertaken. Powers to double the line from Dyce to Ellon had been granted on 24 June 1915 but the impossibility of getting new rails and signalling equipment deferred the plan until after the war, when a short $1\frac{1}{2}$ mile section between Parkhill and a new signal box at Elrick was built by William Tawse for £9,500[2], and completed on 30 May 1920. But renewal of cast-iron bridges by malleable iron, and then steel, had been going on steadily since long before the war and was continued during it[3].

The question of Denburn line toll charges had gone from the Court of Session to the House of Lords, and in January 1919 the Lords upheld the ruling of the Court of Session on the extra mileage issue, and remitted to that court to do "what shall be just and consistent" in the way of fixing terminal charges. Also in January, a 47-hour week for the Inverurie Works was put into operation, following instructions from the Board of Trade, relayed by the Railway Executive Committee[4]. This was only part of a wider ruling – the government had conceded an eight-hour day for railway workers. To the Great North's employees, it was a victory won after long campaigning; to the board, in common with the other Scottish railway boards, it was a dismaying and financially damaging decision, but it had to be obeyed, and a sub-committee was appointed to manage the necessary re-organisation of jobs, working hours and payments. It estimated that the eight-hour day would require 270 additional men, at wages (including the war wage) of £44,045 a year. Soon afterwards, the Railway Executive was demanding that companies should place orders "within the next two or three weeks" for materials and equipment likely to be required within the next eighteen months, in order to help the manufacturers (deprived of war work) to plan ahead. This was followed by an instruction that the companies should take steps for the gradual restoration of full train services, and to co-operate on the provision of competitive services[5]. With victory achieved, railway directors might well have wondered for how much longer they would be subject to the dictates of civil servants; but the government was much concerned with the railways and their future within the whole context of inland transport.

The Railway Strike

In February 1919 the company again declared a dividend of 3% on preferred, and $1\frac{1}{2}$% on converted, ordinary shares. Shareholders might have been relatively content, but after comparative industrial peace on the railways during the war years, with 1919 came an era of tension and confrontation. The companies remained under the control of the Railway Executive and were due to do so until 15 August 1921. Their economic base had shifted radically, due to a vast increase in the wage bill. Now, with the national economy suffering convulsions in the transition from a highly directed war basis back to something like the pre-war commercial, industrial and political conditions (and finding them impossible to replicate), a gulf opened between railway workers and railway managements. Wartime control of the railways had been based on their financial returns in 1913, but in six years the prices of most commodities had doubled, and a scientific calculation of "the cost of living" had been introduced. For the directors, and shareholders, the scale of wage rises had been alarming and there was an open and concerted determination to turn the clock back. One aspect in particular concerned them: the equalisation of pay and working hours across the entire British railway system. Under the Railway Executive, Scottish railwaymen's wages had gone up threefold, compared with twofold for English workers – a difference which reflected the lower previous base as well as the extra costs to the companies[6].

In late September 1919 the intransigence and mutual suspicion came to a head in a national railway strike. Around 2,000 workmen were said to be on strike in Aberdeen, Caledonian as well as Great North. On 28 September the GNS was still running some trains to Ballater, Alford and Macduff. Public opinion was not in favour of the strike, and around 60 to 80 car owners volunteered to provide transport. On 29 September one train, carrying foodstuffs, ran to Fraserburgh and Peterhead. Mail from Inverness was brought on a locomotive, and Aberdeenshire mails were taken from the city by road motor. But the Great North was "generally speaking" closed. Farmers who normally despatched milk daily were turning it into cheese[7]. By 4 October "gradual improvement" in Aberdeen was reported, with one train a day running on most lines, and an increasing number of volunteer workers coming forward. The transport branch of the Ministry of Food was organising transport by sea to Peterhead, Fraserburgh, Macduff and Buckie. Twenty-five naval men were despatched to Aberdeen from Rosyth, as porters, cleaners and (in one or two cases) drivers. The strike committee was reported as "standing firm"[8], but on 5 October a settlement was reached, with promises of wage reviews and mediation on disputed issues.

A new chairman and new initiatives

Sir David Stewart died on October 11, aged 85, after fifteen years as chairman and 28 as a director. The long-lasting Stewart link with the company had exemplified the strong sense of continuity that existed within it. At a special board meeting on 28 October Andrew Bain, his deputy, aged 75, was elected as chairman. With an address given as Hunter's Quay, Argyll, Bain, a keen yachtsman whose fortune had been made in shipping and iron, was the first GNS chairman from outside Aberdeenshire. The meeting also recorded its high appreciation of the officers' successful efforts to cope with the difficulties of a "sudden and almost complete stoppage of work" and their grateful thanks to those employees who had "remained loyal to the Company and performed their own duties and such other work as lay within the scope of their attainments"[9].

Amidst larger issues, the Great North was proceeding with a variety of actions and policies which remained within the board's remit and indicated both a care for maintaining the company's effectiveness and an eye on future developments. In March 1919 a barrier and platform ticket system was initiated at Ellon Station, the first outside Aberdeen. Heywood was asked in April to obtain tenders for building four new locomotives. Haulage on the harbour lines was put up to 4d a ton in May, and two further increases would bring it to 6d a ton by mid-1921. In June another range of executive salary rises gave Davidson an extra £200, to £2,200, Mackintosh, Parker and Willox all got an extra £100, to £800. Heywood went from £750 to £850 and Johnston from £500 to £600. Coal supply was still under government control, and deliveries were irregular because of labour disputes in the collieries. With the resumption of coastal steamer services, locomotive coal was brought to Aberdeen by sea: 3,632 tons in August[10]. Wagons were still being hired from Hurst, Nelson, though in fewer numbers, with a hire charge for July of £151. A deputation from Peterhead was received on 27 June, pressing for a connection to the Boddam line. The directors indicated that if the backers were prepared to guarantee £150,000 for the work, including £30,000 for a new station in Peterhead, the company would be willing to go ahead. This was not at all what the deputation wished to hear, and the plan disappeared from view. For the locomotive committee lineside fires, caused by sparks from engine chimneys, were always a regular topic. The number of instances could vary from two to 120 in a half-year, and in the first six months of 1919 there were 24, with compensation paid to the landowners of £62 18s 10d – an unusually high figure. The GNS was good at resisting the often exaggerated claims for damage in such cases. Its poultry farm is not further recorded in surviving documents, but in September the company was advertising to buy or lease a good farm of not more than 200 acres, situated near one of its stations in Aberdeenshire. A list of farms was submitted to the hotel committee in November, but was deferred, and it does not seem that any purchase was made. The cost of heating Inverurie Works was investigated and found to be a rather daunting £6,300, and it was resolved to get tenders only for the carriage and wagon shops and the stores. As a footnote to this miscellany, the works committee counted 373 clocks in the ownership of the company in 1919, including those in the joint station at Aberdeen[11].

The powerful hand of central authority was always poised above the company. The Railway Executive instructed that all staff should be given a day's paid holiday for 'Peace Day' (19 July 1919) and that those who were required to work on the day should receive an additional day's pay in lieu. In the course of 1919 the Great North board

Pickersgill's class V of 1899 was the company's penultimate locomotive design. Eight more were built in 1910-15 at Inverurie, and Thomas Heywood built eight with superheated boilers in 1920-21 (class F).

decided that six new engines should be ordered, but following an interview between George Davidson and Sir Herbert Walker (Southern Railway), chairman of the Railway Executive, it was decided "in deference to Sir Herbert's wishes" to reduce the number to three, and an order was duly placed with the North British Locomotive Company for three at £10,460 each, on the understanding that if the Railway Executive Committee should alter its view, the order could be changed to six, at £9,860 each. By the end of the year, with the approval of the newly established Ministry of Transport, the additional trio was ordered[12]. Keen to improve statistical records, the Ministry of Transport ordered all companies to provide figures from 1 January 1920 on engine mileage and hours, net ton-miles, commodity traffics, and wagon miles[13]. In July 1920, Lieutenant.-Colonel Murray MP (Liberal, Kincardineshire and West Aberdeenshire) asked about extensions of the Great North to Braemar and Strathdon as supported by the committee on rural transport. The Ministry of Transport replied that these schemes were "under investigation"[14].

Timber merchants met in London in December to co-ordinate resistance to proposed railway rate increases. Foreign competition was returning to the lumber trade. During the war, a maximum rate of 10s a ton had been imposed for the transport of pitwood to Scottish collieries, but the higher pre-war rate was due to be applied from 1 January 1920. It was an important traffic to the the Great North, which had carried 238,328 tons in 1918, equivalent to five 30-wagon trainloads each day[15].

Andrew Bain's first a.g.m., on 17 February 1920, was presented with positive reports despite a disturbed year. Net revenue was £279,608. Doubling of the Parkhill-Elrick section was to go ahead, now at an estimated cost of £25,000. Almost a million – 956,000 – more fare-paying passengers had been carried in 1919 than in 1918, generating £117,000 more in revenue. Passenger trains had carried 42,081 tons of fish. General goods traffic was up by 116,492 tons (it had been a good year for the whisky industry). Livestock traffic was down by 37,450 head, primarily through lack of sheep being transported, due to the failure of the 1918 turnip crop, essential for winter feed[16]. April saw another round of executive pay rises, with Davidson advanced to £3,000, Mackintosh to £1,100, Parker and Willox to £1,100, Heywood to £1165, and Johnston to £900. Other salaried staff also received increases and the total rise in the salary bill was £20,841 4s. A consequence of pay increases was to increase interest in labour-saving devices, and two 15cwt cranes were bought to help with coaling locomotive tenders at Elgin and Keith[17].

One-day tourist excursions were resumed in August 1920, despite opposition from Sir Eric Geddes, the new and imperious Minister of Transport, who claimed there were not enough engines in Scotland to make excursion trips possible. A single fare was charged for the two-way trip along the Deeside line[18]. In June the GNS had had to borrow five elderly 2-4-0 locomotives from the Great Central Railway, but the board considered there were enough suitable engines to run the excursions. The borrowed engines were returned in January 1921. At this time the company was still running some mixed trains, notably on the Lossiemouth-Elgin line[19].

The compensation scheme and the grouping

It was generally accepted that the British railway system needed reorganisation and consolidation, and in government circles at least, that this process was too large, complex, and vital to the national economy, to be left to the companies themselves. At the same time, a parallel issue which affected every railway company was being considered, in private and without consultation, by a government committee headed by Lord Colwyn. With the end of the control period drawing nearer, there was a need to make a financial settlement between the State and the railways, since the provisions of the 1871 Act required the government to return the railways to their owners in the same condition as when they had been taken over. The government no doubt expected that railways would make the most of the opportunity. After six years of exceptionally high usage, with severely limited opportunity for maintenance, repairs and renewals, virtually every one of the 114 companies was in a more run-down condition than it had been in 1913. During 1919 and 1920, all companies had spent heavily in order to catch up on the arrears, and it was apparent that a very large bill was looming. With a brief to ascertain the likely total and to make recommendations accordingly, the Colwyn committee found that the railways might be entitled to between £150,000,000 and £200,000,000 – a very large amount still and a stupendous one in 1921, horrifying the tax-paying public. Its recommendation was for a compromise sum, and for the railways not to make "tenacious insistence on documentary rights". A total compensation of £60,000,000 was suggested.

The Ministry of Transport produced a draft scheme in June 1920, in which the Scottish companies would be combined in a single group, with English and Welsh companies formed into six groups. The proposal for

Milnes-Daimler 20/25 hp two-deck 22-seater bus delivered in April 1907.
The Aberdeen-Newburgh service ran from 1 April 1907 to 1 March 1922. *(Stenlake collection)*

Scotland was immediately opposed by the companies themselves, local authorities, commercial and industrial companies, and the railway unions. The unions feared a reduction in wages and an extension of working hours, while the commercial interests feared increases in the rates and charges. All preferred the idea of Anglo-Scottish links. Aberdeen Town Council and Chamber of Commerce sent members as part of a large Scottish delegation to Westminster on 2 March 1921, to oppose the proposed grouping arrangement. The autocratic Geddes refused to meet them, declaring he had "seen enough deputations from Scotland." The first version of his Railways Bill of 1921 responded by proposing two separate Scottish groups, with the Great North and North British in an East Scottish and the others in a West Scottish system. This was speedily altered in the face of bafflement and derision to the desired "longitudinal" arrangement, in which the Great North was combined with the North British, North Eastern, Great Central, Great Northern and Great Eastern Railways, as one of four large groups, the future London and North Eastern Railway, and this was sealed in the passage of the Railways Act on 19 August 1921, only four days after government control of the railways had formally ended. The Act also left substantial powers of supervision and regulation with the Ministry of Transport, and made it obligatory for the companies to accept £60,000,000 as full payment for wartime wear and tear.

New competition

With the date of 1 January 1923 set for the new groupings to come into effect, the prime task of the board now was to make the necessary preparations for the company's incorporation into a new and vast concern. There was still a railway to run, however, and immediate issues had to be confronted.

After the war the railway buses faced new competition from freelance operators who had bought army surplus vehicles and converted them into buses. The GNS had the advantage of operating postal services[20] but it had to modernise its fleet, with six new Thorneycroft 'J' type buses in 1919, another, plus a Lothian type, in 1920 and six more in 1921. Some services were stopped: the lorry to Culter was withdrawn in 1921; the Huntly-Aberchirder bus was service was extended to Turriff from 31 May 1921 but withdrawn in October through lack of patronage; and the Aberdeen-Newburgh and Aberdeen-Midmar services were withdrawn after 28 February 1922. At the end of 1922 the company had 33 motor vehicles, mostly fitted with bus bodies, and eleven steam lorries, running five regular services and three summer routes. This was equal to what the North Eastern Railway had, and only the Great Western had a larger fleet[21].

One of the few instances of the company pursuing the issue of demurrage came in September 1920 when the Culter Paper Company refused to pay £275 16s on wagons and sheets held for an excessive time. The company began proceedings, but the case ended without a hearing, with the Great North accepting £100. Two other large but not well-disposed customers, the Aberdeen Lime and Commercial companies, were conceded rebates totalling £159 19s 3d, on season tickets for their managers: both rented storage sheds at numerous stations[22].

By February 1921 the entire staff had been incorporated in a grading scheme. Stationmasters were graded 1-6 depending on their station and paid accordingly; thus when the stationmaster at Cambus o' May (Grade 6) was transferred to Pitlurg (Grade 5) his pay went automatically from £160 to £170 a year[23]. Shorter working days and higher pay had brought about an increase of 650 staff and an additional £554,000 a year on the wage bill.

The Great North's hotels, in the post-war years, were moderately successful. From November 1919 a four-person "orchestra" was installed in the Palace Grill Room as a six-month experiment at £500, proved popular, and lasted until the economy drive of 1921. A nine-hole golf-course was added to Cruden Bay's attractions in the summer of 1920 and in that year all the hotels were said to be in profit. The company had its own refreshment rooms at Aberdeen (a rent of £300 a year was paid to the joint committee), Ballater, Elgin and Keith, but refreshment rooms at a number of other stations including Craigellachie and Banchory were leased to tenants; the Banchory building was so decrepit in April 1921 that the works committee proposed to pull it down, but this was rescinded and the tenant allowed to keep going[24].

In May 1921 the company agreed to pay the North British Locomotive Co. an extra £5,454 10s 11d for the six new engines, due to increases in costs during construction[25]. With strikes and disputes endemic across the coal industry through 1921, the maintenance of coal stocks was a constant preoccupation. On 17 May, the GNS had 4,149 tons on hand, down to 2,585 tons by the 31st, with 1,367 tons awaiting delivery, and the stores committee was looking at whether foreign coal might be imported. Lack of fuel reduced the workshops to a 40-hour week, and like other railways, the Great North dabbled with oil firing, installing equipment on a single engine. Coal stocks fluctuated through the year while the stores superintendent struggled to keep the levels around 4-5,000 tons. From October, with only 1,669 tons in stock, and 41,931 tons on order, the situation began to improve. The oil-fired engine was converted back to a coal-burner in January 1922[26].

The approach to Elgin Station in 1937. The goods yard entrance was to the left. By this time, the LMS station was operated by the LNER as part of economy measures instituted in the 1930s, finally achieving the objective of a joint station which was discussed many times by the Great North and Highland.
(Great North of Scotland Railway Association)

The end of government control, and the wages battle

Direct government control, via the Railway Executive Committee, came to an end on 15 August 1921, but the passing of the Railways Act four days later meant that the powers of the Ministry of Transport and of its ancillary organisations, like the wages boards, still left railway boards with limited command of their affairs. On 9 August the GNS directors had approved the company's amalgamation into the Eastern Group, on the understanding that it would have the right to appeal to the Amalgamation Tribunal if the terms were not agreed[27].

Through 1921, cost-of-living increases made to wages in previous years were falling, as prices came down in the trade recession. Other retrenchments were being made, with bonuses paid to engineering shopmen being progressively withdrawn between October 1921 and January 1922. The stationmaster at Persley was transferred to Hutcheon Street and not replaced: the station was opened only between 7.25 am and 7.20 pm, staffed by a junior clerk under the stationmaster at Bucksburn. In September 1921 the National Union of Railwaymen held a meeting in Edinburgh to protest against proposals by the Scottish companies to modify the national agreement of 1919. All 1920 pay increases were to be withdrawn, special payment for night duty abolished, boys were to become men for payment purposes at 21 rather than 18; the eight-hour day was to be scrapped, except in the busiest yards; locomotive men were to have a ten-hour day; and Great North and Highland signalboxes were to be worked on a ten-hour day basis, "with a spread-over of twelve hours"[28]. In November the GNS joined with the other Scottish railways in submitting these proposals to the central wages board, which remitted the question to the national board. There was no proposal to cut executive salaries, and for at least one man on the Great North, pay was still rising: William Johnston, whose salary had been increased to £900 in April 1920, now received a further £100, while the chairman and his deputy, with the general manager and one other officer, were permitted something of a jaunt to attend the International Railway Congress held in Rome in April 1922[29]. With grouping negotiations looming up, Andrew Bain, now aged 77, relinquished the chairmanship in February 1922 and his deputy Alexander Duffus took over[30]. The company's last chairman, Duffus also represented a link with the first generation of Great North directors, as a partner in the law firm of Wilsone, Duffus – the same practice, under changed names, as that of Alexander Jopp in the 1840s.

By 24 January 1922 the cost-of-living index had fallen from 119 in June 1921 to 99 and the bonus was accordingly reduced by 4s a week (adults) and 2s a week (juniors) from 1 January. The national wages board was considering the Scottish companies' case for basic wage reductions. Johnston had gone to represent the Great North company and Davidson reported to the board on the proceedings. One of the arguments against the universal eight-hour day had been that the workload was unevenly spread between town and country stations. Traders were lined up to affirm that carriage rates were too high and must be reduced, through lower costs, or the railways would lose even more traffic to the roads. Countering this, C.T. Cramp of the National Union of Railworkers pointed out the recent large fall in costs, with items like steel rails and steam coal at less than half their 1920 prices. On 25 January 1922 the board issued its decision, approving a reduction in wages for every five-point fall in the index from 1 April of 2s instead of the previous 1s a week, though not to go below the standard rate; also that youths should be paid the boys' rate to the age of 20 rather than 18 (the companies had wanted 21), but to the chagrin of the companies, the eight-hour day was left unassailed, apart from minor adjustments. That same month, however, the Great North had received a payment of £135,715 from the Treasury as its share of the first payout of the £60,000,000 allocated to wartime wear and tear. £3,971 had been held back in reserve. The final amount received by the company was £360,951, 0.6% of the total[31].

The Great North added a last flourish to its Aberdeen-Inverness service in 1922. It never owned a dining car, but that year a borrowed North British restaurant car was run on the morning train from Aberdeen to Inverness and the returning mid-day service, providing breakfast and lunch[32].

Grouping arrangements – the last days of the Great North

A special meeting of shareholders was convened in November 1922 for the final grouping arrangements to be explained by Duffus. The Great North would be merged with the North British, North Eastern, Great Eastern, Great Central and Great Northern Railways, and he would be a member of the committee appointed to arrange the terms of amalgamation, on a basis of the free net revenue of 1913, with certain adjustments for "unfructified" (unspent) capital, and capital; expenditure since 1913. The total adjusted free revenue of the six companies in 1913 was £13,841,549, of which the Great North's contribution was the smallest, at £269,159. The Great North's debenture stock was to be transferred to the new company, on the same terms. GNS 5% and 6% redeemable, and 4% lien stock would be included in 4% First Guaranteed Stock of the new company, and GNS 4% guaranteed would be 4% Second Guaranteed. Preference stocks would be converted at the existing rates of interest; and every £100 of GNS preferred converted ordinary would become £60 of Preferred Ordinary, at 5%. For the deferred converted ordinary, he held out every probability of a 2½% dividend, which would provide the same result as 1913 – £1 10s for every £100. One member of the old GNS board would join the new board, Duffus himself. The Railway Companies' Association had recommended that the equivalent of four years' fees be paid to redundant directors, and the shareholders approved the sum of £6,000. The Labour MP for West Ham inquired in Parliament if this money came from public funds and was informed that it was from the company's assets, and that some companies were giving retiring directors considerably more[33]. There was little in the way of valediction, but the Rev. Dr Bruce, of Banff, rose to say that they parted with such an old friend as the Great North of Scotland Railway with a pang of regret[34].

For the staff, the grouping simply meant a change of corporate name and of paymaster. George Davidson, who had combined the post of solicitor with that of general manager, became Solicitor (Scotland) to the London and North Eastern Railway, at the Scottish divisional offices in Edinburgh. A curious aspect of the grouping was that the Great North lines became an isolated section of the London & North Eastern Railway, separated from the rest of the system by the Caledonian line. Inheriting the old North British running powers on this line, the London and North Eastern Railway continued to run trains from Edinburgh and Dundee to Aberdeen. Keith and Boat of Garten remained frontier stations. Sir Malcolm Barclay-Harvey suggested that the grouping came just in time to save the Great North: "A railway which depended to such a large extent … on short distance traffic was bound to be very hard hit by the new motor competition," and he doubted whether it could have stood alone much longer[35]. But, even without the whole exercise being framed and strong-armed by the government, some form of large-scale amalgamation among the companies would have been inevitable. Helped by its geographical isolation, the Great North lived on in spirit if not in name, clad in London and North Eastern Railway uniform and livery, but still very much as it had been, for several decades after its formal dissolution. Into the 1950s, a few ex-GNS locomotives still drew trains that connected with the original Highland line at Boat of Garten, where a large notice on the gable of the platform building continued to advise passengers that the best way to the south was via Aberdeen.

Cruden Bay 1930s: a study in decline. The main station building has burned down and the tramway wires have been removed. A trailer van still stands on the tramrails. *(Stenlake collection)*

PART TWO – COMPANY AND COMMUNITY

CHAPTER 22
Perceptions of the Great North

From bad to good? A reassessment

The traditional characterisation of the Great North as a very bad railway which became a very good one was held up to question in the foreword. Twenty-one chapters on, it is possible to take an informed view of the company's policy and practice, and to see where the broad generalisation has some truth and where it distorts the actual situation.

By the mid-1840s, when people in Aberdeen and its hinterland began to take a serious interest, railways had two prime sources of appeal. It was apparent that they could play an unprecedented role in improving communication between different parts of the country. Also it was clear that although they cost a lot of money to build, there was money to be made from them, since ownership of a railway joining two or more cities gave control of the traffic between those places, and the opportunity to earn profits long after the initial investment had been paid off. And there were of course communal as well as personal benefits – railways brought down the price of many commodities, especially coal, and helped the growth and diversification of commerce. Furthermore, if Aberdeen did not set about getting its own railways, other people in other places would bring railways to Aberdeen. For a clever lawyer like Alexander Anderson, well-connected in the city's commercial life and with a grasp of finance, there was every reason to seize the moment. At the time of gaining its Act in 1846, the Great North appeared in a strong position to dominate railway development across the entire north of Scotland.

The actual weakness of that position has been explored. Had the proposers been willing to spread the shareholding more widely, they might have raised the starting capital, even in 1846-47. Railway construction did not come to a universal stop in the late 1840s, and the Great North line had no competitor. The lines which still went ahead at that time were those, like the Caledonian and North British (and Aberdeen) Railways, in which there was a powerful will to get the work accomplished. The Great North's seven-year hiatus was entirely of its directors' making. It had a lasting effect, allowing the Highland lines to get under way and to claim almost two thirds of the original GNS route, and leaving the Great North with the "branch policy" and the accompanying failure to collaborate with other railways.

This combination of personal self-interest and short-sighted commercial judgement formed the real "badness" of the GNS in its first decades. But the critics of the 1890s and after focused on its passenger train services. Even discounting Ahrons's absurdities, their comments – made during a rather smug and confident period – were overstated. The Great North's unprecedented – indeed previously scarcely imaginable – transformative effect on the mobility of people and goods within its region is abundantly clear. In terms of service, the company deployed its limited resources as effectively as possible: on the branches, the initial service was often greater than the actual traffic proved to justify. Its use of the electric telegraph for train control was ahead of its time, and its "glacial" speeds were not untypical – the Inverness & Nairn trains also averaged 20 mph, as did many others – and were required both for essential economy and because of the original lightweight "unfished" rails. It was far from alone in treating its passengers, many of them unaccustomed to railway travel, in somewhat dragoonish fashion. From the crisis year of 1865, the nature of the problem was fully understood, and the process of improvement was far from being instantaneous. Without the hard work put in under Duncan's and Leslie's chairmanships, Ferguson and Moffatt would have found it impossible to achieve the reforms of the 1880s, and even so, Ferguson's first few years were lean ones for employees and shareholders.

Contemporary levels of complaint about the Great North's service in its first 30 years do not appear greater than for other Scottish railways, and the company's prime denigrators were its Inverness railway opponents. In Aberdeen, it enjoyed considerable prestige between 1854 and 1864, and again from the 1880s, as one of the city's biggest and most commercially successful enterprises. The joint station, when completed, was a source of civic pride from 1867 until around 1880, by which time the population and its own traffic were becoming too large for it. As far as occasional chicanery went, the GNS had nothing to teach the other companies, and the main lesson they might have taken from it was the debilitating effect of keeping a weak and foolishly complacent chairman in office for far too long.

Passengers and the Public

Every level of society used the railway – convicts under escort to Peterhead Prison (from 1888), schoolchildren, fishwives, farmers, landowners, soldiers, merchants, businessmen of all sorts, seasonal labourers of both sexes, holidaymakers, tourists, cattle drovers. Most went third class, which from the 1850s to the 1890s was not a comfortable experience, in unheated, wooden-seated carriages, but much better than sitting on a cart or an outside seat on a road coach, as well as quicker. Standards of comfort were more robust in those days, and it was

A crowded platform at Cairnbulg, 1900s. The station was briefly named Inverallochy when opened in 1903. *(Stenlake collection)*

only later in the century, when cushioned seats began to appear, that complaints came from lines with unimproved carriages. Like all railways, the GNS sought to provide for public requirements, and its working timetables and advertisements show that special or extra trains were put on for town holidays, farmhands' feeing fairs, special events and evening excursions, as well as for the influx and return of fishery and other seasonal workers.

One unwanted side-effect was new opportunities for Aberdeen's criminal element. In the early days, 'thimbleriggers' were said to await trains from the north, ready to decoy innocent country folk into pubs where they would be conned and relieved of the contents of their purses[1].

In its efforts to combine a sufficient service with containing its costs, the GNS certainly inflicted delays on passengers, caused both by the running of mixed trains and by long waits at the numerous junctions. Some of these delays were unavoidable, though the company was also accused of deliberately timing parliamentary trains to prevent passengers from using them on connecting services. In 1875 the fare from Alford to Aberdeen was 2s 5d by parliamentary train, and 3s 7d third class. But it was noted that "the parliamentary trains do not run in connection with each other, so third class travellers to Aberdeen pay 3s 7d[2]." There was the famous inconvenience at Aberdeen: Vallance refers to the "intolerable position[3]" around 1857, though his only source is James Merry's letter, and the difficulties of through passengers at Aberdeen were certainly no worse than those of people changing stations in Glasgow or trains at Perth. No railway could ever run to the satisfaction of everyone.

An incidental but revealing sidelight on the attitude of the travelling public comes from the ninth half-yearly report of the Aberdeen Tramways Company, in April 1877. It was not doing too well, having "increased the travelling facilities, but the public did not appreciate it or require it." The inside fares had been raised to 2d but had to be cut back to 1d because of loss of custom. The number of cars on the Queen's Cross route was cut from

Buckie was a medium size station with considerable fish traffic and the number of employees reflects that. The stationmaster is, as usual, sitting in the centre of the front row and is wearing a full-length coat. (Douglas Flett)

five to three, and on the Kittybrewster route from four to two, and the number of horses halved, from 70 to 35. In 1876 the trams (still horse-drawn) had carried 1,162,434 people, earning £5,572, or 1.15*d* per trip[4]. Many people evidently preferred a no-frills service at cheaper prices.

In general, though, especially on longer journeys, public expectation of greater comfort and convenience was growing. Provision of ladies-only compartments became a national issue in 1887, and in reply to a Board of Trade circular, William Moffatt reported that the company would provide one on as many trains as was practicable; and that the staff would always try to make special provision where possible[5]. Smoking compartments were introduced, initially in new first class carriages, from July 1883. They would have leather seats in order not to absorb fumes, and older carriages were to be converted when they came in for refitting[6]. A complaint that Sir George Macpherson-Grant (a Highland Railway director) and Mr Campbell of Balliemore were persistent smokers in non-smoking compartments on Strathspey trains was remitted to the secretary to write a suitable letter. In that year it was also decided to cushion the previously wooden seats of third class carriages[7]. It was October 1891 before footwarmers were ordered for third class carriages, with 500 at 10*s* 6*d* each plus a charge of £290 for enlarging the "baths" in which they were prepared[8].

Accidents to passengers were relatively rare and mostly minor, and the company was prompt to pay out against claims which it considered reasonable and justifiable, though always aware of the possibility of over-claiming or even fraudulent demands. Doubtful claims went to court and were often settled beforehand for a modest sum. After a slight collision at Rothiemay on 17 July 1886, when the driver and guard of an Up train forgot they were due to cross an Aberdeen-Keith special, one passenger asked for £50 on account of a broken rib and internal injuries. The company claimed he had suffered only a cut on the cheek and offered £10. On this occasion the passenger sued, and the Sheriff awarded him £30[9]. Fraudulent travelling was regularly prosecuted, but ministers might be spared – when the Rev. A.F. Thompson of Strichen was found travelling between Inveramsay and Aberdeen in a first class carriage with a third class ticket, the company accepted that it was an "oversight" on his part[10].

Vandalism was occasionally reported, with stone-throwing at insulators on the telegraph poles condemned as "too general" a practice by the Sheriff at Banff when he fined a boy five shillings in July 1886, but sometimes there were more serious incidents. A stone weighing about half a hundredweight was seen on the line near Pitlurg in April 1898. A local man, John Wilson, was awarded £1 by the company for removing it, and the boy who put it there, William Dickie, was sentenced to ten strokes of the birch by Sheriff Robertson[11]. In an odd case in 1894, a law clerk brought a Court of Session case against the Great North for compelling him to sit in a particular compartment on the Lossiemouth-Elgin train, for which he had a season ticket. The company's reason was that a group of young men "such as the pursuer" were in the habit of damaging the window straps, and needed to be kept under the supervision of the guard[12]. The stout leather straps for adjusting the window openings were favourite targets, being popular as razor strops.

Like the other railway companies, the GNS was an unwilling contributor to local rates and taxes, with the feeling that the valuation put on railway property was unfairly high. In 1870 it paid £5,009, in 1879 it paid £8,467 and by 1899 the amount was £12,779. These payments were used as a reason for refusing requests for charitable donations. The only regular exceptions were the hospitals which frequently had to deal with its injured employees: Aberdeen Royal Infirmary, Aberdeen Convalescent Hospital, and Dr Gray's Hospital in Elgin all received annual sums. Small subsidies also went to the GNS Ambulance Association, the Railway Benevolent Institution, and the GNS Workmen's Friendly Society. Otherwise charitable gestures were so rare as to stand out. In 1885 the company agreed to carry 200 tons of stone from Kemnay for nothing (usual charge £12 10*s*), on behalf of the Relief Committee for the Unemployed in Aberdeen. Donations to Cruden Bay Golf Club had an element of self-interest, but a surprising one is a donation of £10 to the layout of Fochabers Golf Course in 1906. In 1917 the company was asked for special facilities for a collector for the Blind Asylum to travel on its trains, and it was agreed to provide a ticket at ordinary or season rate, with the collector's boy attendant charged only half-fare although aged over twelve; and in 1918 a special donation of £50 was made to the Aberdeen YMCA 'Hut Week'. Ballindalloch Station waiting room was also made available to the parish minister for evening services every second Sunday[13]. There were no donations to political parties, but like some other railway companies the GNS supported the National Free Labour Association, an anti-trade union and anti-strike organisation, for a few years around 1906, with an annual donation of £5 5*s*. Refusals were the norm: in 1889 the company refused a request from the Committee of Organisation of Fortnightly Holiday Trips for Poor Children for a lower charge than the Railway Clearing House rate of child's single fare plus a quarter for return tickets[14].

Shippers and Traders

1854, the year in which the railway opened to Huntly, was the first year in which Huntly fatstock was supplied to the London Christmas market. Improvements in stock breeding on the one hand, and transport on the other, demonstrably complemented each other. Early positive results of the line were also celebrated at a dinner given by Kennethmont farmers to the corn merchants who had put up granaries at the station: a special train took the diners out and home again[15]. For tenant farmers, however, while the advent of the railway made it easier to bring in lime and other fertilisers, and to send out their produce, it also increased the value of their land and their rents went up. This may have been a contributory reason for the lack of local investment in branch lines: less than 10% of the Banff Macduff & Turriff Junction Railway's £150,000 capital was raised locally[16].

Influenced by the location of towns, the disposition of river valleys and the best areas of arable land, the GNS's pattern of lines was not ideal for cross-country traffic. In the north, apart from the Aberdeen-Keith and Maud-Peterhead lines, east-west movement of goods required wagons to be taken to Kittybrewster, re-marshalled, and re-despatched, making a journey of many miles compared to the actual distance. Here was the main reason for the long-standing demand for a central Buchan line, with Huntly-Turriff-Maud the most obvious route. In the south the position was reversed, with the Alford Valley and Deeside railways running east-west, and no north-south link. Rail traffic from Deeside to places beyond Inverurie had to take the long way round. With goods charged by mile of railway, this made such internal journeys as Aboyne-Alford, or Fyvie-Fraserburgh, expensive, and helps to explain the high usage of road traction engines in Aberdeenshire.

Apart from the broad category of 'general merchandise', coal, timber, stone, whisky and distillery by-products, agricultural produce, fertilisers and fish were the staples of the Great North's goods traffic, and the company provided siding space and dedicated branches for larger users. Its main problem was to supply enough wagons for peak periods without an overstock at other times. Traders' own wagons, numerous on some railways, were few. One local factor was the continuing use of peat as domestic fuel: a good summer for peat cutting would bring a noticeable reduction in coal traffic. Relations with customers appear to have been cordial on the whole, despite the reputation for charging high rates, and William Moffatt's drive for smartness in operations undoubtedly extended to the goods side as well. The most inveterate complainers were the Aberdeen Commercial and Lime companies, and while they certainly caught the Great North in the wrong on more than one occasion, it should also be noted that both these companies had strong connections with the Aberdeen Harbour Commission, which – once the Great North had joined the Railway Clearing House in 1866 and begun to apply through rates to and from the south – was in some respects a commercial rival to the railway companies. During the review period of railway rates around 1890-92, much discussion centred on the relative costs of delivering coal to inland places: if the coal came via Aberdeen Harbour, the GNS charged full local rates; if it came by the Caledonian or North British, the lower 'through' rate was applied.

The staff

The Great North had 1,258 employees in 1875, 1,478 in 1885, 2,080 in 1895, and 3,528 in 1921 – of whom 3,076 were men, 238 women, 189 'male junior' and 25 'female junior'[17]. It was common for men to spend their entire working lives, 50 years or more, with the company, and this certainly helped to promote a sense of tradition and loyalty. Until 1919 there was very little in the way of industrial trouble.

There was also relatively little trouble with staff misconduct. Between June 1897 and January 1902, for example, only thirteen cases were recorded, mostly of petty theft. Moffatt's insistence on smart working, with some station stops as brief as 30 seconds, no doubt kept everyone on their toes. Occasional instances of fraud are noted, usually small sums taken by individuals, though clerks at Waterloo and Mintlaw were found in 1863 to be combining in altering invoices and sharing the proceeds[18]. One of the larger defaulters, Robert Macdonald, goods clerk at Elgin, was jailed for fifteen months in 1870 for embezzling £143. For some reason, such cases seem to have been most frequent in the 1880s, a typical example being A.B. Matthew, agent at Huntly, who absconded with £35 from the station cash in July 1889. Drunkenness was an inevitable problem: William Ferguson, though admitting he was not a teetoller himself, preached abstinence as did most railway chairmen. The engine driver and guards of the 11.15 am Up goods from Aberdeen were dismissed in March 1867 for being drunk, and the traffic committee resolved that sale of drink to employees at the company refreshment rooms be strictly forbidden[19].

Stationmasters, usually referred to as agents, frequently were also local postmasters, and the agent at Longmorn was disciplined in 1899 for using company staff to deliver letters. Some were prominent in their communities:

Some of the houses constructed, on Harlaw Road, Inverurie, to accommodate workers who moved from Aberdeen. (*Great North of Scotland Railway Association*)

when George Strachan, agent at Banff, was transferred to Peterhead in 1898, well-wishers presented him with a marble clock and a purse of sovereigns[20]. On some railways, notably the Highland, stationmasters often retailed coal, paraffin etc., but this does not seem to have been a practice on the Great North. The company sold coal to its officials and servants at the contract price for station coal plus half the carriage rate to their stations, a concession also given to workshop staff at Inverurie[21].

The GNS had its own Workmen's Friendly Society, founded in 1854. Members paid a shilling a month, and in 1870 its income was £320 14s 9½d with expenditure of £318 17s 6d, on sickness benefit and funeral money, with the smallest sum being 3s 4d, and the largest £16 13s 4d. Its reserve fund in November 1875 amounted to £500, and the committee asked the board's opinion on how the interest on this amount, and the company's donations to it, should be applied in future. The finance committee felt that the fund was rather small and suggested that interest and future donations be split between building up the reserves and making higher payouts, and that the weekly subscription should not be reduced[22]. In 1893 the Friendly Society had 1,110 full members, and 49 half-members (boys) and its income was £718 from members and £50 from the directors; total payout was £682. From 1870 there was also a Waymen's Friendly Society, a smaller body, similar to the older one except that any excess in its funds over £50 was distributed among the members each year. In 1893 it had an income of £200 and disbursed £150. For staff with money to save, the GNS also had a Savings Bank, originally a provident society, set up by John Stewart in 1869, but reconstituted in 1893. It paid 4% interest on deposits up to £500, and 3% on larger amounts. By the end of 1893 it had 401 depositors and funds of £36,888.

Apart from the aid of the friendly societies, sometimes benefit concerts were arranged to raise funds for bereaved families; a concert in the Northern Friendly Society Hall in February 1887 for the widow and family of a member of the locomotive department, presided over by James Manson, was noted as the second within a short time[23]. Similar events took place in the 1890s. Events of this kind were intended only for the railway community, but officials' wives joined in staging a grand public bazaar in the Music Hall, Aberdeen, to raise funds for the Railway Benevolent Institution, in December 1893. Mrs Moffatt, Mrs John Stuart, and others had stalls and a "book of the bazaar" was produced, among its contents being John S. Stuart's

'Rambling Reminiscences' of his many years with the GNS. William Walker put on picture shows, 'The Railway Chase', 'The Railway Incident', and 'Life in the Railway Signal Box'[24]. Lord Provost Sir David Stewart, in a speech to mark the event, shed some light on railway amenities in non-corridor trains: "They could not forget the time when they were married, when they were obliged to the guard for a quiet compartment for themselves and their partner for life. (Applause and laughter)". With musical interludes and a shooting gallery, it was hoped to raise £1,600, but total receipts were £777[25].

Membership of the Aberdeen Mechanics' Institute (founded 1824) cost 2s a year, and the GNS paid half for any of its employees who joined[26]. William Cowan was a director of the Institute. In 1898 the company arranged for the training of ambulance teams by the St. Andrew's Ambulance Association, and presented a silver cup for an annual competition[27]. William Pickersgill organised weekly lectures for his staff, and in April 1899 he was presented with a group photograph of the Running Department employees. The presentation was made by Alex Tait, the oldest driver, and the locomotive foreman, A. Harvey, praised the superintendent's coolness, tact and forbearance, remarking that it was a good feature of the GNS that the top officials worked in harmony and that it had contented employees[28]. Their contentment was slightly disturbed in 1901 when, prompted by a circular from the Board of Trade, the issue of engine drivers' health was addressed. A medical test was required at the age of 60 and every two years after that. An age limit for drivers was considered but dropped, when it was found that no other company had one, except for the Great Eastern Railway (70 years). Like the eyesight tests noted in chapter 16, these 'health and safety' steps were suspected as ways of getting rid of ageing men[29].

Pensions were paid only to officials who qualified to join the Superannuation Fund, managed by the Railway Clearing House. In 1894 the Great North had 266 members registered, who paid in 2½% of their annual salary, with the company contributing a similar amount[30]. Retiring allowances were paid to other staff on a grace and favour basis. Between 1888 and 1891, only three are recorded, and very long service was required before an award. In 1891 two retiring station agents received five shillings a week "at the board's pleasure" after 30 and 25 years' service. William Dowell, a wayman retiring in 1899 aged 64 through injury, received 3s 6d a week. Previous recipients had usually been awarded 7s 6d. In an unusual case, the widow of James Petrie, late bank agent in Dufftown and a director of the Keith & Dufftown Railway, was given a donation of £25 in 1898 due to her indigent circumstances.

Perquisites were few. When a circular was passed among the Scottish railway companies suggesting reduced fares could be offered by each to employees of the other four, the GNS was the only one to give a positive answer. Moffatt was willing to agree if the others did, but they all refused[31]. To celebrate Queen Victoria's Diamond Jubilee in 1897, all staff were given a day's paid holiday (to be taken by arrangement with the departmental head). At most stations with enough staff to make up a party, yearly gatherings were held. 1866 appears to be the first year in which the board subsidised such an event, a combined GNS/Deeside affair in Aberdeen[32]. Employees of both companies at Keith held a joint annual festival. The GNS Banff and Macduff staff also combined for a festival, noted in December 1882 as a large gathering. The absence of directors and senior staff suggests that it was a self-help event[33]. Elgin staff also had an annual gathering with around 200 people attending, and Provost Black, a GNS director, as a frequent guest and speaker; and Fraserburgh had an annual ball, with around 70 couples present. For a time at least in the expansive 1890s, the locomotive department joined in the fashion, among railway companies, of an annual trip – in 1893 it was to Elgin, with the party of 1,350, including "lady friends", carried in two special trains leaving at 6.20 and 6.30 am and going via the coast line. In Elgin, they marched from the station to the town hall, behind a band, stopping at the Town & County Bank to give three cheers for Provost Black; and later there was dancing "in and out of doors[34]." The high point of GNS social gatherings was of course the series of events held in January and March 1898, four grand parties, each entertaining around 2,000 people.

Very occasional awards were made for exceptional service in the prevention of accidents. In 1898 driver W. Robertson of the 2.48 pm from Elgin was given £5 for promptly stopping his train when it was switched into a siding in error by signalman McIvor[35]. Admission of corporate responsibility for deaths or injuries incurred by employees on duty was never made, and the verdict of "own rashness", as given in the Strathspey Railway's first accident when the pointsman at Ballindalloch was killed while uncoupling moving wagons, was typical. It was repeated in 1914 when William McWilliam, porter at Tillynaught, jumped on the running board of a carriage to get at the luggage and parcels before the train had stopped, fell, and had to have a leg amputated. The company refused compensation on the ground that he had broken Rule 23 in the rule-book, and was backed up by the Sheriff-Substitute. An appeal to the Court of Session was successful, however, the judge ruling that he should receive compensation because "He was performing his duty in an indiscreet and wrong manner, but still performing it[36]." Court verdicts were not always predictable. The widow of foreman platelayer William Silver sued the company for £4,500 after he was killed by a breakdown train travelling on the 'wrong' line between Kittybrewster and Woodside, on 29 January 1893. The GNS pleaded that he was "culpably late" on duty, and "culpably failed to carry a lamp." A jury awarded Mrs Silver £300 and her expenses[37]. Voluntary payments were sometimes made in the case of deaths. When J. Grant, train register boy at Elgin, and son of the stationmaster at Cromdale, was killed in 1920, his father asked for £100 and received an *ex gratia* £75. A more unusual case in January 1921 was that of Driver Willox, who died on his engine between Aberdeen and Holburn Street Stations, of "excitement and shock" having run down and killed a shunter. His widow was given £300[38].

Shareholders and directors

The original shareholders of the GNS were its directors and a relatively small group of other lawyers, factory owners and men of business in Aberdeen and its county. Most if not all were nominal shareholders, with the 5% deposit money on their £50 shares advanced on their behalf by the local banks. Many intended to borrow money to pay for the successive calls on their shares and when it became clear that the return on the investment might be less than the cost of borrowing, they transferred their shares to other parties, or simply ignored their obligation. When the £50 shares were cut down to £10 shares in 1851, few committed to buying the new cheaper ordinary shares. As a result, the board had to embark on the first of many issues of preference shares, with a specified dividend yield, in order to compete with other companies looking for investment funds. This had the effect of widening the range of ownership, as new share issues needed to be marketed nationally through the network of share brokers and stock exchanges, and also of bringing in shareholders who had no links with north-east Scotland and whose interest in the company was purely financial. There was far more investment capital in England than in Scotland, and from the first preference issue onwards, the Great North acquired a substantial number of shareholders in the great railway investment centres of Liverpool and Manchester. While all railway companies found it necessary to introduce preference shares, the GNS was unusual in that the capital value of its range of special shares became three times that of the ordinary shares. When the company was doing well, or appeared to be doing so, the ordinary dividend, to which in theory there was no upper limit, might out-top the preference shares, but this only happened during the illusory years leading up to the crisis of 1865.

From the later 1880s, the Great North achieved stability in its dividends and its share prices. As a relatively small company with steady results and no serious prospect of large growth, trading in its shares was normally at a low level, with little fluctuation in prices and even on the Aberdeen Stock Exchange very little trading in its ordinary shares went on.

Membership of the board broadened somewhat from 1867, with a couple of directors to represent the interests of shareholders in Lancashire, Glasgow and Edinburgh, but it remained essentially a north-eastern group, composed of businessmen, country landowners and representatives of burghs like Elgin and Banff. Unlike the Highland Railway it had few members of the nobility, a weakness at a time when the Lords was the predominant house of Parliament. The 5th Duke of Richmond had helped the company get on its feet in 1852-54, but kept his distance after that, and William Ferguson's letter book shows how he tried to get the Earl of Kintore to influence the 6th Duke at a crucial time for the coast line and goods rates Bill in 1881 (the duke remained elusive). Lord Aberdeen, though active on the local front, did not involve himself in parliamentary matters for the company.

Although directors were formally elected by the shareholders, in practice their appointment was closely controlled by the board. This was often condemned as "oligopoly" but there were some justifications. The Aberdeen Railway had an unfortunate experience in 1848 when Colonel William Fraser, appointed to its board, proved to be a cantankerous, interfering and interminably time-wasting member who was got rid of with some difficulty[39]. One wonders if the GNS would have had less trouble with Alexander Copland in the 1880s and 1890s if he had been invited to join the board, but he might not have been a co-operative member – John Stewart had certainly not been forgotten. A divided board was unlikely to be effective, and a balance had to be found between collegiate spirit and the directors' responsibility to scrutinise the running of the company. During the post-1880 years of stability it was common for men to propose themselves or others for a Great North board vacancy. Men – it was always men – of sound judgement, solid character, and personal wealth, were looked for. It helped, too, if they were prominent in a significant industry. In January 1883 William Ferguson wrote to J.G. Smith, distiller of Glenlivet, to ask if he would agree to be nominated as a director. Noting that Smith had only £375 of preference

(A) stock at the time, he recommended a purchase of ordinary stock, a good investment at £54 for a nominal £100-worth. Ferguson himself had £4,000 of ordinary stock, well above the necessary minimum but "there has been *talk* about Directors having only a small investment" (in a subsequent letter he referred to "busybodies") and he hoped that Smith would take "a fair amount[40]". Smith duly joined the board, adding £500 of ordinary stock to his holding.

The last big initiative of the GNS board was the proposed amalgamation with the Highland Railway in 1905. After the failure of that scheme, the board was content to maintain its business in good order – which it did very effectively – and complete the major project of the joint station at Aberdeen. From August 1914 the company's future was really out of its hands and for Bain and Duffus the main task was to hold things together under state control, and to ensure that the final dispensation reflected the company's worth.

The east end of Keith Station about 1900 showing the original overall roof, designed to be opened up at the west end to accommodate the line to Elgin. In the event, Elgin trains had to make do with a platform added on the north side. The wooden post behind the leftmost man carried a signal. (*Great North of Scotland Railway Association*)

CHAPTER 23 Power and Provision

First orders, 1854 – 1859

As a regional railway, the Great North had to provide adequate motive power and rolling stock to meet the demands of goods and passenger traffic. Chronically short of funds in its first years, it was always seeking to avoid spending cash. As noted in Chapters 3 and 4, it tried whenever possible to make suppliers take part-payment in shares, and the decision to do without second class may have been to save the cost of building second class carriages. Many stations were built of wood, as were most goods sheds. Stone locomotive sheds were built at Kittybrewster and Huntly. Twelve 2-ton cranes at £22 10s each, also weighing machines for goods and luggage, from Pooley & Co., and station clocks from Alexander Mitchell of Glasgow. Seven 2-4-0 passenger locomotives were delivered from Fairbairns of Manchester by the end of July, but five 2-4-0 goods engines, essentially the same design but with driving wheels of 5ft rather than 5ft 6in diameter, did not appear until June-October 1855, and there were no cattle trucks until fifteen were delivered in December 1854, with eighteen more to follow.

Class 1 2-4-0 no. 7 was one of the locomotives delivered for the opening of the line in 1854. Seen here after rebuilding in *c.*1883, though still with brakes only on the tender, it was the last of the class to be withdrawn, in 1900. (*Great North of Scotland Railway Association*)

No. 13 was one of the two 0-4-0T locomotives built for the steep gradient on the Waterloo Branch in 1856. Latterly, they were used for shunting at Keith and Elgin, surviving on the Great North until 1916 when they were sold for industrial use. (*Great North of Scotland Railway Association*)

The Edinburgh-born engineer Daniel Kinnear Clark, aged 32 in 1854, was responsible for the design and purchase of the Great North's first engines. In July 1855 Clark resigned following a dispute with the board over his failure to live in Aberdeen, and his assistant J.F. Ruthven took over. In Ruthven's brief time as superintendent (he resigned in May 1857) four more passenger engines of Clark's design were delivered from Fairbairns – presumably favourable payment terms outweighed the view that Nos. 1-7 were not well built[1] – and two small 0-4-0 WT engines, from Beyer, Peacock of Manchester, for working on the steep line between Waterloo and Kittybrewster.

The rolling stock roster in November 1856 comprised fourteen engines, eleven first class and 30 third class carriages, 248 open wagons, 20 covered vans and 50 cattle trucks. A year later there were a further four engines, five more firsts, fifteen more thirds, 25 more open wagons, ten more covered vans and fifteen more cattle trucks; also six brake vans, two carriage trucks, five horse-boxes, five sheep trucks, five goods brake vans and two brake wagons[2]. That the extra stock was needed can be seen by the comparative figures to 31 August 1856, and 31 August 1857[3]:

	1855-56	1856-57
Passengers	313,611	410,290
General goods (tons)	22,065	29,278
Coal (tons)	15,498	25,762
Lime (tons)	5,889	7,857
Stone (tons)	4,872	12,424
Timber (tons)	10,527	10,678
Manure (tons)	7,971	8,856
Cattle	18,578	19,817
Sheep	13,521	14,914
Pigs	684	1,145
Calves	571	438

From the opening of the line as far as Keith in October 1856, four trains ran each way daily, plus the single Sunday mail and passenger train:

	Passenger	Mixed/ Parliamentary	Passenger/ Mail	Mixed
Waterloo dep.	8.00 am	11.00 am	3.00 pm	4.50 pm
Keith arr.	10.50 am	2.05 pm	5.40 pm	7.50 pm

	Passenger/ Mail	Mixed/ Parliamentary	Mixed	Passenger
Keith dep.	7.00 am	10.05 am	1.20 pm	4.20 pm
Waterloo arr.	9.45 am	1.15 pm	4.30 pm	7.20 pm

The best service ran at an average speed of 20 mph. For passengers paying the parliamentary fare of 1*d* a mile, there was only a single train each day. With the advent of the Inverness & Aberdeen Junction line from 18 August 1858, there was no improvement, except that a goods service took through wagons to and from Inverness, leaving Aberdeen at 4.55 am and Keith at 3.00 am. In the winter of 1858-59, the GNS timetable offered[4]:

	Passenger	Mixed/ Parliamentary	Passenger/ Mail	Mixed
Waterloo dep.	8.00 am	11.00 am	3.00 pm	5.15 pm
Old Meldrum dep.	8.28 am	11.40 am	3.05 pm	5.50 pm
Turriff dep.	7.15 am	11.00 am	–	5.15 pm
Keith arr.	10.50 am	2.05 pm	5.40 pm	8.15 pm
Inverness arr.	2.05pm	5.25 pm	9.00 pm	–

	Passenger/ Mail	Mixed/ Parliamentary	Mixed	Passenger
Inverness dep.	3.50 am	7.00 am	–	12.45 pm
Keith dep.	7.00 am	10.30 am	1.20 pm	4.50 pm
Turriff dep.	7.15 am	11.00 am	–	5.15 pm
Old Meldrum dep.	8.28 am	11.40 am	3.05 pm	5.50 pm
Waterloo arr.	9.45 am	1.30 pm	4.25 pm	7.50 pm

Years of expansion, 1859 – 1864

Ruthven was succeeded by his works manager, William Cowan, who had come to the GNS as a driver in 1854 but had served an engineering apprenticeship with the Arbroath & Forfar Railway. Cowan's first design was a 2-4-0 of which nine were built by Robert Stephenson & Co. of Newcastle between December 1859 and May 1861, in time for the opening of the Dyce-Mintlaw line. These had 5ft 1in driving wheels and were used for both goods and passenger work. Twelve 2-4-0s had been intended but the final three were completed to a new design as 4-4-0s, the first passenger engines in Scotland to have a leading bogie. These appeared in January-February 1862, followed by six between May 1863 and January 1864. They were no more powerful than their predecessors, but the pivoted bogie gave better running over the curving and lightly laid tracks particularly on the Speyside line. One of them, No. 31, suffered a boiler explosion at Nethy Bridge on 13 September 1878, and it transpired that the boiler had not been examined for 7½ years and had a serious design flaw, which had to be remedied in seventeen other engines, and meantime their boiler pressure was reduced from 140/120 psi to 100 psi[5].

Railway companies were liable to prosecution if their engines emitted excessive smoke, and tended to use coke as fuel, which was much more expensive than coal. To the Great North, far from any pit-heads, fuel costs were a serious concern even in good times. Many railways were experimenting in the 1850s with ways of improving coal combustion and reducing smoke, and Daniel Kinnear Clarke had patented a steam-jet system which blew air into the firebox, and appears to have been quite successful, saving about 2lbs of coal per mile. The GNS adopted his system, beginning with engine No. 17 in 1859, and it was applied to all the company's engines until 1890. Royalties would normally have been payable to the patentee, but the GNS got it free, on the understanding that the engines would be in effect demonstrators of the system to other companies[6].

Cowan's class H of 1862-64 were among the first 4-4-0s in the country, although the bogie was mounted on a rigid pivot. They were particularly needed for the curves on the Speyside line. No. 29 is shown as rebuilt in December 1880, photographed in workshop grey. (*Great North of Scotland Railway Association*)

In March 1860 the board reported that of 678 carriages and wagons, none were under repair; three new engines had been delivered and three were on order, with six more to come when the Formartine & Buchan line opened in 1861. Extension of branches raised the Great North's train miles to 279,183 in 1861, compared to 192,694 in 1858; though with 27 rather than eighteen engines, engine mileage fell slightly.

A further improvement initiated by Cowan was Krupp steel tyres, progressively fitted to the locomotive stock from 1862, their cost charged to the revenue account. The GNS was something of a British pioneer in this respect. The original rails of the main line did not last very long; by the end of 1864, 21 miles at the southern end had already been replaced with heavier, fish-jointed rails and Alexander Fraser reported that the rest of the line would need to be replaced within three to six years. He was also renewing the fencing along the line, replacing the original Scotch fir fence by stone walls or galvanised iron wire fixed to iron straining posts, with intermediate posts of larch. The cost of this, spread over three years, was two-thirds to revenue, one-third to capital[7]. In 1883 it was reported that 21 miles 675 yards of new rails had been laid in the February-July half-year, with 40 miles of lightweight "un-fished" rails still requiring renewal. With currently good prices for steel, it was hoped to complete the work inside two years, and the cost of £35,000 was to be charged to a renewals account, paid off over six years from 1885[8].

From 1 February 1863 the Great North took over working the Banff Portsoy & Strathisla Railway, soon to be renamed as the Banffshire Railway, which owned four small locomotives, all built by Hawthorns at Leith, and transferred to the GNS as Nos. 37-40. Nos. 37 and 38 were 0-4-2 tanks, which survived until 1885 when they were sold to the contractors of the coast line. The other two were 0-4-2 tender engines, of which No. 3 became GNS 39 and No. 4 became 40. In February 1864 the Deeside line needed additional engines and wagons, and the traffic committee transferred No. 39 to it for £2,100[9]. It was renumbered as No. 7 of the Deeside Railway. From 1 July 1863 the GNS also took over working of the Morayshire Railway, which possessed four engines. Of two 2-2-0T engines from 1852, only one was operative, but not used by the GNS; but two 2-4-0ST, of 1859 and 1861, taken over as Nos. 41 and 42, were kept in service until 1885 and 1883 respectively.

As of 31 January 1864, the GNS had 42 engines, classified as eleven passenger, 25 goods and six tanks, inclusive of the Banffshire and Morayshire engines; the passenger engines being the Clark designs supplied in 1854 and 1857. It had 28 first class, 78 third class and twelve composite carriages, sixteen luggage vans, five horse boxes, two carriage trucks, seventeen goods brakes, three brake wagons, 99 cattle trucks, four sheep vans, 181 covered vans, 607 open box wagons and 126 low-side wagons. In the course of the year, Milne reported on additional rolling stock required: six engines (Cowan had requested twelve), three first class, two composite and six third class carriages, two brake vans and 100 open wagons and in November the engines were ordered, along with 83 wagons – seventeen for locomotive coal, the rest for the Fraserburgh line – four first class and composite carriages, and four third class[10].

Years of making do, 1866 – 1879

In March and April 1866 a new supplier, Neilsons of Glasgow, delivered six 4-4-0 engines, urgently needed despite the financial stringencies of the time, following the opening of the Fraserburgh line in 1865. Ten years would pass before the Great North bought any further engines. Following the lease of the Deeside Railway in September 1866, its engines were transferred to the GNS stock. It had owned eight but only seven remained at the time of the transfer, one 0-4-2T of 1854, and five 0-4-2s built by Hawthorns of Leith, including the ex-BP&S engine, now Deeside Railway No. 7, all of which went into GNS stock as Nos. 39 and 50-53. A further 0-4-2, built by Dodds of Rotherham in 1854, was taken over but never put into Great North service.

Considering that snow was a regular occurrence and often blocked cuttings on the lines, the Great North was slow to adopt snowploughs, preferring to dig out snow-blocks. In 1867 however, it was decided to use ploughs, and Alexander Fraser went to inspect the Highland Railway's snowploughs, recently designed by William Stroudley. He was concerned about clearances: the ploughs ran four inches above rail level but trough girders on GNS bridge-decks were higher than that. By January 1868 the bridges on the main line were altered[11], and two ploughs were ordered. By 1909 four ploughs were at work on the Buchan lines alone, noted as "in continuous operation" during the heavy snows of December[12].

Cowan's class K was introduced in 1866, a larger version of class H. As built they had no cabs, just a simple weatherboard. They were rebuilt about 1890 with cabs and larger boilers, and withdrawn between 1921 and 1925. The last to go was No. 45A, after participating in the Stockton & Darlington centenary cavalcade. *(Stenlake collection)*

With the Deeside stock included, the Great North's roster at 31 January 1868 comprised eleven passenger, 35 goods and seven tank engines; 43 first class, 113 third class, and fourteen composite coaches, plus sixteen passenger vans and five horse boxes; 25 goods brake vans, three brake wagons, 111 cattle trucks, four sheep vans, 194 covered vans, 927 goods wagons and 193 low-side wagons.

With these in the course of 1868 it carried 203,818 first class, 1,384,213 third class passengers (the vast majority at parliamentary fare), and 4,540 season ticket holders. Goods trains carried 186,810 tons of minerals and 258,106 tons of merchandise. Passenger train miles were noted as 548,988, and goods 374,723[13] (including Morayshire and Aboyne & Braemar figures).

In the decade between 1866 and 1876 the company was operating with an increasingly elderly and over-stretched locomotive fleet, a fact that later comments on its service ignored. By 1871, of the 53 engines, 27 were ten years old or more, and fourteen were noted as non-effective[14], leaving 39 to cover the full range of services, including the Strathspey and Fraserburgh lines. Only four were rebuilt, the ex-Morayshire and Banffshire tank engines, but a great deal of 'make-do and mend' went on at Kittybrewster. As of 31 January 1871 the company still had 171 passenger carriages plus nineteen luggage vans, five horse-boxes and three carriage trucks; and 1,535 goods vehicles plus 31 service vehicles[15].

The rebuilding programme

The company had increased its stock of goods wagons but still could not meet demand: a letter from James A. Beattie of Turriff in November 1872 complained of several days' delay in supplying wagons for his wool traffic. Milne replied to regret the inconvenience and hoped there would be no further ground for complaint[16]. In March 1876 the first of six "new improved" engines from Neilsons must have been greeted with relief. They were the first GNS locomotives to have cabs, and the first to have six-wheel rather than four-wheel tenders[17]. During 1878-79 a further twelve were added, all 4-4-0 types from Neilsons, intended for mixed traffic; and nine of the oldest were withdrawn or scrapped. Twenty-five years from its opening, the GNS now had 62 engines (56 of them deemed effective); 48 first class, 131 third class and 21 composite carriages, nineteen luggage brakes, nine carriage trucks, eight horse boxes, 1,569 open wagons, 192 covered vans, 150 low-side trucks, 34 goods brake vans, eight brake wagons, 44 fish trucks (fish trucks are listed from 1875, when 50 were supplied), and 20 ballast wagons. In 1879 the company carried 220,383 first class, 1,768,413 third, and 1,468 season ticket holders. Mineral traffic accounted for 283,151 tons, and merchandise for 351,405 tons. Passenger train miles amounted to 593,704, and goods train miles to 510,988[18].

Five more years passed before any further increase was made to the locomotive stock, though from 1880 a systematic programme of rebuilding older types, usually with cabs and new boilers, was begun, giving them a new lease of life and increased haulage power. In June 1883 an agreement was signed with the Westinghouse company for the supply of automatic air brake equipment. James Manson replaced Cowan as locomotive superintendent in October that year, and his first design for the GNS incorporated Westinghouse brake pumps. Thereafter, progress in installing automatic brakes on passenger stock was steady if not rapid, and by March 1893 it was anticipated that all carriages would have automatic brakes within the next few months[19]. Manson maintained the practice of using 4-4-0 engines but initiated inside cylinders and other changes with his first designs, Nos. 63-68, built by Kitson & Co., of Leeds, and delivered in August-October 1884. With 6ft driving wheels, they were intended for express work in accordance with the speeding-up of services then taking place. Between May 1884 and June 1885 nine 0-6-0 tank engines were supplied by Kitsons, for branch work – in another Manson innovation, these were the first engines in Britain to have folding cab doors, a valuable safety feature. In February and December 1887 the two engines built at Kittybrewster appeared, Nos. 5 and 6 (the original 5 and 6 now on the duplicate list, with construction costs fully written off), their boilers and wheels bought in from manufacturers. These were the only GNS engines until 1920 to carry names: *Kinmundy* and *Thomas Adam* respectively, after the chairman and his deputy, though the names were removed around 1907[20]. It is a little surprising that the publicity-minded William Moffatt did not introduce names for locomotives; perhaps the somewhat austere Manson did not care for the idea.

Concerns about contagious disease and a better awareness of hygiene were passed on by the Board of Trade, and in December 1890 the locomotive superintendent was instructed to build 50 meat vans to a new plan, at an estimated cost of £150 each[21]. Though the overall wagon stock went up from 1,997 in 1879 to 2,482 in 1891, merchandise tonnage rose in the same period by 22.5% and minerals by 19%; and Aberdeen traders were still complaining at the end of 1891 about the shortage of wagons. Tenders were put out for a further 150[22]. Another

Class N no. 5 *Kinmundy*, **first of the two locomotives built at Kittybrewster works in 1887, although 'assembled' might be a better term as several parts including the boiler were bought in. Class N was similar to class G but with a larger boiler. Both engines survived until the 1930s.**

indication of the rise in merchandise traffic can be seen in the expansion of Wordies, the railway carters. When first established in Aberdeen in 1852, they had around 20 horses. In December 1888 they had 140 carts working from the GNS goods depots in the city.

A striking difference between 1879 and 1891 is shown in train mileage: while goods mileage had risen to 675,012, passenger train mileage had soared to 1,158,783. Total passenger revenue in 1891 was £187,823, up by just over a third on 1879, and numbers had risen by 37%, while train mileage had almost doubled. Goods revenue, by contrast, had risen by 25.9%, total tonnage carried by 20.5%, and mileage by 32%. While these figures take no account of the diminishing number of mixed trains, it is plain that the goods service was more profitable. In 1903, earnings per passenger train mile were 41.88*d*, in 1906 40*d*, and in 1912 43.2*d*, while the goods figures were 74.46*d*, 79.01*d*, and 82.32*d*. A further significant contrast is seen between the first class figures of 1879 and 1891, down by nearly half, suggesting a considerable switch in travelling habits just around the time that third class got cushions[23]. Many new carriages to Manson's design were introduced in the 1880s to replace worn out stock and handle the increased traffic. Six-wheel chassis replaced 4-wheel ones and comfort was improved.

The journal *Engineer* in May 1890 carried engravings of an O-class 4-4-0 Great North engine, built by Kitson to Manson's design, noting that on some occasions engines of this class had run from Aberdeen to Huntly, 40 ¼ miles, in 42 minutes. The latest order was for three similar engines but with bigger wheels, 6ft 6½in rather than 6ft 0½in, and an eight-wheel, 3,000 gallon tender enabling it to run from Aberdeen to Elgin without stopping for water[24]. In 1878 Cowan had introduced an alphabetic classification system for engines, primarily to avoid confusion since the numbers of withdrawn engines were now being re-applied to newly-built ones, and Manson introduced a three-grade power classification system, first to third, later extended to comprise also 'special' (probably for Royal Trains) and 'harbour' operations.

A decade of expansion, 1890 – 1899

Taking over from Manson in August 1890, James Johnson was at first mainly concerned with the on-going rebuild programme, but in late 1893, responding to the requirements of the suburban services, nine 0-4-4T engines were

Johnson class S 4-4-0 No. 82, built by Neilson & Co., 1893, and withdrawn in December 1951.
(Stenlake collection)

supplied by Neilsons of Glasgow and proved effective on these very tightly-timed trains, running them until the subbies were finally terminated in 1937. Also in 1893 five new passenger 4-4-0 engines, class S, were delivered by Neilson, who from now on were the Great North's preferred manufacturer, becoming part of the North British Locomotive Co. in 1903. Concentration on one supplier perhaps helped with the standardisation of parts; unlike some companies at the time (the Glasgow & South Western Railway for example), the Great North used a standard, interchangeable boiler design on new and rebuilt engines during the Johnson and Pickersgill years. Johnson introduced the GNS's first first lavatory carriages in 1895, still 6-wheeled and only with internal corridors, and added considerably to the stock of standard 6-wheelers. Coinciding with Pickersgill's arrival in 1895 a substantial locomotive-building programme began, with 31 new 4-4-0 engines added by the end of 1899 (in fact 36 were ordered, but Pickersgill's Class V of 1899 was cut back from ten to five, with the other five sold to the South Eastern & Chatham Railway in late 1899 straight from Neilson, Reid at £3,300 each, making a profit of £1,250 for the GNS[25]).

At the locomotive department's annual social gathering in the Albert Hall, Aberdeen, on 27 December 1895, William Pickersgill announced that the GNS now had 100 locomotives, which consumed 52,000 tons of coal a year and 118 million gallons of water. At 31 January 1896 the company actually had 99 engines, including seven of his new T-class 4-4-0, with sliding shutters on the cab sides to keep out wind and weather[26]. It had 369 passenger carriages and 283 other vehicles for running with passenger trains, presumably trucks and vans fitted for automatic braking. In 1895, first class passengers numbered 105,877, with receipts of £12,564; third class totalled 3,048,449 (£136,459) and there were 2,624 season ticket holders (£15,743). Mail and parcels brought total passenger train receipts up to £210,851. Merchandise carried amounted to 461,514 tons, and minerals to 409,906 tons, with receipts of £132,950 and £46,683 respectively, plus £14,717 for livestock transport. The total number of goods vehicles was now 2,836 plus 52 service vehicles. On a track mileage of 36 double and 280 single lines, the number of passenger train miles run was 1,357,331, and of goods trains, 757,686[27].

Carriages had been varnished until 1883, their colouring gradually fading to a dark brown. In 1883 Manson introduced mahogany coaches, painted in purple lake, and in 1896 a more attractive colour scheme appeared, the lower panels in purple lake and the upper panels in cream[28]. The cost of the new corridor carriages built at Kittybrewster in 1897 was £661 each for four first class carriages, with lavatories, and £611 for fifteen composites,

Pickersgill class T No. 108 of 1898, as LNER 6908 at Elgin, in the 1930s. It ran until November 1951. *(Stenlake collection)*

noted as £174 and £164 less than outside builders' tenders. Standard goods wagons at the time cost £66 and 100 were ordered in 1897. The *Railway Magazine* noted in late 1897 that the new fast trains between Aberdeen and Inverness were doing very well, and that owing to the high speed with which they were run on the Great North line, it had been decided to introduce bogie carriages, although the current six-wheelers were "perfectly up to date, with electric light"[29]. Passenger stock was becoming much more expensive with the introduction of steam heating and the nine corridor bogie coaches ordered in 1898 were estimated at £980 each[30]. Oil lighting was still in use but the company had begun experiments with Stone's electric lighting system in 1896, using seven carriages on the Deeside suburban service, and it was noted that with success the GNS "will jump the gas age", going straight from oil to electricity. By December 1897 the GNS had 50 carriages fitted with electric lighting. The 'Deeside Express' in the late 1890s was noted as having eight or nine 6-wheel semi-corridor coaches, with large windows, and comfortable seating. The morning express left Ballater at 8.30 and was due in Aberdeen at 9.40, at an average speed of 37 mph, including six stops[31].

Aberdeen's suburban services demonstrate both the opportunities and problems offered by urban expansion around the turn of the 19th century. Both the Donside and the subsequent Deeside trains were immediately popular with the public, but the introduction of electric trams, beginning with the Woodside-St. Nicholas route on 22 December 1899, initiated a decline, with a 54% drop in Woodside's traffic in 1901 compared with 1890. In 1901 the Aberdeen Suburban Tramways Co. was formed, and though the Great North opposed its Bill in 1902, it was granted routes to Bieldside and Bankhead, competing with the railway. Moffatt had asserted that the subbies ran at a "dead loss", with receipts for Donside at 1s 7d per train mile and for Deeside at 2s 2d, whereas operating costs were 2s 4d in each case, so that train-mile receipts of 2s 6d or more would have been necessary to make a profit. Despite that, investment went on – spacious six-wheel carriages were provided, some with electric lighting; in 1903 a new station was opened at Persley, and in 1904 fares were reduced and additional trains put on to counter the new trams. Still in mid-1905 falls of 12% on Donside and 16% on Deeside traffic were estimated by the GNS. William Ferguson had once remarked that a railway is not a charity, and his shareholders might reasonably have wondered why Aberdeen's commuters and the paper factories were being subsidised. While that specific question has not been addressed, historians have noted a general tendency among railway managements at this time to think in terms of 'service' rather than absolute profit. Also, of course, the GNS had invested in suburban services since 1887 and no self-respecting company would just tamely give up in the face

The growth in size of the company's locomotives is illustrated by a Cowan class C of 1878 and a Pickersgill Class V of 1899. *(Great North of Scotland Railway Association)*

of new competition (the 'subbies' ran until 1937). The railway company had one weapon in its buses – trams were vulnerable to bus competition, and in 1905 the Suburban Tramways Co. agreed not to push its line beyond Murtle if the Great North refrained from running competing buses.

The twentieth century

By the end of 1900 the locomotive stock had risen to 115 – this and the extent of double track, now at 63 miles with 273 miles of single line, plus the ongoing work at Inverurie – reflects the high investment of the later 1890s. There were now 422 carriages for passenger use, plus 306 "passenger train vehicles". First class passenger numbers were 104,995, with receipts of £13,938; while third class rose to 3,372,792 with receipts of £153,120, and season tickets to 2,839 (£17,723). Total passenger train receipts were £242,467. On the goods side were 3,483 vehicles plus 73 service vehicles. Merchandise carried exceeded half a million tons at 508,805, with receipts of £150,245; and minerals amounted to 470,650 tons, yielding £52,021. Livestock transport contributed £15,283. Passenger train miles amounted to 1,472,973, and goods to 789,551. Post Office van No. 3, purchased from the London & North Western Railway in 1886, was reported as too decrepit for use, and broken up[32].

In late August 1904 the Great North rose to the kind of challenge railwaymen relished – working the three special trains required for Buffalo Bill's Wild West Show tour, from Aberdeen to Peterhead, Fraserburgh, Huntly and Elgin. Formed of 20, 21 and nineteen vehicles respectively, including five sleeping cars, with the longest train measuring 395 yards, they needed special arrangements for sidings and crossing points. Running at half-hour intervals, they went from Huntly to Elgin via the coast, and then passed on to the Highland[33].

Two steam rail-motors were built at Inverurie in 1905, using mechanical parts from Andrew Barclay of Kilmarnock and vertical boilers from Cochrans of Annan. Used on the Lossiemouth and St. Combs branches, though achieving 60 mph on trial[34], they proved unreliable and in November 1906 the decision was taken to split them into separate engine and carriage units. The tiny engines were converted to stationary boilers by March 1912, one at Inverurie Works, the other at the Palace Hotel[35]. The top end of the company's motive power was used to run excursion trains: the half-day Strathspey excursion became the Great North's fastest booked service, running the 67.8 miles from Aberdeen to Craigellachie non-stop in 88 minutes at an average speed of 46.2 mph in 1908, and the 64 miles from Aberdeen to Dufftown at an average of 47.4 mph in 1909. But daily schedules showed a slow-down from the 1890s, with the best Down service, the 6 am Aberdeen-Elgin via the coast, arriving at 8.20; and the best Up being the 10.22 am from Elgin via Craigellachie, arriving in Aberdeen at 12.55 pm. Aberdeen to Inverness trains were taking 3 1/2 hours, with the best time via the coast, worked by Highland Railway 'Bens'[36].

At mid-decade, 31 January 1906, five elderly engines from Cowan's time had been withdrawn, reducing the locomotive stock to 110[37]; the track mileage figures were unchanged from five years earlier and the rolling stock figures virtually the same, with the addition of 20 goods vehicles. During 1905 first class passenger numbers had risen slightly to 113,382 with receipts of £12,010. Third class numbers were 3,841,247 with receipts of £155,310, and 3,186 season tickets yielded £19,733. Merchandise tonnage had fallen back to 413,370, with receipts of

£140,264, while the less profitable mineral tonnage had jumped to 565,122 (£65,915). Livestock contributed £14,750. Efforts to hold down or reduce train mileage resulted in passenger trains running 1,493,993 miles and goods trains running 668,972[38].

Five years on, at the end of 1910 another five old engines had gone, but four new Inverurie-built 4-4-0s had been added to bring the total to 109. Six bogie composite carriages were built for the Inverness trains in 1908, with steam heating, and bogie vestibule coaches were also built for through running between Elgin and Glasgow Buchanan Street[39]. There were 427 passenger carriages and 309 other passenger train vehicles; with passenger numbers in 1910 being 103,332 first class and 3,274,000 third. Goods vehicles totalled 3,619, and total merchandise carried amounted to 435,001 tons, and minerals to 553,155 tons. The trackage figure given by the company was 64 miles double and 269 single, and passenger train mileage was 1,515,567, with goods mileage at 663,087[40].

It is rather odd that the biggest locomotive building programme in the Great North's history should have happened in the years just before the completion of its own new works. By the time these opened in 1902, the company had few immediate needs and was anyway engaged in an economy drive. Apart from assembling the two railcars, Inverurie built no new engines until 1909, and only eight between then and 1920. Rebuilding of older engines was the main activity, continuing the programme begun in 1881. Twenty-four were rebuilt or adapted between 1903 and 1915, and a further 30 between 1916 and 1922. Inverurie also carried out routine maintenance, accident repair, and carriage & wagon construction and maintenance, but even so its total output between 1902 and 1922 can hardly have justified the capital invested. By 1920 the passenger carriage stock had increased by 42 from 1905, and the number of goods vehicles had gone up by 122. Had the confidently-expected Highland merger been achieved in 1905, things would have been very different.

When Thomas Heywood arrived in May 1914 the prime power was Pickersgill's 39 post-1895 engines, of which five had been equipped with superheating. Apart from continuing the re-boilering programme, Heywood also oversaw steam heating fitted to most passenger engines and carriages. Had the war not put a stop to such things, further speeding-up would have taken place – in the summer of 1914 the 4.45 pm 'Deeside Express' to Ballater ran non-stop between Aberdeen and Torphins, taking 33 minutes for 23 miles, and detaching a slip-coach at Banchory, but this exercise was never to be repeated. The four Aberdeen dock engines were acquired in 1915, and worked intensively. In August 1920 £5,768 7s 8d was paid to Manning, Wardle for repairs to them. No. 116 (re-numbered 30 in August 1915) was the last Great North engine in active service, not withdrawn until April 1960[41]. In 1917 Heywood altered the colour of Great North locomotives from green to black, perhaps as a wartime economy measure, though green was never restored. In April 1918 the locomotive committee authorised superheating for a further four engines, and a licence was obtained from the Superheater Company for superheaters to be installed either in the GNS's works or by third parties[42].

As of 31 December 1919 the company recorded 97 4-4-0 engines and 22 tank engines. Passenger carriages (first and third) numbered 398, plus 69 composites, two Post Office vans, 75 luggage/parcel brake vans, eighteen

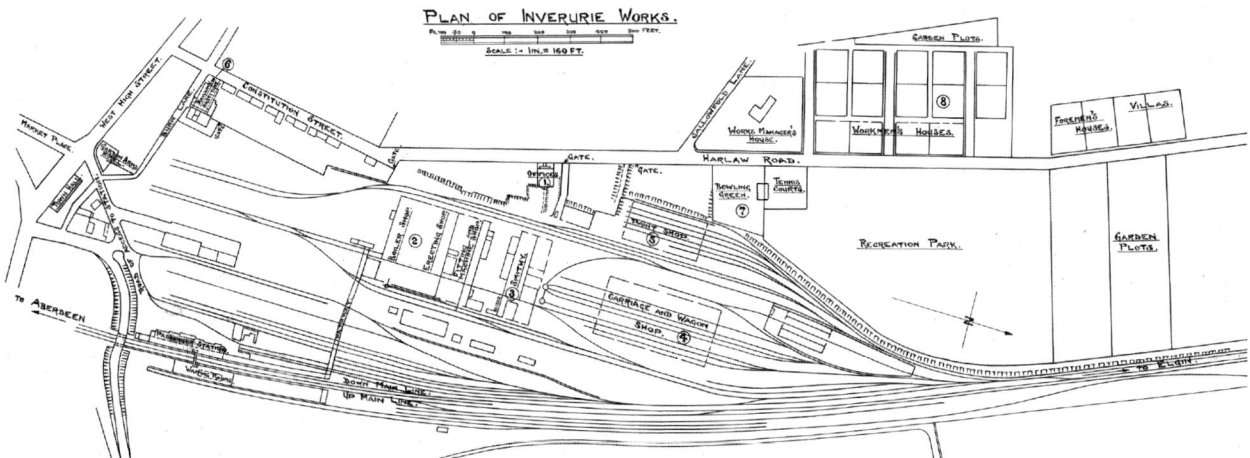

Plan of Inverurie Works showing the various shops in the centre, the new station bottom left and the workmen's housing top right.

Preserved Class F No. 49 *Gordon Highlander*, **built by the North British Locomotive Co. in 1920. It was originally painted black. Withdrawn from service in 1958.** *(Stenlake collection)*

carriage trucks, 24 horse boxes and 192 miscellaneous vehicles. Goods vehicles comprised 2,745 open 8-12 ton trucks, 41 12-20 ton trucks, 89 covered vans under eight tons, 350 covered vans of 8-12 tons, 260 cattle trucks, 81 rail/timber trucks, 72 brake vans and one miscellaneous vehicle. For works purposes there were 86 ballast wagons, seven mess & tool vans, two breakdown cranes, and one travelling crane. There were eleven road motors for goods and parcels, and 36 buses. This rolling stock carried 144,649 first class and 3,389,374 third class passengers, 929 first class and 3,208 third class season ticket holders, and 292,536 at workmen's fares. General merchandise amounted to 620,927 tons, coal and coke to 95,787 tons, and minerals to 69,906 tons. Livestock numbered 341,969. The engines ran 1,307,420 passenger train miles and 872,488 goods train miles, with shunting, light engine working and piloting accounting for a further 727,246 miles[43].

In March 1920 100 10-ton covered vans were ordered from the Metropolitan Carriage & Wagon Co., for £43,550, and eight of what would be Heywood's final locomotive design for the company, the class F 4-4-0s of 1920-21. Although equipped with superheating, steam heating, and dual Westinghouse and vacuum brakes to work Highland Railway stock, this was an old-fashioned design for its period, as compared for example to the Highland's *Snaigow* 4-4-0, though they worked competently on GNS lines, up to 1958 in the case of the longest-lived, No. 49 *Gordon Highlander*, which is preserved. Six were built by the North British Locomotive Co., and only two at Inverurie, for unexplained reasons. All carried names, either of directors or their residences, the exceptions being No. 45, *George Davidson*, and 46, *Benachie*.

The Great North built 162 engines, plus the two rail-motors, and acquired eleven from absorbed companies. By 1900 27 had been withdrawn, and between then and 1923 a further 21 went for sale or scrap[44]. At the end of 1922 three of the Neilson 4-4-0s of 1866 were still on the roster, and all engines of Manson's time and later were still in service.

Sacks and ropes

Provision for a railway company covered a multitude of items. Among the details which the staff had to control was the usage of sacks and ropes, both being items liable to loss or retention by customers. Sacks were hired from Chisholm & Co. of Perth, who supplied 4-bushel grain sacks at $\frac{1}{2}d$ per sack for journeys under 50 miles, $\frac{3}{4}d$ over

50 miles, and 1*d* if going outside the GNS system, the charges being passed on to the users. Ropes also had to be watched over (as did tarpaulins). A daily record of ropes received and forwarded survives from October 1914-June 1916, listing ropes, bearers and pins returned, mostly to stations in the Caledonian and Glasgow & South Western Railway coalfield areas. Each company had its own identifiable ropes, the GNS having a red and a tarred thread in one strand, and a tarred thread in each of the other two strands. Every length (minimum 25 yards) also had a metal ferrule stamped with the rope number and the company's initials[45].

Royal Trains

The regular stays at Balmoral of Queen Victoria, Edward VII and George V meant that the Deeside line was frequently used by royal personages (Patrick Barnett was said to have accompanied over 200 royal journeys up to his retirement in 1906), and the Great North had set procedures for dealing with the Royal Train, or with special saloons attached to scheduled trains, and the 'Queen's Messenger' trains. Barclay-Harvey noted some arrangements: "On the single part of the line no train was allowed for at least twenty minutes before the Royal Train was due to pass. On the double line all trains meeting it had to slow up to ten miles an hour. Each section had to be cleared for the train fifteen minutes before it was due and no-one except the station staff was allowed on the platform of any station while it was passing. All facing points had to be clipped and padlocked twenty minutes before the train reached them, and all level crossing gates (of which there were many) also locked till it had passed." Unlike most other railways, the GNS did not send a pilot train ahead of the Royal Train, but these precautions were ample[46]. The Great North took over the train at Ferryhill, where civic and railway dignitaries paid their respects, in somewhat inconvenient fashion from the lineside, as the junction had no passenger platform, though a temporary platform was put up to enable the Lord Provost to greet the Shah of Persia in 1889.

Special decoration of stations and engines was only done for ceremonial occasions, as with King Edward VII's visit to Aberdeen to mark the University's 400th anniversary in 1906, though a crimson carpet was kept at Ballater Station to roll out on the platform for royal arrivals (surprisingly, the station remained a fairly rudimentary structure until enlargement in 1893-96). The farthest-travelled passenger carriages of the GNS were seven vehicles, including the company's own 'royal saloon', sent to Ollerton, on the Great Central line between Chesterfield and Lincoln in September 1903 to bring Edward VII and his entourage to Ballater.

The Great North was the only Scottish railway to have a specifically royal carriage. Saloon carriage No. 1 was built at Kittybrewster in 1897 as a general-purpose first class saloon car, for hire to travelling parties. With the accession of Edward VII it was completely refurbished for the king's use. Electrically lit, with hot water radiators, and mounted on two four-wheel bogies, it was a state-of-the-art vehicle of its day, and fortunately remains preserved[47]. In 1907 a "unique" third class bogie saloon, 48 feet long, was built at Inverurie, which could be divided into two, for parties of 32 and seventeen, or opened out for larger groups, and its equipment, "at once complete and elegant" included folding tables for refreshments to be taken. There was said to be increasing demand for such accommodation from wedding and sports parties[48] and the split-up railcars were also used for this purpose.

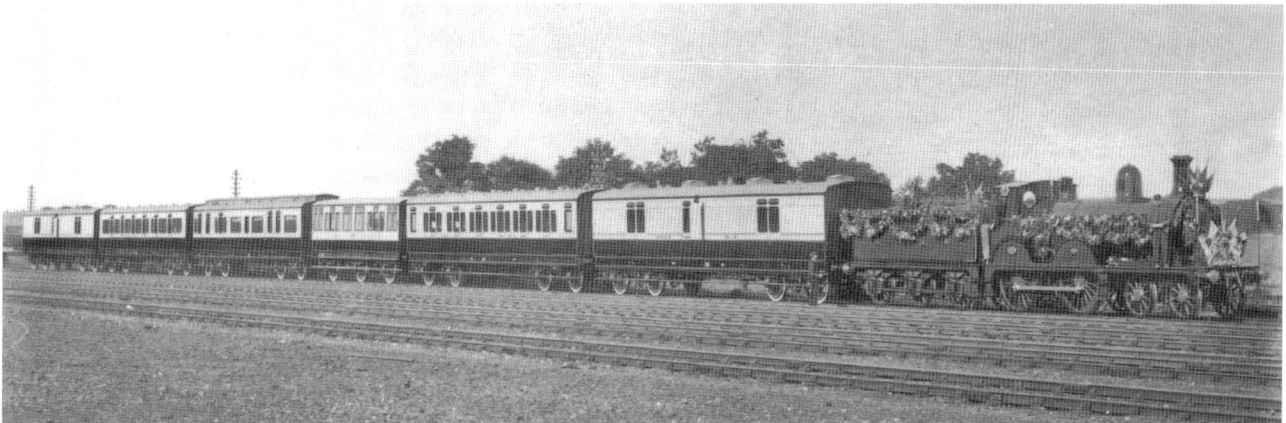

The Great North was asked to provide a complete train for King Edward VII on several occasions. A bogie saloon, the fourth vehicle, built in 1898, was refitted for his use. An older saloon plus some new stock made up the rest of the train. Decoration was applied only for formal events, like the king's visit to Aberdeen in 1904. (*Great North of Scotland Railway Association*)

TIMELINE OF THE GREAT NORTH

Pre 1840

1805 Aberdeenshire Canal opened to Waterloo Quay.

1836 Arbroath & Forfar Rly incorporated, 19 May.

1837 First surveys for a line south from Aberdeen.

1840s

1840 Dundee & Arbroath Rly opens.

1844 Aberdeen Railway announced, 3 April; 'Great North of Scotland Railway' (Perth) prospectus, 24 April.

1845 'Great North Railway' announced, 4 February, with revised name of Great North of Scotland Railway , 8 March. GNS agrees purchase of Aberdeenshire Canal.
Aberdeen Rly and Scottish Midland Junction Rly Acts, 31 July.

1846 Acts for GNS line, 25 June; for Deeside Rly to Aboyne 6 July; for Alford Valley and for Eastern Extension to Fraserburgh and Peterhead, 14 July, for Morayshire Rly, 16 July.
Dee Viaduct collapses, 28 September.

1847 Amalgamation of GNS with Aberdeen Railway authorised by Act of 9 July.

1848 SMJR opens, Perth-Forfar, 2 August.
Aberdeen Railway opens Guthrie-Montrose, and Bridge of Dun-Brechin, 1 February.
It leases Arbroath & Forfar Rly, 1 February.

1849 Sir James Elphinstone elected GNS Chairman. Aberdeen Railway board reformed.

1850s

1850 Aberdeen Railway opens to Ferryhill, 1 April.
Amalgamation Act of 1847 with GNSR repealed, 29 July.

1851 GNS Amendment Act gets royal assent, 3 July, capital reduced.
Robert Milne appointed Secretary of GNS, August.

1852 Morayshire Railway opens Elgin-Lossiemouth, 10 August (public service from 11th).
New Deeside Railway Act, 28 May; construction begins 5 July.
First sod cut on Huntly line, 25 November.

1853 Deeside Railway opens, Ferryhill-Banchory, 7 September (public service from 8th).
Daniel Kinnear Clark appointed GNSR Locomotive Superintendent.
Queen Victoria's first journey on the Deeside Railway, 13 October.

1854 Kittybrewster-Huntly line opens, 12 September (goods), 20th (passengers).
Aberdeen Railway opens Guild Street Station, 2 August.
GNS Amendment Act authorises Kittybrewster-Waterloo line and harbour tramway to Guild Street, 24 July.
Inverness & Nairn Rly Act, 24 July.
GNS Workmen's Friendly Society founded.

1855 Huntly-Keith line authorised, 25 May.
Banff, Macduff & Turriff Jct and Inverury & Old Meldrum Jct Rlys authorised, 15 June.
Kittybrewster-Waterloo opens for goods traffic, 24 September.
Kinnear Clark resigns, James Folds Ruthven appointed locomotive superintendent.
Agreement with Inverness & Aberdeen Junction Railway for its line to Keith, 20 October.

1856 Passenger traffic Kittybrewster-Waterloo, from 1 April.
Inverury & Old Meldrum Junction Rly opens, 1 July.
Huntly-Keith line opens, 10 October.
New Alford Valley Act, 23 June.
Aberdeen and Scottish Midland Junction Rlys amalgamate as Scottish North Eastern Rly, 29 July.
Robert Milne appointed GNS general manager.

1857 Banff Macduff & Turriff Jct Rly opens, Inveramsay to Turriff, 5 September.
Banchory & Aboyne (Deeside Extension Rly) Act, Keith & Dufftown Rly Act, Banff Portsoy & Strathisla Rly Act, Banff, Macduff & Turriff Extension Act, all 27 July.
Inverury & Old Meldrum Junction Rly leased to GNS, 1 September.
Morayshire Rly Act, for Orton-Dandaleith.
Ruthven resigns, William Cowan appointed locomotive superintendent.

1858 Inverness & Aberdeen Junction Railway meets GNSR at Keith, 18 August. Morayshire Railway opens Orton-Rothes, 23 August; Rothes-Craigellachie, 24 December.
Formartine & Buchan Railway Act, 23 July.
GNSR retrospective Act for lease of Old Meldrum line, 11 June.

1859 Alford Valley Railway opens, Kintore-Alford, 21 March (Official opening 30 July).
Banff Portsoy & Strathisla Rly opens, Grange to Tillynaught, Banff and Portsoy, 2 August.
Aboyne Rly opens, 2 December.
Banff Macduff & Turriff Jct Rly is renamed Aberdeen & Turriff Rly, 19 April.
Formartine & Buchan Rly Diversion Act (via Ellon), 19 April. GNS Consolidation Act, 21 July.

1860s

1860 Banff Macduff & Turriff Extension Rly opens to Macduff (Gellymill), 4 June; is incorporated with GNS.
GNS sells back its stake in Inverness & Aberdeen Junction Railway.
Morayshire Rly authorised to build direct Rothes line, 3 July.

1861 Formartine & Buchan Railway Rly opens from Dyce to Mintlaw, 18 July.
Strathspey Rly Act, Dufftown-Abernethy, 16 May; Morayshire Rly authorised to build Spey Bridge link at Craigellachie, 17 May.
Elgin-Rothes opens for goods, 30 December.
Fiddich Viaduct collapses, 9 July.
Scottish North Eastern Railway backs Scottish Northern Junction line.

1862 Morayshire Railway opens Rothes-Elgin to passengers, 1 January.
Formartine & Buchan Rly opens to Peterhead, 3 July.
Keith & Dufftown Rly opens 19 February (goods), 21 February (passengers).
GNS acquires the Deeside Rly and takes an interest in Montrose & Bervie Rly.
Scottish Northern Junction Act, June 30.

1863 Strathspey Rly opens Dufftown to Nethy Bridge, and Morayshire Rly opens Dandaleith-Craigellachie, 1 July.
Banff Portsoy & Strathisla Rly renamed Banffshire Rly in Act of 21 July, which also confirms working of line by GNS (from 1 February) and extension to Portgordon.
GNS takes over working of the Morayshire Rly, 1 July.
Acts of 21 July substitute Maud for Mintlaw as junction for Fraserburgh and authorise GNS 'Circumbendibus' and Banff Macduff & Turriff Extension, line to Macduff Harbour.
Scottish North Eastern Railway absorbs Dundee & Arbroath Rly.
Inverness & Perth Junction Rly opens, 9 September.
GNS joins Railway Clearing House.

1864 Scottish North Eastern Railway Denburn Valley Line Act, June 23, repeals 'Circumbendibus' line Act of 1863.
Merger discussions with the Scottish North Eastern Railway.

1865 Formartine & Buchan Rly opens Maud-Fraserburgh, 24 April.
Peterhead Harbour Branch opens, 9 August.
Aboyne & Braemar Railway and 'Strathspey Junction' line Acts, 5 July.
GNS financial crisis: Shareholders' Committee looks into company affairs, April.
Inverness & Aberdeen Junction Railway and Inverness & Perth Junction Railway amalgamate as Highland Rly, 29 June.

1866 Strathspey Rly. opens to Boat of Garten, 1 August. Aboyne & Braemar Rly opens Aboyne-Ballater, 17 October.
GNS Amalgamation Act of 30 July: merger of Aberdeen & Turriff, Alford Valley, Banff Macduff & Turriff Extension, Formartine & Buchan, Inverury & Old Meldrum Jct, Keith & Dufftown, and Strathspey Rlys with GNS, also 999-year lease of Deeside and Deeside Extension Rlys (operative from 1 September 1867).
Scottish North Eastern Railway amalgamates with Caledonian Rly. Orton-Rothes line closed, 1 August.
Alexander Gibb resigns, succeeded by Alexander Fraser.

1867 Opening of Aberdeen Joint Station and Denburn Valley line, 4 November.
Banffshire Rly amalgamates with GNS, 1 August (Act of 12 August).
GNS lease of Deeside Railway begins, 1 September. GNS board reformed: Elphinstone resigns, John Duncan elected chairman, February.
Alexander Fraser resigns, succeeded by Patrick Barnett as engineer.
W.B. Ferguson appointed secretary, Robert Milne is "manager of traffic."

1868 GNS struggles to maintain solvency.

1869 Four men killed in snow-clearing accident, 28 December.
GNS Provident Society, later Savings Bank, started.

1870s

1870 Banff Macduff & Turriff Extension Bill for extension to Macduff, December.
1871 John Duncan replaced as GNS chairman by William Leslie, October.
1872 Extension to new terminus at Macduff opens, 1 July.
Government purchases GNS telegraphs for £26,000.
1873 GNS Preference Shares Act authorises capitalisation of dividend arrears into a new 4% preference stock.
1874 Aberdeen's first trams run.
Three men killed in Arnage collision, 12 March.
1875 GNS absorbs Deeside Railway, 31 August.
1876 GNS absorbs Aboyne & Braemar Rly, 31 January.
Further Powers Act of 13 July gives retrospective authorisation of amalgamation of Deeside and Aboyne & Braemar Rlys (from 31 August 1875).
1877 GNS Further Powers Act, 28 June, authorises station enlargements and expansion of Kittybrewster Works.
1878 Alexander M. Ross appointed goods manager.
Manure carriage dispute begins.
1879 Leslie dies, February; William Ferguson of Kinmundy elected chairman.
Earl of Aberdeen's Railway proposed, Udny-Methlick.

1880s

1880 Milne and W.B. Ferguson resign, William Moffatt appointed general manager and secretary.
A.G. Reid appointed superintendent.
1881 Morayshire Railway-GNSR Amalgamation Act, 11 August, backdated to 1 October
1880. Manure carriage dispute re-activated.
1882 Act for coast line, Portsoy-Elgin, 12 July; 'Various Powers' Act, for part-doubling of Deeside line, and Stock Consolidation Act, 19 May.
Inverythan Bridge collapse, 5 killed, 27 November.
1883 First sod cut on Portsoy-Elgin line, 24 April.
Cowan resigns, James Manson appointed locomotive superintendent, October.
Cheap Trains Act.
Parcel post service introduced.
1884 Coast line opens Portsoy-Tochieneal 1 April; Elgin-Garmouth 12 August.
Fraserburgh-Rosehearty Rly Act, 28 July.
GNS and Highland Railway Acts authorise exchange of traffic at all junction points.
1885 First express trains, Elgin-Aberdeen.
1886 Coast line completed, open for goods on 5 April, passengers 1 May.
Grange triangle completed, Grange Sth-Grange Nth, 3 May.
Seven-year agreement with Highland Rly.
Through carriages run between Aberdeen and Inverness.
PO sorting carriages introduced.
1887 Suburban service introduced, Dyce-Aberdeen.
Act of 19 July retrospectively allows connecting link at Grange.
1888 Cullen Viaduct collapses (December), line restored by 15 January 1889.
Two killed in runaway accident at Kintore, 11 September.
Railway & Canal Traffic Act requires revision of goods rates.
1889 Mechanical tablet exchange introduced, May.
Regulation of Railways Act. Goods charges controversy.

1890s

1890 Manson resigns, 12 August; James Johnson joins as locomotive superintendent, 25 August.
Garve & Ullapool Rly Act, 14 August.
Scottish railway strike: GNS men remain at work.
GNS buys Palace Hotel, Aberdeen.
1891 Parkmore limeworks siding, Dufftown goods branch.
Palace Hotel opens as GNS establishment, 22 August.

1892   Railway (Rates & Charges Order Confirmation) Act, 20 June.
      Deeside line doubled to Culter.
1893   GNS (Various Powers) Act, 24 August, includes Boddam Branch and Cruden Bay Hotel.
      Garve & Ullapool Railway Abandonment Act, 24 August.
      GNS board decide to build new locomotive works at Inverurie.
      Provident Society is transformed into GNS Savings Bank, and company joins Railway Clearing House Superannuation Fund.
      Drummuir accident 29 December, one man killed.
1894   Deeside suburban services begin, July.
      New offices open in Guild Street.
      Johnson resigns, William Pickersgill appointed locomotive superintendent.
      Board of Trade requires phasing out of mixed trains.
      First sod of Cruden line cut on 8 September.
      Aboyne accident, 4 January, one man killed.
1895   Cruden Bay Hotel plan approved.
      Locomotive men agitate over working hours.
1896   GNS introduces corridor carriages.
      Its proposal to take over Aberdeen Tramways Company is frustrated.
      Light Railways Act, 14 August.
1897   Boddam Branch opens, 2 August.
      Buckie (Cluny Harbour) Act, 12 August.
      Western suburban line authorised, 15 July.
1898   Building of Inverurie Works begins.
      Cairnie Junction exchange platform in use from 1 June.
      Staff receptions held, January and March.
1899   Interlocking and block working completed throughout system.
      Cruden Bay Hotel opens, 1 March; tramway opens June.
      Deeside line doubling to Park completed, 28 August.
      Aberdeen Joint Station Act, 9 August.
      Light Railway Order for St. Combs line, 8 September.

1900 – 1909

1900   Double line completed between Aberdeen and Keith.
      Mortlach Distillery extension.
      A.G. Reid resigns, succeeded as superintendent by William Deuchar, February.
1901   Carriage & wagon dept established at Inverurie.
      Investigation committee on directors' actions.
1902   Locomotive dept. established at Inverurie (move completed 11 May 1903); new station opens, 10 February.
      New Elgin Station completed.
      First sod of St. Combs Railway cut, 12 September.
1903   St. Combs Branch opens, 1 July.
      Inverurie Loco Works FC founded.
1904   GNS road bus services begin between Ballater and Braemar, 2 May.
      Ferguson dies, Sir David Stewart elected chairman.
1905   Amalgamation with Highland Railway proposed.
1906   GNS Order authorises bus services, 26 June. Moffatt retires.
      George Davidson becomes general manager and Thomas Mackintosh secretary.
      Patrick Barnett resigns, succeeded by James Parker.
      Highland Railway amalgamation called off.
1907   Orton-Rothes line lifted.
      'Three Rivers' tours inaugurated, June.
      New goods yard begun at Market Street.
      Two men killed in Fiddich Viaduct accident, April.
      National railway strike averted, October.
1908   New suburban platforms in use at Aberdeen Joint Station.
      Through running of engines Aberdeen-Inverness from 20 April.
1909   A.M. Ross, goods manager, retires; S.R. Willox appointed.

1910 – 1923

1910 Portsoy Harbour line lifted.
  GNS purchases Station Hotel, Aberdeen.
1911 National rail strike again averted.
1912 New wage agreements concluded.
1913 Much discussion of new light railways, with negative results.
  Pickersgill resigns, December.
1914 Thomas E. Heywood appointed locomotive superintendent, February.
  Company placed under control of Railway Executive, 4 August.
1915 Rebuilding of Aberdeen Joint Station completed, September.
  Locomotive haulage at Aberdeen Harbour finally begins.
1916 GNS assists Highland Railway with wartime working.
1917 GNS joins Scottish railways' pooled wagon scheme.
  Wartime traffic peaks; new timber sidings installed.
1918 Lenabo Airship Station Branch, 2 December.
  Deuchar retires, William Johnston appointed as superintendent.
1919 GNS men join in national railway strike, September.
  Stewart dies, Andrew Bain elected chairman, October.
1920 Parkhill-Elrick double track completed, May. Excursion trains resume.
1921 Government control ends, 15 August.
1922 Bain resigns, Alexander Duffus elected chairman, 21 February.
  GNS board seeks staff pay reductions and extension of working hours.
  Shareholders approve arrangements for incorporation of GNS into the eastern group of companies.
1923 From 1 January GNS is merged into the London & North Eastern Railway.

APPENDIX 1

The Case of Signalman Mann, 1909-11

Mann's workplace was the signal box at Fraserburgh Station. The duties of the signalman were described by William Deuchar, the superintendent, as "very light" – there were around eighteen trains a day (shunting was not mentioned). By an agreement of 30 December 1909 the box was advanced from third class to second class status, and its duty hours fixed at ten per day, with no meal break. The previous arrangement had been a twelve-hour day, with two meal hours, and a 40-minute booking-off in the evening. Mann's wages were raised in line with the upgrading of the box, by one shilling a week in the first year, and two shillings in subsequent years. Mann however indicated to the stationmaster that he preferred the twelve-hour arrangement, with breaks, to the ten hours without, and with Deuchar's consent this was allowed. Following statements made by Rothney that the agreement regarding hours was not being strictly adhered to, and that Mann was being forced to do unpaid overtime, Mann was seen by Deuchar, on a visit to Fraserburgh, together with the stationmaster. Questioned, he said he was pleased with the former arrangement regarding hours and breaks. Following this interview, on 16 April 1910 Mann wrote a letter to the Fraserburgh stationmaster which said, "I am quite satisfied with the present arrangements." In Rothney's account of this meeting, Deuchar warned Mann that unless he ceased troubling the sectional conciliation board, he (the superintendent) would "require to take serious steps" and have him transferred elsewhere. Rothney continued to maintain that Mann was not satisfied, and on 30 May 1911 George Davidson saw Mann and Rothney together. At that meeting, Mann said he did not wish to withdraw his letter to the stationmaster, and that he was quite satisfied. Rothney wanted to go further into aspects of the case, and Davidson suggested that Deuchar should be present. In his evidence to the Royal Commission on Railways Davidson said Mann "was really anxious to get the whole thing dropped and stated to me that he did not want any alteration in his hours. We shook hands, and the incident terminated." Davidson told the Commission that there was no disaffection on the Great North, and when asked if any men had come out in the recent trouble, he said, "No, we never heard of it." Deuchar, describing his side of the story to the Commission, said his talk with Mann had been friendly, and denied Rothney's suggestion that this had been one of many intimidations: "… relations between me and the signalmen and other grades in my department are, and always have been, perfectly harmonious and the men are quite contented." It does not seem that Rothney could produce clear evidence to contradict that statement.

This individual case, considered by the Royal Commission of 1911, is of interest because of the unusual amount of detail recorded. Even so, much can only be surmised. It can be seen as an account of heavy-handed management determined to circumvent conciliation procedures and lean on any employee who complained, or as the behaviour of an officious union activist determined to put the company officials in the worst light and perhaps putting words into another man's mouth. The unfortunate Mr Mann appears to have been caught between the two sides, willing to make complaints to the union but failing to reiterate them in front of senior managers. One might have some sympathy with him, in that era when trade unionism was very new, and the company officials exercised dictatorial powers. On the whole, the evidence tilts against the company, since Rothney is scarcely likely to have invented Mann's complaints out of nothing. But he does not appear to have been able to establish any other actual cases of intimidation.

Davidson was able to provide the Commission with evidence of relatively quick resolution of one request, "complete agreement" within six months. Rothney claimed that counter-petitions were coerced, something Davidson denied. Conciliation board 'C' received a petition on wages and hours on 19 April 1909, signed by twelve men, purporting to be on behalf of all waymen and foreman waymen. On 28 May a further petition was received from twelve men in the Aberdeen district, asking for an increase in wages. Board 'C' met on 29 June to consider these two requests, and on the same morning the company's chief engineer handed Davidson a third petition, signed by 75 foremen and 175 waymen, protesting that the petition of 19 April had been put forward without the knowledge or consent of the great majority, and that to adopt it would be retrograde and against the men's best interests. When the conciliation board met, the men's side were informed of this, and agreed to withdraw all issues except that of wages. Consideration of this was deferred for a fortnight, and on 28 July a settlement was agreed. Davidson insisted that the counter-petition was "quite unexpected" and denied that men were coerced into signing it. Unless one takes the crudely patronising view that the majority of GNS employees were simply turkeys refusing to vote for the abolition of Christmas, it is clear that company-employee relations were not clear-cut. On the men's side these might include dislike of self-appointed activists, a preference for individual action, an identification with the company (William Ferguson's handshakes had not been forgotten) that brought with it a certain deference to the managers, a reluctance to ask for 'favours', and a fear of socialism, often represented as next to godlessness; as well as a belief that for far too long they had been overworked and underpaid, and that only united action would remedy things. On the management side, there was a 60-year tradition of firm control and discipline, a sense that authority, if challenged, should bear down hard, and perhaps a genuine concern that that the whole system of rules and regulations, not least for safe and secure working, might collapse.

All might have agreed with the Scottish poet John Davidson (1857-1909): "It's just the power of some to be a boss, And the bally power of others to be bossed" (from *Thirty Bob a Week*).

APPENDIX 2

A profile of the Great North in 1913

Directors: Sir David Stewart (chairman), Andrew Bain (vice-chairman), Thomas Adam (Aberdeen), W. Rose Black (Elgin), Theodore Crombie (Culter), Garden A. Duff (Hatton Castle), Dr Robert Farquharson (Finzean), James Grant (Glen Grant), J.M. Henderson (Wimbledon), Sidney Herbert (Stonehaven), David G. Irvine (Liverpool), Earl of Southesk (Brechin)

Route miles:	334½
Double track:	80 miles 682 yards
Total trackage including sidings:	519 miles 1,562 yards
Authorised capital:	£5,360,757 17s 8d
Loans & debentures:	£1,733,764 16s 3d
Total:	£7,094,522 13s 11d
Total expenditure on capital account:	£6,234,908 9s 11d
Capital uncreated:	£150,000 (shares), £50,000 (loans)

	Gross receipts	Expenditure	Net receipts
Railway	£532,581 8s 6d	£281,769 11s 4d	£250,811 17s 2d
Road services	£10,702 8s 6d	£9,958 0s 2d	£744 8s 4d
Hotels	£41,397 5s 9d	£31,400 17s 9d	£9,996 8s 0d
Miscellaneous			£9,063 11s 4d
Total	£584,681 2s 9d	£323,128 9s 3d	£270,616 4s 10d

	Passenger numbers	Passenger traffic receipts
First	102,586	£9,968 10s 6d
Third	3,541,154	£170,410 19s 5d
First class season ticket	588	£6,192 8s 7d
Third class season ticket	2,254	£13,234 16s 11d
Workmen (weekly tickets, actual journeys)	225,780	£1,540 3s 7d
Mail receipts		£26,385
Parcels & merchandise		£44,648 18s 6d
Total passenger traffic receipts		£272,375 17s 6d

	goods tonnage	average receipt per ton
general merchandise	567,3777	6s 4½d
coal	381,536	2s 6d
minerals	92,777	2s 6½d
livestock (head)	375,933	

Goods tonnage breakdown:
lime 11,026 tons; stone 62,685 tons; timber 56,797 tons; grain 96,097 tons; potatoes 4,523 tons; manure 44,858 tons; fish 10,226 tons; whisky 14,579 tons

Goods receipts

general merchandise	£180,212 11s 9d
less cartage costs of £12,637 12s 1d	£167,607 19s 8d
coal, coke	£47,645 16s 10d
other minerals	£11,777 15s 2d
livestock	£18,407 6s 10d
Total goods receipts	£245,438 18s 6d

Breakdown of expenditure

Maintenance & renewal of way and works	£40,973 2s 8d
Maintenance & renewal of rolling stock (engines)	£18,942 11s 1d
Maintenance & renewal of rolling stock (carriages)	£9,324 5s 4d
Maintenance & renewal of rolling stock (wagons)	£12,471 14s 4d
Locomotive running expenses	£81,901 6s 6d
Traffic department	£84,024 4s 8d (£58,607 in wages/salaries)
General charges	£13,711 9s 8d*

*including directors, £2,100, and salaries of general manager, secretary, clerks; also fire insurance premium £1,350, and superannuation/pension payments, £2,946)

Engine and train miles

	coaching	goods
Total train miles:	1,538,451	705,999
Total shunting miles	53,387	346,075
Total engine miles including shunting and light engine working:	2,835,159	

Rolling Stock

Engines

4-4-0 tender engines	97
0-6-0	9
0-4-4	9
0-4-0 tank engines	2
total	117

Goods Vehicles

goods wagons 8-12 tons	2,902
goods wagons 12-20 tons	16
covered vans under 8 tons	102
covered vans 8-12 tons	270
cattle trucks	265
rail & timber trucks, including twin trucks	34
brake vans	72
miscellaneous	1
total goods vehicles	3,662

Road motors

goods & parcels	8
passenger	35
Total road motors	43

Coaching Vehicles

first & third class carriages	401
composite carriages*	69
Post office vans	2
luggage & parcel brake vans	75
carriage trucks	16
horse-boxes	20
miscellaneous	200
total coaching vehicles	783

* total carriage seating capacity:
first class 1,811; third class 18,103

Works vehicles

ballast wagons	94
mess & tool vans	6
breakdown cranes	2
travelling cranes	1
miscellaneous	1
total works vehicles	104

Houses & cottages

for company servants	442
other houses & cottages	371

APPENDIX 3

William Ferguson's American links

When William Ferguson received the freedom of the royal burgh of Inverurie in 1902, at the age of 79, the town's provost offered a few details of his life to date:

"If Dr. Ferguson will permit me, I would like to give an outline of his personal history as far as it bears on the honorable position which he holds among us today. Dr. Ferguson's education was completed at Marischal College at Aberdeen, in 1840. His business training began in Leith and Glasgow, from 1840 to 1852; then he emigrated to Liverpool, where he remained a couple of years. In 1854 we find him a partner of Robert Benson & Co., American bankers and general merchants, in London, in which business he continued for eight years, after which he returned to Liverpool as a partner in the business of Messrs. Cropper, Ferguson & Co., and later by himself. He conducted the business in Liverpool from 1862 until 1872, when he retired to Kinmundy, to which he succeeded in 1862, on the death of his father. Dr. Ferguson is an LL.D. of the University of Aberdeen, and a Deputy Lieutenant and Justice of the Peace of the county, besides being a Fellow of two learned societies and a valued member of the General Assembly of the United Free Church, from 1873 to 1900, without a break."

Robert Benson & Co. (a predecessor of Kleinwort, Benson) was a Liverpool finance company with considerable railway interests. Robert R. Benson was a promoter of the Liverpool & Manchester Railway in 1828, and an associate of Theodore Rathbone, a fellow Quaker and prolific railway investor. The young Ferguson was very much in a railway *milieu*. Bensons were involved in the financing of American railways, and the company moved to London in 1852. In 1856, Ferguson, by then a partner, went to the USA to view the works of the Illinois Central Railroad, for which his company was the British agent. In honour of his visit, one of the new railway townships in Marion County was named Kinmundy (and still is). Ferguson is reputed to have written a book about his visit, *America by River and Rod*, but efforts to locate a copy have so far drawn a blank. It is clear, though, that he brought much more expertise on railway matters to his role on the Great North than might be expected from an Aberdeenshire laird.

SOURCES AND BIBLIOGRAPHY

ARCHIVES AND LIBRARIES

Aberdeen City Archives (ACA)
Aberdeen Central Library (ACL)
Aberdeen University Library (AUL)

National Archives of Scotland (NAS)
National Library of Scotland (NLS)
Post Office Archive (PO)

OFFICIAL PUBLICATIONS

Edinburgh Gazette (*Ed. Gaz.*)
Hansard see Parliamentary Papers

London Gazette (*Lond. Gaz.*)
Parliamentary Papers (PP)

SERIAL PUBLICATIONS, JOURNALS AND NEWSPAPERS

Aberdeen Free Press (*Abdn. F.P.*)
Aberdeen Weekly Journal (*Abdn. Jnl.*)
Caledonian Mercury (*Cal.Merc.*)
Daily News
Dundee Courier & Argus (*Dund. Cour.*)
Glasgow Herald (*Glas. Her.*)
Leeds Mercury
Morning Chronicle

Morning Post
Railway Gazette (*RG*)
Railway Magazine (*R.M.*)
Railway News
Railway Times (*RT*)
Scotsman (*Scmn.*)
Scottish Railway Gazette (*SRG*)
Transport History

PAMPHLETS AND BOOKLETS

Great North of Scotland Railway Association abstracts:
Fenwick, K., 'Post Office Sorting Carriages'
Smith, Ron, *Towiemore*. Dyce, 2009

Waterman, J.J., *The Coming of the Railway to Aberdeen*. Aberdeen, 1979

BOOKS

1. Books about the GNS and associated lines

Barclay-Harvey, Sir Malcolm, *A History of the Great North of Scotland Railway*. Dinnet, 2nd edition 1949

Cook, R.A., *Great North of Scotland Railway and Highland Railway Historical Maps*. Caterham, 1975

Farr, Alfred, *The Royal Deeside Line*. Newton Abbot, 1968

Fenwick, Keith, *Railways of Keith & Dufftown*. Aberdeen, 2013

Fenwick, Keith, Flett, D., and Jackson, D., *Railways of Buchan*. 2008

Fenwick, Keith, *Great North of Scotland Railway Carriages*. Lightmoor, 2009

Ferguson, W., *The Great North of Scotland Railway: A Guide*. Aberdeen, 1881

Fletcher, Peter, *Directors, Dilemmas and Debt*. Aberdeen, 2010

Gordon, Hugh, *Great North of Scotland Locomotives*. Clophill, 2008

Great North of Scotland Railway Assoc., *150 Years of the Great North*. Aberdeen, 2004

Jackson, D., *Royal Deeside's Railway*. Aberdeen, 1999

Jackson, D., *Rails to Alford*. Dyce, 2006

Jackson, D., *The Speyside Line*. Turriff, new ed. 2006

Jones, Keith, *Cruden Bay Hotel and Its Tramway*. Aberdeen, 2004

Jones, Keith, *The Subbies*. Aberdeen, 1987

Jones, Keith, *The Joint Station, 1867-92*. Aberdeen, 1992

Ramsay, Alexander, *Guide to the Great North of Scotland Railway*. Banff, 1854

Ross, John, *Travellers' Joy*. Elgin, 2004

Sangster, A., *Story and Tales of the Buchan Line*. Poole, 1983

Scott, W.J., *Little & Good*. Aberdeen, 1898

Stephenson Locomotive Society, *Little and Good: The GNSR*. Durham, 1972

Vallance, H.A., *The Great North of Scotland Railway*. Dawlish, 1965

2. Other Books

Acworth, William, *The Railways of Scotland*. London, 1890

Acworth, William, *The Railways and the Traders*. London, 1891

Acworth, William, *Elements of Railway Economics*. Oxford, 1924

Ahrons, E.L., *British Locomotive Practice & Performance*, vol iii. Cambridge, 1952

Alderman, Geoffrey, *The Railway Interest*. Leicester, 1973

Anderson, William, *The Howes o' Buchan*. Peterhead, 1865

Bagwell, Philip S., *The Railway Clearing House in the British Economy, 1842-1922*. London, 1968

Bagwell, Philip S., *The Transport Revolution from 1770*. London 1994

Barnard, Alfred, *The Whisky Distilleries of the United Kingdom. 1887*, new ed. Edinburgh, 2008

Baxter, David and Mitchell, Peter (eds.), *British Locomotive Catalogue 1825-1923, Vol. vi.* Southampton, 2012

Biddle, Gordon, *Historic Railway Buildings*. Oxford, 2003

Bremner, David, *The Industries of Scotland*. Edinburgh, 1869

Campbell, R.H., and Dow, J.B.A., *A Source Book of Scottish Economic & Social History*. Oxford, 1968

Carnie, William, *Reporting Reminiscences*. London, 1902

Carnie, William, *Aberdeen Reminiscences*. Aberdeen, 1906

Checkland, S.G., *Scottish Banking: A History 1695-1973*. London, 1975

Cobb, M.H., *The Railways of Great Britain: A Historical Atlas*, 2nd ed., Shepperton, 2006

Cranna, J., *Fraserburgh Past & Present*. Aberdeen, 1914

Cummings, J., *Railway Motor Buses and Bus Services, 1902-33*, vol. 1.

Cummings, A.J.G, and Devine, T.M., *Industry, Business and Society in Scotland since 1700*. Edinburgh, 1994

Deas, Francis, *The Law of Railways as Applying to Scotland*. Edinburgh, 1873

Dewick, T., *Atlas of Railway Station Names*. Hersham, 2002

Ellis, C. Hamilton, *British Railway History*, 2 vols. London, 1974

Findlay, J.T., *A History of Peterhead*. Peterhead, 1933

Fraser, W.H., and Lee, C.H., *Aberdeen: A New History*. Phantassie, 2006

Freeman, M.J. and Aldcroft, D.H. (eds.), *Transport in Victorian Britain*. Manchester, 1988

Hamilton, J.A.B., *Britain's Railways in World War I*. London, 1967

Henderson, J.A., *History of the Parish of Banchory-Devenick*. Aberdeen, 1890

Henderson, J.A., *History of the Society of Advocates in Aberdeen*. Aberdeen, 1912

Highet, Campbell, *Scottish Locomotive History, 1831-1923*. London, 1970

Keith, A., *1,000 Years of Aberdeen*. Aberdeen, 1972

Lewin, H.G., *The Railway Mania*. London, 1936

Mavor, James, *The Scottish Railway Strike 1891: A History and Criticism*. Edinburgh, 1891

Milne, John, Aberdeen, *Topographical, Antiquarian and Historical Papers*. Aberdeen, 1911

Mitchell, Joseph, *Reminiscences of My Life in the Highlands*, vol 2 (1884). Reprinted Newton Abbot, 1971

New Statistical Account of Scotland. Vol. xii, Aberdeenshire. Edinburgh, 1845

Ottley, George, *Bibliography of British Railway History*. 2nd ed., London 1983 and 2nd supplement (Boyles, Searle & Steggles) York, 1998

Oxford Dictionary of National Biography. Oxford, 2004

Paget-Tomlinson, E., *The Railway Carriers*. Lavenham, 1990

Parris, H., *Government and the Railways in the 19th Century*. London, 1965.

Pattinson, J.P., *British Railways*. London, 1893

Pratt, Edwin A., *British Railways and the Great War*, 2 vols. London, 1921

Quick, Michael, *A Chronology of Railway Passenger Stations in Great Britain*. Oxford, 2009

Ransom, P.J.G., *The Victorian Railway and How It Evolved*. London, 1996

Reed. M.C. (ed.), *Railways in the Victorian Economy*. Newton Abbot, 1969

Robertson, C.J.A., *The Origins of the Scottish Railway System, 1722-1844*. Edinburgh, 1983

Ross, David, *The Highland Railway*, 2nd ed. Catrine, 2010

Ross, David, *The Caledonian: Scotland's Imperial Railway*. Catrine, 2013

Ross, David, *The North British Railway: A History*. Catrine, 2014

Ross, David, *The Glasgow & South Western Railway*. Catrine, 2014

Simmons, Jack, *The Railway in Town and Country, 1830-1914*. Newton Abbot, 1986

Simmons, Jack, *The Victorian Railway*. London, 1991

Simnett, W.E., *Railway Amalgamation in Great Britain*. London, 1923

Slaven, A., and Checkland, S., *Dictionary of Scottish Business Biography*. Aberdeen, 1993

Smith, A., *A New History of Aberdeenshire*, 2 vols. Aberdeen, 1875

Weir, R., *History of the Distillers' Company, 1877-1939*. Oxford, 1995

Wilson, Harold, *The Travelling Post-Offices of Great Britain & Ireland*. Derby, 1996

Wrigley, Chris, and Shepherd, Johnathan, *On the Move: Essays in Labour & Transport presented to Philip Bagwell*. London, 1991

NOTES AND REFERENCES

1. 1830s – 1846, FIRST MOVES

1. *Aberdeenshire: New Stat. Account*, 96.
2. *Ibid.*, 66.
3. *Milne, Aberdeen*, 338. *Abdn. Jnl.*, 17 April 1844; *Cal. Merc.*, 18 April 1839.
4. Simmonds, *The Victorian Railway*, 93.
5. *Cal. Merc.*, 23 March 1844.
6. *Scmn.*, 27 April 1844.
7. *Dund. Cour.*, 26 March 1844.
8. *Scmn.*, 27 April 1844.
9. See advertisements in *Dund. Cour.*, 11 February, and *Glas. Her.*, 24 March 1845.
10. *Morn. Chron.*, 22 March 1845.
11. Father of Sir George Gibb, a distinguished General Manager of the North Eastern Railway.
12. *Abdn. Jnl.*, 2 October 1844.
13. *Dund. Cour.*, 29 October, *Scmn.*, 6 November 1844.
14. *Abdn. Jnl.*, 27 November 1844.
15. *Abdn. Jnl.*, 1 May 1844.
16. *Aberdeenshire: Third Stat. Account*, 97.
17. Headed by Lord Dalhousie, it existed for barely a year before its functions were curtailed and re-allocated to the Board of Trade.
18. *Abdn. Jnl.*, 26 March 1845.
19. *Abdn. Jnl.*, ibid.
20. *Abdn. Jnl.*, 25 June 1845.
21. *Abdn. Jnl.*, 25 June 1845., NAS BR/GNS/1/1.
22. See NLS, Rapkin's plan of Aberdeen, dated 1854 by NLS but evidently drawn some years previously.
23. NAS. BR/GNS/1/1. Committee, 3 March 1845.
24. NAS. BR/GNS/1/1, committee 31 March 1845.
25. The Banffshire lines were also known as the Dufftown, Keith, Fochabers & Portgordon Railway, one of the further-flung schemes promoted by John Learmonth, chairman of the North British Railway.
26. *Abdn. Jnl.*, 5 November 1845.
27. NAS. BR/GNS/1/1. Board, 9 December 1845, 17 March 1846. Fletcher, *Directors*, 9, notes a meeting that month in Elgin, at which the Perth & Inverness promoters offered most favourable terms to the GNS if it stopped at Elgin, but they were firmly rejected.
28. ACA. DO 14/5, 'Personal Reminiscence of John Stewart', 6, says the purchase was made to buy off its opposition.
29. ACL. Canal Acts; *Aberdeenshire, New Stat. Account*, 70.
30. NAS. BR/GNS/1/1. Committee, 14 October 1845. Jopp, like Alexander Anderson, was one of the founders of the North of Scotland Bank in 1836. The canal company's second issue of shares, at £20 each, was an early form of preference share, with priority over the original £50 shares until their dividend reached £1 a share, after which point further proceeds would be distributed evenly. This carrot evidently failed to attract.
31. I have not been able to establish this, though it might explain why Grainger & Miller never actually worked for either the Aberdeen Railway or GNS. See also *Cal. Merc.*, 22 January 1846.
32. PP 1846 (73). 3rd report on classification of railway Bills. ACA. Co 14/5. 'Personal Reminiscence of John Stewart', 4, says that the AB&E Bill was withdrawn after a hint from the parliamentary committee to the promoters that it would not be passed.
33. *Abdn. Jnl.*, 20 May 1846.
34. NAS. BR/GNS/1/1. Committee, 20 April 1846. His leech-like propensities would later be applied to the Inverness & Aberdeen Junction Railway.
35. NAS. BR/GNS/1/1. Committee, 18 January 1846.
36. A solicitor, not the William Leslie who later was chairman.
37. *Cal. Merc.* 24 August 1846; NAS. BR/GNS/1/1. Board, 21 July 1846.
38. NAS. BR/GNS/1/1. Provisional committee, 1 April 1845.
39. Mitchell, *Reminiscences*, 168; Fletcher, *Directors*, 15.

2. ACTS AND INACTION, 1846-1850

1. NAS. BR/GNS/1/1. Board, 6 and 27 August, 22 September 1846. PP 1847 (164) Report of Commissioners of Railways on Bills. In 1858 the GNS was advertising the Woodside estate for sale at the "further reduced" price of £5,500. See *Abdn. Jnl.*, 6 January 1858.
2. *Abdn. Jnl.*, 17 June 1846.
3. *Abdn. Jnl.*, 30 September 1846.
4. NAS. BR/GNS/1/1. Board, 3, 10 November 1846.
5. *Abdn. Jnl.*, 6 January, 17 February, 12 May, 8 September 1847.
6. PP 1847 (164) Report of Committee on Railways.
7. *Abdn. Jnl.*, 29 September, 27 October; *Standard*, 12 October 1847. It came in two wagons, with 24 horses needed to pull them. Simpson's ironworks closed in 1849.
8. *Cal.Merc.*, 23 February 1848.
9. *Abdn. Jnl.*, 1 December 1847; NAS. BR/GNS/1/1. 2nd o.g.m, 30 November 1847; Board, 4 April 1848.
10. NAS. BR/ABN/1/23. Board, 26 October 1847.
11. *Abdn. Jnl.*, 2 February 1848.
12. *Abdn. Jnl.*, 3 May, 7 and 14 July 1848.
13. Quoted in *Abdn. Jnl.*, 27 September 1848.
14. *Abdn. Jnl.*, 6 December 1848.
15. The Bank lost over half its capital in 1847-48, mostly through withdrawal of funds by its

directors and managers for unsuccessful railway speculation. Paterson, the manager, was replaced by Westland. See Fletcher, *Directors*, 17.

16. *Abdn. Jnl.*, 11 October 1848.

17. *Abdn. Jnl.*, 6 December 1848, 3 January 1849.

18. AUL. Thomson 94/2. Printed statements of Blaikie, Pirie, Davidson.

19. AUL. *ibid.*

20. NAS. BR/ABN/1/18. The company had contracted with Blaikie Brothers for rail chairs at £8 10s per ton, £2-£2 5s more per ton than on neighbouring lines. The contract was signed for Blaikie's by Thomas Blaikie's 16-year old nephew.

21. *Abdn. Jnl.*, 3 January 1849. Sir James had been shown not to have the requisite shareholding to qualify as a director.

22. *Abdn. Jnl.*, 24 January, 7 February 1849.

23. NAS. BR/GNS/1/1. Board, 31 January, 16 and 24 February 1849.

24. NAS. BR/GNS/1/1. Board, 29 March, 30 April 1849.

25. NAS. BR/GNS/1/1. Board, 31 August, 3, 13 September 1849.

26. *Abdn. Jnl.*, 28 March 1849.

27. *Abdn. Jnl.*, 19 September, *Glas. Her.*, 21 September 1849. But *Dund. Cour.*, 19 September 1849, says construction was not yet finished and that public opening of the "extended branch" was to coincide with opening of the main line as far as Portlethen.

28. *Cal. Merc.*, 29 November 1849.

29. *Abdn. Jnl.*, 5 December 1849.

30. The station would have been 20ft higher on the north side than on the south side. See Milne, *Aberdeen*, 343.

3. COMPANIES AT WAR, 1850-53

1. NAS. BR/GNS/1/1. Board, 20 October, 27 November 1849.

2. *Abdn. Jnl.*, 20 March, 23 October, 20 November 1850.

3. *Abdn. Jnl.* 1, 15 May 1850. Keith, *1,000 Years of Aberdeen*, 471ff.

4. *Abdn. Jnl.*, 22 May, 5 June 1850; *Lond. Gaz.*, 2 August 1850, 2131f.

5. NAS. BR/GNS/1/1. Directors' meeting 15 March 1850.

6. AUL. O'D Misc. 1.

7. NAS. BR/GNS/1/1. Board, 4 December, 29 November 1850, 25 March 1851.

8. NAS. BR/GNS/1/1. Board, 4 December 1850, 16 January 1851.

9. *Ed. Gaz.*, 15 October 1850, 868, 10 June 1851, 462. *Abdn. Jn.*, 2 October 1850.

10. PP 1851 (555) Warrant from Commissioners of Railways, 10 July ; *Cal. Merc.*, 4 August 1851.

11. *Abdn. Jnl.*, 23 October 1850.

12. *Cal. Merc.*, 28 April, *Abdn. Jnl.*, 5 May 1851.

13. NAS. BR/GNS/1/1. Board, 10, 18 October 1851.

14. *Glas. Her.*, 10 October 1851.

15. See Ross, *Caledonian*, 55ff.

16. *Abdn. Jnl.*, 12 November, *Cal. Merc.*, 27 November 1851.

17. PP 1863 (492). Railway returns 1862. See also Fletcher, *Directors*, 47.

18. The Board of Trade return still recorded the authorised capital as £1,407,440 in 1855, see PP 1856 (2114).

19. *Abdn. Jnl.*, 3 November 1852.

20. NAS. BR/GNS/1/1. Board, 2 December 1851.

21. *Cal. Merc.*, 26 November 1851.

22. NAS. BR/GNS/1/1. Board, 29 July 1852.

23. NAS. BR/GNS/1/1. Board, 28 May; Committee of directors, 5 June, 29 July 1852. See also Ross, *North British*, 35ff.

24. *Abdn. Jnl.*, 5 May 1852.

25. ACA. DO 15/5 'Personal Reminiscence of John Stewart', 9; NAS BR/GNS/1/1. Board, 29 July 1852.

26. *Abdn. Jnl.*, 7 July 1852.

27. At the Elgin staff concert and dance in December 1892, James Grant's son recalled how the carriages and wagons were delivered by road, but the engines came by ship to Lossiemouth, and "one of them before it was landed went through the bottom of the ship." *Abdn. Jnl.*, 24 December 1892.

28. NAS. BR/GNS/1/1. Board, 26 October, 5 November 1852.

29. NAS. BR/GNS/1/1. Board, and 7th ordinary meeting, 29 November 1852.

30. NAS. BR/GNS/1/1. Board, 18 December 1852.

31. *Abdn. Jnl.* 30 June, 27 October 1852.

32. *Abdn. Jnl.*, 16 March 1853.

33. NAS. BR/GNS/1/1. Directors' committee, 18 March, 8 and 22 April 1853.

34. NAS. BR/GNS/1/1. Board, 5 August, 2 September 1853.

35. NAS. BR/GNS/1/1. Robert Milne's letter to the Aberdeen Railway Board, 27 August 1853.

36. *Abdn. Jnl.*, 30 March 1853.

37. *Abdn. Jnl.*, 11 January 1854.

38. Farr, *Deeside Railway*, 14ff. Prior to opening day it was noticed that vandals had lifted off a rail, shortly before a contractors' guest train came along. *Morning Post*, 5 September 1853.

39. NAS. BR/GNS/1/1. Board, 4 and 18 November 1853.

40. NAS. BR/GNS/1/1. Board, 23 September, 7 October 1853.

41. *Abdn. Jnl.*, 8 November 1854.

42. *Ed. Gaz.*, 24 March 1848, 150.

43. NAS. BR/GNS/1/1. Board, 5 August 1853.

44. *Abdn. Jnl.*, 30 November 1853.

45. AUL. O'D Misc. 4. 'HR-GNS Quarrels'.

4. THE OPENING, AT LAST, 1854-57

1. *Abdn. Jnl.*, 2 November 1853.
2. *Abdn. Jnl.*, 2 November 1853.
3. *Abdn. Jnl.*, 22 March 1854. Noted in Fletcher, Ph.D. thesis. See NAS. BR/GNS/1/1. Board, 17, 18 May 1854
4. William Moffatt recorded in a *R.M.* interview, October 1899, 289ff, that John Ellis, chairman of the Midland Railway, noted the GNS's non-use of second class carriages while on holiday at Pittodrie House, and recommended it to the Midland. But Ellis died in 1862 and the Midland Railway did not abolish second until 1875.
5. NAS. BR/GNS/1/1. Board, 25 November, 9 December 1853, 6 January 1854.
6. NAS. BR/GNS/1/1. Board, 6 January, 3 March 1854.
7. AUL. O'D Misc. 12; NAS BR/GNS/1/1. Board, 28 April, 5 May 1854.
8. *Abdn. Jnl.*, 22 March, 24 May, 14 and 28 June 1854. See also ACA. DO 14/5, 'Personal Reminiscence of John Stewart', 14.
9. PP 1854 (1850), Report on Railway Accidents, August-October 1854.
10. *Cal. Merc.*, 21 September 1854.
11. Ramsay, *Guide to the GNSR*, 9.
12. *Twenty-one Aberdeen Events of the 19th Century*, 50.
13. PP 1854 (1850), Report on Railway Accidents, August-October 1854; *Dund. Cour.*, 29 September 1854.
14. *Abdn. Jnl.*, 20 September 1854. Quick, *Stations*, notes Kinaldie was open for southbound trains in November.
15. PO. 32/19A.
16. *Abdn. Jnl.*, 8 November 1854.
17. *Abdn. Jnl.*, 1 November 1854, 18, 25 April 1855.
18. *Abdn. Jnl.*, 22 March 1854.
19. *Ed. Gaz.*, 10 November 1854, 987.
20. *Abdn. Jnl.*, 18 October, 6 and 13 December, *Cal. Merc.*, 30 November 1854. NAS. BR/RAC (S)/1/14. Report to GNS ordinary general meeting, 30 November 1854. See also Ross, Highland Railway, 19-23 for details of the negotiations.
21. *Abdn. Jnl.*, 2 May, 24 October; 17 October 1855.
22. *Abdn. Jnl.*, 31 October 1855.
23. *Abdn. Jnl.*, 4 June 1856.
24. *Abdn. Jnl.*, 31 October, 20 December 1855.
25. *Abdn. Jnl.*, 19 September 1855, *Dund. Cour.*, 2 January, *Cal. Merc.*, 15 April 1856.
26. PP 1856 (2114). Report on Railways for 1855; *Abdn. Jnl.*, 25 June 1856.
27. *Abdn. Jnl.*, 2 July 1856.
28. *Abdn. Jnl.*, 29 October 1856.
29. *Abdn. Jnl.*, 15 October 1856.
30. NAS. BR/KDR/1. Preliminary meeting, 21 October, provisional committee, 5 December 1856.
31. NAS. BR/RAC(S)/1/14, address to ordinary general meeting, 29 October 1855.
32. *Abdn. Jnl.*, 11 February 1857.
33. *Cal. Merc.*, 8 November, *Abdn. Jnl.*, 19 November 1856.
34. *Scmn.*, 19 November 1856.
35. PP 1857 Session 1 (69). Report of Board of Trade on Railway and Canal Bills, 1857.
36. *Abdn. Jnl.*, 25 June 1856.
37. AUL. O'D Misc. 11. Quoted in John R. Allan's 1954 radio script, 'Little but Good: Hail & Farewell to the GNSR.'
38. *Abdn. Jnl.*, 2, 20, 25 July 1857.

5. DEESIDE AND BEYOND, 1857-1860

1. NAS. BR/KDR/1. Directors 2 January, 5 September 1857.
2. *Abdn. Jnl.*, 5 May 1858.
3. *Abdn. Jnl.*, 9 September 1857.
4. PP 1857-58 (117). Board of Trade Report on Private Railway Bills, March 1858.
5. *Abdn. Jnl.*, 11 November 1857.
6. *Abdn. Jnl.*, 18 November 1857.
7. *Abdn. Jnl.*, 25 November 1857.
8. *Abdn. Jnl.*, 10 November 1858.
9. *Abdn. Jnl.*, 24 March 1858.
10. *Abdn. Jnl.*, 11 August 1858.
11. NAS. BR/GNS3/3. Keith Station agreement of 9 November 1859.
12. NAS. BR/GNS/*ibid.* The horse was not GNS property. It always hired horses.
13. NAS. BR/GNS/1/3. Board, 12 July 1857.
14. Ross, *Highland Railway*, 27.
15. *Abdn. Jnl.*, 29 December 1858.
16. Vallance, *GNSR*, 37; *Abdn. Jnl.*, 28 September 1859.
17. NAS. BR/KDR/1. Directors, 19 October 1858., *Abdn. Jnl.*, 28 September 1859.
18. NAS. BR/KDR/1. Directors, 15 October 1859.
19. *Scmn.*, 1 February, 1859.
20. *RT*, 2 November 1857, 1562. The journal was a consistent critic of the GNS branch policy.
21. *Abdn. Jnl.*, 17 November 1858.
22. 30 July had been planned, see Quick, *Stations*; but a derailment prevented services until 2 August.
23. *Abdn. Jnl.*, 5 December 1860.
24. *Abdn. Jnl.*, 26 October, 2, 9, 30 November 1859; *Cal. Merc.*, 26 September, 11 November 1859.
25. *Abdn. Jnl.*, 26 October 1859.
26. *Abdn. Jnl.*, 6 April, *Cal. Merc.*, 26 September 1859.
27. *Abdn. Jnl.*, 28 December 1859.
28. Quoted in *Abdn. Jnl.*, 28 December 1859.
29. *Abdn. Jnl.*, 3 October 1860.
30. See Ross, *Highland Railway*, 27.
31. *Abdn. Jnl.*, 4 April 1860.
32. *Abdn. Jnl.*, *ibid.*
33. *Abdn. Jnl.*, 18 April 1860. In this year the Deeside goods station was also linked to the harbour rail tracks.

34. NAS. BR/GNS/23/57. Inverness & Edinburgh Steam Packet Co. journals.
35. *Cal. Merc.*, 21 July 1859.
36. *Abdn. Jnl.*, 6 June 1860.
37. *Abdn. Jnl.*, 25 July 1860.
38. Wilson, *The TPOs*, 194; Fenwick, 'Post Office Sorting Carriages'; PO 32/19A, 'GNS Arbitration re Mails'.
39. *Abdn. Jnl.*, 3 October 1860.
40. NAS. BR/SNER/1/1. Directors, 7, 25 September 1860.
41. NAS. BR/KDR/1. Directors, 31 August 1860.
42. NAS. BR/KDR/1. 6th ordinary general meeting, 28 April, Board 31 August, 17 October, 28 November 1860.
43. NAS. BR/KDR/1. Directors, 21 December 1860.
44. *Abdn. Jnl.*, 5 December 1860.
45. *Morning Chronicle*, 11 May 1860.
46. NAS. BR/FBR/1/1, noted in Fletcher, *Directors*, 48f. *Abdn. Jnl.*, 10 October 1860.

6. MANOEUVRES AND MACHINATIONS, 1860-1862

1. NAS. BR/SNER/1/1. Board 27 April 1859.
2. *Abdn. Jnl.*, 18 April 1860, 10 July, 25 September, 21 October 1861. See also Wrigley & Shepherd, On the Move, 77ff.
3. ACA. 'Personal Reminiscence of John Stewart', 2. In an obituary of Stewart in 1887 it was said he lost £45,000 in the breach with the ASN company; nevertheless he bought the Craigiebuckler estate from the bankrupt John Blaikie in 1860, only to sell it again in 1865 because of the depreciated value of his GNS shares.
4. *Abdn. Jnl.*, 24 July 1861.
5. *Glas. Her.*, 13 July 1861; NAS. BR/STY/1. Joint meeting, 1 August 1861.
6. NAS. BR/STY/1. Directors, 18 October, 22 November, 27 December 1861.
7. *Abdn. Jnl.*, 30 October 1861.
8. *Dund. Cour.*, 22 January, *Cal. Merc.*, 22 February 1862.
9. NAS. BR/STY/1. Directors, 20 June, 18 July, 19 September, 6 October; Finance & general purposes committee 9 December 1862.
10. *Abdn. Jnl.*, 25 September 1861.
11. *Dund. Cour.*, 30 November 1861, *Cal. Merc.*, 6 March 1862.
12. *Abdn. Jnl.*, 19 March 1862.
13. NAS. BR/SNER/1/1. Directors' meeting, 6 November 1861.
14. NAS. BR/SNER/1/1. Directors, 4, 18 December 1861.
15. NAS. BR/SNER/1/1. Board, 7 February 1862.
16. *Abdn. Jnl.*, letter from Smith and Robertson, 12 February 1862.
17. *Abdn. Jnl.*, 26 March 1862, letter from George Reith and the SNER Denburn Committee.
18. *Abdn. Jnl.*, 14 May 1863. Duncan later said that the SNER had described the Extension line as "worthless" (*ibid.*).
19. *Abdn. Jnl.*, 19 February 1862.
20. NAS. BR/SNER/1/1. Directors' meetings 7, 19 February, 4 March 1862; Lease committee, 12, 17, 25 February 1862.
21. *Abdn. Jnl.*, 12 February 1862, advertisement to Deeside Railway shareholders.
22. *Abdn. Jnl.*, 14 May 1863.
23. *Abdn. Jnl.*, 28 May, *Dund. Cour.*, 7 July 1862.
24. *Abdn. Jnl.*, 2 April 1862.
25. *Abdn. Jnl.*, 18 February 1863.
26. *Dund. Cour.*, 3 December 1862, 28 April, 25 May 1863; *Abdn. Jnl.* 18 February, 29 April 1863.
27. PP 1863 (492). Railway returns 1862; *Abdn. Jnl.*, 19 February 1862.
28. *Abdn. Jnl.*, 6 April 1862.

7. THE BRANCH POLICY, 1862-1864

1. NAS. BR/SNER/1/1. Directors' meetings, 19 August, 13 September, 7 October 1862.
2. *Abdn. Jnl.*, 1 October 1862.
3. NAS. BR/SNER/1/1. Directors, 23 October 1862; *Abdn. Jnl.*, 1 April 1863, report of ordinary general meeting.
4. *Abdn. Jnl.*, 15, 19 November, 17 December 1862. *Ed. Gaz.*, 14 November 1862, 1722f.
5. *Dund. Cour.*, 1 May 1863.
6. *Abdn. Jnl.*, 20 May 1863.
7. *Abdn. Jnl.*, 2 April 1862.
8. PP 1863 (492). Railway returns for 1862.
9. Findlay, *History of Peterhead*, 283.
10. Anderson, *Howes o' Buchan*; *Abdn. Jnl.*, 9 July 1862.
11. Peter Fletcher points out that even that was based on a net revenue of only £1,388, and was probably intended to encourage new investors.
12. *Abdn. Jnl.*, 1 April 1863.
13. NAS. BR/STY/1. Directors, 25 June 1863, 14 February 1862.
14. NAS. BR/STY/1. Joint meeting, 25 June 1863.
15. NAS. BR/STY/1. Finance & general purposes committee, 4 August 1863.
16. *Morning Post*, 21 April 1846.
17. NAS. BR/GNS/1/5. Board, 15 September 1863.
18. NAS. BR/SNER/1/2. Traffic committee, 17 and 23 September 1863.
19. *Dund. Cour.*, 14 November, *Abdn. Jnl.*, 30 September 1863.
20. *Abdn. Jnl.*, 15 July, 23 September 1863.
21. *Abdn. Jnl.*, 30 September 1863.
22. NAS. BR/GNS/1/5. Board, 21 January, 19 February; Traffic & finance committee 2 and 9 February 1864.

23. *Abdn. Jnl.*, 23 March 1864.
24. NAS. BR/GNS/1/5. Traffic and finance committee, 23 February 1864.
25. *Dund. Cour.*, 14 November 1863.
26. NAS. BR/STY/1. Third ordinary general meeting, 13 November 1863. Sir James was known in the House of Commons as 'the Admiral', presumably on account of his constituency rather than for strategic vision.
27. NAS. BR/GNS/1/5. Board 4 September, special board 9 November 1863.
28. NAS. BR/KDR/1. Directors, 6 November 1863.
29. NAS. BR/GNS/1/5. Board, 15 January 1864.

30. NAS. BR/GNS/1/5. Board, 8 September, 8 December 1863, 19 January 1864.
31. NAS. BR/GNS/1/5. Traffic & finance committee, 22 November, 30 December 1863.
32. *Aberdeen Jounal*, 30 September 1863.
33. NAS. BR/GNS/1/5. Board, 11 December 1863.
34. NAS. BR/GNS/1/5. Special board, 8 March; Board, 18, 29 March, 1864.
35. *Abdn. Jnl.*, 23 March 1864.
36. NAS. BR/GNS/1/5. Board, 31 March 1864.
37. NAS. BR/GNS/1/5. Board, 3 March 1864; *Abdn. Jnl.*, 23 March, 27 April 1864.

8. COLLAPSE, 1864-65

1. NAS. BR/GNS/1/5. Traffic and finance, 19 April, 14 and 21 June 1864. Board, 22 July 1864.
2. NAS. BR/GNS/1/5. Special finance committee, 30 August 1864.
3. NAS. BR/STY/1. Board, 29 July 1864.
4. NAS. BR/STY/1. Finance and general purposes committee, 19 August; ordinary general meeting, 29 November 1864.
5. NAS. BR/KDR/1. Directors, 11 November 1864.
6. NAS. BR/KDR/1. Directors' report for 11th ordinary general meeting, 11 November 1864.
7. NAS. BR/KDR/1. Adjourned ordinary general meeting, 8 February 1865.
8. Jackson, *The Speyside Line*, 6, notes that the original SSR Act of 1861 allowed for a connection from Ballifurth, two miles north of Nethy Bridge, to the Inverness & Perth Junction Railway at Dulnain Bridge.
9. NAS. BR/STY/1. Board 13 December 1864; 31 March 1865.
10. *Abdn. Jnl.*, 21 September 1864.
11. NAS. BR/GNS/1/5. Board, 23 September; SNER/1/2. Directors, 24 November 1864.
12. NAS. BR/GNS/1/5. Special board, 14 November; Traffic & finance committee 22 November 1864.
13. NAS. BR/GNS/1/5. Board, 23, 28 September 1864.

14. NAS. BR/GNS/1/5. Board, 14 October 1864.
15. *Abdn. Jnl.*, 5, 12 April, 17 May, 19 July 1865. The Queen's views were never made public: in 1875 it was rumoured that she was "not unwilling" for a Caledonian line to run north from Alyth to Braemar. See Carnie, *Aberdeen Reminiscences*, 183.
16. *Abdn. Jnl.*, 30 May, 29 August 1866.
17. *Morning Post*, 19 October 1866.
18. See O.S. 6in maps, 1866, 1900.
19. Peter Fletcher's calculation.
20. *Abdn. Jnl.*, half-yearly report, 29 March; NAS. BR/GNS/1/5. Board, 10 March 1865.
21. *Abdn. Jnl.*, 22 March 1865.
22. NAS. BR/GNS/1/5. Special board, 21 March; *Abdn. Jnl.*, 29 March 1865.
23. NAS. BR/SNER/1/5. Traffic committee, 26 October 1865.
24. *Abdn. Jnl.*, 3 May 1865.
25. *Abdn. Jnl.*, 10 May 1865.
26. *Abdn. Jnl.*, 30 November 1864.
27. *Abdn. Jnl.*, 26 April 1865.
28. Smith, *A New History*, ii, 1129.
29. *Dund. Cour.*, 25 September 1865, directors' report. NAS. BR/SNER/1/3. Board, 10 November 1865. From 1881 the Montrose & Bervie was absorbed by the North British Railway.

9. REMEDIAL MEASURES, 1865-1867

1. NAS. BR/GNS/1/5. Board, 13 January 1865.
2. *Abdn. Jnl.*, 17 May, 27 September 1865.
3. AUL. O'D Misc 4. GNS-HR documents. In any case the Inverness & Nairn could not have made an agreement that bound the Inverness & Aberdeen Junction Railway.
4. *Dund. Cour.*, 24 June 1865.
5. *Abdn. Jnl.*, 4 October 1865, 11 April 1866.
6. *Abdn. Jnl.*, 9 October 1867, report of half-yearly meeting.
7. The 'Personal Reminiscence of John Stewart' in the Aberdeen city archives is a short account by his

friend, the Rev. J.T. Hagen, of the Great North's history, with details contributed by Stewart, followed by an appreciation of Stewart's spiritual qualities as a devout Baptist, none of which are evident in his involvement with the GNS.
8. NAS. BR/SNER/1/3. Ways & works committee, 28 November 1865, 19 January 1866; BR/GNS/1/5. Board, 6 June 1865.
9. NAS. BR/SNER/1/3. Directors, 10 November 1865. See also Ross, *Caledonian*, 92ff.
10. *Dund. Cour.*, 1 December 1865.
11. *Abdn. Jnl.*, 29 November 1865.

12. NAS. BR/STY/1. O.g.m., 29 November 1865.
13. NAS. BR/GNS/1/5. Board, 24 April 1866.
14. *Abdn. Jnl.*, 27 June 1866.
15. One of the members of the parliamentary committee was James Merry MP, who showed in his questioning of Robert Milne that he had not forgotten his shutting-out at Waterloo Station in 1858.
16. NAS. BR/GNS/1/6. Board 24 July 1866; Traffic & finance committee 28 March 1867.
17. Jackson, *The Strathspey Line*, 41.
18. NAS. BR/GNS/1/6. Board, 9 October 1866.
19. *Abdn. Jnl.*, 31 October 1866.
20. *Abdn. Jnl.*, 3 October 1866.
21. NAS. BR/GNS/1/6. Board, 23 October 1866.
22. NAS. BR/STY/1. O.g.m., 13 November 1866.
23. *Abdn. Jnl.*, 28 November 1866.
24. NAS. BR/GNS/1/6. Special board, 14 November; Finance committee 3 November, 1 December 1866.
25. NAS. BR/GNS1/6. Board, 29 January 1867.
26. NAS. BR/GNS/1/6. Finance & works committee, 13 February, 9 May 1867.

27. NAS. BR/GNS/1/6. Special meeting, 12 March 1867.
28. NAS. BR/GNS/1/6. Finance committee, 14, 21, 26 January; Board 29 January, 4, 21, 28 February 1867. Peter Fletcher notes that in January 1867 69.2% of the GNS's raised capital was in preference shares or debentures requiring guaranteed payments; "a very high – even dangerous proportion."
29. Addressing the Aberdeen staff's annual soirée on 2 February 1894, Ferguson recalled that when he became a director he was living in Liverpool, and "did not open his mouth at meetings" until 1875.
30. NAS. BR/GNS/1/6. Adjourned e.g.m, 5 February, Board, 9 May 1867. Elphinstone had stood for Aberdeenshire in 1866 but lost to a Liberal opponent. He regained his Portsmouth seat in 1868, serving until 1880. His all-too-apparent failings as a chairman underline the importance of that role. Figureheads were not enough.

10. A SLOW RECOVERY, 1867-1875

1. *Abdn. Jnl.*, report of Glasgow shareholders' meeting, 20 March 1867. It was at this time that the Highland was promoting a line from Fochabers to Garmouth, for which powers expired in 1869.
2. *Abdn. Jnl.*, 17 April 1867.
3. *Abdn. Jnl.*, 24 April, 2 October 1867.
4. NAS. BR/GNS/1/6. Board, 15 August 1867.
5. *Abdn. Jnl.*, 2 October 1867.
6. *Abdn. Jnl.*, 6 November 1867.
7. *Abdn. Jnl.*, ibid.
8. In 1871 the agent of the Liverpool steamer and his assistant were given free passes over the GNS, "so long as the steamer continues in the trade", and the Aberdeen Steamship Co. paid half the costs of a traffic canvasser at Inverness until March 1874. NAS. BR/GNS/1/9. Finance, traffic & works committee, 24 August 1871, 5 March 1874.
9. NAS. BR/GNS/1/6. Board 17 October 1867.
10. *Abdn. Jnl.*, 17 June 1868. Perhaps "second class" means "comparable to second class".
11. *Abdn. Jnl.*, 20 February 1868.
12. *Abdn. Jnl.*, 8 July 1868.
13. Directors' report, March 1868; *Glas. Her.*, 13 July 1868.
14. *Abdn. Jnl.*, 12 August, 21 October 1868.
15. NAS. BR/GNS/1/7. Finance committee, 23 April, Report to ordinary general meeting, 8 October 1868; Fletcher, *Directors*, 92.
16. *Abdn. Jnl.*, 13 January, 17 March 1869.
17. *Dund. Cour.*, 16 September 1868.
18. See *Abdn. Jnl.*, 25 October 1871, 5 November 1873.
19. *Abdn. Jnl.*, 25 October 1871.
20. Noted in *R.M.*, January 1954. Vallance, 'GNSR: A Centenary Retrospect'.
21. NAS. BR/GNS/1/8. Finance & works committee,

18 February 1869. See also Fletcher, *Directors*, 89ff.
22. PP 1870 (C42). Board of Trade report on accidents, July-December 1869.
23. *Scmn.*, 7 April 1870.
24. *Abdn. Jnl.*, 6 April, 5 October, 21 December 1870.
25. *Abdn. Jnl.*, 7 December 1870.
26. *Railway Times*, 8 April; *Abdn. Jnl.*, 5 April, 11 October 1871.
27. PO 11/74 and 11/2.
28. *Glas. Her.*, 21 October, *Abdn. Jnl.*, 25 October 1871; NAS. BR/GNS/1/9. Special finance committee, 8 June 1871.
29. *Abdn. Jnl.*, 3 April 1872.
30. PP 1873 (316). Telegraph companies (purchase).
31. NAS. BR/GNS/1/9. Board, 11 January, 25 July, Finance, works & traffic committee, 8 February, 8 August, 17 October 1872.
32. NAS. BR/GNS/1/9. Board, 30 May 1872, 24 July 1873.
33. *Abdn. Jnl.*, report of 40th ordinary general meeting, 9 October 1872.
34. NAS. BR/GNS/1/9. Board, 27 June, Finance, works & traffic committee, 16 May 1872.
35. PP 1872 (C.642).
36. NAS. BR/GNS/1/9. Finance, works & traffic committee, 26 June, 10 July 1873.
37. NAS. BR/GNS/1/9. Finance, works & traffic committee, 24 July 1873, 10 June 1875. How did newsboys operate in non-corridor carriages? The reference to them as being "on trains" is explicit.
38. NAS. BR/GNS/9. Finance, works & traffic committee, 11 December 1873, 14 May 1874. *Abdn. Jnl.*, 24 March 1875.
39. *Abdn. Jnl.*, 8 and 15 October 1873.
40. *Dund. Cour.*, 13 March 1874.

41. PP 1874 (64).
42. PP 1874 (C.1015). Board of Trade report on accidents, January-April 1874, Pt 2.
43. NAS. BR/GNS/1/9. Board 5, 12 March 1874.
44. *Abdn. Jnl.*, 5 November 1873.
45. *Scmn.*, 4 November 1875.
46. Cranna, *Fraserburgh Past & Present*, 467.

47. NAS. BR/GNS/1/9. Board, 18 February, 18 March; Special committee, 8 April 1875.
48. *Dund. Cour.*, 16 September, 1 October 1875.
49. NAS. BR/GNS/1/9. Board, 5 August 1875. Millegin was never a station.
50. PP 1876 (C.1540). Railway returns, 1875.

11. NEW DEPARTURES, 1875-1880

1. Fraser & Lee, *Aberdeen: A New History*, 82.
2. *Dund. Cour.*, 11 December 1875.
3. *Abdn. Jnl.*, 27 October 1875.
4. *Abdn. Jnl.*, 16, 23 February, 29 March 1876.
5. PO 11/2, Record of contracts; *Abdn. Jnl.*, 27 September 1876, 4 April 1877.
6. *Abdn. Jnl.*, 21 February, 28 September 1877. AUL O'D Misc. 5. Board report, 6 December 1877.
7. *Abdn. Jnl.*, 15 September 1877.
8. *Abdn. Jnl.*, 13, 21 February, 3 March 1878. PP 1871 (374) (374-1) Report of Select Committee on Railways. *Abdn Jnl.*, 13 March, 15 April, 4 May, 8 June, 16 October 1878. PP 1878-9 (C2218). 5th annual report of Railway Commissioners, 7. AUL O'D Misc. 12 has a dossier on the case.
9. *Dund. Cour.*, 4 May, *Abdn. Jnl.*, 13 July 1878.
10. *Abdn. Jnl.*, 28 September 1877, report of 50th ordinary general meeting
11. *Abdn. Jnl.*, 28 March 1879.
12. *Abdn. Jnl.*, 23 May 1879.
13. *Abdn. Jnl.*, 26 September 1879.
14. *Abdn. Jnl.*, 23 October, 7 November 1879.
15. NAS. BR/GNS/2/1.
16. Directors' report for 25 March 1880. Carnie, *Reporting Reminiscences*, about Shirley Brooks's novel *The Silver Cord* (1861). Carnie, Milne and Brooks all knew one another.
17. This "passive resistance" to the law earned the GNS a mention (p. 173) in A.T. Hadley's *Railroad Transportation*, an international survey published in New York in 1885.
18. To appoint an outsider was a bold step; soon after Moffatt's appointment a letter from "An Englishman" criticising the GNS's "decidedly too high fares" observed that, "it is almost impossible for a stranger to receive a patient hearing on local affairs in Aberdeen" (*Abdn. Jnl.*, 29 October 1880).
19. See Appendix 3.
20. AUL. OD L2 GNS Fer g 'GNS memoranda from August 14, 1880. The outcome of the venture is not recorded.
21. *Abdn. Jnl.*, 27 May 1880.
22. *Dund. Cour.*, 24 September 1880. This stock was already authorised under Acts of 1864 and 1877 but had not been issued.
23. NAS. BR/GNS/1/11. Board, 12 January 1882.
24. *Abdn. Jnl.*, 2, 20 December 1880, 8, 17 February 1881.
25. NAS. BR/GNS/1/11. Finance committee, 8 September 1881.
26. AUL. O'D Misc. 1. *Abdn. Jnl.*, 19 November 1880. The 6th Duke was described by a Conservative historian as an "amiable but ineffective nonentity", but he expected to have his way in Banffshire.
27. *Abdn. Jnl.*, 20 December 1880, 11, 20 January, 17 February 1881; PO 11/2, Record of contracts.
28. *Abdn. Jnl.*, 7 March, 23 September 1881.
29. *Abdn. Jnl.*, report of parliamentary committee hearings, 19 May, 26 March 1881.
30. AUL. O'DL2 Fer c. Letter of 28 May 1881.
31. *Scmn.*, 13 May 1881. This was also a tussle between landowners: the Cluny Estate, next to Seafield's, had made the new harbour and wanted the railway.
32. PP *Hansard*, 30 May 1881.
33. *Abdn. Jnl.*, 22 August 1881.
34. *Abdn. Jnl.*, 23 September 1881.
35. PP 1881 (C.3096). Royal Commission on Agriculture, 462.

12. NORTHERN RIVALRIES, 1881-1887

1. Ferguson, *The GNSR*, xv, 64, 132.
2. The pervasive influence of the Baird family in 19th-century Scotland has yet to be properly assessed. One member, George Baird of the Gartsherrie Ironworks, was proprietor of the Strichen estate.
3. *Abdn. Jnl.*, 9 June, 23 September 1881.
4. *Abdn. Jnl.*, 16 October 1882, 31 October 1883
5. *Abdn. Jnl.*, 15 December 1881, 10 February 1882.
6. AUL. O'D Misc 1. Letter to Skene, Lewis & Bilton WS, Edinburgh, solicitors to the trustees; letter from Ferguson to Bryson, noting Lord Seafield had "uncourteously declined" a request to take photographs of Cullen House and grounds, and Bryson himself had "interrupted" Blyth and a survey party: "a proceeding which under the peculiar circumstances of the case I thought very unlike what I would have expected from the representative of a nobleman."
7. NAS. BR/GNS/1/11. Parliamentary committee, 3 May 1882.

8. *Abdn. Jnl.*, 25 April 1883.
9. *Abdn. Jnl.*, 12, 23 September 1882.
10. NAS. BR/GNS/1/11. Financial committee, 30 November 1882.
11. In December 1881 the Highland Railway had refused to hand over the cattle train despite the GNS's "proper and legal" request. See NAS. BR/GNS/1/11. Law committee, 30 November 1881, also Ross, *Highland Railway*, 63, 161.
12. *Abdn. Jnl.*, 14, 24 March 1883.
13. *Abdn. Jnl.*, 28 November, 1 December 1882, 24 March 1883. NAS. BR/GNS 1/11. Board 8 February, Finance committee 22 February 1883. The £10 10s was returned by Mrs Cosmo Gordon, who had founded the hospital with her husband in 1879 and preferred to defray the whole expenses herself.
14. *Abdn. Jnl.*, 2 July 1883; see also Barclay-Harvey, *GNSR*, 63f; *R.M.*, February 1948. In 1887 the charge for QM trains was altered to 1s 6d per mile of railway, see NAS. BR/GNS/1/12. Finance committee, 26 May 1887.
15. NAS. BR/GNS/1/11. Financial committee, 17 June 1883.
16. AUL. O'D Misc. 14 'HR and GNS Quarrels', letter from Dysons to Moffat, 28 September 1883.
17. NAS. BR/GNS/1/11. Finance committee 17 May; Board, 13 December 1883.
18. AUL. O'D Misc. 14, Marquis of Huntly's memorandum.
19. Letter of 21 July 1883, quoted in *Transport History* 2, 1969, Sinclair, N., 'The Aviemore Line'.
20. NAS BR/GNS/1/11. Parliamentary committee, 10 November 1883.
21. *Abdn. Jnl.*, 29 April, 22 May 1884.
22. AUL. O'D Misc 1, letter to Ferguson, 10 December 1883.
23. NAS. BR/GNS/1/11. Finance committee, 2 February, Board 31 May 1883. See also Ross, *North British*, 83, 86, 90, 115, 121.
24. AUL. O'D Misc. 5, assorted documents.
25. *Abdn. Jnl.*, 8 October 1883.
26. Though the Highland Railway charged 1.33d per mile for third class on mail trains.
27. AUL. O'D Misc. 1. *Abdn. Jnl.*, 22 September 1883, 21 September 1885.
28. PP 1885 (134) Fish conveyed inland by railway.
29. NAS. BR/GNS/1/11. Board, 16 October 1884, 1 December 1885, 23 March 1886.
30. *Abdn. Jnl.*, 13 March, 19 September 1885.
31. NAS. BR/GNS/1/12. Finance committee 28 September, 23 November 1887, 30 December 1891, Board 31 December 1890. *Abdn. Jnl.*, 5 November 1888.
32. NAS. BR/GNS/1/11. Minutes of joint meeting, 15 October; Board, 13 November, Finance committee 24 December 1884.
33. NAS. BR/GNS/1/11. Finance committee, 24 December 1884.
34. *Abdn. Jnl.*, 22 September 1887.
35. NAS. BR/GNS/1/11. Finance committee, 21 September 1882, 1 November 1883, 24 December 1884.
36. NAS. BR/GNS/1/11. Financial committee, 1 April 1886.
37. *Abdn. Jnl.*, 24, 26 November 1884.
38. NAS. BR/GNS/1/11. Finance committee, 28 May, 11 June; Special board, 9 July 1885.
39. *Abdn. Jnl.*, 31 December 1886; 5 July 1887.
40. Use was restricted to the hours of 6-7 am and 2-3 pm, with a maximum load of five wagons.
41. NAS. BR/GNS/1/11. Finance committee, 19 March 1885. It was not built until 1905.
42. NAS. BR/GNS/1/11. Finance committee, 11 June 1885, 20 January 1887.

13. A SERVICE REFORMED, 1885-1889

1. *Abdn. Jnl.*, 6 May, 26 June, 18 July; NAS. BR/GNS/1/11. Special board, 18, 22 June, 1, 9 July 1885.
2. PP 1886 (C.4718). 12th annual Report of Railway & Canal Commissioners. *Abdn. Jnl.*, 19 September 1885.
3. PP 1886 (C.4826). Railway returns, 1885.
4. *Scmn.*, 12 October 1885, 10 November 1886, 6 October 1887, 7 March 1889.
5. NAS. BR/GNS/1/11 and 12. Board 1 April, 24 June, 22 July 1886.
6. NAS. BR/GNS/1/31.
7. NAS. BR/GNS/1/12. Finance committee 20 January 1887. If it was available in 1887, it cannot have been of positive use to the GNS, as we hear no more of it.
8. *Abdn. Jnl.*, 8 April, 6 May 1885. The Highland at the time was earning £26,200 a year from mail traffic.
9. PO 32/64A; *Glas. Her.*, 9 March; NAS. BR/GNS/1/11. Finance committee, 5 August; *Abdn. Jnl.*, 11 August 1885; GNSRA. Fenwick, 'P.O. Sorting Carriages'; Wilson, *The TPOs*, 195.
10. Wilson, *ibid.*
11. NAS. BR/GNS/1/12. Finance committee 15 April, 10 June, Board 22 June 1886.
12. GNSRA. Fenwick, 'P.O. Sorting Carriages'.
13. *Glas. Her.*, 10, 19 March 1886.
14. *Abdn. Jnl.*, 18 August, 17 September 1886.
15. *Abdn. Jnl.*, 13 November 1866, 22 September 1887.
16. *Abdn. Jnl.*, 15 March 1888.
17. Acworth, *Railways of Scotland*, 131. Incidentally, GNS shares were known on the London Stock Exchange as "haddocks".
18. PP 1894 (12). Sea Fisheries of the UK.
19. *Abdn. Jnl.*, *ibid.*
20. Barnard, *Whisky*, 198. He bought the first first class ticket issued between Carron and Cromdale, 20 years after opening of the line.

21. Barnard, *op. cit.*, 474. The station opened as Dalbeallie on 1 July 1899.
22. NAS. BR/GNS/1/12. Finance committee, 23 November 1887.
23. Quick, *Passenger Stations*.
24. *Abdn. Jnl.*, 8 January 1887.
25. *Abdn. Jnl.*, 18 February 1887.
26. *Abdn. Jnl.*, 3 May 1887, 6 March 1889.
27. *Abdn. Jnl.*, 17 May 1887.
28. *Abdn. Jnl.*, 23 October 1889. PP 1890 8th Report of Fishery Board for Scotland (1889).
29. *Abdn. Jnl.*, report of half-yearly meeting 22 September 1887. The footbridges were of wood, to a standard pattern.
30. *Abdn. Jnl.*, 2 August 1888.
31. *Abdn. Jnl.*, 5 December 1887.
32. *Abdn. Jnl.*, 18 March 1887. The erecting shop could only hold four engines and half the work was done out in the open. See Acworth, *Railways of Scotland*, 121.
33. NAS. BR/GNS/1/12. Board, 26 May, Finance committee, 8 June, 17 August, 23 November 1887.
34. NAS. BR/GNS/1/12. Finance committee, 9 May, 22 August 1888.
35. AUL. O'D Misc. 5. Board of Trade report, 29 September 1888.
36. *Abdn. Jnl.*, 12, 27 September 1888.
37. NAS. BR/GNS/1/12. Finance committee 22 June 1887.
38. *Abdn. Jnl.*, 12 December 1888.
39. *Abdn. Jnl.*, 13 July 1887.
40. PP 1881 (374) (374-1). Report from select committee on railways.
41. PP 1890-91 (423). Report on classification of merchandise traffic and schedule of maximum rates for the Ayrshire & Wigtownshire, Callander & Oban, Great North of Scotland, and Highland Railways.
42. *Abdn. Jnl.*, 12 February, 5, 20, 28 March; NAS. BR/GNS/1/12. Finance committee, 5 June 1889.
43. Manson informed William Acworth personally of this decision: see *The Railways of Scotland*, 166. Highet, *Scottish Locomotive History*, 126, suggests the idea of the catcher might have originated with Ferguson or Moffatt.
44. Barclay-Harvey, The GNSR, 105f. Manson's 'catcher' was used on the Highland, Callander & Oban, Northern Counties Committee (Northern Ireland), the North British between Usan and Montrose, and perhaps other lines.
45. *Abdn. Jnl.*, 25 September 1889.
46. *Abdn. Jnl.*, 5 June, 16, 23, 25, 28 December 1889, 27 March 1890; NAS. BR/GNS/1/12. Board, 11 December 1889.

14. PUSHING AT THE FRONTIER, 1890-1892

1. *Dund. Cour.*, 11 October 1889. The same article said of the Highland Railway, "… a worse-worked railway, or a more disobliging, it would be difficult to find this side of Pekin."
2. Acworth, *Railways of Scotland*, 119; *Abdn. Jnl.*, 30 September 1897, quoting *Daily Chronicle*; Scott, *Little & Good*, 6.
3. *Abdn. Jnl.*, 24 January, 17, 19, 24 February 1890.
4. NAS. BR/GNS/1/12. Finance committee, 16 January 1889.
5. *Abdn. Jnl.*, 26 September 1889.
6. *Abdn. Jnl.*, 10, 30 May 1889.
7. NAS. BR/GNS/1/12. Board, 26 February; *Glas. Her.*, 25 April 1890.
8. NAS. BR/GNS/1/12. Special board, 1 November, Board 6 November, 4 December, Finance committee 20 November 1889.
9. NAS. BR/GNS/1/12. Law committee, 17 December 1890.
10. NAS. BR/GNS/1/31. Joint committee, 9 September 1890.
11. See Ross, *Highland Railway*, 72f, though its suggestion that the GNS letter is "strongly redolent of blackmail" overstates things.
12. *Abdn. Jnl.*, 27 March 1890.
13. *Abdn. Jnl.*, 4 April 1890.
14. *Abdn. Jnl.*, 30 April, 6 May 1890.
15. NAS. BR/GNS/1/12. Special board, 9 April 1890.
16. *Abdn. Jnl.*, 2 October 1890.
17. *Dund. Cour.*, 27 June; NAS. BR/GNS/1/12. Finance committee, 27 August 1890.
18. NAS. BR/GNS/1/12. Board, 12 August, 10 September 1890.
19. *Abdn. Jnl.*, 7 October 1890.
20. *Abdn. Jnl.*, 8 December 1890.
21. NAS. BR/GNS/1/12. Finance committee, 24 September 1890.
22. *Abdn. Jnl.*, 25, 31 December 1890.
23. *Abdn. Jnl.*, 13 January 1891.
24. PP 1890-91 (388) Licensed premises (Scotland) return.
25. NAS. BR/GNS/1/25. Hotels committee, 28 January, 16 March 1891.
26. *Glas. Her.*, 22 June 1891. The interdict was contested, but made perpetual on 15 July 1892, see *Glas. Her.*, 16 July 1892.
27. *Abdn. Jnl.*, 10 March 1892. NAS. BR/GNS/1/25. Hotel committee, 2 September 1891.
28. *Abdn. Jnl.*, 20 June 1890; NAS. BR/GNS/1/12. Law committee, 4 November 1891.
29. *Glas. Her.*, 11 March 1891.
30. See Ross, *Highland Railway*, 72f. The GNSR had been interested at the time, but failed to get a *locus standi* (right to representation) with the committee.
31. NAS. BR/GNS/1/12. Special board, 25, 29 April 1891.
32. PP *Hansard*, statement by Sir William Harcourt, Chancellor of the Exchequer, 9 March 1893.

33. NAS. BR/GNS/1/12. Law committee, 18 November 1891; PP *Hansard*, 1 March, 31 May 1892; 9 March 1893.
34. William Ferguson had travelled the Dingwall & Skye line in 1874 and knew the territory at first hand. See AUL. ODL2 GNS Fer n 'Notes on Inspection of the Line'.
35. NAS. BR/GNS/1/12. Board, 25 February, Financial committee, 6 May 1891.
36. *Abdn. Jnl.*, 12, 24, 26 March 1891.
37. *Abdn. Jnl.*, 26 March 1891. Peter Fletcher suggests, plausibly, that shareholders were becoming irked at the amount spent on the company's efforts to expand its routes.
38. *Abdn. Jnl.*, 25 July 1891.
39. NAS. BR/GNS/1/12. Finance committee 21 October, 4, 18 November 1891.
40. *Abdn. Jnl.*, 29 August, 14 October 1891.
41. NAS. BR/GNS/1/12. Board, 2 December 1891.
42. *Abdn. Jnl.*, 29 August 1891.
43. *Abdn. Jnl.*, 23 September, 1 October, 5 November 1891.
44. *Abdn. Jnl.*, 16 November 1891.
45. PO 32/64A, GNSR 1890-92.

15. A MODEL LINE, 1892-94

1. *Abdn. Jnl.*, 24 March 1892.
2. PP 1892 (187). Joint committee on railway rates and charges, pp 623-5.
3. PP 1892 *ibid.*; *Abdn. Jnl.*, 5 May 1892.
4. PP 1892 *ibid.*, 632ff. The GNS maximum rates were confirmed in the Railway Rates & Charges Order No. 23 (Great North of Scotland Railway) Confirmation Act, 20 June 1892.
5. PP 1892 (C.6695). Report on signalling.
6. *Abdn. Jnl.*, 26 January 1893; *Dund. Cour.*, 22 September 1892.
7. *Abdn. Jnl.*, 18 November 1892.
8. *Abdn. Jnl.*, 26 January 1893.
9. NAS. BR/GNS/1/25. Hotel committee, 25 January 1893.
10. *Abdn. Jnl.*, 31 December 1892.
11. *Abdn. Jnl.*, 29 March, 25 January 1893. See also *JTH*, new series, vol ii, no. 2, September 1973, 65ff. P.J. Cain, 'Traders vs Railways'.
12. PP 1893-94 (385) First report of select committee on railway rates and charges, 58.
13. See Acworth, *Elements of Railway Economics*, 161.
14. PP *Hansard*. Commons, 28 April 1893, 5 July 1894; PP 1893-94 (385) First report of select committee on railway rates and charges, 117.
15. *Abdn. Jnl.*, report of half-yearly meeting, 21 September 1893.
16. *Abdn. Jnl.*, 11 January 1894.
17. *Abdn. Jnl.*, 3 June 1893.
18. *Abdn. Jnl.*, 22 March 1894.
19. *Abdn. Jnl.*, 30 December 1893, 5 January, 27 February 1894.
20. *Abdn. Jnl.*, 10 May 1894.
21. *Scmn.*, 14 , 16 November 1893.
22. *Glas. Her.*, 15 November 1893; *Abdn. Jnl.*, 28 April 1894.
23. *Abdn. Jnl.*, 22 March 1894.
24. *Abdn. Jnl.*, 29 September, 4 October; *Scmn.*, 10 September 1894.
25. *Abdn. Jnl.*, 20 September 1894.
26. *Abdn. Jnl.*, 21 November, 6 December 1894. See also Ross, *Highland Railway*, 74.
27. *Abdn. Jnl.*, 14 January, 2, 11, 16 February 1895.

16. DIVERSIFICATION, 1895-1897

1. *Abdn. Jnl.*, 16 February, 21 March 1895.
2. *Scmn.*, 18, 23, 29, 30 May, *Abdn. Jnl.* 30 May, 1895.
3. *Abdn. Jnl.*, 13 July 1895.
4. Keith, *1,000 Years of Aberdeen*, 477, says that the GNS collaborated with the East Coast, but its trains connected with both.
5. *Dund. Cour.*, 8 August 1895.
6. *Abdn. Jnl.*, 2 September, 17 October 1895.
7. *Abdn. Jnl.*, 13 August, 11 September, 9 October 1895.
8. *Abdn. Jnl.*, 21 October, 6 November 1895.
9. *Abdn. Jnl.*, 4 December 1895.
10. NAS. BR/GNS/1/25. Hotels committee, 30 January, 27 November 1895.
11. *Abdn. Jnl.*, 14, 19 December 1895.
12. *Abdn. Jnl.*, 16 April 1896.
13. *Scmn*, 17 July 1896.
14. *Abdn. Jnl.*, 6 August, *Dund. Cour.*, 10 August 1896. Scott, *Little & Good*, 23, noted in 1898 that the special duty of GNS conductors on trains west of Elgin "is to see that no unkempt Gaels from local Highland stations set their defiling feet within the doors of these vehicles".
15. Keith, *1,000 Years of Aberdeen*, 477.
16. *Glas. Her.*, 5, 6 November 1896.
17. PP 1897 (77). Report on Bills. See also Ross, *Highland*, 89, and *North British*, 162, 165.
18. *Glas. Her.*, 9 December 1896.
19. *Abdn. Jnl.*, 8 June, 8 July 1896.
20. *Abdn. Jnl.*, 4 June 1894.
21. *Abdn. Jnl.*, 29 May 1896. Findlay, *History of Peterhead*, 284.
22. *Abdn. Jnl.*, 16, 23 July, 7 August 1896.
23. *Abdn. Jnl.*, 19 March, 11 April 1896.
24. *Glas. Her.*, 19 February 1882; *Abdn. Jnl.*, 1 October 1896.
25. *Abdn. Jnl.*, 11 August 1896.
26. *Abdn. Jnl.*, 12 August 1896.

27. *Abdn. Jnl.*, 17 August, 10 September 1896.
28. *Abdn. Jnl.*, 28 September 1896.
29. *Abdn. Jnl.*, 17 September 1896.
30. *Abdn. Jnl.*, 30 July, 5 September 1896.
31. The *Abdn. Jnl.*, 24/11/96, stated this connection would be at Angusfield but the tramline did not extend so far.
32. ACL. Notice of Light Railway Order Application, 23 December 1896. PP 1898 (55) Report of Proceedings of the Board of Trade under the Light Railways Act, 1896.
33. *Abdn. Jnl.*, 24 November, 3, 16, 31 December 1896.
34. *Ed. Gaz.*, 16 February 1897, 158.
35. PO 11/9, 11/3. NAS. BR/GNS/1/14. Finance committee, 17 March 1897.
36. AUL. OD Misc. 11. Letter of 8 May 1906 from Jameson's, solicitors of Elgin, to Walker & Ironside, civil engineers of Aberdeen.
37. NAS. BR/GNS/1/14. Finance committee, 28 April,

25, May, 18 August, 10 November 1897, 27 April 1898. PP 1900 (Cd 148, 200, 211). Smith, *Towiemore*, 7, notes that Towiemore was first a siding for the Drummuir lime quarries from 1 June 1863, renamed Botriphnie by December 1884, closed between 10 July 1890 and 8 April 1895, extended and renamed Towiemore from 1 January 1898. It did not have a passenger service until the London and North Eastern Railway era, 1924.
38. About a mile and a half on towards Carron, a private halt called Knockando had been provided for the Grant family since 1869: it was now renamed Knockando House.
39. *Abdn. Jnl.*, 19 November 1896. NAS. BR/GNS/1/14. Special board, 3 March 1897. *Ed. Gaz.*, 1173ff, 24 November 1896. Such stock conversion was made by all Scottish railways except the Highland Railway. Seee Ross, *G&SWR*, 133, 234.

17 A SPIRIT OF EXPANSION, 1897-1899

1. *Glas. Her.*, 21 July, *Dund. Cour.*, 14 August 1897.
2. *Abdn. Jnl.*, 8 May 1896.
3. *Abdn. Jnl.*, 10 February, 18 March, *Dund. Cour.*, 10 April 1897. The Board of Trade recorded the syndicate's scheme as "rejected", see PP 1899 (105).
4. *Abdn. Jnl.*, 27 April, 4 May 1897.
5. NAS. BR/GNS/1/14. Finance committee, 18 August 1897.
6. *Abdn. Jnl.*, 16 September 1897.
7. NAS. BR/GNS/1/14. Finance committee, 11 November 1897.
8. PP 1898 (C8788), 1900 (Cd 70), 1901 (Cd 488). Reports of Railway & Canal Commissioners. *Scmn.*, 5 December 1900. The GNS had once wanted to apply a similar charge for the Denburn line.
9. *Abdn. Jnl.*, 16 February 1898.
10. NAS. BR/GNS/1/14. Finance committee, 2 March 1898.
11. *Abdn. Jnl.*, 12, 14 January 1898.
12. See report of stationmasters' dinner, AUL. O'D Misc. 5. William Walker had seen the Lumière film in 1896. Unfortunately his GNS sequence has not survived.
13. *Abdn. Jnl.*, 24 January 1898. "Little and good" was used by the Rev. W.J. Scott as title of his 1898 booklet, warm in its praise of the company.
14. *Abdn. Jnl.*, 1 July 1898.
15. *Abdn. Jnl.*, 17 February 1898.
16. *Abdn. Jnl.*, *ibid.* and 10 March 1898.
17. *Abdn. Jnl.*, 17 March 1898.
18. Saltoun had supported the Rosehearty line, which would have traversed his land. A main reason for its never being made was landowners' refusal to donate ground for it.
19. *Abdn. Jnl.*, *ibid.*
20. These had been received in February. NAS. BR/GNS/1/14. Finance committee, 2 February 1898.

21. *Abdn. Jnl.*, 7, 24 April, 13 June, 1 July 1898.
22. NAS. BR/GNS/1/14. Finance committee, 2 March; Special board 20 April 1898.
23. *Abdn. Jnl.*, 30 September 1897.
24. NAS. BR/GNS/1/14. Finance committee, 31 August; *Isle of Man Times*, 10 September 1898.
25. *Abdn. Jnl.*, 1 October 1898; NAS. BR/GNS/1/14. Finance committee, 14 September 1898, 5 July 1899.
26. *Dund. Cour.*, 7 October 1898.
27. PP 1900 (105). Proceedings of Board of Trade under the Light Railways Act 1896.
28. PP 1899 (C. 9538). Proceedings of Board of Trade under the Light Railways Act 1896.
29. NAS. BR/GNS/1/14. Finance committee, *Abdn. Jnl.*, 15 November 1899. The Board of Trade was still recording it as a live scheme in 1901, see PP 1902 (198).
30. *Abdn. Jnl.*, 25 April, 20 December; NAS. BR/GNS/1/14. Finance committee, 2 August 1899; traffic committee, 11 December 1906.
31. *Abdn. Jnl.*, 22 September 1898.
32. *Abdn. Jnl.*, 28 December 1898, *Glas. Her.*, 2 January, *Abdn. Jnl.*, 2 March 1899. The two tram bodies were found in use as sheds in 1988, and restored into a single No. 2, now kept at the Grampian Transport Museum in the former station at Alford.
33. NAS. BR/GNS/1/25. Hotels committee, 14 September 1898, 2 August, 11 October 1899, 28 February 1900.
34. *Abdn. Jnl.*, 8 October 1898, 2 February 1899. PP 1899 (116).
35. *Abdn. Jnl.*, 25 April, *Glas. Her.*, 12 July 1899.
36. Jones, *The Subbies*, 4.
37. PP 1900 (187). Workmen's trains in Great Britain.
38. *Abdn. Jnl.*, 31 May, 5 June; *Glas. Her.*, 12 July 1899. NAS. BR/GNS/1/14. Finance committee, 13 September; Special board, 4 December, Board 20 December 1899.

18. THE OLD ORDER GOES, 1900-1907

1. *Scmn.*, 13 September 1900.
2. NAS. BR/GNS/1/14. Board, 4 February 1900.
3. NAS. BR/GNS/1/14. Special board, 18 April, Finance committee, 24 October 1900.
4. NAS. BR/GNS/1/14. Finance committee, 18 January 1901.
5. NAS. BR/GNS/1/14. Board, 12 March, Works committee, 15 July; Finance committee, 21 May; Works committee, 16 December 1901.
6. *Scmn.*, 11 February 1902.
7. PP 1904 (Cd 1973).
8. NAS. BR/GNS/1/14. Board, 12 March, 27 August 1901.
9. NAS. BR/GNS/1/14. Board, 27 August, 19 November 1901.
10. *Scmn.*, 2, 10 September 1901.
11. PP 1902 (400). Return on stockholders.
12. *Scmn.*, *ibid.*
13. *Scmn.*, 10, 12, 27 September 1902.
14. *Scmn.*, 25 March 1903.
15. A photograph in the Fraserburgh Harbour Commissioners' collection shows railway tracks on the quays of the South Harbour in "the late 1800s", though none are shown on the O.S. maps surveyed in 1869 and 1901. Cranna, *Fraserburgh Past & Present*, 337, refers to the "railway jetty" as part of the improvements to the South Harbour in the 1880s. These lines may have been laid and lifted between 1880-1900.
16. AUL. O'D Misc. 5.
17. *Scmn.*, 29 February 1904.
18. *Scmn.*, 8 March 1904. Many of the details regarding road motor services are taken from Cummings, *Railway Motor Buses, I.*
19. Wear and tear on tyres was a problem, and a mileage deal was negotiated with tyre suppliers. *Scmn.*, 22 March 1905, report of half-yearly meeting.
20. *Scmn.*, 6 April, 30 August 1904.
21. See PP 1906 (Cd.7681) proceedings of the Royal Commission on Motor Cars, 574f.
22. NAS. BR/GNS/1/17. Special board, 19 February 1907.
23. NAS. BR/GNS/1/17. Board, 17 October 1905.
24. *Scmn.*, 17 November 1905, 16 January 1906.
25. *Scmn.*, 5, 19 February 1906.
26. *Scmn.*, 8 March 1906; NAS. BR/GNS/1/17. Board, See also Ross, *Highland Railway*, 91f.
27. *Scmn.*, 21 March 1906. NAS. BR/GNS/1/17. Locomotive committee, 26 June 1906.
28. NAS. BR/GNS/1/17. Board, 18 September 1906.
29. *The Times*, 9 July 1906, notes Moffatt as a director of the Atlantic, Quebec & Western Railway of Canada.
30. NAS. BR/GNS/1/17. Board, 3 April 1906.
31. NAS. BR/GNS/1/17. Board, 17 April, 1, 5 May; locomotive committee 6 March 1906.
32. NAS. BR/GNS/1/17. Board, 18 September 1906.
33. NAS. BR/GNS/1/17. Locomotive committee, 6 March 1906; Board 22 January 1907, letter to the general manager of the Caledonian Railway: "It is understood that the transference of the goods stations will be proceeded with forthwith". *Scmn.*, 17 December 1907.
34. NAS. BR/GNS/1/17. Special meeting of conveners, 13 July 1906.
35. *Scmn.*, 27 August, *Glas. Her.*, 12 December 1901.
36. NAS. BR/GNS/1/25. Hotels committee, 26 February, 8 October, 19 November 1901, 11 February 1902.
37. NAS. BR/GNS/1/17. Hotels committee, 26 February, 20 March, 4 April, 1906.
38. *Scmn.*, 18 March 1908; NAS. BR/GNS/1/17. Traffic committee, 30 October 1906.
39. NAS. BR/GNS/1/17. Board, 10 July 1906. PP 1906 (Cd 2882). Railway & Canal Commission.
40. NAS. BR/GNS/1/17. *ibid.* Nine years would elapse before this happened.
41. NAS. BR/GNS/1/17. Stores committee, 2 October 1906, 8 January 1907.
42. *Scmn.*, 31 December 1906, 20 March 1907, report of half-yearly meeting.
43. NAS. BR/GNS/1/17. Board, 19 February 1907.
44. *Scmn.*, 28 May 1907.

19. NEW KINDS OF DISPUTE, 1907-14

1. PP 1909 (Cd 5927), 1911 (Cd 5937) Summaries of Accidents. PP 1912-13 (Cd 6174, 6474) Summaries of Accidents 1912-13. The exception is thought to have been Old Meldrum.
2. *Scmn.*, 28 August, 9 September 1907.
3. *Scmn.*, 18 September 1907.
4. *Scmn.*, 18, 28 March 1908.
5. NAS. BR/GNS/1/17. Stores committee, 19 February, conveners' committee 21 February; Hotels committee 4, 12 March 1907.
6. *Scmn.*, 11 August 1908.
7. Abdn. F.P., 21 April 1908. Noted in Jackson, *The Speyside Line*, 23. The experiment was not repeated.
8. Ross, *Highland Railway*, 92.
9. *Scmn.*, 18 November 1908.
10. Abdn. F.P., 21 April 1908. Jones, *The Joint Station*.
11. *Scmn.*, 7, 18 September 1912.
12. ACA. DD/1/100. 'Oor Railway Station', 29 May 1911.
13. *Scmn.*, 19 February 1913.
14. NAS. BR/GNS/1/21. Board, 29 July, *Scmn.*, 19 July 1913.
15. NAS. BR/GNS/1/21. Board, 23 September 1913.
16. PO 32/162A; 121/196.
17. A steam tug towed small barges upriver to Waterton, just east of Ellon, for a time. See Raffaeli, Dave, 'The Ythan: A River in History' on the Aberdeen University website.

18. *Scmn.*, 18 February 1910.
19. *Scmn.*, 14, 21 December 1909.
20. *Scmn.*, 16 December 1909, 1 June 1910.
21. Weir, *History of the Distillers' Co.*
22. Vallance, *GNSR*, 52.
23. *Scmn.*, 30 July 1910; 15 March 1911.
24. NAS. BR/GNS/1/21. Hotels committee, 30 September 1913.
25. *Scmn.*, 14, 18 January 1910.
26. *Scmn.*, 6 November 1909.
27. *Scmn.*, 17, 19 August 1911. This represents a changed situation from 1892, when Buckie's coal all came by sea.
28. PP 1912-13 (Cd 6016). Royal Commission on Railway Conciliation Scheme of 1907.
29. *Scmn.*, 1, 21 September 1911. See also Appendix 1.
30. *Scmn.*, 28 September, 22 November 1911.
31. PP 1913 (116) Railway companies (staff & wages) return.
32. *Scmn.*, 28 June 1912.

33. PP 1913 (Cd 7037) Railway Conciliation Scheme. Statement of Settlements under the Revised Conciliation Scheme recommended by the Royal Commission on the Conciliation and Arbitration Scheme of 1907 as amended by the Railway Conference Agreement of 11 December 1911, 268-80.
34. NAS. BR/GNS/1/21. Board, 15 July 1913.
35. NAS. BR/GNS/1/21. Board, 9 September, 7 October 1913.
36. NAS. BR/GNS/1/21. Board, 16 December 1913, locomotive committee, 27 January, 17 February 1914.
37. NAS. BR/GNS/1/21. Stores committee, 21 October, 18 November; Finance committee 4 November; Traffic committee 2 December; Board 16 December 1913; Finance committee, 27 January 1914.
38. NAS. BR/GNS/1/21. Ordinary general meeting, 17 February; *Scmn.*, 18 February 1914. See also Appendix 2.
39. *Scmn.*, 24 June 1914.
40. NAS. BR/GNS/1/21. Board, 28 July 1914.

20 THE GREAT NORTH AT WAR, 1914-1919

1. Pratt, *British Railways and the Great War*, i, 919.
2. NAS. BR/GNS/1/21. Board, 25 August, 22 September; Locomotive committee 22 September; Board 20 October 1914.
3. NAS. BR/GNS/1/21. Board, 17 November 1914.
4. NAS. BR/GNS/1/21. Locomotive committee, 21 October 1914; Pratt, *op. cit.*, ii, 921.
5. *Ed. Gaz.*, 24 November 1914, 1413f; *Lond. Gaz.*, 25 June 1915, 6164.
6. NAS. BR/GNS/1/21. Locomotive committee, 20 October, 1 December; Board 17 November 1914, Law & parliamentary committee 19 May 1915.
7. NAS. BR/GNS/1/21. Board, 15 June, 3 August 1915, 22 August 1916.
8. *R.M.*, October 1915.
9. NAS. BR/GNS/1/21. Conveners' committee, 7 September, 2 November; Board, 14 December 1915.
10. *Scmn.*, 14 December 1915.
11. NAS. BR/GNS/1/21. Board, 19 May 1914, Locomotive committee, 3, 24 August; Finance committee, 24 August, 19 October 1915.
12. NAS. BR/GNS/1/21. Finance committee, 19 October 1915; Conveners' committee, 31 October 1916.
13. NAS. BR/GNS/1/21. Board, 12 December 1916.
14. NAS. BR/GNS/1/21. Stores committee 19 October, 16 November 1915.
15. NAS. BR/GNS/1/21. Board, 14 December 1915.
16. NAS. BR/GNS/1/21. Stores committee 31 July 1917, Conveners' committee, 7 September 1915, Stores committee 11 December 1917.
17. NAS. BR/GNS/1/22. Stores committee, 11 June 1918.
18. NAS. BR/GNS/1/21. Board, 1 August, 19 September 1916.
19. NAS. BR/GNS/1/21. Locomotive committee, 11 December 1917.

20. NAS. BR/GNS/1/22. Board, 19 February 1918.
21. NAS. BR/GNS/1/21. Law & parliamentary committee, 7 November 1914, 11 January, 12 December 1916.
22. NAS. BR/GNS/1/21. Law & parliamentary committee, 30 January 1917.
23. NAS. BR/GNS/1/21. Board, 19 September 1916, 9 January, 15 May 1917.
24. *Scmn.*, 23 February 1916, report of a.g.m. on 22nd.
25. NAS. BR/GNS/1/21. Board, 9 January, 26 February 1917.
26. NAS. BR/GNS/1/21. Board, 21 August, 18 September, 10 October, 13 November 1917; Law & parliamentary committee 29 January, 9 July 1918.
27. NAS. BR/GNS/1/21. Finance committee, 20 March 1917; BR/GNS/1/22. Hotels committee, 15 March 1918.
28. NAS. BR/GNS/1/22. Locomotive committee, 9, 30 July; Stores committee 12 November, 10 December 1918.
29. NAS. BR/GNS/1/22. Board & committee minutes, June-July 1918.
30. It was "wanted back at Aberdeen". See letter from assistant locomotive superintendent of Highland Railway, quoted in Ross, *Highland Railway*, 97.
31. See Ross, *op. cit.*, 69.
32. NAS. BR/GNS/1/22. Locomotive committee, 14 May; 19 February; Board, 30 July, 20 August 1918.
33. Construction of the massive breakwaters at Peterhead, by convict labour, was suspended during the war: the Railway Executive wrote to the GNS, who had nothing to do with the matter, to ask if the contractors' works could be used by convicts to repair wagons and tarpaulins. NAS. BR/GNS/1/21. Board, 17 April 1917.

34. NAS. BR/GNS/1/21. Conveners' committee 6 March, traffic committee 16 May 1917.
35. *Scmn.*, 20 February; NAS. BR/GNS/1/22. Traffic committee, 30 July 1918.
36. Pratt, *British Railways and the Great War*, ii, 921ff.
37. *Scmn.*, 20 February 1918, report on ordinary general meeting on 19th; NAS. BR/GNS/1/22. Finance committee, 20 August 1918.
38. NAS. BR/GNS/1/22. Law, parliamentary & finance committee, 6 September 1921.
39. NAS. BR/GNS/1/22. Finance committee, 20 August 1918.
40. NAS. BR/GNS/1/21. Board, 15 May 1917; BR/GNS 1/22. Board, 21 August 1917, 29 January 1918; Pratt, *op. cit.*, ii, 920.
41. PP 1919 (Cmd. 227). Committee on rural transport (Scotland), 10.
42. NAS. BR/GNS/1/22. Board, 20 August 1918.
43. NAS. BR/GNS/1/22. Board, 10 December 1918.
44. NAS. BR/GNS/1/22. Board, 18 February 1919. 45. *Lond. Gaz.*, supplement 7 June 1918, 6735; *Ed. Gaz.*, supplement 1 April 1920, 996.
46. Pratt, *op. cit.*, ii, 921ff.

21. THE FINAL YEARS, 1919 – 1923

1. *Scmn.*, 19 April, 2 May, 9 June 1922.
2. NAS. BR/GNS/1/22. Board 14 October 1919.
3. NAS. BR/GNS/1/22. Works & permanent way committee, 28 January 1919.
4. NAS. BR/GNS/1/22. Locomotive committee, 7 January 1919.
5. NAS. BR/GNS/1/22. Board, 7 January, 18 February; 28 January. Traffic committee, 28 January 1919.
6. *Scmn.*, 3 March 1921.
7. *Scmn.*, 29, 30 September 1919.
8. *Scmn.*, 4 October 1919.
9. NAS. BR/GNS/1/22. Special board, 28 October 1919.
10. The Board of Trade had issued an order that all bunker coal to Peterhead, Fraserburgh, Banff, Macduff and Buckie *must* be sent by sea, from 30th June. NAS. BR/GNS/1/22. Traffic committee, 29 July 1919.
11. NAS. BR/GNS/1/22. Board, 16 September; Hotels committee, 25 November; Locomotive committee, 11 November 1919; Works committee, 6 January 1920.
12. NAS. BR/GNS/1/22. Locomotive committee, 8 July, 9 December 1919.
13. NAS. BR/GNS/1/22. Board, 6 January 1920.
14. PP *Hansard*. Commons, 20 July 1920.
15. *Scmn.*, 24 December 1919.
16. *Scmn.*, 18 February 1920.
17. NAS. BR/GNS/1/22. Board, 13 April 1920; Locomotive committee, 8 June 1920.
18. *Scmn.*, 11 August 1920.
19. NAS. BR/GNS/1/22. Locomotive and Traffic committees, 6 July 1920; Locomotive committee, 25 January 1921.
20. The bus conductors got a useful bonus for parcel handling, sharing around £20-£30 a month.
21. Cummings, *Railway Motor Buses*, 18ff.
22. NAS. BR/GNS/1/22. Traffic committee, 28 September 1920, 15 February 1921. Law, parliamentary & finance committee, 19 July 1921.
23. NAS. BR/GNS/1/22. Traffic committee, 15 February 1921.
24. NAS. BR/GNS/1/22. Hotels committee, 25 November 1919; Law & parliamentary committee, 6 June 1920; Works committee, 5 April, 31 May 1921.
25. NAS. BR/GNS/1/22. Locomotive committee, 31 May 1921.
26. NAS. BR/GNS/1/22. Locomotive committee, 17, 31 May, 19, 28 June, 4 October, 1 November 1921.
27. NAS. BR/GNS/1/22. Board, 9 August 1921.
28. *Scmn.*, 26 September 1921.
29. NAS. BR/GNS/1/22. Board, 20 December, 1 November 1921.
30. *Abdn. Jnl.*, 21 February 1922.
31. NAS. BR/GNS/221. Board, 24 January 1922; Simnett, *Railway Amalgamation*, 265.
32. Barclay-Harvey, *The GNSR*, 222.
33. PP *Hansard*. Commons, written answers, 27 November 1922.
34. *Scmn.*, 18 November 1922.
35. Barclay-Harvey, *The GNSR*, 224.

22. PERCEPTIONS OF THE GREAT NORTH

1. *Abdn. Jnl.*, report of police commissioners, 20 December 1854.
2. Smith, *A New History*, ii, 1301.
3. Vallance, *The GNSR*, 33.
4. *Scmn.*, 24 April 1877.
5. NAS. BR/GNS/1/12. Board, 12 October 1887.
6. Finance committee, 12 July 1883.
7. NAS. BR/GNS/1/11. Finance committee, 8 August 1883. Letter from Moffat to Ferguson, 22 December 1883, noted in AUL. OD C2.6, O'D r 3, 'Railways & Geography in N.E. Scotland', 9.
8. NAS BR/GNS/1/12. Finance committee, 21 October 1891.
9. *Abdn. Jnl.*, 21 October 1886, 17 February 1887.
10. Finance committee, 17 April 1884.
11. NAS. BR/GNS/1/14. Finance committee, 13 April 1898.
12. *Glas. Her.*, 14 May 1894.
13. NAS. BR/GNS/1/17. Traffic committee, 16 October 1906.
14. NAS. BR/GNS/1/12. Finance committee, 3 July 1889.
15. *Abdn. Jnl.*, 14 March 1855.
16. Rent rises in line with productivity predated the railway: it is possible that many tenant farmers had little to spare for investment.
17. PP 1921 (Cmd. 1494). Staff employed at 19 March 1921.
18. NAS. BR/SNER/1/1. Traffic committee, 30 December 1863.
19. NAS. BR/SNER/1/6. Traffic committee, 28 March 1867.
20. *Abdn. Jnl.*, 23 February 1898.
21. NAS. BG/GNS/1/14. Finance committee, 9 April 1901.
22. *Abdn. Jnl.*, 7 December 1870; NAS. BR/GNS/1/9. Finance, works & traffic committee, 11 November 1875.
23. *Abdn. Jnl.*, 21 February 1887.
24. Three years before the Lumière brothers' pioneering essay in cinematography, they would have been magic lantern shows.
25. AUL. OD H Rail g, 'The R.B.I. Bazaar.' *Abdn. Jnl.*, 22,23, 25 December 1893. John Stuart recalled the first cab in Aberdeen, in the 1840s: "a yellow-painted conveyance with the door in the back, with 'The Wonder' emblazoned in a panel. But some people called it a minibus, as distinct from the omnibus" – perhaps the first use of the word 'minibus'.
26. *Cal. Merc.*, 26 March 1862.
27. NAS. BR/GNS/1/14. Finance committee, 12 October 1898.
28. *Abdn. Jnl.*, 10 April 1899.
29. NAS. BR/GNS/1/14. Finance & traffic committee, 19 November, special board, 31 December 1901.
30. *Abdn. Jnl.*, 3 February 1894.
31. *Scmn.*, 12 August 1895.
32. NAS. BR/GNS/1/6. Board, 8 January 1867.
33. *Abdn. Jnl.*, 25 December 1882.
34. *Abdn. Jnl.*, 5 June 1893.
35. NAS. BR/GNS/1/14. Finance committee, 6 July 1898.
36. *Scmn.*, 14 March 1914. One wonders if the "smart working" at stations encouraged such actions, though the stationmaster had warned McWilliam on a previous occasion.
37. *Glas. Her.*, 17 November 1893, 17 March 1894.
38. NAS. BR/STY/1. Board, 23 July 1863; BR/GNS/1/22. Law, parliament & finance committee, 26 October 1920; Locomotive committee 25 January 1921.
39. AUL. O'D Misc. GB 0231 Ms3697/1/14/4.
40. AUL. O'D Misc 4. Letter of 12 January 1883.

23. POWER AND PROVISION

1. See Gordon, *GNSR Locomotives*, 1. This chapter draws to a considerable extent on Gordon for locomotive information.
2. *Abdn. Jnl.*, 12 November 1856, 18 November 1857.
3. *Abdn. Jnl.*, Directors' report, 18 November 1857.
4. *Abdn. Jnl.*, 8 December 1858
5. Jackson, *The Speyside Line*, 33. Gordon, *GNSR Locomotives*, 7.
6. Gordon, *op. cit.*, 2.
7. *Abdn. Jnl.*, 24 September 1862; NAS. BR/GNS/1/1. Board, 29 January 1863.
8. *Abdn. Jnl.*, half-yearly report, 15 September 1883.
9. NAS. BR/GNS/1/5. Traffic & finance committee, 16 February, board 4 March 1864.
10. NAS. BR/GNS/1/5. Traffic & finance committee, 8 November 1864.
11. Directors' report, 19 March 1868.
12. NAS. BR/GNS/1/6. Board, 20 May, 18 July 1867; *Scmn.*, 21 December 1909.
13. PP 1868-69 (286). Railway returns.
14. *Abdn. Jnl.*, 5 April 1871.
15. PP 1872 (C.651) Railway returns.
16. AUL. O'D Misc. 1.
17. Baxter, *Locomotives*, 229; *Abdn. Jnl.*, 29 March 1876.
18. PP 1880 (C.2596) Railway returns for 1879.
19. NAS. BR/GNS/1/11. Finance committeee, 14 June 1883; *Abdn. Jnl.*, 29 March 1893.
20. Gordon, *op. cit.*, 27.
21. NAS. BR/GNS/1/12. Finance committee, 17 December 1890.
22. NAS. BR/GNS/1/12. Finance committee, 2 December 1891.
23. PP 1880 (C.2596) and 1892 (C.6713), Railway returns.
24. Noted in *Abdn. Jnl.*, 31 May 1890.
25. NAS. BR/GNS/1/14. Finance committee, 22 November 1899.
26. Scott, *Little & Good*, 39. This feature was not retained.
27. PP 1896 (Cd 8181). Railway returns for 1895.
28. An authoritative history is given in Fenwick, *GNSR Carriages*.
29. *R.M.*, vol 1, July-December 1897, 472.
30. NAS. BR/GNS/1/14. Finance committee, 3 August 1898.

31. *Abdn. Jnl.*, 15 January 1896; *R.M.*, *ibid.*; *R.M.*, January, March, June 1934, S.R. Yates, 'Notes on Scottish Locomotives and Railway Working'.
32. PP 1901 (Cd 691). Railway returns, 1900. NAS. BR/GNS/1/14. Finance committee, 3 January 1901.
33. AUL. O'D Misc 5.
34. *R.M.*, June 1934, 429. S.R. Yates, 'Notes on Scottish Locomotives & Railway Working'.
35. NAS. BR/GNS/1/17. Board, 27 November 1906; Gordon, *op. cit.*, 60.
36. *R.M.*, June 1934, 430. S.R. Yates, 'Notes on Scottish Locomotives & Railway Working'.
37. The company's return says 113.
38. PP 1906 (Cd 3106). Railway returns 1905.
39. *R.M.*, June 1934, 429. S.R. Yates, 'Notes on Scottish Locomotives & Railway Working'.
40. PP 1911 (Cd 5796). Railway returns, 1910.
41. Baxter, *Locomotives*, 242.
42. NAS. BR/GNS/1/22. Locomotive committee, 16 April, 30 July 1918.
43. NAS. BR/GNS/1/22. Annual report for 1919.
44. Figures taken from lists in Baxter, *Locomotives*, 229-244.
45. AUL. OD f L2 GNS Gre d; PP 1872 (364). Report from joint select committee on railway amalgamation.
46. Barclay-Harvey, *The GNSR*, 179.
47. It is at the Scottish Railway Museum in Bo'ness.
48. *Scmn.*, 3 June 1907.

INDEX

Towns and villages are in the general index, but for specific references to stations, see under 'Stations'. Locomotive references are grouped under 'Locomotives'. 'Timeline entries are not indexed. References to illustrations are in bold type.

Boddam, 101, 140, 141, 150, 152
Botriphnie, 244
Bouch, Thomas, 75
Boyndie siding, 122
Braemar, 76, 97, 143, 164, 165, 175f, 189, 194, 238
Brake vans, passengers in, 115, 125
Brand, Charles, 52, 56, 72, 141, 152
Brassey, Thomas, 22
Brebner, John, 42, 44
Brechin, 12, 18
Bridge of Gairn, 75, 76, 88, 91f, 156
Brodie, Mr, 16, 234
Brooks, Shirley, 103, 240
Brown & Marshall, 33
Brown & Murray, 18
Brown, Rev. George, 157
Bruce, Thomas C., 40, 81, 92, 106, 115
Brunel, I.K., 37
Bryce, James, 142
Bryson, W.G., 108, 240
Buchan Line (see also Formartine & Buchan), 91, 95, 101, 103, 105, 169, 176, 180, 184, 213
Buckie, 67, 69, 101, 105f, 108, 113, 119, **121**, 122, 137, 140, **146**, 176, 177, 193, 246, 247
Buckie Extension Railway, see Coast line
Buffalo Bill's Wild West Show, 218
Burgess, David, 77
Burghead, 14, 16, 28, 32, 50, 129f
Burnett, Newell, 34, 87
Burnett, Sir Robert, 110
Bus services, **25**, 82, **164**, **165**, 167, 175, 184, **189**, **196**, 245, 247

C

Cadenhead, William, 2, 30
Caithness Commissioners of Supply, 16
Caledonian Canal, 140
Caledonian Mercury, 11
Caledonian Railway, 11, 13, 17, 27, 41, 82, 83, 85f, 88, 93, 95, 100, 101, 109, 110, 113, 116, 120, 121, 125, 131, 136, 138, 149, 153f, 156, 158, 162, 167, 172, 180, 182, 184, 185, 186, 193, 204, 221, 245
Campbell, Miss Kate, 157, 168
Canadian Pacific Railway, 138
Cardhu distillery, 151
Carriages, livery, 216
Carron, 66, 151
Cathcart, Lady Gordon, 108
Cattle traffic, 91, 98, 109, 122, 176, 204, 241
Central Buchan Railway, 139, 148, 184, 204
Chaytor, Henry, 28
Chisholm & Co., sack hirers, 220
Churchill, Lord Randolph, 106
Churchill, Winston, 177

Circumbendibus, 62, 71, 150
Clark, David, 12
Clark, Daniel Kinnear, 32, 34, 36, 210, 211
Clarke, Seymour, 28
Cluny, 165, 175
Cluny estate, 240
Coal traffic, 99, 102, 137, 162, 187, 188, 197, 205, 246, 247
Coast line, **30**, 77, 78, 83, 86, 97, 105f, 107, 108, 109, 113, 120, **123**, 134, 135, 145
Cochran & Co., 218
Colwyn, Lord, 194
Commercial Bank, 76, 93
Consolidated Pneumatic Tool Co., 163
Copland, Alexander, 105, 116, 126, 136, 207
Corgarff, 170
Council of Education in Scotland, 161
Court of Session, 27, 31, 43, 60, 91, 102, 110, 123, 128, 133, 134, 141, 145, 154, 157, 193, 203, 206
Cowan, William, 71, 72, 94, 97, 100f, 113, 206, 211, 214
Crachie Mills, 151
Craib, William, 145
Craigellachie, 13, 27, 52
Cramp, C.T., 198
Crathes, 12
Creosote plant, 186
Cripps, Henry, 106, 113
Cromarty, 50, 54
Cruden Bay, 68, 169, 183, **199**, 203
Cruden Bay Brick and Tile Works, 141, 169
Cruden Bay Hotel, 141, 145, 152, 157, **168**, 176, 187, 197
Cruickshank, omnibus operator, 165
Cubitt, William, 12, 25
Cullen, 50, 108, 113, **114**, 123
Culter, 59, 100, 140, 164, 196
Culter Paper Co., 116, 197
Cuminestown, 148
Curling halts, 122

D

Dailuaine distillery, 116, 122, 151, 180, 181
Dalhousie, Lord, 234
Davidson, George, 167, 172, 177, 178, 179, 185, 188, 194, 195, 199, 227
Davidson, Patrick, 69
Davidson, Robert, 11
Dean, William, 138, 161
Dee, River, 11, 12, 22
Dee viaduct, 17, 22
Deeside & Alford Extension Railway, 38, 42
Deeside Express, 219
Deeside Extension Railway, 42, 44, 59, 64, 65, 68f, 90, 92, 237

Deeside Railway, 14, 16, 19, 22, 23, 24, 27, 28f, 33, 36, 37, 38, 39, 41, 42f, 44, 49, 58, 59, 63, 64, 68f, 70, 75f, 77, 84, 88, 90, 91, 92, 93, 97, 98, 99, 101, 108, 124, 169, 212, 213, 235, 236;
Opening, 31;
Leasing of line, 59f, 84;
Amalgamation with GNS, 59f
Denburn Valley line, 13, 22, 25, 28, 31, 42, 50, 55, 57, 59, 60, 62f, 65, 71, 72, 74, 82, 86, 89, 125, 158, 186, 192
Denison, Edmund, 28
Deuchar, William, 160, 170, 186, 227
Deveron, River, 40, 48, 67, 160
Dingwall, 188
Dodds, Rotherham, 213
Don, River, 11, 14, 31, 55, 98, 124, 186
Dornoch Light Railway, 158
Dougall, Andrew, 81, 110, 111, 117, 119, 130, 133, 143, 145
Drummuir, 109, 151
Dubton, 18, 20
Duff, Maj. Gordon, 47
Dufftown, 41, 56, 67, 76, 104, 122, 131, 144, 148, 151, 156
Duffus, 129
Duffus, Alexander, 198, 199, 208
Duncan, John (blacksmith), 127
Duncan, John (chairman), 27, **28**, 33, 38, 42, 43, 45, 59f, 64, 69, 70, 74, 75, 76, 77, 82, 83, 84, 86, 87, 88, 90, 92f, 97, 201
Dundee, 13, 39, 60, 111, 137
Dundee & Arbroath Railway, 11, 12, 39, 67
Dundee & Perth Railway, 13
Durris, 187
Duthie, Mrs, 163
Dyce, 14, 38, 103, 125, 164, 186
Dyson & Co., 110f

E

East Coast route, 11, 12, 13, 19, 20, 21, 28, 29, 111, 113, 121, 129, 130, 143, 147, 153, 158, 243
East of Scotland Junction Railway, 14
Eastern Counties Railway, 35
Echt, 139, 149, 150, 152, 155, 156, 165, 175, 189
Edinburgh, 27, 32, 68, 74, 87, 122, 129, 155, 186, 207
Edinburgh & Glasgow Railway, 11, 54
Edinburgh & Northern Railway, 11, 12f, 19f, 23
Edinburgh Perth & Dundee Railway, 23, 27
Edmonson Ticket Works, 172
Edward VII, King, 168
Electric Telegraph Co., 34, 37, 201
Elgin, 13, 26f, 28, 29, 32, 34, 36, 37, 46, 47, 52, 81, 92, 104, 106, 109, 110, 111, 112, 113, 115, 117, 119, 122, 125, 127, 129, 130, 131, 133, 140, 142, 145, 152, 207, 219

Front cover: The terminus at Macduff, opened in 1872, with a train about to leave. (*Stenlake collection*)

Back cover: A-class engine No. 63, James Manson's first locomotive design for the GNS (1884) with a train at Elgin in the 1900s.